5117

D0871577

Nations and Cities

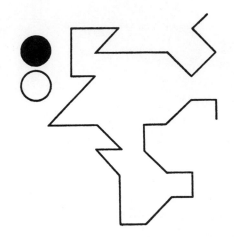

Lloyd Rodwin

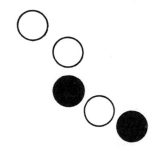

Nations and Cities

A Comparison of Strategies for Urban Growth

HOUGHTON MIFFLIN COMPANY · BOSTON

New York   Atlanta   Geneva, Illinois   Dallas   Palo Alto

To

CHARLES ABRAMS

Pathbreaker

whose wit, wisdom, and generosity

have nourished two generations

of urban reformers

in this country and abroad

Contents

vii

List of Figures

Introduction

BEFORE WORLD WAR II almost no one wanted the central government to determine how cities should grow. Today, only a generation later, national governments throughout the world are adopting or being implored to adopt urban growth strategies. This change is the most significant innovation in urban development policy in the last two decades.

Two problems in particular now spur urban growth strategies. These are, first, the social costs of current metropolitan growth patterns and second, the disparities between growth centers and depressed areas. Each of these problems is separable yet interrelated. Each represents a different malady of development, yet the treatment for one affects the other. And, in different parts of the world, these problems or some combination of them are already impelling action, if not a clear policy, at the national level.

If it is any consolation, we can trace the blame for these two problems to social and economic progress. We have learned how to keep more people alive; and the productivity of our economy and the ingenuity of our technology allows them a more or less satisfactory survival. This "progress" has sparked an unparalleled population explosion, a vast migration of people, and a radical transformation of living patterns.

At present, between 50 and 60 million people are being added to the world's total population every year. This rate of growth will become 75 million a year in 1975, and 125 million in the year 2000. At that rate, the world's population will reach 4,000 million in 1975, and some 6,000 million at the turn of the century. By then 60% of the world's population will probably be urban. Thus, an urban environment, tolerable both from the physical as well as the socio-economic viewpoint, will have to be provided in the last five decades of the twentieth century for thirteen times as many people as in the previous 150 years; to do so, the rate of construction in the next fifty years must average almost 40 times that of the past.[1]

Economic progress further exacerbates these consequences, at least at the outset. Rising income and expectations lead to more families, increasing migration, mounting traffic struggling through outmoded street systems, and acute shortages of housing, schools, and other public services. Prices soar as a result of the pressure of an expanding demand for space and facilities on a supply that is relatively inelastic and inadequate. Massive migration and population changes disrupt both rural and urban living patterns. They contribute to the tensions aroused when low and moderate-income families, especially minorities, wanting higher status and more power, seek better jobs, homes, schools, and neighborhoods. They also accentuate the cold war carried on between suburban communities and central cities and increase pressures on the central city for more and costlier services.

Not surprisingly, complaints about the city abound in almost all countries. There are outcries against overcrowding and ghettoes, against the pollution of air and water, against the poor quality of physical environment in general. There is dissatisfaction with the access to jobs and with the quality of health and educational services and community facilities. There is concern about the huge investments required for urban infrastructure in the large cities. There are objections to land speculation, to unsightly and often inefficient land uses, and to patterns of growth which tend to concentrate more and more people and wealth in two or three regions while development elsewhere is stunted.

That these problems are unleashed by beneficent forces and thaι the city itself is the indispensable crucible for change and economic progress do not make these problems any less frustrating or explosive. Nor is coping with them easy even for the richer countries, despite the fact that they have more capital, more skilled specialists, and more highly developed political, economic, and social institutions. For, much of the basic equipment and institutions in their cities is obsolete; and over the years a powerful array of interests has become wedded to the way things are, so that many of the desired changes, which otherwise might be feasible, take a long time to materialize. In the meanwhile, innovations in transportation and technology are fast bringing about *megalopolis*— vast urban agglomerations of linked metropolitan areas—which aggravates the situation still further.

Concern over the question of "imbalanced" urban development is by now widespread. The intimately linked problems of metropolitan development and lagging regions are the subjects of debates in many kinds of countries—big and small, densely or relatively sparsely populated, and with mixed or socialist economies. Mexico City in Mexico, Caracas in Venezuela, Rio de Janeiro and São Paulo in Brazil, Lagos in Nigeria, Tripoli in Libya, Bombay and Calcutta in India, Djakarta and Surabaja in Indonesia—are but a few examples of urban areas where formidable metropolitan development problems and startling differences in cultural patterns and standards of living exist between the leading cities and the hinterlands. These contrasts are perhaps the most visible and the most poignant expression of the gaps that must be overcome in the course of the development of these countries.

There are comparable "discrepancies" in the wealthier countries. Great Britain is troubled by the scale and pattern of growth of London and Southern England and the damaging effects of this growth on Scotland, Wales, the Northeast, and the Northwest. France is attempting to limit and decentralize the growth of Paris, and at the same time to promote the growth of lagging regions, especially in the West and Southwest. In Italy the north-south issue has become the classic symbol of neglect and decay which writers cite to haunt the conscience of their nation. In Turkey, once the empire was stripped away, turning inward toward the interior and away from Istanbul became a quest for modernization and national identity as well as for development. For Israel, urban growth policy has taken the form of a challenge and a dream of developing the Negev. The Soviet Union has had a policy for decades to curb and reorganize the growth of Moscow and to encourage development in other areas, especially beyond the Urals. Japan is making a major effort to counter the burgeoning of Tokyo and Osaka and the virtual stagnation of Hokkaido and other regions. In India, China, Poland, Yugoslavia, and many other countries the aim in varying guises is to reduce and rechannel growth in the big cities and redress the balance for more backward regions.

In the United States, the problems of urban growth have taken on additional dimensions. The rapid shifts of families and jobs to the suburbs have crippled the central cities of metropolitan areas and have led to national measures to arrest the trend. But the accelerated movement into the metropolis of an underprivileged and, to a large extent, black population is spurring further outmigration of whites and is exacerbating the more traditional conflicts between the central city and its suburbs by transforming them into racial and poverty issues. At the same time, the inundation of central cities by population from the South, Appalachia, and elsewhere is converting these cities into new kinds of lagging regions, at once more visible and more explosive than the social and economic quagmires from which their impoverished residents have come.

It is increasingly evident that these problems range far beyond the boundaries and capabilities of the city and region. This is so whether we are concerned with the growth or redevelopment problems of New York, Paris, London, Istanbul, Caracas, or any of the other major metropolitan areas of the world; and it is all the more true for the poorer regions of nations, such as Turkey's East, France's West, Britain's North, or the United States' South. Only central governments have the resources and the power of redirecting public and private investment decisions to influence these growth patterns. This explains why pressures are mounting for nations to do "something" about these matters. Indeed, the issues are rapidly gaining priority and neglect of them will be increasingly dangerous.[2]

As yet, however, very little is known about the urban growth strategies of nations, about the policies and means they have evolved to come to grips with these issues. The aim of this book is to help correct this deficiency by providing an analysis of the relevant policies and methods, the underlying theories, and the experience on these matters. The study begins with an examination of the principal urban growth options and the problems which the adoption of urban growth strategies may entail. It next examines those clues and suggestions that can be gleaned from current theory and research. These ideas are then explored in more detail in five case studies. Finally, the book concludes with some reflections on the inferences which might be drawn from these experiences.

The way the case studies came to be selected may be of interest. I first got involved in this subject some twenty years ago when I became interested in the British policy of building New Towns.[3] The more I studied this experience, the more I was persuaded that its most significant aspect was the light it shed on the complexities of devising urban growth strategies. As pioneering and as challenging as the New Towns policy was, the British, nonetheless, had not yet come to grips with the basic questions of how, where, on what scale, and for what purpose was urban growth to be encouraged. Subsequent professional work in several other countries, especially Turkey and Venezuela, convinced me that these same questions were critical for the poorer countries, too. For many reasons, however, they have been slighted by economists, city and regional planners, and other specialists in the fields of planning and development.

The general neglect of these questions tempted me not only to write this book but to employ case studies based in part upon my experiences in the countries mentioned above. To deal with the subject more exhaustively I also made plans to explore urban growth policies in eastern Europe, Israel, Italy, and the Netherlands. I found, however, that I was dangerously overextended. Because of the constraints of time and my profound ignorance of their languages and cultures, I could not hope to acquire intimate knowledge of all these areas. It seemed wiser to restrict the case studies to countries where I had done extensive professional work or where I had devoted considerable time to the study of their national strategies—enough at any rate to acquire some intimate knowledge, or at least the illusion of having such knowledge. These countries were Venezuela, Turkey, Great Britain, France, and the United States.

The case studies are intended to amplify and also to test the more general ideas on urban growth strategies which are developed in Chapters I and II of this volume. More specifically, they examine how policies evolved in these countries, what goals were sought, what methods were employed, how and why programs differed and resembled each other, how successful the efforts have been, and what lessons can be drawn from these experiences. These case studies also illustrate different facets of urban growth strategies. For example, the Venezuela case points up the problems of formulating such a strategy at the regional level. The Turkish case shows the nature of the problems at the national level. Great

Britain's experience is an example of a permissive approach in a decentralized political system without an explicit physical development strategy, whereas the French case illustrates the evolution and pursuit of a relatively explicit national strategy under a hierarchical administrative setup. Finally, the case of the United States points up the value of such a strategy even in an egalitarian environment with a "mature" urban system and is of particular importance because it may foreshadow some difficult issues which other countries will encounter in the future.

To be sure, these countries do not illustrate all of the significant activity in this field. But these case studies do bring together a fairly wide and significant range of experience, and, as far as I know, this has not been done before.

Nations and Cities

Through the years, a man peoples a space
with images of provinces, kingdoms, mountains, bays,
ships, islands, fishes, rooms, tools, stars, horses, and people.
Shortly before his death, he discovers that
the patient labyrinth of lines traces the image of his own face.

JORGE LUIS BORGES

I

Urban Growth Options[1]

The conviction that urban growth does not take place the way it should is no longer the view of merely a few sensitive intellectuals and professional urbanists. It has become one of the dominant beliefs of the age. If somehow we could determine the best locations for urban growth, and could steer economic activities and families into those areas and away from less desirable ones, we would have powerful weapons for changing our environment. Instead of being stricken or overwhelmed by movements of population and economic activity, we could help communities and regions adjust more effectively to these changes.

At present, we have neither accurate tools with which to anticipate urban growth nor the equivalents of thermostatic devices with which to alter its direction and scale. Market mechanisms are supposed to perform these functions. However, when there are sluggish or inflexible adjustments to price signals, differences between private and public costs, and inadequate or wrong information, these market mechanisms work badly. And, for groups living outside the economy or for groups which are unresponsive to economic rewards and penalties, they do not work at all. To make

3

the mechanisms perform better, we would need more relevant information, some effective incentives and controls, and a reasonable consensus on what we want to occur.

Such efforts imply feasible urban growth options—ranging from limited efforts to encourage or discourage growth in particular regions to attempts to achieve specific national urban growth patterns. There are a number of precedents for these kinds of programs. Both the United States and the Soviet Union have attempted to bring about broad sweeping changes in regional growth patterns. In the nineteenth century, the United States resorted to subsidies and internal improvements to develop the West; in the twentieth century, the Soviet Union invested in infrastructure and industrial development to promote the regions east of the Urals. Turkey's shift of its capitol from Istanbul to Ankara, although undertaken for military and political reasons, relieved the pressures on Istanbul and promoted development of its hinterland. Still other nations, such as Britain and France, have devised elaborate systems of controls and incentives to change the patterns of growth in their expanding and declining regions. There is also an increasing fund of experience growing out of programs to accommodate migrants from rural areas. These programs have varied from complex plans for developing an entire city and region, as in the case of Ciudad Guayana in Venezuela, to minimum provisions for such essentials as a small tract of land, a central source of water, and instructions showing individuals and groups how to build the simplest kind of dwelling with local materials, as in the case of Puerto Rico.

THE CASE FOR CONCENTRATED DECENTRALIZATION

A policy designed to influence urban growth presupposes no particular philosophy or ideal of development. It could attempt to promote either one huge center, a few major centers, a network of decentralized communities, or some combination of these. The decision-makers in each country would have to decide far more explicitly than now which policy would suit their problems, their values, and their goals of development. Controversy would be inevitable, for the distribution of cities of varied sizes[2] would affect

4

many factors — costs, employment, regional growth, birth rates, productivity, military security, and national unification.

A variety of considerations, however, tend to favor metropolitan concentration. Some regions offer only limited development opportunities, thereby making a thoroughgoing policy of dispersion impossible. Also, few countries have enough resources to develop all communities and regions, so some principle of selection is unavoidable. On the other hand, growth in big cities (those with populations of about 100,000 or more) appears to have a better chance of becoming self-propelling. This is especially true of cities with some initial advantages, such as an exceptional harbor, a salubrious climate, superior transport, access to a potentially rich hinterland, or a resource ripe for exploitation. Such assets offer a matrix of possibilities which, if successfully tapped, will create additional advantages and opportunities. Some of the more important of these are: a larger and more specialized labor force, more adequate credit and exchange facilities, increased business and professional services, improved roads and utilities, more diversified job opportunities and a wider range of consumer services. The interaction of these developments widens the market and generates external economies. It also spurs new enterprises, sparks worldly ambition and competitive effort, transforms surrounding agricultural activities, and helps to reinforce the cycle of growth.

In addition, big cities attract migrants and induce drastic changes in traditional attitudes. Job opportunities or illusions beckon; so do the jostling crowds, the bazaar-like shops, and the rich mixture of sights, sounds, and human experience. Patterns of family expenditures change, standards of demand rise, the birth rate tends to decline, the origins of class or caste lose some of their significance, and innovations find an easier welcome. No one knows for certain to what extent the size of the metropolis, as compared to such factors as increased income and education and new patterns of work and living, encourages change.[3] Future research should reveal much about these matters. Meanwhile, from what we have observed of urban trends in economically advanced countries, we have a strong suspicion that a shift from the traditional rural economy to that of the large city is conducive to a variety of changes as well as to economic progress.

5

Big cities, however, have well-known disadvantages. Approximately 50 to 70 percent of the total capital available for investment goes into overhead capital or infrastructure.[4] Many of these costs are higher in large cities. Moreover, with most of the facilities of these cities overtaxed, the marginal costs of further congestion, or of simply accommodating a much larger population, are likely to be high. Partly for these reasons, many persons oppose further big-city development and propose as a feasible alternative planned decentralization. These proponents of decentralization believe that:

> cheap land, lower densities and shorter distances should mean simpler standards and technology for all kinds of social and civic facilities, utilizing rough, impermanent materials, personal labor and capital otherwise untapped, and other resources from the more or less non-monetized sectors of the economy. From this viewpoint, decentralization in one form or another is essentially a resource-saving device.[5]

There are still other objections to big-city growth policies. The most important of these have been raised by people who do not oppose big-city growth in principle, but believe that the price of such growth should not be neglect of the pressing needs of poorly developed regions. Because of the inherent advantages of big-city growth, many of the poorer countries have been neglecting their underdeveloped areas. This has led to a politically unacceptable and potentially explosive dualism:

> a peasant agriculture and handicrafts sector using simple labor intensive techniques where manhour productivity is extremely low, and where one-half to four-fifths of the population earn their incomes; and a plantation-mining-and-manufacturing sector using advanced techniques where manhour productivity is high but where only a small part of the population is employed .... Both sectors are usually distinct geographically as well as technologically and economically. Sometimes they represent quite different regions. Nearly always the two sectors appear in a contrast between one or a few large and growing cities and the surrounding countryside....[6]

Aspects of this dualism, although less extensive in scale, can also be found in backward regions of wealthy countries. Appalachia and the Deep South are the most well-known examples in the United States.

6

This dualism is responsible for an inefficient allocation of capital. The resulting losses are hard to estimate but are nonetheless real. They involve not so much the increasing costs for overhead and relief of congestion in the expanding large cities as the potential costs of failure to exploit resources and other investment possibilities in the lagging regions. In big cities, opportunities come more easily within the line of vision of investors, whereas in backward areas inadequate information makes it difficult to spot attractive investment possibilities.[7] Even when information is available, prospects are still apt to be obscure. Investment returns must be gauged over a long period. But during the first few years when predictions are somewhat surer, the returns may be low, though thereafter they may more than balance initially higher returns elsewhere. Moreover, to investors, big cities connote success, whereas lagging regions are associated with high risks and dubious prospects. Given these circumstances, it is not surprising that investors tend to underestimate opportunities in backward areas.

An effective way of confronting these problems of urban and regional growth is to create or expand a few key cities in each of the lagging regions and to do the same in the more prosperous regions. In the case of the former, the aim would be to promote growth; in the case of the latter, it would be either to accommodate growth or to assist in the transformation or renewal of the existing metropolis. Where location permits, it might even be possible to have the new city (or the expanded city) serve all of these purposes. Such a concentration of effort would make it easier for the centers in the lagging regions to compete with the big cities and even to help spark a transformation in the agricultural and cultural patterns of the hinterland.[8] The development of these centers in the lagging regions, and of the new centers in the growing regions, would also permit the largest metropolitan areas to cope more effectively with the population avalanche which now threatens them.

Of course, much of the success of this policy depends on the proper selection of urban growth centers. But other factors, too, will influence the outcome. Investments in these centers may be premature or unwise. Individual firms may see no advantage in shifting their location until the necessary infrastructure exists, whereas the provision of such facilities may not always induce the desired entrepreneurial activity.[9] Probably only one or two centers can be developed at the outset in very poor countries, or in each of the depressed regions of economically advanced countries, and perhaps even in the largest metropolitan areas. This is because the size of the market restricts the number of activities and because very limited resources will be available under most circumstances. But as the economy grows and regional markets expand, more and larger urban centers will then be feasible. Notwithstanding the very real difficulties involved, the promotion of such regional and sub-regional centers may have a better chance for adoption than a plan that neglects either the critical needs of the lagging areas or the growth and reconstruction requirements of the metropolis. Moreover, this strategy will surely prove more effective in promoting various development goals than would either entirely dispersing growth or entirely concentrating it in very large cities.

POLICY IMPLICATIONS

To carry out such a program, a *national urban growth strategy* is necessary. The development and administration of such a strategy would require a small, high-level professional staff of policy and research specialists to work in a national agency and in each of the major urban growth centers. Although this approach would not be foreign to the political tradition of most countries, the creation of an urban growth strategy national in scope would be a new experience for city and regional planners.[10] By training and experience their function has been to help formulate local development goals and to devise policies and control mechanisms for achieving local and regional development objectives. To design an urban growth strategy for the nation would require local and regional planners to learn new skills and perspectives.

An urban growth strategy would also require new efforts in economic planning. Most developing countries now have some sort of economic policy agency or planning mechanism for promoting growth. These agencies generally define economic goals, evaluate available resources and economic opportunities, and suggest appropriate policies—fiscal, monetary, budgetary, exchange, and development. For the most part their analyses are aggregative and formulated in terms of trends and the requirements of output, employment, income, savings, investment, and other factors. On occasion, these agencies may plan specific locations for such capital investments as roads, multipurpose valley programs, resettlement projects, harbor installations, and irrigation schemes. More recently, national plans are providing special tax and credit incentives to induce firms to locate in backward or lagging regions. But the measures designed by these national agencies are often too unfocussed and limited in character to achieve substantial results. An additional limiting factor is the desire to achieve high growth rates. Recognizing that for the short-run the most efficient and productive regions are those which are already developed, the agencies tend to concentrate their programs there and neglect less developed areas. Sheer ignorance also plays a restrictive role. Thus, location analysis is usually slighted or at best only briefly touched on, if considered at all. In general,

> economic development plans concentrate on capital use. They do not as a rule include a plan for land use as such. Decisions as to land use are left to private investors, local governments, and to central government implementing agencies within the framework of capital allocation which is provided in the economic development plan. Presumably, if an appropriate allocation of capital is obtained, the appropriate allocation of management, labor and land will follow substantially.[11]

As a result of this convenient assumption, economists have generally neglected such questions as where and on what scale growth should occur and how these growth complexes might affect each other. Moreover, though the situation is changing, most economists now working on plans for economic development have not been specifically trained, and have only a marginal interest, in the urban or regional aspects of development.

The gulf between physical and economic planning further complicates matters. Until recently, the low esteem in which local and regional planning was held has inhibited most top-rank graduates in economics and the other social sciences from developing a serious interest in this field. Also, development economists function in a different administrative sphere and use different methods of analysis than do city and regional planners. The conventional reaction of the economist to the city planner, especially in developing countries, is to wonder whether the economy can afford the luxury of civic sculpture or whatever other "uneconomic" frills he imagines the city planner is contemplating. The city planner, on the other hand, is not infrequently scornful of the economist for his use of glib generalizations based on unrealistic assumptions and his deficient understanding of the practicality and regional effects of his decisions. Neither image is flattering or just, yet each continues to influence attitudes.

Recently, however, there has been a remarkable growth of interest in urban and regional studies. First-rate minds are entering the field. The upsurge promises to produce a new breed of urban specialists: not just economists and city planners, but geographers, sociologists, anthropologists, and political scientists who understand one another's models and ways of thinking and take these into account when engaged in research or policy-making. Questions that could not be adequately answered before the rise of this interdisciplinary approach to urban development will now become the subjects of extensive research.

There are already a number of crucial items on the research agenda. One of the most important concerns the aims of development. There are growing doubts about our ability to establish meaningful priorities when there are multiple goals. Our mathematical models have less relevance when decision-makers "satisfice" rather than "optimize," which current research suggests is often the case. There is evidence that inadequate account is taken of what is feasible and of what people realistically want. And, the conventional criteria do not give us sufficient information on which to base urban and regional development strategies. It will not do to think simply in terms of income levels, employment, and growth rates. Although a variety of urban alternatives may be consistent with a specific group of economic targets, some of them may prove more likely than others to achieve the desired ends. It only begs the question to assume that the proper patterns will sort themselves out automatically. Whether they will in fact do so is precisely what is at issue.

We shall also have to evaluate the potentials of different urban growth centers. In the past the emphasis in economic policy has been "vertical," that is, on developing particular sectors of the economy such as transportation, power, agriculture, education, and forestry. This emphasis neglects the symbiotic character of a region and the interdependence of its diverse "systems" of activities. The allocation of funds to local and state authorities is rarely the result of careful studies of the development possibilities of various urban regions or even of estimates of the complementary requirements resulting from proposals for development in these areas. The consequences of this neglect can be seen in studies and reports on the problems of implementing development: the promotion of agricultural projects without marketing facilities, ports without feeder roads, power installations without market outlets, and industries without adequate shopping, housing, educational, and community facilities.[12] These errors would be substantially reduced if the vertical estimates were supplemented—or corrected—by parallel "horizontal" evaluations of the most significant regional needs and growth problems.

The indirect effects of national policies must also receive some attention. We know that urban development may be influenced by changes in tax policy, agricultural development, land reform, tariffs, transportation rates, amortization allowances for plants and equipment, and the location and priority schedules for infrastructure investments. But these influences, as a rule, are unintended consequences of efforts to do something else. To the extent that urban growth objectives could be set in advance, the effects of some of these policies and programs could be examined and, when appropriate, adjusted to serve these objectives better.

HYPOTHETICAL INSTITUTIONAL REQUIREMENTS

What are the hypothetical institutional requirements for a national urban growth strategy and what are the problems such a strategy would be likely to encounter? Some first approximations can be hazarded, provided we make certain assumptions about the character and functions of the central government. An effective urban growth strategy presupposes the existence of: 1) a stable government; 2) some intelligence mechanisms to analyze problems and suggest roles which the government should play; 3) some central power over the principal incentive and control mechanisms, including those affecting the allocation of capital; and 4) a relatively efficient civil service. The economy, however, might be private, public, or mixed.

To devise an urban growth strategy, an urban or regional organization would have to be established sooner or later, either in the chief executive's office, or in a national planning agency, or in some national agency for public works and urban development. Its primary function would be to recommend a growth strategy to the chief executive, the appropriate legislative committees, and other designated officials. It would also have to monitor such a strategy once adopted. To carry out these functions, the organization would be required to evaluate urban growth goals and ways of realizing them, define the major regions of the country, identify existing or potential growth centers in these regions, and specify the methods to be used to help these centers grow. These methods might utilize a variety of approaches: penalties and controls to limit the expansion of the very largest cities or metropolitan areas, as well as grants, tax incentives, and other premiums to induce private investment into those centers designated for growth. In the course of these efforts, it would probably be necessary for the organization to acquire reliable information about the functions, migration and growth patterns, and development possibilities of the country's principal urban regions. The agency would also have to assess the government plans for transportation, power networks, and resource utilization and the prospects for major industrial, agricultural, and village developments. This information would help the staff to propose policies tailored to the needs of different regions. These studies and policy proposals would also put private investors in a better position to judge the potential of particular growth centers.

For most countries, these efforts set the outside limits on what might be feasible within the first few years. Other countries, however, desiring or already possessing more comprehensive planning systems, might want to go further and establish program linkages which would encompass all the key agencies of their central governments. Under such an arrangement, the principal central government departments, particularly those concerned with development, would have to prepare a series of plans, programs, budgets, and schedules dealing with current operations and targets. These activities, as well as the development programs of local and regional authorities, would have to be evaluated in relation to the nation's urban growth strategy. Some local agencies, and perhaps even some agencies in the central government, might need help in preparing their plans and projects and in relating them to other programs. To serve these functions, a special unit would be created. Its staff, composed of "all-around" trouble shooters and area specialists, would advise local agencies, coordinate programs, and cut through red tape. They would also perform an invaluable feedback function by reporting to the central agency on local plans and needs, on the effectiveness of growth programs, and on problems that otherwise might be overlooked.

New techniques for allocating capital would also be needed. One important innovation might be the creation of regional capital budgets. They could be prepared in a relatively simple way. The proposed budget, involving the urban development projects of all the departments of the central government, would be transferred to a set of forms indicating the regional incidence of capital expenditures. (When appropriate, provincial and local investments might also be included.) By using *development maps,* it would then be possible to see at a glance the locations of both past and proposed capital expenditures. In time, the standardization of forms and classifications would permit the computerization of this entire process. These maps would provide valuable and easily understandable information on the implicit development policy of the nation. They would also make it easier to compare development goals, complementary requirements, and actual progress.

Problems of Implementation

The particular national urban growth strategy adopted by a country will deviate from the proposed model according to that country's special needs and situation. At least three problems, however, will confront almost all of these programs. First is the critical question of personnel. Specialists in this area are rare, and, as we have observed, few have received appropriate professional training. Second is the problem of the level of intellectual capital. It is debatable whether we know enough about urban growth strategies either to deal with them effectively or to secure the necessary understanding early enough to avoid doing more harm than good. The third problem is the fear that the proposed innovations in policy may contribute to further political centralization. This would be especially unfortunate for countries which are already suffering from "apoplexy in the center and anemia at the edges."

Mention of these difficulties will arouse varied reactions. Some people will brush the problems aside; some will consider them easily solvable; there are others who will regard them as decisive arguments against the adoption of any national strategies for urban growth. Certainly there is enough substance in these views to cause responsible persons to hesitate and weigh the consequences. One of the dangers in many countries, particularly the underdeveloped ones, is the desire to bite off more than can be chewed. Even such economically advanced countries as Britain and France have experienced difficulties in bringing such programs to a successful conclusion.

But the choice between all or nothing may not be necessary. Some of the hypothetical recommendations can stand alone. For some countries it may be enough simply to create a high-level national agency concerned with devising an urban growth strategy, without establishing a more intricate planning system. Other countries may want to undertake thorough regional studies or establish a mechanism for regional budgets. Still others may wish to go much further, for surely the argument for more extensive action is not without appeal. Decisions are daily being made which fix tomorrow's patterns of development. Many governments might prefer to make these decisions consciously.

II

Choosing Urban Regions for Development[1]

A country which embarks upon an urban growth strategy must soon decide which regions are the right ones for development. No doubt, political considerations will shape the final decision. But errors have to be minimized, for they can hobble or even destroy a program. Some helpful criteria for the choice of these regions are therefore desirable — if only to suggest the kinds of compromises that might reasonably be made.

Unfortunately, few theoretical or empirical studies have probed the subject directly and those that have leave much to be desired. Of the economic concepts, the most relevant are concerned with comparative advantage, growth, location, and programming rules and techniques. In addition, there have been a number of urban growth studies undertaken mainly by geographers, historians, and economists. The more traditional deal with questions of urban hierarchy and rank size relationships, but there have also been some illuminating investigations of urban history, peripheral hinterlands, and growth centers.

In examining this literature, our aim is to devise an initial set of guidelines for the selection of urban growth regions, after explaining the limitations of current concepts and drawing whatever insights we can from them.

The Relevant Economic Concepts

The Limitations of Comparative Advantage

No one, not even the most fanciful utopian visionary, ever assumes that development should be spread evenly throughout a region or a nation. On the contrary, it is generally taken for granted that most development should and will take place where it is comparatively advantageous. If development were guided by the *principle of comparative advantage,* there would be no need for criteria to determine where growth should take place. Regions, like countries, would import the things they could buy more cheaply and sell the things they could produce more cheaply. Those regions that could perform these economic activities most advantageously would experience the greatest growth. Presumably, optimum development patterns would emerge from conventional market behavior.

Whatever may be the pros and cons of this doctrine, clearly it would not be of much help in deciding where to provide development incentives or where to make infrastructure investments. The assumption is that such public decisions would be made only after private investment decisions had already occurred. Development policy then would merely follow the dictates of the market, reinforcing the direction of growth rather than altering or initiating it.

The comparative advantage thesis may also be questioned because it presupposes the traditional assumption of equilibrium theory; namely, the efficient adjustment of supply and demand when market prices equal economic (or opportunity) costs. To be sure, these adjustments do occur under the hypothetical conditions of perfect competition. But in the actual market many of the these posited conditions are absent. This is especially true in developing countries where high unemployment, exchange crises, and other disequilibria constitute serious prima facie evidence of economic maladjustments.

16

In addition, the doctrine of comparative advantage takes no account of economies of scale. As a consequence, it overlooks the reductions of cost, the growth of demand, and the improvements in efficiency and quality which may result as production increases and new activities and services burgeon. Many countries also consider it dangerous to depend on the pattern of prices and fluctuations of international raw material markets. Most of them prefer a more diversified economy, one that can more readily assume other functions should changing trade conditions make this necessary. Unfortunately, as Hollis Chenery and others have noted, modification of the comparative advantage thesis to take account of these objections would rob the doctrine of much of its practical value. This is because one has to make "an explicit analysis of the growth process itself before it is possible to determine, even theoretically, where comparative advantage lies; market prices and current opportunity costs are no longer sufficient."[2]

The Growth Economists

These difficulties have led many economists to reject the doctrine of comparative advantage, or at least its customary expressions. Their models relax equilibrium assumptions and allow for internal and external economies of scale and for long-range changes in the quantity and quality of production. These more realistic assumptions lead to quite different inferences for policy. Thus, growth economists contend that to obtain a pattern of production and trade which maximizes income over time requires not "laissez faire" but the encouragement of the most influential growth sector(s) of an economy — such as that which occurred in the past of timber in Sweden, cotton textiles in Great Britain, and railroads in the United States, France, Germany, Canada, and Russia. Investment prospects, they would add, depend on spreading the effects of the expansion of these "leading sectors" to complementary activities.

Beyond this point, the policy recommendations of the growth economists diverge. They may be roughly divided into two major groups.[3] Some favor the simultaneous expansion of a number of interrelated sectors *(balanced growth)* because of the interdependence of the economy and the need for a significant widespread change. Others advocate concentrated, sequential growth patterns (*imbalanced growth*). They do so partly because of certain inelasticities (limited capital, managerial ability, and technological innovations) and partly to induce linkages which will spur further development, either "backward linkages" based on inputs, such as import substitution, or "forward linkages" involving outputs, such as encouraging more varied uses of existing products or services.[4]

The Location Theorists

We might be much further ahead in ways of handling growth strategies if the leads furnished by the growth economists were explored in more detail by the theorists concerned with the location of economic activities. But their principal approach, with few exceptions, has been from the point of view of equilibrium theory with extensions to take account of transportation and trade variables. Location theory, therefore, is subject to the same criticisms that the growth economists make about equilibrium theory and comparative advantage. Its limitations are best illustrated by citing W. Isard, the foremost scholar in this field. In his major work on location theory he touches on the problem of determining "the optimum spatial distribution and hierarchy of cities of different size," and he specifically poses the question: "Given a network of cities and corresponding patterns of land use, along what channels should changes in the structure of this network and these patterns be fostered in order to attain a situation closer to optimum?"[5] But, after a brief discussion of the agglomeration aspects of location theory, he concludes that there is "little to say beyond the obvious; units are attracted to or repelled from cities according to a simple comparison of advantages and disadvantages generated by these cities."[6]

Programming Rules and Techniques

There are also a number of programming rules and techniques that are being used today in national planning to guide investments in development projects, but their merits vary depending on the uses to which they are put.[7] The least versatile of these rules (or criteria) and the ones making the least demands on skill and data are the *minimum capital output ratio* and the *capital labor ratio.* They are used to identify the development projects which would require the least capital, measured respectively in relation to output and labor. Two other tools of even greater utility, requiring still higher skills and better data, are, first, the *marginal productivity criteria,* which attempt to measure and rank the contributions of specific projects to the national product and, second, the *marginal growth criteria,* which adjust the marginal product by taking into account future effects, especially on savings and re-investments in particular. Finally, the most versatile of all and the most difficult to apply are the *programming techniques.* These attempt to develop, on the basis of specified goals, a consistent and optimum allocation of resources among a number of feasible economic activities. Due allowance is made for resource limitations, the expected demand for goods and services, and the probable effects of new investments on the economy.

When data is not available, which is often the case, the simpler ratios are usually employed. But they can hardly be used with much confidence, since they rely on a number of erroneous assumptions. The notions that capital is the only scarce resource and that there are no variations in efficiency by sector are two examples of these misconceptions. Another objection to using the simpler ratios in selecting urban development regions is that they would make the choice of regions dependent upon specific project investment analyses. Should the decision-maker have to select regions in advance of such project analyses, as he may often be required to do, these simpler ratios would be inapplicable.

The programming techniques, when backed up by sound information systems and highly versatile computing capabilities, add a powerful technique to current analytical methods. Nonetheless, they cannot cope with intangibles or non-quantitative considerations. This imposes severe limitations on any evaluation of costs or benefits or of such constraints as the preference for one type of growth sequence rather than another because it economizes on managerial ability or can spur political action.[8] Programming techniques are also often made irrelevant either because of the assumption of linear relationships or because of empirical difficulties, such as those involved in estimating training effects and economies of scale. Yet these are precisely the problems that crop up when one is attempting to compare the effects of specific incentives or infrastructure investments. The difficulties of comparison are all the more intractable when the estimates are required for a wide range of hard-to-define investment complexes in several different regions.

Regional Programming Models

Despite the difficulties, programming techniques have proven sufficiently attractive to tempt location theorists to experiment with regional applications. Indeed, some of the more optimistic spirits think it may soon be possible to devise operational interregional input-output models. They expect to be able to formulate equations describing the combination of economic inputs of different types of activities in regions which, in turn, will account for the total output of goods and services regionally or nationally. In the course of describing one of these models, Benjamin Stevens observed that they

> are basically ... identical in form to the non-spatial models of Leontief except that the inter-industry matrix is expanded by the inclusion of inter-regional relationships; each input is specified as coming, not just from a particular industry, but from a particular industry in a specific region. As is usual in input-output, the coefficients in the matrix are assumed constant. Thus, fixed proportions of each good are assumed drawn from each region no matter what the pattern of outputs. This, coupled with the usual condition that there be fixed factor proportions in the production of any good — makes an inter-regional input-output system completely determinate. Once a bill of goods is specified there is no choice mechanism for optimizing shipment patterns or substituting factors to achieve a more efficient allocation of available resources.[9]

If these interregional matrices were easier to construct and relatively reliable, they might be of considerable value. They could depict existing economic relationships within and between regions and trace the national and interregional effects of specified investments in particular regions. Their weaknesses, however, include neglect of price effects and of technological changes, egregious aggregation of industry categories, and unrealistic linearity assumptions. In addition, it is not only hard to get data for these models but the need for regional coefficients substantially increases the computational problems. These flaws make one skeptical of their immediate, not to mention their long-term, usefulness.

A related prescriptive technique, interregional linear programming, permits the exploration of cases where regional "location and transportation costs are allowed to vary and where transportation is included in the productive system as a consumer of factors."[10] But even Louis Lefeber, who believes this method holds promise, acknowledges that "because of the complexity of spatial adjustment, investigations which involve a large number of locations, goods and factors result in a prohibitively large number of choice variables; hence an investigation of spatial allocation embracing many details cannot be undertaken without suitable simplifications."[11] On the other hand, Stevens, another pioneer in the use of this tool, thinks his model would enable the analyst to trace the differential effects of locational decisions, such as those involved in the building of major public works or the development of a steel plant or some other private installation.[12] But, in fact, neither of these models would disclose which regional pattern was the optimum. More specifically, they would not indicate how, or where, new regional concentrations should be developed or where significant new infrastructure investments should be made. Thus, these efforts, too, are of limited value for our purposes.

URBAN GROWTH STUDIES

Urban Hierarchies

Let us turn now to the studies dealing more directly with urban growth. One of the basic research efforts in this area is the work on the nature of central place hierarchies of W. Christaller, A. Lösch, and others. They have shown how one can derive an *order of cities* based on the market areas or hinterland of a territory. They have also noted that "corresponding to each order there is both a definite number of functions which each city of that order performs and a population size typical for each city of that order."[13] This hierarchy reflects the results of myriad efforts to maximize markets, to minimize travel effort and costs, and to take advantage of economies of urbanization and of scale.

A second empirical relationship purports to link urban size and rank. Generally referred to as *the rank size rule*, it suggests that the population of cities in an array of cities by size within a defined territory is inversely proportional to its rank. In other words, the second largest city is one-half the largest, the third largest is one-third, the fourth is one-fourth, and so on.[14]

We know something about the underlying factors in these two relationships. Christaller's urban hierarchy constitutes one type of non-symmetrical or skewed distribution of cities by size. The rank size formula represents another. There are several reasons why one should expect skewed distributions of cities (though not necessarily a relationship conforming to the rank size rule). Most urban areas perform simple service, manufacturing, marketing, and government functions. This is why the bulk of our cities are small. Only a relatively small number of urban sites have an exceptionally favorable location or resource endowment. These advantages, if exploited by vigorous leadership or favored by happy accidents, will be further reinforced by economies of scale and agglomeration. The subsequent growth of these areas will augment their income and purchasing power and spur the proliferation within them of a wide range of market and service-oriented enterprises, as well as activities serving national and international markets. Generally, such a combination of favorable conditions is essential to the formation of large metropolitan areas. Sheer inertia will then tend to sustain them. Indeed, Herbert Simon has shown that a class of skewed distributions may emerge if net urban growth is simply proportional to the size of the urban population.[15] To be sure, changes in the specific types of population distributions will occur through changes in growth rates and migration. But the non-symmetrical patterns will still persist, since the imbalance in opportunities and incentives which influences migration flows also generates skewed distribution.

The significance of the rank size rule is that it attempts to formulate a precise hypothesis concerning the specific form of this skewed distribution. If this rule accurately depicted urban size relationships, we could try to project the future size of the largest city and then calculate the sizes of the other cities by their rank. We could thereby identify potential growth centers and even establish population growth targets for specific cities. However, the evidence in support of the rule, as formulated, is quite skimpy. In the United States, Poland, Belgium, India, China, and Brazil, the rank size rule seems to have only limited applicability. In other countries, such as Austria, Sweden, Japan, Mexico, Spain, and Peru, its applicability is even less.[16]

It is possible to adjust the rank size formula by computing the exponent that would best fit the available data on the sizes of cities. But it would still be questionable whether such a modified version could prove reliable for projections.[17] For the rule would remain subject to the same limitations of the original formulation. First, the basis for the definition of territory is unclear. Neither the research on central place hierarchies nor the rank size rule provides adequate guidance on boundaries. As E. M. Hoover has noted, "the ascending series of orders of places could be carried on up to the largest city in the world or else arbitrarily chopped off at any given smaller size or confined to a smaller area."[18] Second, it would not be easy either to define the boundaries or to estimate the future population of the largest city; and any errors would affect the projections for the other cities. A third, and even more serious, weakness is that the rank size rule describes, in effect, an equilibrium model. It presupposes an urban system in which the growth rates of cities in relation to each other do not change. But over time the relative growth rates do change, as evidenced by the changing sizes and ranks of places like Houston, Lyon, Ankara, and a great many other cities. The rank size rule provides no guidance for anticipating these changes.[19] Nonetheless, despite the frailties of this concept, the hierarchical distribution of cities is a stubborn fact. This suggests that any national policy to equalize the sizes of cities would be very risky, if not ill-advised, for it would require the reversal of persistent and powerful trends.

Urban History, Peripheral Hinterlands, and Growth Centers

Still other suggestive hints can be gleaned from a number of historical studies of the patterns of urban and regional development. One of the most important of these is N. S. B. Gras's analysis of the metropolitan economy. The core of his view is that the metropolis, in addition to having a healthful climate and an efficient location between consumers and producers, "must possess a *hinterland,* a tributary of adjacent territory, rich in natural resources, occupied by a productive population and accessible by means of transportation."[20]

This perspective illuminates B. F. Hoselitz's polar categories of "generative" and "parasitic" cities.[21] Strictly speaking, most cities are *generative* in Hoselitz's sense. Their hinterlands prosper when they prosper because they perform functions for the hinterlands on which they depend for supplies and markets. The *parasitic cities,* on the other hand, are rare. Only Batavia and Rio de Janeiro among contemporary cities have been identified as such, and on rather flimsy evidence.[22] By definition, these cities do not encourage regional economic growth and development. They perform negligible functions for their hinterlands which, at best, serve them only as limited supply areas and as insignificant markets. As a consequence, the growth of these hinterlands is limited or impeded by such neglect.

Developing this relationship further, W. F. Stolper has maintained that in advanced countries every consumer has some access to the market area of each good, whereas in the hinterland of Brazil and of most other underdeveloped countries such access is remote or non-existent.[23] Providing such access through improvements in transportation and communication is generally necessary to open hinterlands as supply and market areas. Often these improvements also help to raise the productivity of the surrounding agricultural regions and even to channel the flow of capital from the more successful agricultural enterprises into local trade and manufacture.[24]

If, however, access cannot be improved, there may be severe penalties. Peripheral areas are often *lagging regions.* The North of Britain, the West of France, the South of Italy, and the East of Turkey are some typical examples. This tendency has prompted T. W. Schultz to formulate his well-known locational matrix hypothesis.[25] It asserts that urban, industrial, and rural activities situated in areas peripheral to the dominant economic center are destined to be at a distinct disadvantage as long as such center-periphery relationships persist.

Still other studies of lagging regions, as well as the experience of grappling with their problems, have made many decision-makers reluctant to place too much reliance on migration as a way of helping these regions.[26] It arouses too much resistance and sometimes creates more problems than it solves. It also takes a long time to curb the population growth of these regions and to transform their economy. Partly for this reason, the idea of *urban growth centers* has developed special appeal.

Interestingly, the original notion of *growth poles*, as formulated by F. Perroux, referred only to influential economic activities — firms, groups of firms, and industries. Perroux was not especially interested in urban or regional growth centers.[27] As his doctrine acquired currency, however, the concept was used more loosely. The notion of urban growth centers became popular and was soon used interchangeably with the term "growth poles." Strictly speaking, however, only the term "urban growth centers" has a geographic connotation. It refers to the concentration (or implantation) of growing and influential economic activities in a particular geographic center or along a major transportation axis. There has been an increasing recognition of the ability of urban growth centers to generate numerous advantages for their population and economic activities. Among such advantages are more varied public services, lower costs, more plentiful labor, more attractive job opportunities, and desirable investment, educational and cultural effects. The fact that the size and the characteristics of the activities are ambiguous, the costs and benefits uncertain, and the factors which determine the location of successful centers not at all clear does not discourage use of the concept. On the contrary, its ambiguity contributes to its suggestiveness as well as to its misuse. And, despite pleas for more rigorous definitions, the situation is unlikely to change much until we know more about the sequences or stages by which growth and urban development spread to lagging regions and more about the type of urban patterns and policies that exert the maximum influence on lagging hinterlands.[28]

THE DERIVATION OF CRITERIA

Our review of the relevant literature in the field has given us a better sense of what it is that we do and do not know. The findings, although limited, reinforce some of our earlier surmises which were discussed in Chapter I. Let us now consider how these findings can help us to devise an initial set of criteria for the selection of urban growth regions.

Our most important insights come from the growth theorists. They remind us that because of limited resources we must abandon hopes of achieving simultaneous development or equal growth rates in all regions or in all sectors of a region. We cannot even seek theoretically optimum growth rates, for we do not know how to define or to translate such optimum rates into meaningful or reliable operational specifications. Our efforts must have a more pragmatic purpose: to help a few urban centers reach some roughly estimated "critical size" that would induce "dynamic external economies"[29] and other desirable regional development effects.

These aims may be accomplished, the growth doctrines suggest, by encouraging some of the leading economic growth sectors of a nation to locate in the urban regions selected for expansion. If significant and sustained growth is to occur, the selection of these regions must take into account the feasibility of attracting such activities. Moreover, it would be prudent to ensure that the growth activities encouraged were those which either had, or might obtain in the future, a reasonable prospect of comparative advantage in these regions.[30] At this juncture, the programming rules and techniques might also provide some help since they make it possible to compare the productivity and other investment characteristics of proposed projects. Knowledge of input-output relationships should also be helpful to administrators trying to induce further development in the region by promoting a range and sequence of investments in related infrastructure and economic activities.

The studies of market areas, urban hierarchy, and metropolitan hinterlands underscore the function of urban growth regions as innovative and economic seedbeds for much larger hinterlands. This suggests another important criterion for the choice of urban growth regions. The regions selected for further development should be those which, with relative economy, could improve their access to large, resource-rich, or densely populated hinterlands. To apply this criterion, evaluations would have to be made of the probable cultural and economic consequences of proposed development programs in different regions. In particular, these evaluations

26

would have to consider the number of families affected and the likely changes in consumption and saving patterns and in social and other relationships. To be sure, few of these changes can be traced with precision. But, if an essential aim is to transform traditional attitudes and values, it is important to estimate how effectively different regional developments serve this end.[31]

Emergencies and critical problems, such as foreign exchange shortages or high unemployment, also have to be taken into account. In selecting regions as well as in determining the pattern of their development, the capacity (and willingness) of a region to contribute solutions to these problems should surely rank among the prime requisites. Evaluation, however, will not be easy since a variety of remedies may have to be considered, such as exploitation of the region's export potential of raw materials or agricultural products, the stimulation of import substitution activities, the attraction of labor-oriented industries, the encouragement of "tourism," and minimum infrastructure investments.[32]

Still another closely related, but even less tangible, criterion is the effect of different regional development programs on general public attitudes. Have the schemes the possibility of changing the citizen's, not to mention the decision-maker's, image of himself and his country? Can they arouse the public's imagination sufficiently to set in motion a whole new series of aspirations? It would be foolish to neglect these possibilities. Investment in a particular region may well yield poor returns, yet warrant high priority. A region, such as southern Italy or the Negev in Israel, may be so backward, neglected, or difficult to develop that it acquires symbolic value. It is as though a nation has stubbornly chosen to pit its energies and will against insuperable odds. Such programs, of necessity, must be unique exceptions, but it is worth remarking that over the long run they may speed up general development rather than retard it.

It would be difficult and perhaps even impossible to assign weights to the tangible and intangible criteria just discussed. Nevertheless, decision-makers must somehow ponder and estimate the relative significance of these considerations in their countries in arriving intuitively at some initial judgment. Any extensive development planned for selected regions will take a number of years to promote. Therefore, while tentative programs may be started based on existing knowledge and judgment, more detailed studies could be gotten underway. Then, at some later stage, when one has acquired a better sense of development prospects, these programs and their planned sequences can be reviewed and either stepped up or contracted.

To facilitate this subsequent review, the main goals ought to be reexamined closely. There is ample evidence that most countries want to maximize growth rates and to increase per capita income. But these general goals are subject to a variety of constraints.[33] Some of the more important of these are: minimum levels of consumption; implicit discount rates of future returns; desired distribution (or desired rate of change in the distribution) of income by class and region; and minimum acceptable levels (or minimum rate of decrease of the levels) of unemployment by class and region. Other restrictions emerge from projected defense requirements and from the need for internal consistency in resource allocations, such as specified exchange balances and execution of programs within available or potentially available resources of capital and of managerial and administrative ability. An even more important limitation today may be a preference for certain ways of carrying out programs, such as emphasis on decentralization and participation as well as on system maintenance. Moreover, since growth problems are not always clearly understood, the aims are likely to change significantly over time. Nations will certainly add new goals, weight them differently, specify less or additional constraints, or spell out the implications more or less precisely. Nonetheless, it is useful for a country to reexamine its more important objectives to see how different alternatives, including urban development alternatives, might affect the choice and scale of sector and urban investment programs.

More refined comparative analysis of the problems and of the long-term prospects of the leading regions will also be essential in order to evaluate development alternatives and to make program recommendations. This would presuppose evaluations of the principal characteristics and capabilities of the population. It would involve projections of trends in the main economic activities, in population, income, investment, and consumption. Knowledge of the demand and supply implications for related activities in the "leading regions" would also be necessary. It would be useful, too, to try to estimate the probable impact of existing national development policies on sectors within the selected regions as well as the induced effects of the regions' development on the national economy. Where data and circumstances permit, even the presently inadequate and unrealistic inter-industry and interregional input-output matrices and programming methods might be employed, if used mainly to direct attention to interacting relationships and significant implications which might otherwise be overlooked.[34]

In addition, if there is to be a more refined evaluation, the boundaries of the urban development regions will have to be carefully defined.[35] This job is a treacherous one and likely to beget friction and differences of opinion. There is no easy solution. At the outset, some rough ad hoc demarcations of the leading metropolitan and resource development regions could probably suffice. The nucleus of each region, even in later stages, should probably be some existing or potentially important urban complex; and the outer limits of the boundaries might be mapped on the basis of the hinterland which appeared likely to approximate the market or influence zone of this complex. The actual boundaries could conform as closely to these limits as data-gathering opportunities permitted.

But what about those regions which are not scheduled for large-scale urban development? One might argue that, if left to their own devices, they would fare no worse than in the past. This may or may not be true, but in any case, it is not a tenable political position. Most of these areas cannot be entirely neglected; yet neither can they be adequately served. In one attempt to simplify this problem, the regions of southern Italy were divided into three categories: areas of integral development, areas of partial development, and areas of emigration and rehabilitation.[36] But such classifications, especially if they are negative or neutral, arouse acrimonious controversy, for the effects that these labels induce are often akin to self-fulfilling prophecies. Partly for this reason, Britain changed the name of its lagging regions from "depressed areas" to "Development Areas."

However, a few things can be done to aid these other lagging regions without undertaking a major regional development program. By means of agricultural and community development projects, land reform, and self-help schemes, migration to large cities may be reduced to somewhat more manageable levels. It might also be possible to subsidize sufficiently the cost of transportation to bring many families living in lagging regions within reasonable commuting distance of growth centers. Much could also be done to ease the shifts of population that do occur. Training programs could be set up, accurate information on expanding areas disseminated, and, where resources permitted, minimum assistance payments provided during the period of relocation. Investments in health and education, in social rather than in economic overhead capital,[37] might also be emphasized in these regions. Such investments would contribute to development as well as to welfare. Finally, some areas might only need help for a short period or might require more moderate assistance, whereas in other areas some uneconomic investments and tax bonuses might be inescapable. In short, some positive and some token efforts and a great deal of consummate political skill will be essential. Success will depend on the balance struck between economic progress and social welfare and on a sensitivity to those repercussions that can upset a theoretically rational development program.

Once these major decisions have been made, what next? If urban growth policies are to achieve their long-range goals, key officials in all agencies engaged in sector development will have to relate their own programs to these policies. Better coordinating and feedback mechanisms will be required to deal with problems and errors before they become too serious. To influence the contours of growth programs and to project infrastructure and land use requirements, detailed market, cost, manpower, and industry feasibility studies will be needed. And, effective tax benefits, incentive programs, and other credit measures may also prove necessary to spur development in designated areas.

All of these things are important, but without significant public consensus and political support, the program's budgetary requirements and other needs may never be obtained or, if obtained, may be whittled away by attrition and negligence. Appointment of a distinguished and skillful administrator may be one means of countering this tendency. "Reform-mongering"[38] may be another, and grass roots participation a third. In the past, the vision of transforming a hinterland or of building great new cities has played a powerful role in propelling nations forward: the settlement of America's West, the Turkish move to Ankara, the development of Russia beyond the Urals are but a few examples of this. Today, if proposed, such undertakings would be labeled as mere "show piece" psychology, and yet they actually worked. Somehow, urban and regional growth strategies must be spelled out, enlarged, dramatized, and made more visible. For they, too, have this potential for sparking unsuspected energies and therefore need to be made to work.

National Planning of
an Urban Growth Region:
The Experience of Venezuela[1]

Once an urban region has been selected for development, what happens next? What specific studies are required and what policies have to be set? What steps are necessary to put the program into effect and what problems are likely to arise in the process? Some of these measures and difficulties have already been discussed in general terms. It will be clearer and certainly more interesting to examine an actual case, the development of Ciudad Guayana in the lower Orinoco valley of Venezuela (see Figure 1).

In the past forty years, Venezuela has undergone a great transformation. At the start of the oil boom of the 1920's, the country was a rural nation with a population approximately 80 percent non-urban. By 1961 almost 60 percent of its population was urban and Venezuela had become a nation of city dwellers. Its population growth of 3 percent a year, one of the fastest in the world, has been outpaced by the even more rapid growth of its major cities: Caracas, Maracaibo, Barquisimeto, Valencia, and Maracay. From 1926 to 1961, the population of Caracas, the capital city, increased four times the rate of increase of the total population; it also shifted from a little more than twice to three times the size of Maracaibo, the next largest city and the largest center of oil production. But severe problems accompanied economic progress. Investment of oil revenues in public works, coupled with the growth of services and consumer industries, induced a vast urban migration. This, in turn, resulted in a high rate of unemployment, reaching levels of 20 percent and more. Discontent bred instability, dictatorship, revolution, and finally a coalition government which stressed new policies favoring diversification of development and reform. These new policies sought to establish modern basic industry and thereby reduce the dependence of Venezuela on petroleum. A complementary aim was to promote an urban growth zone in an area other than Caracas or Maracaibo and thus provide a new migration target for the population leaving the poorer regions. Both aims found remarkable expression in the development of Ciudad Guayana and its surrounding region.

While certain features of this experience are characteristic only of Venezuela, or of the problems of a new metropolis, many of the problems confronted and the techniques used are relevant to urban growth regions throughout the world. In addition, the way in which the decisions and programs for Ciudad Guayana evolved[2] in the context of national development goals may suggest how urban growth strategies elsewhere can become part of national development policies.

THE GUAYANA REGION

At first glance, the lower Orinoco valley of Venezuela hardly appears an inviting place to build a great city. Isolated (it is three hundred miles from Caracas), tropical in climate, and generally inferior in agricultural resources, the region stood still while other regions were developing first their agriculture and then their oil deposits and other industries. Nevertheless, Guayana's potential was expected some day to make up for its backwardness. The region is vast. Dominated by broad expanses of savannah and

tropical forest, broken only by treacherous rivers and low mountain ranges, it occupies one-third of Venezuela's total area. Sporadic discoveries of diamonds, combined with memories of gold mining in the nineteenth century, had also created a myth of fabulous riches. As a result, Guayana has long been a beckoning frontier suggesting adventure and opportunity to most Venezuelans.

The myth still persists, and rightly so, for the region possesses extraordinary resources. It has rich deposits of high-grade iron ore and promising possibilities for the mining of manganese, nickel, chromium, gold, industrial diamonds, and even bauxite and aluminum laterite. Within sixty miles of Ciudad Guayana, there are large fields of petroleum and natural gas. The sites for the main economic activities, along the banks of the Orinoco River, provide direct access to the ocean. Running through the heart of the city is a branch of the Orinoco, the Caroní River, which has a hydroelectric potential of about ten million kilowatts. With an abundance of potential power, water, timber, and iron ore, Ciudad Guayana is admirably equipped to be a center of industry.

As recently as 1950, the population on the site of the city was only 4,000. Then, two United States–owned organizations, the Orinoco Mining Company and the Iron Mines Company, built plants in Guayana for iron-ore processing. They also created small settlements there for their staffs. Later the Venezuelan government began the construction of a large steel plant on the Orinoco a few miles west of these centers. In 1960 President Betancourt's administration, recognizing the potential of the Guayana region, created a public corporation to develop it. This agency, the *Corporación Venezolana de Guayana* (CVG), was entrusted with the job of devising a growth strategy for the region. It took over the steel plant, which was still under construction, and the Macagua Dam at the Caroní River Falls. The Corporation also began plans for developing a city in the Guayana region. Through purchase from private owners and through transfer of public lands from other government agencies, it acquired much of the land within the prospective city area. The powers of the Corporation, however, were limited by the activities and jurisdiction of other agencies. Its capacity to act was also handicapped by a shortage of skilled staff members. To help overcome this difficulty, CVG engaged the assistance of the Joint Center for Urban Studies of the Massachusetts Institute of Technology and Harvard University.

Initial Efforts

The site confronting the planners where the city was to be built was an area about 15 miles long on the south side of the Orinoco (see Figure 2). The terrain was vast and in some respects spectacular. It was dominated by the broad Orinoco, the falls of the Caroní, and the heights above both rivers. Scattered over this area were several disconnected settlements. At the western end was the steel plant; at the eastern end the community of San Félix. Within these bounds were Puerto Ordaz, a mining town built by the Orinoco Mining Company for its staff; Palua, another mining settlement; and various smaller developments that sprawled along

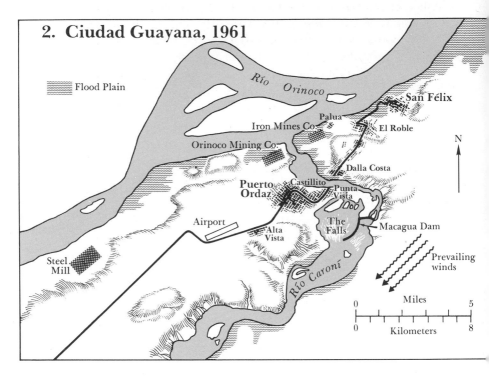

2. Ciudad Guayana, 1961

Flood Plain

Río Orinoco

San Félix

Palua

Iron Mines Co.

El Roble

Orinoco Mining Co.

Dalla Costa

Puerto Ordaz

Castillito

Punta Vista

N

Airport

Alta Vista

The Falls

Macagua Dam

Steel Mill

Río Caroní

Prevailing winds

Miles
0   5

Kilometers
0   8

connecting highways. The Caroní River, running north-south, cut the area in two. A bridge across it was under construction.

One of the planners' first tasks was to estimate the magnitude of the job that lay ahead. Rough schemes had been prepared previously by the Urban Planning Office of the Ministry of Public Works, but these were inadequate. They assumed, for example, that the town would serve about 200,000 to 250,000 people. When the figures were questioned, however, they turned out to be only guesses. A case could just as easily be made for a town of 100,000 or 400,000. The staff needed more accurate information. They had to know the probable sizes of the town in different stages of its development. They required data on the types of industries to be attracted to the region. They had to learn more about the needs and preferences of the existing and future population. Without such information it would be difficult to make land use plans suited to Ciudad Guayana's specific development aims.

But before these studies could be completed, the planners were confronted with a series of urgent problems. Workers looking for jobs were already arriving in large numbers. By 1961 the population of Guayana had mushroomed to 42,000; in 1964 it reached 70,000. The former village of San Félix alone had 45,000 inhabitants. New shantytowns were springing up overnight. There was a clamor for housing, water, sewers, electricity, roads, and schools. The planners could not wait for studies or long-range programs to be completed. Sites had to be found immediately for the temporary settlement of newcomers, for low-rent housing, and for industrial plants. Site plans that had been made earlier and public works that were already in progress had to be redesigned to avoid damaging the long-range interests of the community. These solutions not only needed to be worked out in a hurry; they had to be fashioned with negligible data, a fairly limited staff, and the assurance that if things went wrong, as on occasion they assuredly would, the planners would be the scapegoats for all disaffected elements.

Largely because of the accidental circumstance of their availability, the first Joint Center specialists to arrive on the scene in September 1961 were the physical planners. Faced by a situation that threatened to get out of hand, they and their Venezuelan counterparts quickly initiated studies on topography, vegetation, climate, and the existing activities and patterns of development. They then made some educated guesses concerning the probable sizes of the town over the next fifteen years and the possible location of its major land uses. On the basis of these rough judgments, they reviewed specific projects, already planned or in the early stages of development, to see which, if any, ought to be changed or relocated.

Because it was a serious undertaking to stop any activity, they tried to avoid making a negative decision unless clearly needed to achieve a major objective. One of the immediate issues was the new bridge across the Caroní, on which work was already well advanced. The local population ardently desired the Caroní Bridge. But the planners discovered, when it was too late for any fundamental redesign, that the bridge was too small. The capacity of the bridge should have been twice the original estimate. Since it was destined to be a critical visual element and an important

37

symbol of the future city, the planning staff wanted to make it as meaningful for the residents of Ciudad Guayana as the Ponte Vecchio was to the people of Florence or the Galatea Bridge to the population of Istanbul. The planners sought and won a short delay in construction. This enabled them to design separate lanes for bicycles and pedestrians, thereby protecting them from the automobile traffic across the bridge and reducing congestion.

THE ECONOMIC AND SOCIAL DIAGNOSES

Eventually, the planners were able to begin assessing the principal development alternatives. Their first study was a detailed evaluation of the role Ciudad Guayana would play in the development of the Venezuelan economy and the Guayana region. Over the past twenty-five years the country's economy had been growing at the impressive rate of 7 percent a year, thanks largely to exploitation of its oil resources. The planners estimated that, to maintain this growth rate and to take care of the needs of a population increasing at the rate of 3 percent a year, Venezuela would have to raise its output of goods and services fourfold in the next twenty years. To depend mainly on petroleum would be unsound, particularly because this resource was bound to decline in the long run. Examination of the country's needs, potentialities, and existing industries led to the conclusion that its industrial development should focus strongly on the production of metals, petrochemicals, and machinery. Existing Venezuelan industries, which were largely final-assembly actitivities, required these basic and intermediate products. Their production would not only fill gaps in the domestic economy but would also provide Venezuela with export goods. This evaluation further substantiated the high priority which the national government had assigned to the development of Guayana. It also set the framework for the next step: selecting the specific economic activities to be encouraged in the region.

Criteria were prepared for the screening of these activities[3] and a preliminary list of the more promising industrial projects was then drawn up. The most important of these were iron and steel, sponge iron, aluminum, other metals and metal products, heavy machinery, electrochemicals, and forest products such as pulp and paper. These activities, if located in the Guayana region, could enjoy comparative advantage and could compete successfully in foreign markets. But to do so, they would have to be modern and efficient, and this would require huge capital outlays.

These findings were only first approximations, of course, and the planners continued to study other aspects of Guayana's economic development. They investigated how the functions of the Guayana region might change if Venezuela joined the Latin American Free Trade Association. They examined the relationships of the city's economy to its hinterland and to the changing patterns of urban and regional development in Venezuela. In particular, they intensively reviewed estimates of the projected long-term demand for the products of Guayana's new industries. Because a large proportion of the food for the population was imported from other regions, the planners also initiated a number of agricultural studies and experiments aimed at making Guayana more self-sustaining. In addition, they made a projection of the economic structure of the region. This included an analysis of national and regional demand (consumption, investment, and exports) and supply (production and imports). These data, in turn, formed the basis for estimates of the level and distribution of income.

It was also essential to gauge Guayana's long-term investment requirements.[4] The planners recommended a comprehensive investment program with two phases: one for the period 1963–1966 and one for the years 1967–1975. After being reviewed by the national planning office and slightly modified, it was adopted as part of Venezuela's national plan. On the basis of these projections, a preliminary financing program was established. The total projected investment in the Guayana region over the first ten years was expected to be about 3.8 billion dollars. Of this, the Venezuelan national government itself would provide more than 500 million for the period 1965–1968 and about 1.5 billion for 1969–1975. This amounted to approximately 10 percent of the total Venezuelan public investment in both periods. The rest was expected to come from private capital, both domestic and foreign, and from loans by international agencies. As a result of these investments, it was hoped that by 1975 the Guayana region would provide about a fifth of Venezuela's total manufacturing and export products.

The planning staff also worked out the implications of these findings for employment in basic and service activities and analyzed the accessibility and spatial requirements of these activities. By use of trends in family size and ratios of labor force to population, they were able to make population estimates as well. The economists could then supplement demographic projections with estimates of future population based on anticipated levels of economic activity. The indications were that the city would have a population of close to 100,000 by 1966 and of 400,000 by 1975. (These estimates were later changed to 90,000 by 1966 and 221,000 by 1975.)

Since such a rapidly growing city would face significant social problems, the planners initiated some experimental projects and studies to obtain policy leads. A pilot program was set up to help in-migrants build their own housing. Valuable insights also came from a member of the staff, who lived in one of the barrios of the city, had become friendly with the inhabitants, and had learned a great deal about their ways of life and their responses to the changes going on around them. Other investigations looked into questions of health, nutrition, and family-spending patterns. Still others surveyed migration characteristics, the attitudes of the people toward authority and change, and the relative importance attached to various public services and physical improvements. One novel inquiry surveyed how people of different backgrounds perceived and rated the importance of particular features of their physical environment.[5]

These studies took far more time than was thought desirable, partly because they were given low priority by some officials and partly because of the difficulty of obtaining skilled staff. Nonetheless, the investigations, besides providing essential background information, pointed up the need for a more adequate explanation of the development program to the people of the community. They also highlighted conflicts between the immediate concerns of the residents and the long-range aims of the planners, and stressed the importance of community participation in planning decisions. Above all, they signaled, to some of the top administrators and consultants, failings in the way certain programs were being carried out: in organizing the self-help housing program; in providing jobs for matrifocal (female-headed) families; in helping to create models and special opportunities for those trapped in the "culture of poverty"; and in slighting "mechanisms for those at the bottom to press their needs to those in control or to advance themselves upward through some sort of step by step mobility ladder."[6] As might be expected, the studies produced no immediate effects in some instances other than the raising of policy issues and the sensitizing of key members of the Venezuelan and Joint Center staff to neglected needs; whereas, in other cases, such as the self-help housing program, they led to a radical shift in management.

THE LAND USE STRATEGY

While these studies were underway, the staff also made plans for the layout of the city. These had to be versatile enough to ensure the orderly future integration of scattered settlements and specific enough to provide clear guidelines for the present. The primary objective was to create conditions that would foster economic growth. While holding to this main aim, the planners also wished to minimize investment expenses, recapture the increments in value resulting from the massive investments of the government, make economical and flexible arrangements suited to different stages of the city's growth, and take advantage of the normal forces of the market rather than running counter to them. In addition, they wanted to provide variety and interest in the community's living and social facilities and plan for the needs of families at all income levels. They also sought to establish a high standard of design which would serve as a model for developments elsewhere in Venezuela and attract enterprising organizations to Guayana. Finally, like any other organization, CVG wanted to maintain its organization and, if possible, enhance its power and prestige.

Given these multiple goals, much necessarily depended on the importance attached to them in specific circumstances. After a great deal of discussion, it was decided that first consideration had to be given to housing, education, and the facilities required by the local government, because significant failures in any of these areas could retard the entire program. Consensus, however, disappeared when the discussion turned to more specific questions about housing, schools, and local government. On still other matters there was never any clear agreement. These involved sensitive social questions such as the relative emphasis to be placed on employment as opposed to growth; participation and decentralization as opposed to efficiency; and general welfare objectives as opposed to development. Interestingly, CVG generally stressed economic development goals, centralized administration, and maintenance of the national image of the agency, whereas the Joint Center placed more emphasis on welfare goals, decentralization, and local participation in the decision-making process.[7]

The plans for the city were also influenced by four other considerations: the site was large; the location of the steel mill at the western end made that area the logical center for industrial development; a large proportion of the population was already living near the eastern end; and the most beautiful part of the site lay between the industrial area and the population center toward the south along the Caroní River. These considerations led some key persons to argue that the new city should be built around the steel mill; others hotly disagreed. It was finally decided to build a linear city uniting all of the existing elements. This would be less expensive; and it would also conform to existing growth patterns, encounter less political opposition, and provide greater flexibility and security if the projections proved optimistic.

Transportation

The spread-out character of the city posed some difficult transportation problems. Prospective low density for many years to come made it imperative to reduce the cost and time of travel to the main industrial area, the central business district, the civic center, and other areas frequented by residents. But a high capacity rapid transit system would prove too expensive an investment for the postulated size of the city and the travel distances to be covered. Therefore, the plans assumed that most of the travel would be by automobile: private cars, taxis, buses and *por puestos* (jitneys).

To ensure that the staging and development of the circulation system would link into and reinforce the staging and development of the major land uses, the staff formulated a number of development alternatives and tested them with the aid of a high speed computer. They varied the distribution of population, levels of income, locations for homes and jobs, and choices of travel mode (buses, taxis, *por puestos,* and cars). These studies made it possible to estimate preferred travel patterns and probable traffic volumes for each of the alternatives. They also provided the basis for some of the subsequent calculations of the size and layout of roads, the location and staging of the most important facilities, and the reservation of land for the transportation network.

The solution finally decided upon did not minimize transportation costs. An economic evaluation indicated that when the city's population reached 250,000 approximately 12 to 16 percent of the disposable income of its citizens would be used for transportation.[8] This figure approximates the transportation costs of some American cities: Los Angeles spends 16 percent of its disposable income on transportation; Cleveland, 14 percent; and Chicago, 13 percent. Because income in the United States is generally higher than in Venezuela, such travel costs would be a greater burden to the citizens of Ciudad Guayana. This burden is inherent in the present low density settlements and the considerable distances between the industrial areas in the west and the main residential areas in the east. In view of the constraints, there was probably no other feasible or less expensive solution. But the planners hoped that, as the residential areas grew westward toward the industrial center in the future (see Figure 3), the journey to work and the accompanying costs would decline.

Specialized Centers

There was little difficulty in deciding where to place the major industrial area in Ciudad Guayana. The western part of the site was clearly the best location. The steel plant was already there. There was plenty of suitable land around it for building a large complex of heavy industry. The site was usually downwind from the rest of the city so that smoke, odors, and other nuisances would be blown away from the residential sections. It also had good access to land and water transportation, and the truck traffic generated by the industry would be able to reach domestic markets without passing through the city.[9] But the heavy industries that would constitute the principal activities of the region were largely capital intensive and would not furnish enough employment. The planners, therefore, provided additional sites and attractive fa-

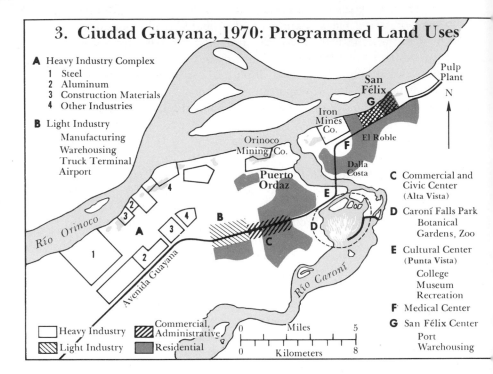

3. Ciudad Guayana, 1970: Programmed Land Uses

A Heavy Industry Complex
1 Steel
2 Aluminum
3 Construction Materials
4 Other Industries

B Light Industry
Manufacturing
Warehousing
Truck Terminal
Airport

Pulp Plant

San Félix

N

Iron Mines Co.

Orinoco Mining Co.

El Roble

F

Puerto Ordaz

Dalla Costa

E

Río Orinoco

Avenida Guayana

Río Caroní

C Commercial and Civic Center (Alta Vista)

D Caroní Falls Park
Botanical Gardens, Zoo

E Cultural Center (Punta Vista)
College
Museum
Recreation

F Medical Center

G San Félix Center
Port
Warehousing

☐ Heavy Industry
▨ Light Industry
▨ Commercial, Administrative
■ Residential

Miles 0 — 5
Kilometers 0 — 8

cilities for light industrial areas elsewhere in the city. These were designed to encourage a variety of other enterprises including the manufacture of consumer goods, a warehousing and truck transportation center, and commercial facilities near the airport. There were also plans for a special training and service center for nearby low-income neighborhoods.

No less important for the future of the city was the building of an attractive cultural center. For Ciudad Guayana, isolated from the leading population centers of Venezuela and unable to compete with Caracas in the scale and quality of facilities and services, it was exceptionally important to create an environment which would attract enterprising managers, professionals, educators, and skilled specialists of all sorts on whom the development of a vital community depends so heavily. Fortunately, an excellent site for such a center was available. It was an area called Punta

Vista. Overlooking the Caroní Falls, the site was one of varied terrain and great natural beauty. Within this area the planners decided to construct a cultural and civic center. Its church and municipal buildings would be located on a common plaza where the most important civic, religious, and ceremonial activities of the city would be conducted. Space was also assigned for an educational complex, containing a technical college, a research establishment, a hotel, clubs, a library, a museum, and other institutions. A large public park was also planned. Surrounding the Falls, the park would offer such facilities as a boat basin and landing, a botanical garden, a zoological garden, and an aviary. Room would also be available for an attractive residential settlement to be built next to the park.

For the main city center, where the principal business offices and retail establishments were to be located, the site selected was an area called Alta Vista. This area stood on a height commanding wide views of the city. Its terrain was level and allowed for inexpensive expansion of the business area. Moreover, it was bordered on three sides by still undeveloped land that was admirably suited for residential areas. If Alta Vista grew as planned, it would become one of the dominant elements in the development of the city. Linking the industrial and residential areas both functionally and visually,[10] it would eventually have the best transportation facilities and maximum accessibility to the greatest volume of purchasing power. In addition, by generating the highest land and building values, it would probably be the most important revenue producer in the city.

To ensure a more rapid development of this area in the early stages, the planners decided to detach the civic center from the cultural center with which it originally had been combined and to locate it instead at the eastern end of the Alta Vista plateau. This decision was also justified on the grounds that there were important functional ties between the city's government offices, courts, and principal business services and establishments. Moreover, at this location the civic center would be visible from all directions as a symbol of civic activity.

Finally, completing the list of specialized areas, a medical center was planned at a site on the eastern side of the Caroní near the

San Félix settlement. It would contain a major hospital, clinics, and allied health services.

The Existing Settlements

The decision to transform Ciudad Guayana into a single community made it necessary to relate the plans for the new industrial areas and the new city centers to the existing communities of San Félix and Puerto Ordaz. To do so, the planners explored the functions which the older settlements might play in the metropolis of the future. San Félix, the community on the eastern flank of the city, was originally a small market town, but its growth had burgeoned with the emergence of new activities. Someday its port would be the principal entry and exit point for the products of the entire southeast region of Venezuela. Meanwhile, San Félix and its adjacent areas of El Roble and Dalla Costa had become the principal centers for migrants to the Guayana region. Puerto Ordaz, on the other hand, continued to function as a residential settlement for employees of the Orinoco Mining Company. But it too had experienced rapid change. Built early in 1950, it was located almost midway between San Félix and the new industrial areas. In the 1960's, speculative development began to flourish and soon spread along the road connecting Puerto Ordaz to the Caroní. Frenzied growth soon converted large segments of the intervening areas into a sprawling slum.

A variety of measures appeared necessary. Improvements in health and waste disposal facilities were required, as well as more schools, housing, social services, and recreational facilities. The markets and commercial area needed to be expanded, transportation facilities and services modernized, and the waterfront redeveloped. To ensure that these steps were taken, staged programs with varying priorities were incorporated in the development plans for Ciudad Guayana.[11]

But a key problem still remained unsolved. How were the developments in the older areas to be related to the growth complex on the western side of the Caroní so that one urban community would ultimately emerge? There were two solutions. The first was to encourage the extension of San Félix and El Roble to the west. Future growth could then be steered and planned

46

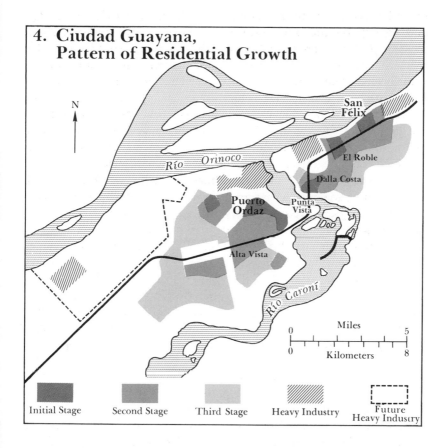

4. Ciudad Guayana, Pattern of Residential Growth

N

Río Orinoco

San Félix

El Roble

Dalla Costa

Puerto Ordaz

Punta Vista

Alta Vista

Río Caroni

Miles
0   5
0   8
Kilometers

Initial Stage   Second Stage   Third Stage   Heavy Industry   Future Heavy Industry

without disrupting existing activities. The second device was to construct a major linear highway which would link disconnected areas and facilitate movement between all parts of the city.

Avenida Guayana

The new highway, Avenida Guayana, offered a special opportunity for the designers.[12] It was to be an important connective element, tieing together the major activities and movements over the entire length of the city. Starting as a heavy duty road in the industrial area to the west, it would change into a boulevard as it passed through the business and civic center; then, sweeping down

47

the hill into the cultural center, it would cross the Caroní bridge and emerge on the other side as a limited access highway. After moving past the residential areas, the highway would circle the medical center on the crest of the eastern hill, only to be transformed once again into a boulevard running through the San Félix area. Probably no other physical element in Ciudad Guayana would be able to show so effectively the relationship of the major activities of the city to each other and to their natural surroundings. And probably no other physical element to be planned was as subject to the control of its designers.

Here was a chance to thread the discontinuous fragments of Ciudad Guayana into a comprehensive whole. Small wonder then that the designers explored every tool at their disposal, from controls on the location and siting of activities and the treatment of natural amenities to the handling of road alignments, paving, lighting, landscaping, densities, height, and signs. The designers even tried to take account of the visual impressions and preferences of the residents of Ciudad Guayana, despite much skepticism in some quarters as to how helpful the reactions of untutored observers might be in such a complex process.[13] Unfortunately, shortages of staff precluded the detailed evaluations and revisions that ought to have accompanied such efforts. And, the problem of providing for a given pattern of land uses for the present was further complicated by the need to plan for probable uses in the future. Partly for this reason, the staff sought to identify the areas and visual elements which required most attention and control. The designers felt that if they could develop criteria and methods for handling "high" and "low" control zones, this would permit concentration on visually and functionally significant areas, such as Punta Vista, the civic center, the skylines, historical monuments, and Avenida Guayana. In addition, the staff considered establishing flexible land use controls, ranging from general zoning and building regulations to more specific and special restrictions for key points in the city. Yet the urban designers were fully aware that, in spite of these efforts, the final results would be far different from their original intent. A metropolis, after all, is the "product of many builders who are constantly modifying the structure for reasons of their own."[14]

IMPLEMENTING THE PLANS

The Corporación Venezolana de Guayana was charged with the responsibility not only of planning the city but also of seeing that it was built. But, almost inescapably, there was more emphasis in the earlier phases of the program on the formulation of objectives and plans (as well as on "firefighting") and, in the later phases, on the policies and steps necessary to realize them. As the plans took shape, however, a number of specific questions had to be answered. What aspects of the plan were to be carried out first? Where and why? In what detail were the plans to be developed? How was the work to be divided between the various ministries and CVG? What role would the local authorities play? How would the development undertaken by the private sector be fitted into the overall program? And how would these efforts be tailored to fit the changing needs of a local population whose characteristics and values were probably inadequately and differently sensed by the Venezuelan and Joint Center staffs? Let us examine how the planners attempted to deal with each of these problems.

Staging and Priorities

Several factors influenced the staging of actual development. One was the insistent demand for improved transportation between east and west. Another was the role of the highway as a generator of new activities. Both set a high priority on the prompt scheduling and proper location of the new artery. In addition, the San Félix–El Roble areas were already expanding in a westerly direction. The policy was to encourage this growth pattern. This made the selection of housing areas for the migrants and the preparation of a zoning ordinance for the city top priority items. It also intensified the pressures to provide an expanded commercial area on the western side of San Félix, which would include a market and bus terminal in addition to the offices, warehouses, and light industry parcels already planned for the port area. This, in turn, influenced the location and staging of roads, utilities, schools, hospitals, and other facilities[15] (see Figure 4).

On the western side of Ciudad Guayana, the most pressing consideration at first was the need to provide space and facilities for the expansion of both light and heavy industry. Soon, however, the preparation of the site for the new business center took temporary precedence. The planners wanted to bring in large department stores and supermarkets, such as Sears and Cada, and headquarter offices, such as those of CVG, so that these strategic establishments would generate other substantial developments in the area. But if the facilities were not ready in time, key firms would probably move to other commercial areas. This prospect threatened the pace of the growth and perhaps even the vitality of the central business district. The staff promptly recommended that the program for the business center be speeded up. (For several reasons, however,[16] this speedup did not occur and, therefore, the prospects for the commercial center have been jeopardized.) These decisions prompted a belated recognition that there was not enough activity at the major commercial center to ensure its dominance and growth potential. After much debate and anguish of spirit, the planners decided, as noted earlier, to shift the civic center away from the cultural center at Punta Vista to the commercial complex at Alta Vista. Even the dissidents conceded that Punta Vista, stripped of its administrative offices, would still be able to function effectively as a cultural and educational complex.

Detailing Plans and Projects

One cannot go too far in the action stage of land use planning without detailed physical plans. The amount of detail, of course, depends on one's requirements. It can be diluted to encompass the entire metropolis or region or it can be pinpointed to deal with important components within a project.[17]

Land use plans were drawn for Ciudad Guayana at scales up to 1 : 10,000. Their function was to delineate the transportation system, major activity areas, density patterns, and the principal visual elements and focal points. Community plans were also made at scales up to 1 : 5,000. These depicted the land uses, streets, highways, public utilities, public service facilities, and other major elements within each sector. A still more detailed set of development unit plans, at scales up to 1 : 500, shifted attention from the nature and intensity of land use to the character of development in terms of building types, uses, and arrangements. Next came the project area plans. These consisted of general specifications which described the main functions of the development areas, the elements within them, the priorities and staging of the operation, and the proposed methods of carrying the project into effect. In the last phase of this process, the detailed drawings were prepared. The basic units for construction were the project areas. A single general contractor, private or public, was held responsible for each of them, and the general specifications and drawings were the contractor's principal guides for design and construction.

Proper sequence and timing are essential for both general and more detailed plans but it is not always easy to prescribe or to follow such schedules. The more general plans should be prepared first. However, in Ciudad Guayana tight deadlines and staff shortages resulted in the community development and project plans being prepared simultaneously.

Even more serious problems can arise with scheduling failures. Sometimes two to four years, and even longer, may be required from the initiation of a project until its actual completion. These requirements must be anticipated in programming. Unfortunately, the difficulties of anticipation are often complicated by changes in programs and projects as new obstacles or opportunities are identified. The price of failure, however, can be high. Enough capital may not be allocated for investment; adequate consideration may not be given to alternative locations and projects; there may be no operational criteria for checking the progress of actual development against planned project schedules; and indispensable complementary facilities may not be provided when and where needed. Many of the early housing and public works programs in Ciudad Guayana bogged down because of these delays. The repeated crises led to friction between the planners and the developers and between the directors and the staff and resulted eventually in the introduction of more systematic scheduling methods.

Capital Budgets

After the detailed plans have converted general goals into feasible programs and targets, these, in turn, have to be transformed into economical and imaginative projects. The approximate cost of these projects must then be established and the benefits evaluated in relation to competing projects and available resources.

In the case of the urban development activities conducted by CVG, the end product of this process was a financial schedule and program. Formulated in different levels of detail and for different periods of time, it could encompass a wide variety of subjects: the capital requirements for individual projects; the estimated investment requirements for all public and private urban development projects for the budget year; the four-year capital investment program corresponding to the requirements set by the national plan; and a ten-to-fifteen-year projected schedule of the probable investments needed to fulfill the program's long-range objectives.[18]

Although these estimates were only first approximations and were likely to improve with time and experience, they reflected the best available information and judgments. It was very difficult to obtain accurate data on costs, particularly for projects scheduled beyond the first year, and to take account of changes that might occur in project details and schedules. Nonetheless, capital budgeting was essential, not only to gauge the order of magnitude of project and program costs and to match proposed outlays with resources, but also to compare objectives, alternatives, and price tags and to provide more objective measures of control and accomplishments.

Inter-Ministerial Relations

What was the role of CVG vis à vis other agencies? Functioning as a regional agency, the Corporación Venezolana de Guayana potentially overlapped every other sector of government. To avoid meddling and conflict, the general policy of CVG was not to take on any jobs that other organizations could be expected to handle more effectively. Major difficulties arose, however, when specific jobs failed to get done. For example, everyone agreed that Ciudad Guayana needed more roads, housing, schools, hospitals, and other facilities. Everyone also recognized that the Ministry of Public Works had more staff and experience in building roads and other public works than did CVG. The same appeared to be the case for Banco Obrero, the government agency for building housing for low-income families. Similarly, the Ministry of Education was better equipped to handle school design and educational programs and the Ministry of Health more capable of supervising the construction of hospitals and public health facilities. The logical solution was to get these ministries to do the things that needed doing in the Guayana region. When the cabinet and the central planning agency (Cordiplan) accepted the CVG investment program as part of the national plan, the other ministries, in effect, had incurred an obligation to use their organizations and resources to fulfill the Guayana portion of the plan. But, because of political pressures and sheer inertia, they were quite content to ignore this obligation, choosing to concentrate instead on their own national programs. The ministries assumed that the resources allotted to CVG for the development of the region limited the need for their own participation, and, except for modest token efforts, they believed their responsibilities lay elsewhere. Unfortunately for CVG, if facilities and services were not available in the Guayana region when required, the program was sure to bog down and CVG was likely to receive the lion's share of the blame, whether justified or not.

To cope with the situation, a number of officials at varying levels within CVG became actively concerned with intergovernmental liaison. They sought more cooperation and flow of information between high-level officials at CVG, Cordiplan, and other ministries. They also tried to frame agreements on respective responsibilities, deadlines, and other forms of interagency collaboration. But when other ministries, despite these efforts, failed to respond to critical needs, CVG found it necessary to develop its own staff and programs.

The Housing Strategy

Housing soon became the thorniest of all problems. The Corporation did not want to get into the housing business. Its top officials had more than enough to handle. They felt that other agencies had the skills, the experience, and the responsibility to do whatever needed to be done. Although many of these same officials were convinced that adequate housing would not be provided by the government housing agency, Banco Obrero, or by private developers, they argued that CVG could not act decisively until this was

53

demonstrably the case. That, in effect, was what happened. In 1962 a housing study by the staff of the Joint Center reported in detail what everyone already knew: that the backlog of needed housing had reached serious proportions and that neither Banco Obrero nor any other organization could handle more than a small fraction of the job alone.

CVG then resorted to a variety of measures to get the necessary housing built.[19] To increase mortgage funds, the Corporation started a savings and loan association. To augment the supply of middle-income housing, it arranged for a non-profit organization, the Foundation for Popular Housing, to put up 854 houses. CVG also offered a special "sales guaranty" to the International Housing Associates, a private building organization, to ensure that 800 additional units would be built with less expensive foreign capital. This supplemented a guaranty by the Agency for International Development against losses resulting from war, confiscation, currency inconvertibility, or devaluation. Speed was of the essence. Unfortunately, the final agreement took two years to negotiate and clear through the various government agencies, and in the end only 200 units were built.

In another effort, CVG made land available to private builders at prices adjusted to the income levels of the people for whom the houses were to be built. It also investigated a number of alternative construction systems in the expectation that one of them might be promoted through guaranty or through joint venture agreements in association with local builders. These studies led to negotiations with prominent industrialists who were interested in the possibilities of large-scale construction involving prefabrication processes as well as more conventional building techniques. Notwithstanding these efforts, the Corporation still found itself obliged to build houses directly. This was because CVG's agreement with the steel workers union had guaranteed that there would be a certain number of houses at stipulated price levels by the end of 1965, and it became increasingly clear that the agreement would be breached unless CVG took direct action.

CVG also felt an obligation to help the poorest migrants cope with their housing problems. Its motives, to be sure, were mixed. There was a genuine desire in some quarters to help these families. It was also clear that key parts of the city had become unplanned settlement zones for the migrants. And these settlements would continue to grow and still other areas might be "invaded" if the migrants could not find suitable places to live. Prudence and pressure, therefore, led the planners to designate a number of places as "reception areas"[20] where migrants could obtain land and minimum public services. The planners insisted, however, on the observance of minimum space standards in the reception areas so that, when the income of these families increased, it would be easier and more economical to remodel or rebuild the houses. (Such rebuilding, with CVG assistance, is already occurring in existing slum areas.)

CVG also experimented with a self-help housing scheme in the El Roble area. The Corporation undertook to provide land, public utilities, schools, loans for construction materials, and technical assistance. After families moved into a sector where lot lines and street rights of way had been staked out, streets were graded, lots leveled, public water taps installed, and electric lines laid out. At the same time, building materials were made available on a credit basis. The next phase of the program was scheduled to start after the community had repaid credits for construction materials and had raised additional funds. CVG would then match the credit repayments and the funds collected to finance further improvements, such as individually piped water systems, street paving, sidewalks, schools, and community centers. Hopefully, as the community became more aware of CVG's policy of reinvesting all repayments in the community itself, there would be a strong incentive to keep the repayment schedule up-to-date until adequate urban standards were achieved.[21]

A Municipal Housing Institute, the equivalent of a local housing authority, was established, too. Its purpose was to supervise the self-help housing program for families of low income which was being supported by funds from the savings and loan association, the Community Development Foundation, CVG, and other sources. With the aid of a government field material testing laboratory, CVG also began studying the use of local building materials. Because of the limited variety of building materials available to the small autonomous builder, the study focussed on the use of precast elements and lightweight building aggregates. The Corporation also planned to look into the possibility of financing a plant to produce basic elements for prefabricated houses. Fortunately, the performance of Banco Obrero has significantly improved in the last few years, and CVG now expects this national housing agency, with the assistance of the Municipal Housing Institute and of private builders, to shoulder most of the housing and construction responsibilities in the future.

Education

In anticipation of possible educational problems, CVG undertook a survey of the region's requirements during the coming decade. Assuming that Ciudad Guayana would have a productive labor force of 150,000 and a population of 400,000 by 1975,[22] the study examined the prospective demand for four elements of the educational system: 1) elementary and high schools; 2) vocational programs to train workers for some of the new jobs that would develop in the region; 3) commercial and rudimentary business training at the secondary level; 4) a technical college serving the recruitment needs of the local industries. Since needs were far in excess of resources, the study dealt only with minimum requirements.

The evaluation showed that it would take three to five years at the earliest to establish a technical college, and, even by 1975, the school could probably turn out no more than a fifth of the required technicians. In the interim most technical personnel would have to be recruited from outside the region. If prompt steps were taken to establish the college, the bulk of the higher level professionals and executives could be obtained from the region within a five-to-ten-year period after 1975. Despite the time, money, and effort needed, the establishment of a post-secondary facility was considered essential because of the political sensitivity which surrounded the recruitment of foreign specialists and because of "the need to maintain incentives for the young Venezuelans coming up through the educational levels." Such an institution would "serve as a powerful symbol that the way to the top [was] not closed off to local middle level workers and their families."[23]

The survey recommended expanding primary and secondary school facilities to the maximum, for it was unlikely that a sufficient number of middle level skilled workers could be recruited from outside the region unless prohibitive wage and incentive schemes were employed. The primary school would have a dual role: to provide an adequate number of students for the secondary school system and to provide the other students with enough basic education to enable them to profit from special training courses in middle level skills. The secondary school program also would serve two purposes: to produce the required number of workers with middle level skills and to furnish a core of graduates to enter the higher institutions.

The recommendations to meet these needs took into account "the present size and condition of the school system existing in the region, the likelihood of expanding and at the same time keeping sufficient quality to yield an education product of any significance, and the necessary balance that must be maintained between different levels and kinds of programs within an educational establishment."[24] They also dealt with school plans and equipment, site locations, construction schedules, reorganization of curriculum materials, scholarships, in-service training, school organization, and recruitment programs.

This analysis of Ciudad Guayana's educational needs and problems was subsequently presented to the Ministry of Education, which, until then, was unaware of the scale of the problem. In the past the Guayana region had received a proportionate share of the educational budget. But the role that the Guayana program was destined to play in national development required radical changes in priorities and programs. Although the Ministry of Education had the principal responsibility for developing such programs, it was beset by pressures for action throughout the country and lacked the resources to cope with all of Guayana's needs. The immediate task was to determine which responsibilities the Ministry was able and willing to handle. This decision would then allow CVG to determine what additional measures it could undertake on its own.

Unfortunately, the necessary collaboration did not develop easily. The help CVG gave to private education (the religious schools) and its history of neglect of public education (presumably because this was the responsibility of the Ministry) had only aggravated past differences. Therefore, in response to the recommendations of its staff,[25] CVG decided to show by its actions its readiness to assist public education. It undertook to provide funds for library and textbook collections in the seven public schools in Ciudad Guayana. (This program has since been adopted in the rest of Venezuela.) It built six more primary schools. It gave grants for milk and lunch funds, for building and curriculum materials, and for playground equipment. It provided technical advisory services for school officials on equipment, programming, visual aids, teacher training, and educational diagnostic tools. It also established the Guayana Center for Educational Research, Planning, and Extension Services with the assistance of the Harvard Center for Studies in Educational Development. The purpose of this organization was to assist CVG and the Ministry in guiding the development of local school systems.

The Guayana educational program still faces a number of perplexing problems. Most serious is the limited cooperation of the Ministry of Education as well as a number of other educational organizations. But the program has been successful in many ways. The number of schools have increased, the quality of the educational services in Ciudad Guayana has shown improvement, "drop outs" have declined, and the prospects for the future are much more encouraging than they were only a few years ago.

Local Government

Tremendous strains were also imposed on Ciudad Guayana's existing local government by the profound transformations the region was experiencing in population, in class relationships, in economic activities, and in values and styles of living. Almost inescapably these strains affected CVG's relations with the local authorities. The normal exercise of the Corporation's power provoked concern and resentment. The Corporation's ownership of most of the land in the local area, its power of expropriation, its authority over what development should or should not occur reduced the scope of local political authority and intensified the feelings of political inadequacy and anxiety of local groups and individuals. Moreover, by speeding the process of development and change, the Corporation was breeding higher standards and expectations. CVG was aware of some of these reactions. It also knew that approximately 195 million dollars in urban infrastructure capital improvements were planned for the four years from 1964 to 1967, with an ultimate investment of 400 million dollars planned for the next fifteen years. At a population level of 300,000, the operation and maintenance of this infrastructure would require almost 10,000 employees engaged in public or quasi-public activities. As many responsibilities as possible had to be turned over to the local officials so that the Corporation could concentrate on those matters which no other agency could handle.

It was one thing, however, to recognize this need and another to agree on what responsibilities could be shifted, and how and when the shifts should occur.[26] This agreement was all the more difficult to achieve because, in Venezuela as in most developing countries, government and politics were extremely centralized and municipal functions extremely limited. Municipalities lacked adequate revenues and had almost no experience in large-scale management. These weaknesses were reinforced by wide educational and status gaps between representatives of the national agencies and local officials and leaders.

CVG explored these problems with the Foundation for Community Development, the government agency assigned to study local problems. The Foundation agreed to collaborate with CVG in drafting new ordinances and in assisting in the development of local institutions in Ciudad Guayana. The Joint Center also arranged for a team of political and social specialists to evaluate the character of existing administrative services and programs within the region and the magnitude and scope of the new facilities and services that would soon be provided. The team studied the present aspirations of the Guayana population and the current civic and political leaders. It also probed into some of the political changes then taking place, their implications for CVG, and the ways in which efforts might be channeled to maximize the prospects of constructive performance by the new municipal officials.[27]

The team's recommendations emphasized the need for an increased number of opportunities for local action and for the expression of local options. The report noted, for example, that the local community could play a greater role in advising and helping CVG to administer housing and public works programs and could undertake neighborhood improvement programs in cooperation with the Corporation. It also urged CVG to give the community more responsibility for such matters as the maintenance of public works; the administration of zoning, building, and subdivision regulations; and the reorganization of the system for land registration and revenue administration.

Coupled with these recommendations were several proposals concerning CVG's organization and activities. One called for a quasi-autonomous Urban Development Section within the Corporation to handle its urban public works. Another suggested the establishment of a formal liaison office to facilitate a flow of information between the local and central government officials of other ministries, the representatives of the local community, and CVG. Still a third stressed the need for improved information services to explain the aims and activities of CVG and the ideas behind its plans. The report also proposed that CVG enlist the aid of some organization, such as the Foundation for Community Development, to organize a training program to prepare local officials for some of their new management responsibilities.

Efforts are now being made to put some of these ideas into effect. It is too early to say how successful they will be. But one lesson from this experience already stands out: an effective urban growth strategy cannot be executed, even in an environment where local political leadership is weak and inexperienced, without first developing a sensitive rapport with the local interests.

Land Policy and Controls

With the exception of the Orinoco Mining Company properties and some small private holdings in the vicinity of Puerto Ordaz, CVG acquired most of the urban land in Ciudad Guayana and about 35 to 40 percent of the land in the Caroní district. The land use planners figuratively rubbed their hands in glee at this prospect, for public land ownership presumably gave them more freedom to decide the initial use and price policy of the land. Perhaps even more important, through earned income and increases in land values, particularly in the new commercial areas, the planners hoped to recover most of CVG's investments in plant, facilities, and services, with a reasonable profit to boot.

As is often the case, the freedom and advantages proved to be less real than anticipated. CVG's administrative burdens were heavy and key officials were reluctant to get entangled in extensive real estate management. Some of them feared the everpresent possibility of corruption. Credit impediments loomed, too, since it was not customary to finance improvements without land serving as a security for debt. Still others felt that private land ownership, with prospects of speculative profits, was not only traditional in Venezuela but essential. They believed that private ownership was necessary to induce more rapid private building, commercial growth, and perhaps even industrial development, and to generate jobs and income which, after all, was one of the main aims of the program. A final argument was that sale of the land might partially erase the image of Ciudad Guayana as a government-owned city.

Other officials demurred. Because the Corporation was functioning as a public entrepreneur, they felt it was taking great risks and had an obligation to protect and even earn a fair return on its investment. They believed the investments already made were in jeopardy unless CVG faced up to some unpleasant realities. As matters stood, its plans were in danger of being eroded by illegal private building activity and lack of coordination and communication. CVG could try to meet some of these problems head-on, by establishing more effective links between the planners, the local regulating agencies, and the principal development officials and by trying to promote greater understanding of the purposes of its plans. But CVG had to recognize that, ultimately, the administration of zoning, building, and other related ordinances would be the responsibility of the local council, and, despite all of CVG's efforts, the local council might not prove sufficiently sympathetic or cooperative.

From this point of view, public land ownership was the principal means by which CVG could preserve the essence of its plans, at least for a reasonable period of time. It would allow CVG to place restrictions on the land sold and regulate use through leases and similar mechanisms. The Corporation could keep the land needed for public purposes out of the private market. Above all, public ownership offered CVG the prospect of capturing a reasonable share of the income and the concentration of values it helped to create. In the United States and elsewhere, where there are significant local taxes on the capital values of real estate, the public shares the increases in value even when land and improvements are privately owned. But in Venezuela, as in most developing countries, local revenues were negligible and most communities had no real estate property taxes of any consequence.

The arguments on both sides were telling, and so some experienced real estate economists were called upon to help frame a more flexible solution. Since the commercial land and some of the better quality residential and industrial land were likely to be the most profitable areas, the advisors urged CVG to retain this land and to sell the remainder, subject to restrictions on its use and on the transfer of title. They also emphasized that if it became necessary to sell certain parcels in the commercial locations, CVG's benefits could still be retained either by making it a partner in some of the enterprises or, more probably, by withholding strategically located parcels from sale.

The same economists were also asked to suggest methods of setting land prices and leasehold terms and to review the proposed strategy and stages of development. Interestingly, after careful evaluation, they endorsed the decision to build a single integrated city.[28] In addition, they devised a flexible system for setting land prices, based on the price of housing, the desired density patterns, and the employment and income effects of subsidized prices in attracting specific economic activities. They also recommended that CVG encourage the construction of low-density and low-priced houses in the outer fringes of the commercial center before developing its inner areas, even though the utility costs would be higher and less people would surround and enliven the center. They supported this strategy on the grounds that CVG would thereby obtain a much greater share of the gains in land values and would also avoid a serious urban renewal problem in the future since the commercial center would otherwise be surrounded by low-density houses of poor quality.[29]

Promotional Activities

One of the main aims of CVG's planning efforts was to encourage the growth of private economic development and thereby increase the income and initiatives of the population. A decisive test of CVG's success would be whether it did in fact create a physical environment and services that were attractive to investors and entrepreneurs. That this was already the case at an early stage is clear from the increasing interest displayed by a variety of business interests and by the decisions of firms, such as Phillips Petroleum, Reynolds, U.S. Steel, and others, to invest or extend their investments in the Guayana region. But a program still had to be devised to deal with the mounting series of inquiries and to kindle the interest of other business enterprises in undertaking specific investments.

To begin with, how were routine inquiries and follow-up to be handled? What informational materials were needed to answer the usual questions of investors? To what extent would local officials and business interests be drawn into the promotional effort? What were the policies of the government and of CVG for providing technical and financial assistance for new enterprises and what changes might be advisable? Still another set of questions concerned the efforts to promote the program outside the office. How much time should the CVG staff spend in meeting with business organizations in Venezuela and abroad? Should offices be established in Latin America, the United States, Europe, and elsewhere? Finally, and perhaps most important, what fields of potential investment warranted the highest priority and what resources were required and likely to be available for these purposes?

Even while these questions were under consideration, certain promotional activities had already been initiated. For example, in several cases CVG in cooperation with the Venezuelan Corporation for Development (CVF) had furnished special assistance to encourage new activities. It had provided inexpensive land on prepared sites, helped in the preparation of market and feasibility studies, and aided on occasion in obtaining investment capital, tax benefits, custom duty exemptions, and CVF leaseback arrangements for plant and equipment. In unusual situations when there was a justification and request for participation, CVG had provided equity capital in the form of joint ventures. These then were some of the general tools that could be deployed in appropriate circumstances.[30] Such promotional activities were being handled by some of the members of the economics staff who had special knowledge of particular industries such as pulp and paper, aluminum, and chemicals. Since these arrangements were working well, it seemed best to continue them with only marginal assistance from outside specialists.

The remaining critical high priority activities were housing, construction materials, the heavy machinery complex, and the business center. An approach was tailored for each of these activities, but the lack of staff severely curtailed actual promotional efforts.[31] Development of the commercial center proved to be the most pressing problem. The planners placed major emphasis on the search for an entrepreneurial group to take responsibility for the center. A private firm would not only save CVG about 2.5 million dollars in capital investment funds, it would also help CVG avoid getting enmeshed in the details of development and administration. However, the planners decided to prepare at least some of the initial plans for the center, and if necessary, to erect key buildings there. All of this activity involved time-consuming details of coordination. The promotion staff found themselves actively involved in such matters as the planning of architectural projects, the provision of basic services, the working out of leasing arrangements and improvements, the preparation of contracts, and the ironing out of inevitable legal complications.[32]

These activities had first priority and consumed most of the staff's energies. Other efforts were pursued when time permitted or reluctantly held in abeyance. Thus, the staff did manage to clarify standard office operating procedures and to prepare several brochures providing basic information about the region and describing selected investment opportunities and types of assistance available. But needed changes in the government's policy on taxes, loans, and other types of assistance were not systematically investigated, and sheer lack of time led to the neglect of two important fields of action: the promotion of foreign investments and the promotion of smaller, labor-intensive industries.[33]

Cultural Problems of Implementation

Enough has been said about the efforts of CVG in a half dozen different areas to illustrate the range and complexity of an effective implementation program. But perhaps the most difficult aspect of implementation lies in the way general ideas and programs are adapted to particular circumstances. Most social environments are far more complex than initially suspected. It requires an exacting combination of skill and wisdom to work with groups and values which are sometimes subtly different and sometimes radically conflicting, for there are no hard and fast rules on how to identify these differences or how to resolve them assuming they are resolvable. It is largely a matter of sympathetic interest and of sensitivity—heightened perhaps by the realization that neglect of these differences in the past has led to misunderstanding, friction, and failure. Learning the language is often said to be indispensable, as indeed it generally is. However, use of the same language in both the capital city and the local areas may mask tremendous differences in aims and views of reality. Sensitivity here may overcome language barriers that linguistic skills can never correct.

Local habits and values must be sympathetically approached. Plans that ignore or patronize them run the risk of being ignored or patronized in turn. But often local habits are changing and local values are in conflict. A residential area that serves "a just-emerging middle class . . . may create all sorts of difficulties in the mobility process at the bottom of the scale. . . . [A] process which tends to separate the successful individual from his less successful relatives and acquaintances makes it harder for those at the bottom to find the models who would help them learn what we would like them to learn."[34] And designers who can accommodate or reconcile these requirements are rare indeed.

Solutions should be flexible and subject to review at various stages of the process. But economy, understaffing, and time constraints often preclude experimentation or the necessary subsequent tests. Creation of new institutions such as a building and loan association or a housing authority is relatively easy on paper. But getting the legislation, recruiting the staff, and maneuvering an administrative apparatus that operates largely on the basis of social and class ties involves frustrating delays and the constant threat that one's original aims will be vitiated.

Fashioning and carrying out plans and programs that reconcile conflicting interests is often a quixotic enterprise. The planner is held suspect by diverse interests both within and outside his organization, and his motives, his associations, and his activities are constantly under scrutiny. This is all the more so for foreign specialists. They are often considered, and sometimes are, easy dupes, whose friendship, frankness, or naiveté is exploited for purposes that they hardly suspect or even comprehend.

All of this, and more, is part of the problem of implementation in transitional societies. How successfully were these matters dealt with in Ciudad Guayana? Certainly, there was often a quest for instruments and incentives that would nourish local initiative or relieve CVG of responsibilities. The self-help housing program is one example. Land policy is another. The approach to local government responsibilities is a third. Yet much more remains to be done. Fortunately, an urban growth strategy requires many years to devise and to put into effect and there may still be time to modify existing approaches and invent new ones that take better account of local interests.

A final observation ought to be made on the consultant relationships. The Joint Center staff members stationed full-time in Caracas were usually briefed on the social and administrative topography they would have to negotiate. Knowledge of the language or readiness to learn it was a requirement of the job. All members of the staff had to respect, if not thoroughly follow, the administrative style of the client agency; and they were instructed to take no strong public positions in a serious conflict. They knew that if anyone became persona non grata, his usefulness would be at an end, no matter how exceptional his skills. Basic differences of opinion were not discouraged, but they were to be vigorously represented only at the highest administrative levels. A few individuals lost sight of these rules and were either forced to leave or left to brood in splendid isolation. The others, however, functioned effectively subject to these constraints.

CIUDAD GUAYANA IN PERSPECTIVE

Lengthy as it is, this description of the efforts to promote the growth of Ciudad Guayana is far from complete. The political background has not been touched upon. Little evaluation has been made of the quality and effectiveness of the work done. There has been no discussion of the management, organization, and reorganization of the planning office. The personalities of the Venezuelans and their consultant associates, their conflicts in views, the evolution of working relationships, the disappointments and satisfactions of association with this enterprise—all these can only be inferred. The emotional outbursts sparked by the design of a bridge, the location of a sewer, the closing and opening of a road, the choice of a site for a center, the handling of applicants for housing have been accorded no place here. Many other policy issues such as migration, interregional relationships, environmental health, and housing density and tenure have either been omitted or dealt with merely in passing. Only a series of books could adequately explore these aspects.[35] Nonetheless, this abbreviated version may help to acquaint the reader with some of the basic ideas and methods which such an urban growth strategy implies.

After five years of collaboration, the Joint Center left Guayana, parting on very amicable terms with their associates at CVG. Meanwhile, the program is continuing and the city is booming. Reviewing the experience again, one is tempted to ponder its relevance for other countries. In many ways Ciudad Guayana is unique: a new city planted in an isolated frontier region by a comparatively wealthy government (thanks to its oil riches) which had donated the land for the enterprise and had called in expert assistance from an advanced country. For all its uniqueness, however, the Ciudad Guayana project has some useful lessons to offer, especially for developing countries.

1. To succeed in an enterprise demanding a heavy and continuing concentration of national energy and resources in one region requires substantial consensus and political support. Without the impressive reputation and political backing which CVG managed to maintain, especially during the early years when there were little visible results, the program would have foundered. Obtaining the necessary consensus and support presupposes remarkable acumen and leadership, for there are no rules on how this should be done. Yet it is surely one of the vital responsibilities of a nation's top political and administrative officials.

2. Lack of staff is undoubtedly one of the most constricting limitations. The government of a developing country may draw up plans and programs, only to find these impossible to execute for lack of skilled personnel. CVG has not yet adequately

resolved this problem, but it did attempt to fill this gap by pioneering a novel arrangement with foreign universities. This arrangement was not the only one possible, and perhaps not even the best that could or should be worked out elsewhere. It illustrates, however, one imaginative way of reducing the problem of personnel to manageable proportions.

3. Despite skilled technical assistance, there were many problems that went unsolved. These included methodological questions such as the fashioning of more sensitive analytical and land use control techniques for transitional areas, institutional difficulties such as the reduction of financing costs, and technological bottlenecks such as the construction of really inexpensive housing or housing components. Much too much had to be learned on the job by Venezuelans and consultants alike. It is understandable, therefore, that practitioners working under such conditions should feel that research efforts have been scandalously inadequate — especially considering the potential effects of such research in human and economic terms.

4. Even in a relatively well financed undertaking, as in the case of the Guayana program, shortages of time, staff, and knowledge made it impossible to tackle many critical problems. Priorities had to be set and choices made. One of the hardest tasks of a local official and his technical advisors is to determine not only what things can and will be done but also what problems will have to wait. Perhaps one can take some consolation from Hirschman's observation that these inadequacies are not always a disadvantage. Given the nature of the development process, "the pressures and tensions it creates do not necessarily frustrate it, but can be made to help it along."[36]

5. It is often said that programs should experiment, and this is no doubt true. But experimenting is harder than it might at first appear to be. Programs are primarily developed to meet real and pressing needs and administrators cannot often tailor their programs to suit the requirements of experimental design. The scientist recording his results in the laboratory is in a rather different position from the planner who has to make his evaluations in the midst of simultaneous pressures for solving

problems and for maintaining public support. Even in the Guayana program, most of the operations in the field have yet to provide successful laboratories. Still, the "experimental project" or "pilot program" is often a useful device, if such programs are clearly significant ones and are properly evaluated. This means that the "experiments" must be few and critical and that adequate means must be devised for getting "feedback" from them. The advantage of the university connections established by CVG is that significant studies may result from the Guayana experience. Officials undertaking similar programs elsewhere might well ponder the advantages of emulating this approach.[37]

6. Finally, unique as the Guayana program may be, its effectiveness, in large measure, is attributable to certain key elements which can be reproduced elsewhere. Perhaps the most important of these was the emphasis of national policy on the development of a single region and the mustering of an extraordinary political consensus to sustain that emphasis during the critical early years. Another key element was the creation of effective intelligence and implementing mechanisms which made it possible to assess and link the growth potentials of the city and the region with the development goals of the nation. Still another was the joint preparation of economic, social, and physical studies and plans for both the city and region. These helped to encourage private investment, locate and schedule critical infrastructure investments, and guide development decisions. In point of fact, the most significant aspect of the Guayana program was not the resource endowment or the public ownership of land or the comparative wealth of the government. It was these other features—or more accurately—these other features *in combination*.[38]

Devising a National Strategy for Urban Growth: The Experience of Turkey

The Guayana program illustrates what can be done to develop a specific region if there is a significant consensus, fairly ample resources, a readiness to act, and some skilled management. Suppose, however, instead of a relatively clear policy involving a single region, there is only a vague inclination to encourage the planning of metropolitan growth in different parts of a country. Suppose, also, that resources are woefully limited and that there is no clear consensus, at least initially, on how to proceed. What difficulties are likely to be encountered in implementing a program for this kind of situation? Instead of speculating about the answer, let us once again look at an actual case: the experience of Turkey in devising a national urban growth strategy.

THE HISTORICAL BACKGROUND[1]

Initial Policies: Focus on Ankara and Internal Development,
1923–1950

Turkey first attempted to change its pattern of urban and regional development shortly after the establishment of the Turkish Republic in 1923. Its policies were not explicit, nor was the period altogether propitious for such a move. On the other hand, it was the very gravity of the crisis that made these policies feasible at all. Turkey's defeat at the end of World War I had ended over six hundred years of Ottoman rule and had led to the invasion of the country, the loss of its remaining empire, and the crumbling of its economy. The new nation was left with two national urban centers (Istanbul and Izmir), a few relatively well-to-do coastal regions (along the Marmara, the Aegean, and the Mediterranean), and a number of scattered regional centers. With a primitive transportation system and an illiterate, impoverished, backward hinterland containing 35,000 villages, many of which were almost completely insulated from the contemporary world, Turkey's future looked bleak indeed. But rebuilding, especially under inspirational leadership, has a way of sparking new energies. And, fortunately, Turkey had such leadership in Mustafa Kemal.

Inheritor of the remnants of an empire, Mustafa Kemal's historic role was to set in motion the processes of renewal and point Turkey on its future course. Rejecting irredentist dreams, he summoned his country to focus its energies on internal development. His audacious decision to shift the capital from Istanbul, perched on the western boundary of the new frontier, to the town of Ankara, located well within the interior of the central Anatolian plateau, dramatized the goal of developing Turkey's interior and assured a safer location for the government as well. His subsequent attempts to westernize and to industrialize Turkey were designed to destroy old attitudes and create the foundations for a modern, progressive economy. The key elements of the development strategy were the promotion of new industries in the interior, the construction of new community facilities (schools, hospitals, bridges, parks, streets, water facilities, and community buildings), and the building of a national railroad system linking cities and towns throughout the country with the new capital and the Marmara region.

At the outset the government counted heavily on the private sector of the economy to achieve its aims. Hoping to encourage enterprise, it provided subsidies, monopoly privileges, and certain market guarantees.[2] But the formidable risks of investing in the interior of a primitive economy discouraged private investment. So did heavy taxation and the deeply rooted religious and cultural attitudes of contempt for the business man. The exodus of the Greek and Armenian minorities which formerly had dominated Turkey's entrepreneurial elite also had a restraining effect. In the 1930's, when the initial policies had failed to produce the desired results and the urgency of the worldwide economic depression impelled prompt action, the government decided to develop its own enterprises.[3]

In retrospect, it is clear that the policies pursued for almost a generation, first by Mustafa Kemal and then by Ismet Inönü, did achieve some of their main objectives. They helped to strengthen and modernize the country[4] and to stimulate some economic development in the interior. They provided the infrastructure foundations for some of the cities and towns in the different regions. Finally, they produced several growth centers, and one powerful growing point in particular, Ankara. In 1925 Ankara was only a small town of approximately 25,000 people. Twenty-five years later, it was the second largest city in Turkey with a population of 290,000 and the highest growth rate of Turkey's nine cities of 100,000 and over.[5]

Although military security, modernization, and promotion of internal development were the general aims, the government's emphasis on towns and on the construction of railroads, and the special concern for the building of the new capital, gave the diverse investments an urban and eastern focus which produced some dramatic results. In 1927 there were only five cities of 50,000 and over, three in the east and two in the Marmara and Aegean regions. By 1950 there were not only eleven cities of this size, but all six of the additional cities of 50,000 and over were located outside of the Marmara.[6] There was little net migration of population between regions, but there were large intra-regional shifts of population to the larger provincial cities, especially in the east.

The population of Istanbul (in the Marmara region) increased by only 42 percent from 1927 to 1950, whereas, during this same period, the population of Ankara quadrupled and the larger provincial capitals and military centers experienced population increases ranging from 100 percent to 300 percent and more. As a consequence, the Marmara region's proportion of the total urban population (cities of 10,000 and over) dropped from 43 percent in 1927 to 36 percent in 1950.

Despite these accomplishments, the policies had some negative aspects. Financing of the public investments by taxation, rationing, and forced crop collection led to a stationary per capita income between 1938 and 1950 despite a 21 percent rise in national income. Little was done directly for the peasants. Roads were relatively neglected. Many investments had minor economic effects, and general economic activity was inhibited by burdensome taxation. The principal private industrial activities also remained centered in Istanbul and Izmir.[7] Except in Ankara and Adana,[8] the basic industries that existed elsewhere were mainly government plants which depended on subsidies for their survival.

Internal Development without Focus, 1950-1960

Turkey sided with the Allied powers towards the end of World War II, joined NATO after the war, and, starting in 1945, experimented with independent political parties and electoral processes. Soon thereafter, Inönü, the successor of Mustafa Kemal as President and head of the Republican Party, was voted out of office.

From 1950 to 1960, the new group in power—headed by Celal Bayar and his prime minister Adnan Menderes—pursued policies catering largely to interests that had been neglected by the Republicans. Public investment in agriculture increased tenfold. Taxation was lowered; credit and import quotas expanded. The size of the army rose steeply. Price supports, trade deficits, and the public debt increased. The national and provincial highway systems were substantially improved, as a result of the emphasis on mobility by Turkey's U. S. military advisors and the desire to improve marketing facilities for argiculture.[9] Public investments generally had no special regional focus, although efforts were made to embellish Istanbul, Izmir, and Ankara and harbor improvements tended to favor the larger cities. Numerous factories were built in the hinterland areas, partly to provide employment opportunities for prospective migrants and partly for the political appeal of such programs.

This investment binge could not have occurred without lavish assistance from Turkey's allies. The United States alone furnished over 1.6 billion dollars in economic aid between 1950 and 1962. Unfortunately, many of the new activities were poorly conceived. Market considerations were frequently ignored, complementary requirements overlooked, and defaults on agricultural loans forgiven. The government's irresponsibility led not only to mounting debt but to increases in paper currency.[10] The aftermath was dramatic, culminating in inflation, political repercussions, repressive measures, and a military coup.

The social and economic consequences of the policies developed during the fifties had a significant effect on urban development. With improvements in public health (especially the drop in infant mortality) and an increase of income (per capita income rose 24 percent from 1950 to 1960), population growth jumped to almost 3 percent a year compared to a previous rate of less than 2 percent.[11] And, although more machinery was employed and most of the remaining land suitable for agriculture was put under cultivation, farm production failed to increase proportionately. The combination of these factors — the population explosion, the exhaustion of almost all of the good crop land, and the efforts to mechanize agriculture — contributed to a substantial increase in urban migration. Between 1950 and 1960, Turkey's urban population rose from 19 percent to 25 percent. The movement off the land was reinforced by many other influences: the increase of parcellization in some areas and the growth of landed estates elsewhere; the impact of radio, movies, and newspapers; the great increase in the number of peasants inducted into the army; the new road network and bus system which began to break down the isolation of the peasant villages;[12] and the unusually favorable attitudes of Turkish villagers toward cities.[13]

The bulk of the migration was intra-regional, and urban development, too, tended to take place mainly within the same region.[14] These trends continued the pattern that had been set in the three decades following the establishment of the Republic. Since most of Turkey's population still lived on the land, the cities distant from Istanbul increased most rapidly.[15] Especially evident in Ankara; in Adana and Iskenderun in the Çukurova region to the south; in Eskişehir, Konya, and Kayseri in the central plateau; in Trabzon, Samsun, and Zonguldak on the Black Sea; and in Erzurum in the east, this growth sustained the earlier eastward trend of urban development. In 1950 there were eleven cities with a population of 50,000 or over, three of which were in the Marmara region. By 1960 there were twenty-seven cities of this size and only five were in the Marmara region. Medium-sized cities between 50,000 to 100,000 more than tripled in population; cities of 100,000 and over almost doubled. On the other hand, cities of 10,000 to 50,000 increased by less than 40 percent. The populations of Istanbul and Izmir also increased during the decade, and at a higher rate than the national average, but their increases were less than half the average increase of the populations of medium-sized cities.[16] The net effect was to reduce the proportion of the urban population in the Marmara region from 36 percent in 1950 to 31 percent in 1960, an annual rate of decrease equal to twice the rate of the previous twenty-three years.

In short, by 1960 Turkey had a network of cities in which the distribution of population was far less skewed than in the past (see Figure 5). The growth of the regional cities, made possible by improvements in transportation and other government policies, reflected the increase in their populations and markets and their new administrative, trading, and consumption-oriented industrial activities. Istanbul was still dominant, but no longer overwhelmingly so. Ankara contained almost half the population of Istanbul; Izmir almost a fourth; and others like Adana were rising fast. Turkey's urban system was conforming more closely to the rank size pattern of countries such as the United States and Canada. Although many grave difficulties faced Turkey, conditions conducive to more adequate urban and regional development prevailed.[17]

To be sure, there had been errors and setbacks. Most likely, if there had been wiser management of investments in the fifties, returns would have been higher. More focus on specific regional developments coupled with more effective incentives might have

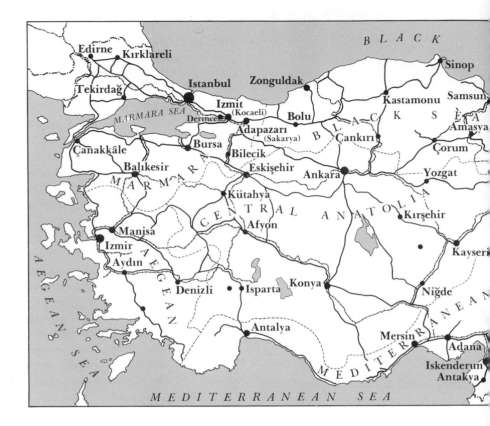

expanded the scope of private activity. In addition, Turkey's vaunted political stability had turned out to be more ephemeral than had been assumed. The Republican Party of Mustafa Kemal had been promptly voted out of office at the first opportunity, primarily for neglecting agricultural, commercial, and other interests. Turkey's first experiment in democracy had lasted only a decade before being upset by a political coup spurred largely by corruption and political maladroitness. On the other hand, judged in terms of the experience of other countries undergoing rapid transformation, Turkey's progress had been real, albeit often uneven and unstable. Whatever the pros and cons might be, this was the heritage of the past and the setting in which the next

76

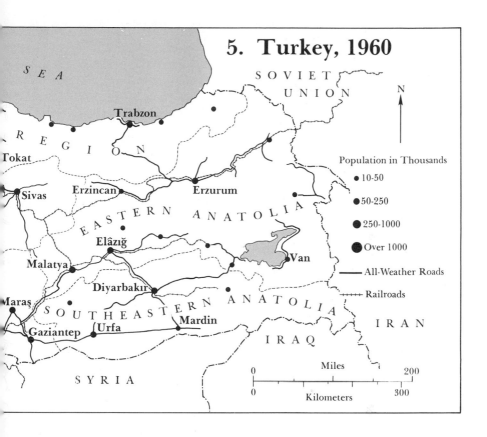

5. Turkey, 1960

S E A

SOVIET
UNION

N

Trabzon

R E G I O N

Tokat

Sivas   Erzincan   Erzurum

E A S T E R N   A N A T O L I A

Elâzığ

Malatya   Van

Diyarbakır

Maraş   S O U T H E A S T E R N   A N A T O L I A

Gaziantep   Urfa   Mardin

IRAN

IRAQ

SYRIA

Population in Thousands

● 10-50

● 50-250

● 250-1000

● Over 1000

—— All-Weather Roads

++++ Railroads

Miles   200

Kilometers   300

experiment in urban and regional development policy was to take place.

THE SHIFT TO REGIONAL PLANNING

The Need for Nourishing Further Regional Growth

Turkey had opened up its interior and changed the rate and location of urban development in different regions by means of powerful, but crude, instruments: the shifting of a capital, the development of a basic transportation system, and the manipulation of infrastructure investments. What it had not done in the past, however, and what was especially necessary now, was to establish more refined mechanisms for nourishing growth, for discovering development opportunities, and for assisting in the encouragement of both private and public activities in key sectors and regions. Such tools were scarcely known and hardly feasible in the past; nevertheless, a need for them had existed. In the fifties, the neglect of market studies, the failure to provide complementary facilities, and the lack of national and regional development strategies had inhibited many enterprises, both those that were undertaken and those that might have been undertaken.

Future urbanization prospects further underlined the need for such tools. Between 1927 and 1960, when Turkey's population rose from 13.6 million to 27.8 million, rural population increased only 81 percent. At the same time, the number of people living in cities jumped from 2 million to 7 million or 250 percent, and the number of people living in the largest cities from 1.1 million to 4.6 million or 335 percent.[18] By 1962 already 10 percent of the population was officially classified as unemployed, and the figure would have been higher if disguised unemployment had been taken into account. Clearly, finding jobs and providing community facilities for future urban migrants was going to be a formidable task, particularly since most of the problems of infrastructure investment of the Marmara region — not to mention those of the other regions — were not likely to be solved for many years.

Meanwhile, the urban revolution had hardly begun, and this, too, was widely and uneasily sensed. Approximately three-fourths of the population was still on the land or in small towns. Many of Turkey's public officials hoped that they could be induced to stay there. Other officials were more skeptical, for none of the nations that were more economically developed than Turkey had maintained such a high rural-urban ratio. The visible trends also belied such optimism. Increase of population, exhaustion of good agricultural land, mechanization of agriculture, and growing industrialization augured a significant reduction of the rural population and a massive migration to the cities. How these trends were to be dealt with was one of the major issues confronting the country's new leaders after they had wrested control from Menderes by means of a military coup. Seeking a possible solution to Turkey's problems, the new government soon turned to national and regional planning.

The Creation of Regional Mechanisms with a Metropolitan Focus

Actually, the first steps were taken just before the outbreak of the revolution. On September 5, 1958 the Turkish Parliament enacted legislation establishing a *Ministry of Reconstruction and Resettlement*. In addition to its responsibilities for housing, building materials, city planning, resettlement, and the administration of two government banks, the Ministry also obtained some broad and vague powers in the field of regional planning. It was given this authority at the instigation of a few zealous planning professionals and government officials who had persuaded key legislators and ministers that such action was long overdue. The Ministry's regional planning functions were lodged in a *Department of Regional Planning* within a larger bureau, the General Directorate of Planning and Reconstruction of the Ministry.[19] The new Department had an obscure status, limited funds, and almost no staff and had been created in a period when the country was close to bankruptcy. Yet it possessed a broad mandate. It could make regional studies, prepare regional plans, and coordinate the activities of other government agencies to achieve these ends.

To help organize the Department, its director arranged through the Ministry for the Organization for Economic Cooperation and Development (OECD) to send a part-time consultant (the author). The main job of the consultant, who arrived in the fall of 1959, was to help the director and his small staff identify the appropriate functions and scope of regional planning in Turkey and the steps necessary to get the program off the ground.

Meanwhile, the director and his associates initiated a few preliminary regional inventory studies of demographic and urbanization trends, patterns of industrial distribution, and natural resource endowment. They also prepared a bibliography of basic maps related to regional planning and divided Turkey into seven planning regions.[20] In setting these boundaries, account was taken of usage, geographical characteristics, flows of economic activity, boundaries of regional service areas of various government ministries, and the statistical convenience of employing provincial boundaries as component elements. The regional boundaries that the Department adopted were considered provisional, for the planners wished to avoid prolonged evaluation and controversy until the essential functions of the program were more clearly defined.

As for the scope of the Department's activities, there were several possibilities. The Department might concentrate on multi-purpose resource development programs, emphasize rural resettlement and village development, or focus on metropolitan growth regions and their hinterlands. Or it might decide to dodge the issue entirely by starting with one or more of these approaches without precluding the use of any of the others.

The choice, however, turned out to be limited. Multi-purpose development schemes were impracticable because they required special organization and financing efforts which were totally beyond the resources and skills of the Department at that time. Village planning and rural resettlement also seemed inadvisable. Other, more powerful, ministries and agencies were already dealing with the problems of villages, resettlement, and resource development and were likely to resent the intrusion of a new and inexperienced organization. This left one major alternative— developing metropolitan regions. Fortunately, the specialists who had promoted the establishment of the Department knew most about urban regions and least about villages and natural resources. Moreover, key officials of the Ministry also made it clear that it was the problems of urban and metropolitan development that most aroused their concern. Under the circumstances, it seemed wise to concentrate on metropolitan development regions and their hinterlands. This would permit the Department to deal with significant problems which no other organization was handling and yet allow it to examine basic aspects of rural and natural resource development in relation to a national strategy for metropolitan development.

This decision led the consultant to suggest three specific tasks which the Department of Regional Planning might perform: evaluating the trends and development potentials of significant growth regions; appraising the massive problems of urban migration that would develop in the future; and devising explicit national policies for regional development.[21] However, nothing of any consequence appeared likely to happen without funds and personnel. Since the Department had neither, its principal efforts over the next year were devoted to resolving these difficulties.

During this period, the director and his associates pondered the organization of the new Department, interviewed potential staff, and pressed for a minimum budget to speed up recruitment. Preliminary studies of urban and regional trends were continued. In addition, tentative arrangements were worked out by the director and his consultant for pilot programs to be undertaken in two or more regions. They also sought assistance from international agencies for technical advisors and training scholarships and made efforts to encourage or expand courses in planning in various Turkish universities.[22]

The results of these actions were hardly dramatic, but they laid the foundations for much of what was to happen later. An informal agreement was worked out with two international agencies — the United Nations and the OECD — to coordinate their efforts in this field and to provide technical assistance and fellowships for the regional planning program. The Ministry and the city of Istanbul also undertook cooperatively to establish a field office in the Marmara region. The municipality agreed to provide office space, equipment, and a budgetary allocation of one million lira (about 111,000 dollars) for regional planning studies. The Ministry, in turn, promised to furnish administrative and technical staff and some additional funds. There were two main reasons for this unique collaboration. Istanbul's officials wanted a regional framework for their urban plans. And, the Ministry staff members were convinced that this was a critical period for the Turkish economy and that what happened in the Marmara was likely to have a tremendous impact on the rest of Turkey because of its demonstration as well as training effects.[23]

The Linkage of Regional and National Planning

The revolution on May 27, 1960 at first created tremendous uncertainty. No one was sure what the future held in store. But, despite the turmoil and indecision of this period, the revolution brought to power people who believed strongly in national and regional planning.

The new leaders felt a need for economic advice. To meet this need, Professor Jan Tinbergen of the Netherlands was appointed the official advisor to the Prime Minister's office on national planning. Then, a meeting to explore the future role of regional planning was arranged between the economic planners attached to the Prime Minister's office and the staff of the Ministry of Reconstruction and Resettlement. At this meeting Professor Tinbergen expressed sympathy with the view presented by the Ministry staff and their consultant that regional as well as social planning should be provided for within the proposed new central planning agency. He agreed that regional planning, by reducing lags in backward regions and encouraging growth centers, especially those with export and tourist development potentials, might help to alleviate the foreign exchange problems of Turkey.[24] When the *State Planning Organization* (SPO) was formally created at the end of September 1960, it did contain a *Department of Social Planning* which eventually acquired responsibility for regional planning.[25]

The creation of the Department of Social Planning soon prompted key officials to consider what the relationships ought to be between the regional planning interests of SPO and the programs in the Ministry of Reconstruction and Resettlement. As might be expected, fears about duplication and conflict were promptly voiced by some persons who felt that regional planning was the mission of the Department of Regional Planning of the Ministry. However, these fears were dispelled, temporarily at any rate, when it was made clear that SPO was not concerned with the operations or details of urban and regional planning. Since its job was to help frame and coordinate economic and social development policies, it would have to work with the Ministry of Reconstruction and Resettlement in the field of regional planning just as it would have to work with other Ministries when dealing with agriculture, transportation, or industrial development.[26]

It is not surprising that overall responsibility for Turkey's urban and regional development rested with two national agencies. Although one generally expects urban and regional plans to be prepared by some local organization, in many developing countries where there are no local agencies able to prepare such plans, a ministry handles these responsibilities. That was the case in Turkey where the Ministry of Reconstruction and Resettlement acquired these functions (except for the cities of Istanbul, Ankara, and Izmir, which had their own city planning staffs). In the evolving planning system the Ministry's regional plans had to serve a dual purpose. In relation to the city and its surrounding hinterland, the plans had to set goals, schedule development, and coordinate sector programs. But in relation to national development, they had to be guided by national goals, coordinated with other programs, and subject to fiscal and other constraints. These issues provoked much wrangling and negotiations. But when they were apparently cleared up, the planners assumed that they could now get on with their job. Unfortunately, they had not reckoned with the weaknesses of the new government and the administrative system.

Other than their opposition to the former Menderes regime and their sympathy with national and regional planning, the military leaders had no fixed objectives. During this period of political uncertainty, investment declined and economic conditions worsened. Finally, after holding power for seventeen months, rewriting the constitution, and arranging for elections, the junta turned over its power to civilian authorities. But no decisive verdict emerged from the polls. The Republicans under Ismet Inönü won a plurality in 1960, but the Justice Party, representing to a large extent the former followers of Menderes, was a close second. Without a clear mandate from the electorate, the support of various splinter parties proved necessary to form a government. The situation did not change until elections were held again five years later in October 1965 and the Justice Party under Suleyman Demirel won a decisive victory.

The instability of the early sixties left its mark on regional planning efforts. During these years, indecision and compromise were the rule. Cabinets were reshuffled and there was a rapid turnover of ministers and key staff. Over a period of three and a half years, the Ministry of Reconstruction and Resettlement had six ministers and six chiefs of the Department of Regional Planning. SPO experienced similar, though fewer, changes in key personnel. Inescapably, this meant shifts in personal and power relationships, blunted initiatives, delays until new officials could be adequately briefed, problems in maintaining support for programs which had little initially to show for themselves, and growing enmities and disillusionment.

It was during this period that the Department of Regional Planning had to take root, survive, and hopefully accomplish something. That it actually did the first two—and perhaps even the third—is in retrospect no mean achievement. Let us see how the planners were able to accomplish this feat.

THE EMERGENCE OF AN URBAN GROWTH STRATEGY

The Decision to Concentrate on the Eastern Marmara and Zonguldak Regions

It will be recalled that the decision to initiate the first regional planning project occurred before the outbreak of the revolution on May 27, 1960. Shortly thereafter (first in June, then again in September) the new ministers and staff chiefs confirmed the decision to proceed with the program.

This was fortunate since several months earlier the OECD had arranged to bring some "resident consultants"[27] to Turkey to serve as assistants to the chief consultant and to help in the development of these programs. Salary schedules of international agencies made it extremely difficult to recruit first-rate senior specialists in this field for long-term service, but because assistants were placed under the supervision of the chief consultant, younger persons could be utilized. This device, a deliberate experiment, turned out to be very advantageous. Not only were the younger assistants able to help local officials, they could also avoid some of the critical pressures resulting from sensitive recommendations by shifting responsibility to the chief consultant.

The first two resident consultants were stationed in Istanbul. Arriving in September 1960, shortly after the revolution, they were bewildered to find that there was nobody in Istanbul for them to assist and advise. For a variety of reasons, including personal animosities between certain central and local government officials, the Marmara Directorate had not been established and, as a consequence, neither funds, staff, nor supplies were available. Fortunately, some unofficial assistance, in the form of temporary staff and space, was provided by the new head of the Istanbul city planning office.[28] In Ankara, the situation was equally bleak.[29] When the resident consultant arrived there in October 1960, there was no regional study underway. Because the head of the Department was overwhelmed by administrative chores, there were only general inventory studies being conducted by an inexperienced staff with no effective guidance. Some of these problems might have been solved if the Department could have subcontracted certain tasks to outside firms, individuals, or universities. But a legislative restriction made this impossible, thus forcing the Department to return available funds to the Treasury. A crisis was imminent. If something was to be accomplished, there had to be a tough-minded reappraisal of what could and could not be done.

The issues came to a head early in 1961. The new minister and his colleagues were advised of a number of steps that the staff and their advisors thought needed to be taken before they could count on any progress.[30] To get the Marmara program underway, the Ministry would have to establish a regional office, appoint a director, and allocate funds for staff and research activity. In addition, the central office of the Department would have to be reorganized and the professional assignments focussed on one region — possibly Zonguldak, Çukorova, or Antalya. To do more, it was emphasized, would be impossible. If an attempt were made, it would fail, and in failing it would squander resources and preclude more effective programs. The minister was warned not to expect great accomplishments since funds were inadequate, staff inexperienced, and data limited. However, it was suggested that the accomplishments would be of sufficient significance to justify a series of public conferences, starting in June, to explain the methods and preliminary findings of the plans to key government officials and leading citizens of the region. To be sure, the proposals were a deliberate challenge and an uncertain gamble for the harried officials of the Ministry. Nonetheless, they decided to move ahead; and it was this decision by the minister, Professor Fehmi Yavuz, and his associates that made possible the subsequent advances in the program.

The Ministry finally established an office in the Marmara, the Istanbul Regional Planning Directorate, to undertake the first regional planning project. Zonguldak, the center of an iron and steel complex on the Black Sea, was selected as the second project, and would be handled by the Ankara staff of the Department of Regional Planning. To show its support of the program, SPO's Department of Social Planning agreed to loan the Department of

Regional Planning two economists to help for a short period on the Zonguldak survey. The UN also arranged for an additional regional planning consultant to come in June to the Istanbul regional office and for a regional economist to come at a later date. Although this assistance helped, there were still serious deficiencies. The Turkish staff had increased, but contained only a few professionally trained specialists of uneven quality. To make matters worse, red tape still blocked action in trivial ways that often produced frustration and resentment. Despite these difficulties, however, the projects moved ahead.

The Proposals for the Eastern Marmara Region [31]

Fortunately, the first stage of the Marmara study was completed on schedule. Several ideas underlay this project. The most controversial was the notion that Istanbul would and should continue to grow. This view was not popular in important quarters. There was strong sentiment, even in Istanbul, in favor of curbing the growth of the city. Moreover, SPO was determined to encourage development in other regions.[32] However, it had also set some ambitious national development goals which had an even higher priority. The government proposed to invest 18 percent of the gross national product to achieve a growth rate of 7 percent, and export goods and capital goods were to receive special encouragement. These plans were likely to be frustrated if the government curbed the Marmara's development. The Marmara region was the country's major market, dominant commercial center, and principal area for manufacturing and for private capital investments. In 1960 it produced about 20 percent of the national income, 40 percent of the non-agricultural revenue, and almost 45 percent of total state revenues. Somehow the Department of Regional Planning and its Marmara office had to devise a development strategy for the growth of the Marmara region which would take reasonable account of these conflicting aspirations.

Among the other considerations influencing the Marmara project was the desire to minimize outlays for expensive infrastructure and to promote activities which would increase productivity and income. The plans also needed to be produced in a hurry; yet they had to be spelled out in enough detail to prove persuasive and useful.

The staff examined the economic functions carried on in the Marmara region and the main activities and requirements of its port. They made a pioneering inventory of urban land use and density in the municipality of Istanbul.[33] They analyzed the population and migration characteristics of the Marmara region, taking account of population increases in the hinterland as well as the number of farm families which the surrounding agricultural hinterland would be capable of supporting at varying levels of living. They also investigated housing and building trends in the region; in particular, the growth of squatter housing (*gecekondu* construction) in Istanbul.

These studies showed that the region's population growth over the next twenty years would be in the neighborhood of 3.3 million: 0.8 million for Istanbul, 1.9 million in rural Marmara, and almost 0.6 million elsewhere in urban Marmara. Even if the rural economy maintained the same level of farm production and even if there was a decline in farm income due to population increase, some 1.5 million persons appeared likely to migrate. And the largest portion of this migration seemed destined to concentrate in the urban areas of the Eastern Marmara. These estimates were necessarily tentative. Many things, including government policy, could alter the scale and the direction of these movements. Nonetheless, the estimates helped to define the dimensions of the population problems which the local authorities would have to cope with in the future.

The next step was to examine the economy of the region. Given the resources available, it was impossible to do this for the entire area of the Marmara. This area, for planning purposes, included the nine vilayets (provinces) of Istanbul, Kocaeli, Sakarya, Bursa, Balikesir, Canakkale, Edirne, Tekirdag, and Kirklareli. First priority was given to the Eastern Marmara, a subregion which included the vilayets of Istanbul, Kocaeli, Sakarya, and Bursa. Accessible by sea, excellently served by rail and road transportation, it seemed the most advantageous location for industrial and commercial development. Its urban centers, particularly Istanbul, Izmit, and perhaps Adapazari, appeared likely to be the focal points of a significant growth complex.

The Istanbul Directorate, thereupon, focussed its initial economic studies on the Eastern Marmara. Agriculture, these studies showed, was the major revenue producer, accounting for 32 percent of the region's revenue in 1960. Its past growth reflected a substantial increase in the area under cultivation (a rise of 2 percent annually from 1950 to 1960) and a shift to industrial and cash crops. And, although most vilayets appeared to have reached or overreached the limits of the areas they could safely cultivate, the switch to cash and industrial crops, which was still taking place, seemed likely to yield higher revenue per hectare than staple crops.

Manufacturing, the second most important economic sector, accounted for 24 percent of the region's revenue. During the fifties its annual rate of growth was approximately 17 percent. This growth, with the continued support of the import restrictions of the fifties, seemed likely to be sustained — and even increased — if offered a little encouragement.

But lack of encouragement was one of the industry's major problems. For several years the municipality had failed to designate appropriate industrial sites despite the growing number of potential investors. The Istanbul Directorate, therefore, decided to study the manufacturing activities of the Eastern Marmara, in hopes of discovering which sectors of the manufacturing economy were expanding and where. They also undertook a series of field surveys to identify the areas inside and outside the metropolitan area which would best serve these needs. The proposed surveys sparked the active collaboration of the municipality of Istanbul and the Istanbul Chamber of Commerce.

But the studies disclosed what had been suspected all along — that the growth of existing manufacturing activities was severely handicapped by the shortage of industrial areas adequately supplied with water, power, and other essential facilities. They also showed that population was spreading throughout the region at relatively low density standards, which would greatly increase servicing costs in the future. These forebodings were reinforced by an analysis of the present and prospective requirements for infrastructure, particularly water, power, and sewage facilities. The prevailing standards were far below European, not to mention "optimum," standards. The condition of the water and sewage facilities was so bad that it constituted a threat to public health, and it was likely to get worse.

Three principal policies were proposed (see Figure 6). The first was to encourage compact or higher density development in the

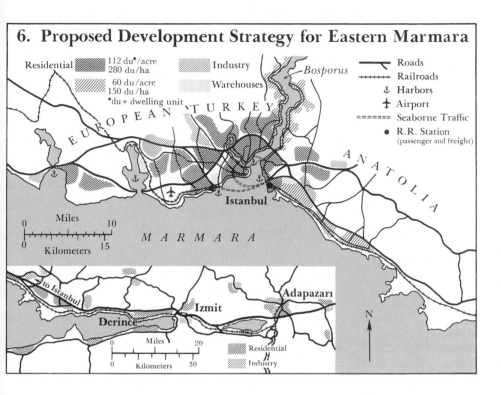

6. Proposed Development Strategy for Eastern Marmara

Residential — 112 du*/acre / 280 du/ha ; 60 du/acre / 150 du/ha ; *du = dwelling unit

Industry

Warehouses

Roads

Railroads

Harbors

Airport

Seaborne Traffic

R.R. Station (passenger and freight)

Bosporus

EUROPEAN TURKEY

ANATOLIA

Istanbul

MARMARA

Miles 0 — 10
Kilometers 0 — 15

to Istanbul

Derince

Izmit

Adapazarı

N

Miles 0 — 20
Kilometers 0 — 30

Residential
Industry

Marmara region and in the metropolitan area. The staff felt it was indefensible to permit, indeed encourage, low density development, considering the increased public investments this would entail for water, power, sewerage, and transportation.

Second, the staff urged that during the next decade or two future development be encouraged on the European (western) rather than the Anatolian (eastern) side of metropolitan Istanbul. This was desirable for several reasons. There were ample and attractive opportunities for development on the European side. On the other hand, further development on the Asian side of the Marmara would produce strong pressures for bridges, tunnels, and roads to relieve traffic congestion, solutions which at this time were far beyond the fiscal capacity of the region and the nation. A preliminary cost analysis showed that providing sites on the European side with water and power from sources on the Asian side would undoubtedly be expensive; but these additional costs were likely to be minor in comparison with those which a more accelerated Asian development might generate. Still another advantage of encouraging development on the European side—but somewhat further west—was that it would help to relieve congestion in the central core of Istanbul. This would assist the city planners of Istanbul in preserving the scenic attractions and amenities of the old city which represented one of its great assets, both for residents and for tourists from other regions and countries. Acceptance of such a policy did not mean there would be no growth on the Asian side over the next decade, but such growth would be far more moderate and thus easier to handle. Eventually, when the country's resources were less strained, the strategy for Asian development could be reassessed.

The third major proposal was to encourage a major growth complex on the far Asian side of the Marmara in the Izmit-Adapazari area, some 100 to 150 kilometers from Istanbul. This proposal was based on the assumption that, because of special locational requirements, particularly a need for orientation to Turkey's internal market, some manufacturing activities had to be located on this side. To avoid dispersed development, the Directorate proposed a specific growth center in an area served by roads and railroads with access to the sea. At this location, there was enough water, an ample potential supply of power, relatively low land costs, and a fairly stable and adequate supply of skilled and unskilled labor. Concentration of growth here would contribute to the decentralization of those manufacturing activities which had to be located outside the metropolitan area of Istanbul, but would not generate huge infrastructure investments that the government could not afford.

A schematic land use plan was prepared for the Eastern Marmara region to provide some guidelines on how to proceed with the staging of development. In addition, a sketch plan was formulated for the Derince-Izmit-Adapazari region. The aims for both were the same: to provide a conceptual framework, a set of assumptions, and some initial suggestions for whatever organization would take responsibility for implementing the plans.

The staff also evaluated and ranked a wide range of essential infrastructure projects (water, power, sewerage, harbor, airport, and highway programs). In doing so, it employed three criteria:

first, whether facilities would encourage industrial activities contributing to higher per capita income and employment; second, whether facilities would reinforce the policy of insuring more compact development; and third, whether facilities would encourage decentralization within the region. The recommendations were so formulated that, depending on the resources available for investment in the region, a choice might be made of the projects to be initiated first.

An industrial survey made it possible to screen the specific firms, by types of manufacturing activities, which would consider the possibility of relocation in an organized industrial district, either within the European Istanbul metropolitan area or in Izmit or in other areas in Anatolia. It also helped to identify the specific land, water, and power requirements of these firms.

Finally, some members of the staff in Istanbul and Ankara examined what might be done to carry out the proposed programs. There was clearly a need for reform in the system of local property taxation, for the creation and extension of the powers of the development authorities, and for revision of the system of land use controls. But these changes were not likely to occur soon. There were, however, some steps which might be taken in the near future. Of these, the staff especially recommended the demarcation of those industrial zones which the private owner could develop, the creation of an organized industrial district in the Eastern Marmara, and the staged provision of essential utilities, such as power and water, in the proposed areas of development. Still other things were suggested which the municipality might do. For example, local officials could expedite building permits, develop a clear policy of land purchase and sales in appropriate areas, and speed up subdivision procedures. The Ministry, in turn, might press the city officials to amend local building and density regulations to ensure greater consistency with the proposed regional land use and development policy.

The Proposals for the Zonguldak Region [34]

Zonguldak, located in the northwestern part of Turkey (see Figure 7), was the other area which the Department of Regional Planning studied. Smaller and less complex than the Marmara, it

7. Zonguldak

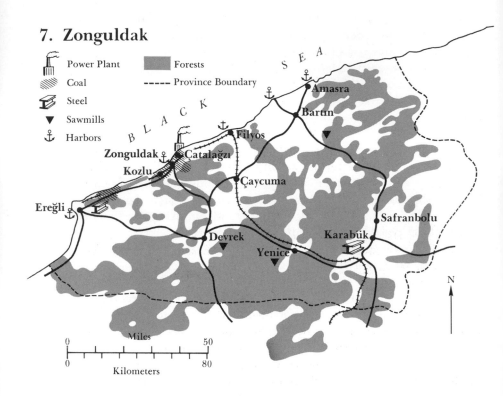

Power Plant
Coal
Steel
Sawmills
Harbors

Forests
Province Boundary

was in many respects an easier region with which to deal. Most of Turkey's coal, iron, and steel production was located in this province. At the time of the study, the steel mill at Karabük was planning to double its capacity which already amounted to half the country's consumption of steel. Even more important, a new steel mill was started at the port city of Ereğli as a joint venture between the government and private and foreign interests. The foreign exchange component of this venture was to be financed by a 139-million-dollar loan from the U. S. Development Fund. In addition, the region had 113 billion tons of proven bituminous coal reserves, and modernization of existing mines was expected to bring about substantial increases in the efficiency of its production, then amounting to 6.3 million tons.

Although coal and steel were the major industries, the region had other resources as well. East of Zonguldak at Çatalağzi was the country's largest power plant. Forests covered 60 percent of Zonguldak vilayet and two sawmills had been built by the Forestry Directorate to exploit this resource. The province of Zonguldak was also favorably situated for inexpensive waterborne transport of commodities abroad, as well as to Istanbul and Izmir, two of Turkey's major market and port centers. Road, rail, and air facilities were inadequate, but they could be upgraded to improve substantially the transportation linkages with Ankara, Bursa, and Istanbul.

However, the studies disclosed a number of serious problems which were impeding the development of the region. The situation in agriculture looked particularly grim. Most of the population lived off the land, but typical holdings were smaller than average, and income and productivity were low. Primitive farming methods, overpopulation, plus a high percentage of tenancy had caused mining of the soil, loss of forest land, and legal complications in the control of urban land use. Migration of "single" men to the steel plants and coal mines created special housing problems. Part-time employment in the mines provided valuable supplementary income for subsistence farmers eking out a living on their small holdings, but it also disrupted family relationships. Mining operations led to land subsidence and the need to control the location of new housing and development. Moreover, although the mines served Turkey's domestic requirements, obsolete pit-head equipment, labor intensive practices, uneconomic pricing policies, and poor management resulted in low productivity and inadequate production. Modernization, however, would create strains since it implied displacing a large proportion of the labor force.

Various ancillary activities generally associated with mining operations and iron and steel complexes in other countries had not developed in this region. There were many reasons for this: gaps in information, lack of confidence in Turkish sources of supply, inadequate infrastructure, the tangled land tenure, poor topography, and sheer inertia. Service activity, too, was abnormally low, even taking into account the relatively low family income. The region's surpassing beauty could easily lend itself to some domestic tourist development, but poor transportation connections and inadequate hotels had hampered the exploitation of this potential. *Gecekondu* construction, too, was increasing, especially in areas subject to subsidence, and schools were unusually poor and crowded. There appeared to be ample power, but water resources were adequate only for present urban needs and the contemplated expansion of steel operations. What Zonguldak lacked most was an organization concerned and knowledgeable about these problems and charged with the responsibility of finding solutions.

Unfortunately, the situation seemed likely to worsen. Tentative population projections indicated that during the next ten years the employable labor force in Zonguldak might increase by 85,000 to 100,000, and by 1980 by perhaps another 100,000 to 150,000. Total population by 1980 was likely to have grown by one-half million. If new economic activities did not develop, agricultural conditions would deteriorate and Zonguldak would begin to export population to other regions, most likely the urban areas of the Marmara, which, as has been noted, would have great difficulty in coping with this migration flow.

Taking account of existing skills, resources, and markets, the staff suggested a number of possibilities for the expansion of existing enterprises. These included fishing, canning, metal pressing, shoemaking, furniture making, cement and building materials production, activities ancillary to the production of steel, and tourism. Other suggestions dealt with the possibilities of crop substitution and soil conservation within each of the four river valleys of the region.

But promotion of these enterprises would require incentives and other forms of assistance. And even a very modest expansion of the economy in some of these directions, it was pointed out, would produce difficult site selection problems and shortages of port, transportation, water, and sewage facilities. The staff, therefore, undertook to identify those sites able to accommodate the growth of economic activities and population and those sites which were not. Some evidence was also produced, on the basis of user requirements, to justify a reconsideration of existing transportation plans and priorities. In addition, the attention of the appropriate ministries was directed to the obvious water and sewage problems. The Department particularly emphasized the need to establish some permanent organization to spur the development of the region's resources. For, in addition to pursuing these studies further, two major jobs remained — the encouragement of more private investment and the translation of recommendations for public action into specific programs.

Results of the Projects

The studies and recommendations for the Marmara and Istanbul regions were formally presented and discussed at four official conferences starting in June of 1961.[35] Key ministers (including at one session the Deputy Prime Minister), governors of the provinces, and leading local and central government officials attended these sessions.

To the professional observer, the imperfections of the studies were painfully obvious. But this was to be expected, given the conditions under which the work was being conducted. In both offices, the studies were run with tiny staffs ranging from ten to fifteen persons, mainly architects and engineers and one or two economists, most of whom lacked any previous experience at all, let alone experience in their specialized field. Their performance on the job was somewhat uneven: some persons worked diligently; some were indefatigible; but there was always a substantial number who plainly lacked skill, ability, or motivation. Of course, salaries left much to be desired. Elementary supplies were often unavailable, and offices were crowded. There were serious gaps in data, and the data which were available had serious quality limitations. Of necessity, the methodology was primitive and the economic and social analyses weak. None of the project proposals were evaluated adequately in terms of cost; and, despite heroic efforts, the prospects of implementation were dubious at best. Nonetheless, as the deadlines approached, the challenge spurred astonishingly devoted efforts and the enthusiasm and pride growing out of this activity soon became contagious.

The intense dedication of the participants was sensed by the conference. The results of the projects, too, surpassed all expectations. A unique experiment in local-central government relations had been successfully managed in the Marmara region. Significant regional development problems had begun to be tackled. Limited as the studies were, they, nonetheless, were able to provide some valuable leads which officials of Istanbul and SPO, as well as other local and central government agencies, could take into account in planning their infrastructure investments. In addition, the staff had learned to work with each other and with the consultants and had obtained valuable experience in sifting and analyzing raw data and in formulating policy recommendations. Moreover, although they had acquired these skills within a short period, they were able to impress some of the ablest and most powerful officials of the government.

The prospects for further progress had also visibly improved. Within a year and a half after the start of the program, the Department of Regional Planning had enlarged its staff to more than thirty professionals and was cooperating with the Department of Social Planning of SPO. Two regional planning studies had been undertaken and in the course of these efforts a number of inexperienced professionals had been trained on the job and had revealed promising capacity for growth and leadership. Some of them had been sent abroad for further specialized training under the auspices of the OECD, the UN, and bilateral technical assistance agreements. Finally, the newly reorganized Central Statistical Institute offered the prospect of an improved information system in the future.

These accomplishments were real and the Turkish officials took pride in them. The programs were praised in the press and warmly applauded by important government officials, university staff, and various professional and business groups. The prestige of the Department of Regional Planning rose, more funds became available, recruitment expanded, and the quality of the staff perceptibly improved. But however real these accomplishments were, the hard truth was that the program still owed its support less to the success of past efforts than to the promise of future achievements. In addition, the progress of the Department had created a new complex of problems which would have to be solved before the previous advances would have any lasting significance.

Questions of Implementation

In the early stages of the program the Ministry preferred to rely on persuasion as the primary means of implementation. The plans had their weaknesses and until more skill and experience were gained, the Ministry thought it best that the plans serve only as optional guides for officials charged with the enforcement of land use controls for the private sector and for officials responsible for infrastructure or other development decisions affecting the regions.

The Ministry's influence could be considerable, however, if and when it chose to exercise its power. The General Directorate of Planning, the same branch of the Ministry which supervised the Department of Regional Planning, was responsible for approving proposed urban and regional plans, and all development plans of private entrepreneurs had to be consistent with these. As yet, many communities did not have urban plans and only two areas had tentative regional plans. Nonetheless, the existing procedures indicated how the Ministry might grapple with some of these problems. The regional plans could identify high priority urban areas, such as Izmit, Adapazari, and Zonguldak, and the Bank of Municipalities, the organization charged with this responsibility, could prepare detailed urban plans within the frame of reference established by the regional development proposals. In addition, if the regional plans were "accepted" by SPO, other ministries might be persuaded to make their investment programs consistent with these plans, and SPO could monitor this adherence through its established control and coordinative mechanisms. The pattern of private investment might also be significantly affected if public services were concentrated in particular growing points of the economy and if tax and credit incentives were adjusted accordingly.

The inadequacy of land use controls raised important implementation questions. Should development be regulated in areas outside of the jurisdiction of cities? How were current density trends to be influenced? What were the best procedures for adjudicating conflicts between public and private interests? And what should be done about land speculation?

Certainly, there was no lack of possible solutions. One staff study suggested that land sales be registered and that the municipality have power over the subdividing, leasing, and purchase of land outside of its boundaries. Another proposed that full costs be charged for infrastructure improvements. Others wanted "compulsory purchase" proceedings speeded up and a public agency created to purchase and resell or lease land at reasonable prices. One of the UN consultants in the Marmara office, a specialist in urban land use controls, prepared a "model code" to show how land uses might be regulated through the use of zoning and subdivision controls. All of these proposals were attractive to physical planners, but each of them involved many tricky substantive and legal questions.[36] For example, the system of negligible local property taxation encouraged speculation and municipal impotence, whereas raising revenue by taxes on land or improvements did not appear feasible as long as rents were frozen. The net effect might be wholesale evasion or rapid deterioration of improvements because it would be unprofitable to maintain or repair property. Thus, it seemed wise to move slowly on these matters and to seek the advice of experienced, legal, administrative, and economic specialists.[37]

Subsequent Programs and Problems

Although the process took more time than had been originally anticipated, the studies that the Department had conducted were eventually revised, updated, and published.[38] But the Department was unable to conduct preliminary feasibility or cost-benefit analyses of project proposals or to keep up with new regional developments. It was even forced to neglect follow-up discussions which would have explained the details of the existing proposals to key public officials in different ministries and to interested private developers.

The Department bogged down on these matters partly because of its astonishing success. Top staff members were promoted to new positions. The head of the Department of Regional Planning was shifted to SPO as head of the Department of Social Planning. The chief of the Istanbul Directorate was made acting chief of the Ankara Department and consequently began to neglect development in the Marmara region. Some of the abler members of the staff were rewarded with fellowship opportunities for training abroad. At about the same time, three of the resident consultants had to be replaced when their tours of duty ended. There was also the usual change of ministers.

Meanwhile, with success came pressures on the Department to broaden its scope of action to include such areas as Çukurova, Antalya, and Eastern Anatolia and such subjects as village development, migration, and requirements of sites for tourist development. How was the Department to handle these additional responsibilities? Its first step was to suspend further work in Zonguldak and the Marmara until other pressures subsided. Then, a few members of the staff were turned into "firefighters." They examined migration trends, conducted important reconnaissance surveys in the eastern region, and helped SPO devise socio-economic indicators for national studies of regional disparities. They also identified tourist development sites along the Mediterranean and the Aegean for the Ministry of Tourism and provided assistance on urban and infrastructure problems in Antalya for the staff of SPO and the Food and Agriculture Organization.[39] All these tasks, however, were merely incidental to the major preoccupation of the Department—the development of Çukurova and its largest urban center, Adana.

Çukurova, a military center in southern Turkey, was a critical region for a variety of reasons. It was not only growing rapidly, it also appeared to have tremendous potential. In the past, its growth had been based on the production of cotton. The principal economic activities of Adana were still concerned with cotton processing, textiles, and wholesaling. With the decline in the price of cotton, however, citrus fruits, cereals, vegetables, and grapes became increasingly important. Forestry resources and, to a much lesser extent, fishing also seemed to offer attractive commercial possibilities. In addition, the region contained two ports. Iskenderun, 135 kilometers southeast of Adana, was the principal outlet for the agricultural products and other goods produced in Turkey's southeastern hinterland. Mersin, 70 kilometers southwest of Adana, had a refinery for crude oil and was the outlet for the goods produced both in the south-central region of Turkey and in Adana. Tarsus, a junction point between Mersin, Adana, and the north, was another focus of economic activity (see Figure 8).

From the very outset, the Department had eyed the region as one of the most significant in the country and as an appropriate theater for its activities. The initiative for action, however, was

8. Adana Region

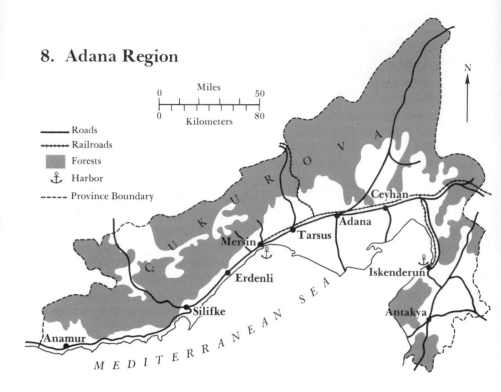

sparked by the prospect of an unusual collaborative effort. SPO, partly because of the influence of the new director of Social Planning, had become strongly interested in the development potentials of this region. The Agency for International Development (AID), the economic and technical assistance agency of the United States, likewise wanted to help promote activities here. Since the staffs of the three agencies were friendly, respected each other, and saw clear advantages in working together, they negotiated an informal agreement early in November 1962.[40]

In substance, SPO agreed to sponsor the study and to assign some of its staff to work on this problem, both in Ankara and in the field. AID agreed to provide eight to ten experts for a period of six months. The Department of Regional Planning was to act as the "agent" for SPO in staffing and managing the operation. The Department would also establish a field office, set up a staff, and, as in the Marmara program, try to maximize the amount of local assistance. In addition, SPO was to get the other ministries to provide additional staff and specialized assistance.

Unfortunately, corrosive disputes soon developed concerning the roles of the participants.[41] Therefore, SPO decided to supervise the entire program itself. Although other ministries were expected to contribute staff, the coordinator of the program was appointed by and solely responsible to SPO. Despite the many problems of administration, the Çukurova program managed to achieve some results. A number of studies were prepared dealing with development possibilities in agriculture, marketing, fishing, canning, forestry, port development, and land use. Subsequent technical assistance decisions of AID were guided by these studies, and they in turn influenced both the programming decisions for the region made by various ministries and SPO's criteria for review of its sectoral investments. But the program acquired no long-run institutional significance. AID experts had little interest in regional planning or staff training. Unlike the Marmara program, there was relatively little local participation and support. To the surprise of no one, shortly after the studies were completed, the Çukurova field office was closed.

In August 1964 a new Undersecretary for SPO was appointed. Eventually, he decided that regional planning was the responsibility of the Department of Economic Planning and shifted the functions away from the Department of Social Planning. This policy was reinforced by the change of government in February 1965 and by the decisive victory of the Justice Party in the following October elections.

TURKEY'S URBAN GROWTH STRATEGY IN PERSPECTIVE

How should one assess the efforts made at the national level to fashion an urban growth strategy for Turkey? The government initiated studies and programs for the Marmara region and for Zonguldak (where some 20 percent of the total public investment took place). Later, it did the same for Çukurova. And it has continued this approach in still other urban regions — pragmatically and intuitively in response to pressures and opportunities. But has the government really fashioned a policy and the means to implement it?

To say that there is *no* national policy would certainly be inaccurate. Such a policy does exist: not a clear one to be sure, perhaps not even an operational one, but a policy nonetheless. It is vague, it lends itself to inconsistency, and it is not quantitatively defined. But it does aim at promoting development in selected urban areas, while reducing, whenever feasible, the social and economic gaps between regions and especially those between the east and west.[42]

Because funds, staff, and time were limited and because there were so many difficult problems to be solved during the early period of the program, the government's initial actions had to be limited. The Ministry of Reconstruction and Resettlement experimented with pilot studies and plans for one or two regions at a time. Attempts were then made by the Ministry and SPO to carry out the recommendations by manipulating tax, credit, capital allocation, and control mechanisms.[43] The focus was on urban growth regions, chosen on the basis of their importance for national growth, the significance of their hinterlands, the estimated effects of the programs, and political pressures. These initial experiments laid the foundations for a more systematic formulation and implementation of urban growth policies in the future.[44] Although modest, they had the great virtue of being feasible. And, for better or worse, they helped to increase the share of public investments in the lagging regions from 11 percent in 1963 to 24 percent in 1965.[45]

The Ministry and SPO are now approaching a point where they may be able to confront some of the larger issues. Since the mid-sixties, the staff and program of the Ministry of Reconstruction and Resettlement have continued to expand. The Ministry numbers over fifty professionals and is involved in a wide range of activities. It has collaborated with SPO in developing data and plans for the regions of the Aegean, Antalya, central Anatolia, and eastern and southeastern Anatolia (the latter in connection with the building of the Keban Dam). It has investigated Turkey's migration, urbanization, and regional development trends and the locational characteristics of Turkey's principal economic activities. It has sponsored some follow-up land use and economic studies in the Marmara, Zonguldak, and Çukurova regions.[46] In addition, the Greater Istanbul Master Planning Bureau, established by the Ministry in 1964, has taken over most of the staff and work of the Istanbul Regional Planning Directorate. As in the past, however, the greatest danger lies in overextension and poor quality, a natural outgrowth of the tendency to confuse expansion with strength and challenging tasks with jobs that can be satisfactorily accomplished.

Some very serious difficulties lie ahead. For if the government is to meet stipulated employment goals, 7.5 million jobs will have to be created by 1975.[47] SPO, on the basis of its investment and production targets, considers it improbable that the urban economy will produce more than 6.8 million jobs. Therefore, in addition to long-term population measures, it has committed itself not only to promoting a higher rate of investment in urban growth centers, but also to improving rural life and to encouraging village development programs and the building of the Keban Dam in southeastern Anatolia. Through these efforts, it hopes to maximize non-agricultural employment in rural regions and thereby reduce urban migration.[48] But the aim is ambitious and unlikely to be fully achieved.

Even if these measures do prove effective, the new and the old metropolitan centers face a population avalanche. Projections made by the Department of Regional Planning suggest that Turkey's 1960 urban population will not only double by 1975, it may even increase by three to four-and-a-half times by 1985; the greatest increases will occur in cities of 100,000 or more.[49] How this population will be accommodated and which metropolitan regions are likely to experience the most serious discrepancies between the number of jobs and job seekers are still largely unknown.

Clearly, the existing government machinery for grappling with metropolitan and regional development faces an enormous challenge in the coming generation. To help the Ministry and SPO meet this challenge, new powers have been made available. A law (No. 933) was passed in the summer of 1967[50] giving SPO special authority to use the development and promotion funds of the budget as loans for promoting high priority sectors (public and private) in the chosen regions of the country. In case of reinvestment, income taxes can also be reduced up to 80 percent, depending upon the sector and region of investment. The law also allows the central government to exercise direct land use control and direct land development for industrial estates and tourist development areas. There is even a special fund in the national budget to assist those local governments experiencing rapid industrialization in coping with problems of land purchase and infrastructure investment. But these new powers must be used skill-fully to succeed and, without radical transformation, the Turkish government is unlikely to develop the necessary administrative flexibility and effectiveness.

CONCLUDING OBSERVATIONS

1. Whatever the inadequacies of educational institutions, one has hardly any alternative but to turn to their faculty or students to find modern perspectives and fresh talent. Efforts to nurture new policies and new ways of doing things tend to foster, and respond to, changes in university programs. For urban growth strategies, this implies attracting able recruits and encouraging new courses and programs in all relevant academic disciplines. Some first-rate staff members were obtained in this way for both the Turkish and Venezuelan development programs. Nonetheless, university collaboration in the first few years proved disappointing in both countries. In Venezuela there was a political conflict between the principal local university and the administration; and Turkey suffered from the lack of sufficiently advanced programs in most of its universities.[51]

As a general rule, unless local institutions are adequate, some training abroad is essential. In addition to formal educa-tion, this should include attendance at professional meetings and short visits to examine programs in other countries. Such changes of environment are particularly valuable for personnel in cultural situations where it is necessary to broaden perspec-tives and to help reorient attitudes and work habits.[52] There is a real danger, of course, that these training programs may lend themselves to abuse. They can become a means of getting rid of a problem personality, a potential competitor, or an incompetent clod. A grant may sometimes become a reward for seniority or for services rendered. The period abroad may be turned into a junket or an opportunity to find a better job at home or elsewhere. But one can anticipate such malprac-tices and even attempt to minimize them.[53]

In the case of Turkey, one of the most successful aspects of its entire program was the effective utilization of the fellowship and travel arrangements of international agencies and of dif-ferent countries with which Turkey had bilateral agreements.

The Department of Regional Planning could not possibly have survived the constant loss of top personnel if, over the years, able members of the staff had not received fellowships for travel and study abroad. This equipped them to handle more effectively the responsibilities that resulted from the abrupt "vertical" and "horizontal" mobility of the Turkish administrative scene.

2. The role of the consultant varies with the circumstances, as can be seen from the experiences of Venezuela and Turkey. He is supposed to provide technical expertise, and sometimes he actually does. But his presence may also serve as a ruse to stall action or as a means of amplifying the ideas of a local expert or program chief who otherwise might be ignored. At times too much attention may be paid to his views, and, on occasion, not nearly enough. But if he is capable and persuasive, he may at certain periods, especially in the early years, exercise exceptional influence in shaping the quality, the content, and the direction of the program. In more advanced stages, as we have seen, his role may shift to that of a specialist supplementing the work of the existing staff.

During the early period, the general consultant cannot function effectively without the support of a few key individuals who have—or who might acquire—prestige and influence. No matter how sensitive, skilled, and knowledgeable the consultant may be, he is an outsider. He must have the help of someone who knows the terrain to run interference and to steer him away, or otherwise protect him, from pitfalls he can neither gauge nor negotiate. Whenever such a successful collaboration occurs, surprising things can happen: the support of the right people can be mustered; better quality staff can be obtained; proper work habits and attitudes have a reasonable prospect of being inculcated.

But such an alliance is often an invitation for hostile cliques or coalitions to form. This may result in the overthrow of both the policies and the offending individual. Thus, it is often a good idea—good as long as it is permitted—for the consultant to keep open some cordial lines of communication with opponents or potential successors and to make it clear that the consultant is serving an institution and the people in power, not a particular individual. Such an avowal or disavowal provides no guarantees. But the consultant may have no other practical option if he is to serve in an environment characterized by conflict and change. Perceptive local leaders are aware of these problems and are often, though not always, indulgent about efforts to keep friends on both sides of the political fence provided that such efforts are handled with prudence and frankness.

3. The author has deliberately omitted any discussion of motivation and personalities, although he is *keenly* aware of their importance. Differences in temperament, family background, education, rank, pay, office arrangements, and similar matters may warp judgments and nourish grievances that will become manifest on the most unexpected occasions. Ways of negotiating an agreement will vary depending on whether one is dealing with a sophisticated administrator, an ineffectual political hack, an insecure bureaucrat, or a doctrinaire research specialist. A key decision-maker may be a Hamlet capable of the most thoughtful philosophical "aperçus" while committing the most deplorable practical blunders. Or he may be a competent craftsman, a thoughtful scholar, a delightful raconteur—indeed all three—and still generate the most passionate resentment because of contemptuous class attitudes or astonishing political naiveté. A man's behavior may be transformed by his wife's neurotic jealousies and frustrations or by the megalomania that sometimes grips ambitious minds.

Yet it would be neither gracious nor just to deal here with these tortuous details, since the judgments of a participant-observer may not accurately mirror reality. Nor would such revelations necessarily serve any purpose, for the character faults themselves cannot easily be corrected. Moreover, though such details may add some realism, they also detract from the experience, make it less general, perhaps even less significant. What may be worth stressing, however, is that these additional considerations—which are complicated, non-quantifiable, and important—must somehow be faced and negotiated with endless patience, humility, and skill if the programs are to be made to work.

Urban Growth Centers versus London: The Experience of Great Britain

British urban policy first emerged near the end of the depression of the 1930's. Because it emerged then, and not during the eighteenth or nineteenth century when Britain's contemporary urban system was growing and undergoing rapid change, the main emphasis of British policy was on the modification rather than the fashioning of an urban system. The policy had deep antecedents, however. Its appearance in the thirties was the result of a convergence of two major nineteenth-century movements of reform. One had originally dealt with the employment conditions of the working class and had gradually evolved into a more general preoccupation with such hazards of modern industrial society as "structural unemployment" in "depressed areas." The other had concerned itself with the living conditions of the poor and had persistently agitated for a healthy, efficient, and attractive urban environment. Through the combined influence of these two reformist traditions, the urban growth strategy of Great Britain was decisively shaped.

The strategy had three basic aims: to curb the growth of population and employment in London and its surrounding region; to increase growth in the more distant peripheral areas; and to change the form of growth of the largest metropolitan regions, particularly London. (Military security, although an important aim at the outset, soon dwindled into insignificance due to technological progress.) Presumably these goals, if achieved, would reduce the diseconomies of the congested metropolis and the unemployment and outmigration trends of the lagging regions. They would spur national, as well as regional, growth, and they would rationalize the form of growth wherever it occurred.

Many tools were devised to obtain these ends. One set, designed largely by urban planners, sought to limit the size of London and reduce its inner densities by the construction of a greenbelt along the perimeter of the city and by the building of small, self-contained New Towns in the outer areas of the metropolis beyond the greenbelt and in the more distant peripheral regions. Another set of devices, designed by economic planners, restricted the building of industrial plants in the London region while providing incentives to firms either contributing to exports or willing to locate their plants in the less prosperous regions. These methods, which have been experimented with for more than a generation, can now be assessed with some historical perspective.

The strategy has succeeded in some respects but not in others. No doubt the efforts were hampered by many constraints. Resources were inadequate. Understanding of the problem was faulty. There were changes in emphasis with changes of the party in power. Energy was diverted by nationalization measures and other simultaneous policy innovations of the government and by efforts to solve balance of payment problems that, at least in the short run, were not altogether consistent with the strategy. Hindsight also suggests that the key programs did not enjoy a high enough priority and that the means employed were not wielded firmly enough to ensure the desired effects.

Yet there has been almost no disposition to give up the quest. On the contrary, the cumulative experience has only sharpened

Britain's desire to make the efforts succeed. Fortunately, because of recent innovations in policy and methods, its urban development strategy now seems likely to produce more successful results. To understand why, let us examine the failures and accomplishments of the past and the problems which still have to be solved. These can tell us a great deal about some of the mechanics and pitfalls of making such an enterprise work.

EVOLUTION OF A GROWTH STRATEGY, 1850–1950

Policy for the Depressed Areas

Throughout the nineteenth century there were sustained efforts to improve the lot of the industrial worker. Led by the unions, the movement initially sought to achieve the legalization of unions and control of the conditions and territory of jobs. Of primary concern were the questions of hours of work, rates of pay, safety, training and apprenticeship, and jurisdiction.

As conditions improved and expectations rose, however, the definition of the problems of labor broadened to include the need for comprehensive assistance and insurance schemes to deal with death, accidents, unemployment, old age, and health. The new issues were of such magnitude that they could not be adequately handled by the union, the employer, or the local community. Therefore, reform efforts spread from labor to political organizations and from local to national activity, as it became increasingly necessary to muster national support in the political arena to achieve their widening assortment of objectives.

Over time, however, it became clear that one of the most intractable of these new issues was the concentration and persistence of heavy unemployment and underemployment in regions with declining industries. Northern Ireland, Scotland, northeast England, Cumberland, Lancashire, Merseyside, and Wales were the areas most affected. The basic industries in these regions—coal mining, iron and steel, cotton and woolen textiles, shipbuilding and repairing, and heavy engineering—were declining over the long term and were especially vulnerable in periods of recession. Some of the reasons for this decline were the shift from rail to roads, the new sources of power, the decline of free trade, the emergence of light market-oriented industries, the impact of external economies, the shift of population, and the self-reinforcing aspects of success and failure. The combined effects of these trends favored the growth of population and of new expanding activities in the South (London, the South East, part of the South West, and the Midlands). At the same time, the older, resource-oriented industries which had developed in the North (the rest of England, Scotland, and Wales)[1] were put at a growing disadvantage.

All of Britain's regions grew throughout the nineteenth century, but its Southern regions grew at a more rapid rate. In 1801 London and the Home Counties contained a little more than one-sixth of Britain's total population. In 1861 they accounted for one-fifth; in 1901, a little more than one-fifth; and in 1961, one-fourth.[2] By the turn of the century, regions in the North were experiencing a decided outmigration.

The problem came to a head in the 1930's. By then there was general recognition that not only were the less prosperous areas losing population and providing a lower level of income per family, but that

> the level of unemployment in them as a group had been consistently about twice that of all other areas in the country as a group and about 50 percent above the regional average. This remained true whatever general conditions were; for example, in 1929 the percentage of unemployment in the five major depressed areas was 14.5 when the average for the rest of the country was 7.3 and in 1931 the figures were 31.3 and 16.5 respectively.[3]

Even when economic conditions substantially improved for other regions in 1939, in most depressed areas unemployment and outmigration still continued to increase.[4]

The conventional economic prescription for dealing with these problems was to bring the workers to the jobs. Presumably, this would increase total employment without either shoring up inefficiency or countering existing trends. Many men and women, of course, did leave the poorer regions of their own accord, but the aim of the prescription was to systematize the movement and reduce the obstacles impeding it.[5] Britain's first attempt to assist the declining regions involved the adoption of such a policy. In 1928 an *Industrial Transference Board* was created. Its task was to advise workers about areas with more attractive employment opportunities and to provide them with the kinds of skills and minimum financial support required to make the transfer.[6] Although originally aimed at shifting workers from coal mining to specific vacancies elsewhere, the program was subsequently extended to other kinds of employees.

For all of its apparent logic, this policy had its limitations. The areas which were most affected by unemployment—Northern Ireland, Scotland, and Wales—were among the most politically sensitive in the nation. Reliance on relocation measures alone meant that the government would make no effort to change the economy or to introduce more productive activities. On the contrary, the nature of the remedy exacerbated the very conditions that it was intended to cure. To obtain the confidence and the patronage of both employers and employees, the exchanges generally recruited the younger, the abler, and the more skilled workers.[7] These efforts, when combined with extensive unassisted migration,[8] drained these areas of their potential leaders, increased the tax burdens of those people who remained, and reinforced the prevailing atmosphere of failure.

The policy makers also had to contend with one other stubborn fact. A great many people simply would not leave the depressed areas. To them it meant leaving their friends, their families, their homes, not to mention other ties or forms of security, all for an uncertain future in an alien environment. They could hardly have anticipated such a move with pleasure or tranquillity. One can comprehend their preference for the joys and sorrows they already knew; their pathetic hope that things might somehow change for the better; and their stolid bitterness when forced to drift into less skillful occupations or even into partial or total unemployment.

During the depression year of 1934 several government investigators examined the amount of "surplus labor" in three regions: the northeast coast, southwest Scotland, and south Wales. These particular areas were not the most hard hit by any means, but they were areas which could be studied in detail and where experiments might be conducted which could then be applied on a more comprehensive basis.[9] Despite the increasing outmigration, the investigators discovered that about 40 percent of the population in these areas was unemployed. This forced the government to recognize that, in spite of the transfer policy, the scale of the problem had reached intolerable dimensions. As a result, that same year the *Special Areas (Development and Improvement) Act* was passed. Under this legislation, the Board of Trade appointed an English commissioner for West Cumberland, the northeast coast, and South Wales, and the Scottish Office appointed a commissioner for southwest Scotland.

It took time, however, to devise solutions. At the outset, it was assumed the emergency was temporary and required only limited efforts. The legislation also excluded the major cities in these areas, thus limiting drastically what could be done. It is not surprising, therefore, that the principal initial measures of the commissioners involved the financing of public works, mainly sewerage and public health facilities. The English commissioner also attempted to encourage more emigration from these areas, but the results proved negligible. His program of grants for land settlements and subsistence farming was expensive and equally ineffectual. There were also some desultory efforts to encourage new development, tourism, and the placement of government contracts in these areas. Finally, in 1935, when most of these measures had proved inadequate and when industrial surveys had established that almost no firms were interested in locating in these areas under the prevailing conditions and forms of assistance, the English commissioner decided to experiment with the development of planned industrial areas, or "trading estates." Similar to those first initiated in the United States, these *trading estates* built standard factories at subsidized rents for small firms. Provision was also made for Treasury loans and grants and limited tax assistance for firms willing to make the move to these areas but preferring to provide their own plant or equipment. Later, financial aids were made available for housing and for improving local services and amenities, as well as for the conversion of wasteland to industrial and recreational areas.[10]

The effect of these measures in the years prior to the war was limited. The basic economic weaknesses in most of the regions remained unchanged. Most of the reduction in unemployment in the late thirties was clearly due, not to the Special Areas program, but to rearmament. By the end of the decade, the program was still restricted to the initial four areas, and a long-range national policy had not as yet been agreed upon.

Nonetheless, much had been learned from the experience of the thirties. It had pointed up the futility of such piecemeal measures as land settlement, public works improvements, and transference schemes. One major new tool, the planned industrial estate, had been created which was destined to play a larger role in future development policy. Finally, the experiments of the thirties had made clear the need for devising more effective long-term policies to change the growth prospects of the North.

When the *Barlow Commission* (The Royal Commission on the Distribution of the Industrial Population) held its hearings in 1939 and 1940, there were strong representations from the commissioners for the Special Areas and from representatives of the depressed regions.[11] They marshaled evidence to show that the changes in industrial structure and in the distribution of population favored light market-oriented, rather than resource-oriented, industries and that London and the Southern regions were benefiting from these changes while the less prosperous areas were being confronted by the cumulative disadvantages. This gap, they emphasized, would continue to widen unless somehow the advantages enjoyed by the South were offset by controls and incentives which diverted some of the growth activities from the South to the North and changed the economic structure of the lagging areas.

Precisely how this should be done, however, was unclear. With mounting evidence of elephantiasis in the South and anemia in the North, the interdependence of these problems could hardly be overlooked; nor, for that matter, could the joint remedies that might theoretically be applicable. On the other hand, given the secular changes in industrial structure and the prevailing time-cost relationships between regions, few pragmatic policy makers were then likely to count on drawing more than a tiny proportion of the South's economic activities to the North. Conceivably, shifting the capital city might have helped. But in a country as tradition-bound as Great Britain, this solution was virtually unthinkable.

Although there was general agreement on the need for a central planning authority to shape national patterns of urban and regional development, there was no consensus on the specific locational strategy or the type of regional and central organizations required. There were also strong differences of opinion concerning the use of positive and negative measures. A great deal of improvisation was still to occur before these issues would be clarified. Nonetheless, the North had now expressed a strong policy position.

With the start of World War II, attention shifted to other matters. War contracts and increased employment temporarily eased the problems of the less prosperous regions. However, the achievement of full employment in most regions made the problem of structural unemployment even more visible. One of the main goals of Great Britain had now become full employment, and it was simply not possible to achieve full employment without first solving the problem of structural unemployment. Moreover, times had changed and the problems of lagging regions were being examined from the point of view of the growth economists. It seemed to make economic sense to utilize idle labor and infrastructure and thus increase regional, as well as national, income.

But no major action was taken until the war's end. Then, in 1945 the Conservative Government passed the *Distribution of Industry Act* which made the Board of Trade responsible for national policy on industrial location with special responsibilities for areas of high local unemployment and designated Development Areas. At the outset, these areas were the former Special Areas (Central Scotland, the North East, West Cumberland, and South Wales); subsequently, the list was enlarged to include Wrexham, south Lancashire, Merseyside, the Scottish Highlands, northeast Lancashire, and the South West.[12] In 1950 the Labor Government passed legislation providing for increased government contributions to the cost of transferring firms and their workers to depressed areas. Both acts also provided loans and subsidies for the establishment of promising undertakings in these areas and assistance for the building of trading estates and the subsidization of infrastructure.[13] These tools were further strengthened by the continuance of two government controls that had been established during the war: one set priorities for building materials and raw materials; the other regulated the issuance of building licenses.

The passage of this legislation made it clear that the country was no longer content with the policy of bringing workers to jobs. The government had now committed itself to bringing jobs to the areas of high unemployment. But, in the course of the next two decades,

114

this policy, too, was to prove inadequate and in need of substantial modification.

Policy for the Cities

While the labor reformers were widening their point of view, the urban reform movement was also broadening its perspectives, but this transformation was a vaguer, more tortuous, and complex process. The crowding and invasion of the city by the poor that had accelerated in the nineteenth century and the slum's ever-present menace of fire, disease, blight, and crime produced fear and indignation everywhere, but particularly among the middle and upper classes. The resulting emotional recoil and efforts at reform have not yet spent themselves; nor, despite a century or more of effort, have they yet ensured relatively healthy, efficient, and attractive environments in which to work and live.

The reformers launched their first attacks against two prevalent nineteenth-century evils: miserable sanitary standards and jerrybuilding. After winning legislation imposing higher and more costly minimum standards of housing and land use, they turned their attention to related issues: the housing shortage, high rents, speculation, the need for cheap transportation, land reform, the lack of adequate open space, and the reorganization of local government and municipal boundaries. Some improvements of conditions followed, partly due to rising income and partly due to reform efforts.

As the cities continued to grow, however, new expectations and new issues arose.[14] Improvements in transport opened up cheap land at the edge of the city. After basic utilities had been installed, private builders put up new homes for middle and higher-income families. Eventually local authorities did the same for low-income families. Shops and other services followed. So did an increasing number of firms starting new or branch plants or relocating old ones. As the city spread, the length, time, and cost of the journey to work increased. When the city grew beyond the boundaries of local control and overlapped the jurisdictions of many other local authorities, questions arose concerning the need for larger and more powerful local governments. Soon the cycle began repeating itself on an ever widening scale.

In the process, access to the countryside became more difficult, while open and recreational space became scarcer and more expensive. Changes in land uses within the city became less feasible, for the rise of population and income increased the pressure for space, bid up land values and the costs of labor and construction, and created financial difficulties in acquiring or providing the land and structures needed for new uses. Modification was possible only when the proposed land uses involved higher income-producing activities than those already on the site. Although the requirements of families and firms changed with rising incomes and population, the city's physical patterns and facilities remained relatively inflexible and increasingly inadequate, especially in relation to the higher quality of services desired. Complaints multiplied about the deficiencies of the urban plant, the low standards, and the mismatch between houses, shops, workplaces, and community and recreational facilities.

London in the late 1930's particularly dramatized these problems. During those years, while the North was struggling to increase its economic activities and retain its population, the London region—with its superior port, transportation, and communication facilities, its huge market, and its diverse centers for business, shopping, and entertainment—continued to attract more population and economic activities. It continued as well to require and obtain more extensive infrastructure and other capital investments to deal with its mounting needs, its congestion, and its ponderous inflexibility.

Experience over the years suggested that adequate solutions were not likely to come from attacks on isolated sectors, such as transportation, housing, industry, or land. But neither was there any likelihood of transforming London or any of the other metropolitan areas into linked clusters of small, self-contained, low-density "garden cities" surrounded by agricultural greenbelts—as had been strongly urged by Ebenezer Howard and his school of urbanists.[15] Between these two poles, however, lay other possibilities, for there were elements in Howard's ideas that could be adapted to the problems of the British metropolis; in particular, his notions of limiting metropolitan size and of transforming the pattern of growth of the metropolitan region. These ideas were within the range of thinking with which the town planners in Britain were familiar; hence, they most readily agreed on the need to decentralize London's growth and to shift some of the excess population and economic activities to small communities in the outer areas of the London region.

Even this more modest approach, however, required some extensive changes in the planning system. Under the prewar administrative mechanisms, which were governed by the Town and Country Planning Act of 1932, there was power to prevent something from being done but not enough power to ensure development along lines and in places deemed desirable. Adoption of plans was time-consuming and difficult, modification was equally cumbersome, and refusal to allow private development carried the risk of charges for compensation. Planning powers were fragmented, being wielded by 1441 councils of counties, country boroughs, and local authorities in rural areas. As a result, "only 5% of England and 1% of Wales were actually subject to operative schemes and there were important towns and cities and large country districts for which not even the preliminary steps had been taken." [16] The new aims could hardly be achieved until there were more adequate financial mechanisms to handle the questions of compensation, larger jurisdictions for local authorities, and a new approach to the strategy of regional development. In short, a revolution was needed in Great Britain's land use and development system.

This revolution came sooner than anyone expected. The threat of war, coupled with the converging problems of the North and South, prompted a series of historic inquiries by royal commissions. The first of these commissions, the *Barlow Commission,* was established in 1939 to investigate the causes and consequences of trends in industrial location and to suggest new policies and administrative machinery. The main recommendation of the Commission was to create a central planning agency. Its job would be to help redevelop congested urban areas, to decentralize or disperse industries and population from such areas, and to encourage a reasonable balance and diversification of industrial development throughout the various regions of Great Britain. The Commission also proposed a number of specific measures. These included restrictions on the location of industry in London, the development of a greenbelt to limit the size of the city, and the encouragement of growth beyond the central area of London. Among the principal devices suggested for encouraging such growth were trading estates, the expansion of existing towns, and the building of satellite cities and new towns.

The recommendations of the Barlow Commission exerted an enormous influence.[17] One reason for their great effect was the bombing of British cities during World War II which reinforced the need for some postwar policy for reconstruction and development. Interest was further sustained by the County of London Plan published in 1943.[18] This essay on rebuilding exercised a powerful emotional impact, with its sanguine proposals for the reconstruction of London, the lowering of densities, and the accommodation of more than a million of London's residents in new towns and expanded small towns in the outlying areas of London.

In 1943, in response to these recommendations, the wartime Coalition Government created a *Ministry of Town and Country Planning* with jurisdiction in the field of housing, local government, and land use. Derived in part from the Ministry of Health and the Ministry of Works and Planning, its general responsibility was to ensure "consistency and continuity in the framing and execution of a national policy with respect to the use and development of land throughout England and Wales."[19] Until the war ended, the new Ministry's actual tasks were few. It administered the housing subsidies and exercised some limited controls over local land use plans and the operations of local governments; mainly, it prepared for the postwar period.

When the first Labor Government came to power in 1946, the powers of the Ministry were enlarged. New legislation, requested by the Minister, facilitated land acquisition by local authorities for housing and planning and provided more generous subsidies at higher standards. Still other legislation authorized the building of New Towns in Great Britain (the *New Towns Act of 1946*) and the reorganization of the land use planning system (the *Town and Country Planning Act of 1947*). The latter shifted the basic planning powers from smaller local entities to counties and county boroughs and obliged them to prepare development plans by 1951 and to revise these plans at least every five years thereafter.[20] It also required industrial firms to obtain permission from the Board of

118

Trade for all new building or extensions over 5000 square feet to ensure that such developments were consistent with national policy on industrial location. The same act dealt with the compensation problem by transferring all development rights to the community and by making all development subject to the permission of either the local planning authority or the central government.[21]

But planning efforts during this period were complicated by the extraordinary volume of additional legislation of major importance passed by Parliament. The bulk of the measures dealt with the nationalization of a variety of industries and institutions: coal, gas, electricity, airlines, railways, medical services, development rights, and the Bank of England. The ambitiousness of these programs imposed a tremendous strain on Britain's administrative apparatus; and because the early postwar years were not only a period of social change but a time of economic crisis as well, this strain was particularly acute.

The economic crisis of the postwar period also had a detrimental effect on development programs. Until 1950 the need for foreign exchange forced the government to weigh almost all capital investment projects on the basis of their short-term effects on dollar earning and dollar saving projects. Although it was argued that the new national policy of urban and regional development would ultimately improve the efficiency of the nation's productive plant, many years would probably elapse before the results became visible. Meanwhile, no one could really be certain that, in addition to all its other programs, the authorities would be able to prepare adequate local development plans, operate successfully the new land policy, build efficient and economical New Towns, and attract industry to large trading estates in the North. All that appeared likely at the time was that the development activities would be expensive, the payback period would materialize far in the future, if at all, and serious problems would probably emerge from pioneering errors, administrative inadequacies, and postwar dislocation.

In addition, the planners still lacked sufficient powers for changing the relative balance of growth in the South and North. Surprisingly enough, the Labor Government did not innovate any central or regional planning mechanisms for the economy, and the Ministry of Town and Country Planning was not an adequate substitute for such an authority. Since the five-year Development Plans were to be prepared locally without benefit of explicit national targets and goals, it was bound to be a fortunate coincidence if they were consistent or took adequate account of interregional relationships. There was still no satisfactory machinery to formulate or to implement national, interregional, or even macroregional development strategies. The British planners were working within a system hitched largely to local efforts involving the manipulation of land uses on the basis of relatively cursory and intuitive information about the phenomena they were supposed to guide.

But, however inadequate British institutions were in relation to the government's professed aims, the new land use planning system and development programs were bold and challenging by comparison with anything attempted in the past. Nor was there at the time enough awareness of or agreement on the need for additional administrative machinery to proceed otherwise.

The Lessons of Experience, 1950–1969

By the end of the war, or shortly thereafter, Great Britain had forged two fairly autonomous planning systems to carry out different aspects of its growth strategies. One system attempted to promote more industrial development in the less prosperous areas of the North. The other tried to control the size and growth of the big cities, especially of London, and to channel a share of their populations and economic activities to the surrounding regions. The ideas upon which both were based were novel, and in a sense experimental, though they had managed to win tentative political acceptance. Except for the control and purchase of development rights, all of the elements of these systems were continued in one form or another by the subsequent Conservative Government. However, the planners ran into some revealing as well as some exasperating difficulties in trying to make the ideas and the administrative machinery work.

Weaknesses of the New Towns Building Program

The policies for building new and expanded cities turned out to be exceptionally significant. First, they cut across the efforts of both the economists and the urbanists to reorganize growth in the North and in the South. Second, these experiences helped to redefine and integrate the dual planning systems, with the result that urban development came to be looked upon as one of the most important instruments for putting both sets of goals into effect. A very brief review of the historical record will explain how this occurred.

The decision to build New Towns was made in 1946. The purpose was to implement the recommendations of the Barlow Commission and the county and regional plans for London. More specifically, the intention was to provide a more effective method and pattern of organizing or decentralizing metropolitan growth, especially at the periphery of the London region. To carry out this policy, the Ministry of Town and Country Planning established public development corporations to build relatively small, "self-contained" communities of approximately 60,000 people. These corporations acquired the land, made the development plans, and hired the contractors that put up most of the houses and shops and many standard industrial plants. Although the corporations avoided jobs normally handled by local authorities, they had the power to build sewer and water facilities when needed and could arrange on occasion for the local authorities to perform various services for which they would be reimbursed. What the corporations did not do directly or through their contractors, they often stimulated and coordinated, or tried to. This role was particularly important for assuring adequate and timely provision of utilities, roads, schools, pubs, and other social facilities and private developments.

Fifteen New Towns were started during the five years following the passage of the New Towns Act. Nine were in the London-Midlands area: Corby, Stevenage, Harlow, Hemel Hempstead, Welwyn Garden City, Hatfield, Bracknell, Crawley, and Basildon. Of these, all—save Corby and perhaps Basildon—were intended primarily to aid in the decentralization of London. The others were judiciously located in different parts of Britain's North: Cwmbran in Wales; East Kilbride, Cumbernauld, and Glenrothes in Scotland; Peterlee and Aycliffe in the North East (see Figure 9). Of these, only Cwmbran, East Kilbride, and Cumbernauld were built to serve the aims of metropolitan decentralization. The other towns had more specialized functions. Basildon, for example, although in the London area, was also expected to repair the ravages of the shoddy speculative subdivisions in Essex. Corby was planned to facilitate the expansion of a steel plant in the Midlands. Peterlee and Glenrothes were communities with modern facilities, presumably for miners. And Aycliffe was started as an effort to keep an isolated war plant in operation after the war by providing suitable housing and community facilities.[22]

As a means of organizing and promoting new development, the New Towns rated high scores. Despite some harrowing experiences during the early phases, the first generation of New Towns proved that public development was a decidedly feasible policy. As examples of physical planning, they were not extraordinary, although one town — Cumbernauld — was a first-rate technical achievement, and one can find examples of highly competent and imaginative architectural and site design in most of the others. And, for all of their limitations, the towns were generally superior in design to other, more typical, suburban developments. As appropriate public investments for the period, however, they could perhaps be challenged, for under different building and management policies they might well have been less costly and maybe even more exciting visually and socially. All of this, of course, is easier to say in retrospect. As of today, the towns are faring well financially. All are, or are soon to be, operating in the black. But our primary concern here is with neither the problems nor the achievements of the New Towns. Of greater importance to us is the role they played in the evolution of Britain's urban growth strategy.

From this point of view, the most illuminating aspects of the New Towns experience were the difficulties encountered because of inconsistencies and ambiguities in the earlier versions of the policy. Some of these difficulties were minor; others were more serious and intractable.

One of the most trying involved the problem of attracting industries. If the towns were to be self-contained and not dormitory suburbs, industry and other economic activities were essential. But getting the industries during the early stages proved to be more difficult than originally anticipated. At first, the towns were not too well known, and, considering their small populations and negligible facilities, they were hardly attractive places in which to locate. Furthermore, the Board of Trade, which then had tremendous influence because of its control over building licenses and development certificates, gave first priority to export activities, no matter where they were located, and the next highest priority to the

Development Areas. New Towns were at the end of the queue. The Board adhered to these priorities because of the perilous economic condition of the country and because of the employment needs of the lagging regions. However, its policy remained inflexible even when the aim was to get industry for some of the New Towns in the North. The Board would help firms move to places like Merseyside or Glasgow, then defined as Development Areas, but for several years (and the change came only after a great deal of pressure) it would not assist firms from Merseyside or Glasgow to transfer to the new growth centers of Lancashire or to the New Town of East Kilbride just south of Glasgow. No other conflict provoked more bitter recriminations between the economic and physical planners or more clearly highlighted the lack of agreement between two independent agencies in the execution of the government's policy.[23]

An equally vexatious problem was the gap in the legislation dealing with the location of economic activities. The Barlow Commission and the Distribution of Industry Bills dealt with industrial jobs. But in inner London the most significant expansion of new jobs was in office and other service activities. This oversight by the economists and the physical planners meant that the basic incentives and controls did not apply to the most important growth sector of London's economy. To make matters worse, the space left by the departing industries proved too expensive for the government to purchase and was taken up by the expanding small industries and office and service activities which were exempt from regulation. Largely for these reasons, hardly a trickle of these activities moved to the New Towns for almost a decade.[24]

These problems indicated flaws in the policy and administrative machinery which, sooner or later, would have to be corrected. At worst, they were symptomatic of a lack of intimate knowledge of the functioning and transformation of the urban economy and an absence of a clear and properly coordinated development strategy. Far more serious, however, was the apparent inability of the program, as it was then conceived, to influence the basic pattern of development of either the North or the South. It was this limitation that was bound to spur some rethinking of ends and means.

Why was the program, as first formulated, so unlikely to achieve a significant impact? The most obvious reason was its gross dimensions—the number, scale, and location of the planned New

Towns. No limit was set initially on how many New Towns might be established, and the initiative for establishing a town could come from either the local or central authorities. The only ceiling was the budget: no more than £50 million could be encumbered in the first five years.

Another factor was the Ministry's implicit decision not to use the New Towns to alter the relative scale of regional development. A good deal of development was going to take place in the London region anyway, the Ministry reasoned, and a portion, especially the portion associated with the decentralization of families and firms, might as well be accommodated in the New Towns. But, although only one out of every four persons in Great Britain lived in the London region at the time, eight New Towns accommodating 430,000 persons were provided for this region alone, while the rest of the country was allotted only seven New Towns for 242,000 persons.[25] If anything, the balance seemed to be shifting even more in favor of the London region.

The same held true for the efforts to encourage the expansion of existing towns. This new program, which was enacted by the Conservative Government in 1952,[26] was also designed to help decongest large cities. It would do this by promoting agreements between large local authorities (which would "export" population) and small towns (which would "receive" them) and by providing land improvement subsidies as "sweeteners" to facilitate the negotiations. Although schemes were initiated for expanding more than fifty small towns near London, Birmingham, Salford, Liverpool, Wolverhampton, the North East, and Bristol, by 1962 about 130,000 persons, or more than 50 percent of those accommodated, were in the expanded towns of the London region, 25 percent were in those of Staffordshire, and less than a quarter were spread out over the rest of the country.[27]

Even if the programs had not been weighted in favor of the South, the effects would have been limited. The building of forty to fifty New Towns simply added "to the 874 cities of approximately 75,000 or less in England and Wales without significantly reducing the ninety-one larger cities or the fourteen cities of 250,000 or more."[28] The fact that the scale and location of the programs were inconsistent with the presumed regional development goals of Great Britain was not more disturbing, perhaps, because the final

124

results were scarcely visible in relation to the national trends of development.

At the heart of the problem lay the significance of the government's commitment to provide an urban growth strategy for the nation. In terms of what was actually happening, this commitment seemed to have little meaning. The way the program was developing implied an acceptance, indeed a reinforcement, of existing regional trends. In part, this was because the idea of New Towns was devised and pushed by physical planners who looked upon them largely as instruments for *accommodating* the growth of regions. The few economists who were interested in a regional economic development strategy and in the problems of overcoming unemployment in the less prosperous areas did not then grasp how the mechanism of New Towns could help to achieve their objectives.

What probably contributed further to this misunderstanding was the form in which the New Towns policy was initially advocated by its proponents. The functions of the towns which they stressed were their role in serving the overspill populations of congested metropolises and their remedial possibilities, such as tidying up the excesses of speculative development or transforming the mining camp environment created by an expanding steel plant. But they neglected to emphasize the most significant role of the New Towns—that of guiding, perhaps even dominating, critical interregional and intra-regional relationships. No doubt the program first had to prove itself and its potential, and certainly the other roles were also important. But the limited resources and the failure to concentrate them at the most significant points made it likely that the program, if not substantially changed, would not achieve maximum leverage.

Weaknesses of the Development Areas Program

During the early years after the war, the Labor Government was fairly successful in diverting industrial jobs to Northern Ireland, Scotland, northern England, Wales, Devon, and Cornwall. These peripheral areas of Britain's North contained only 20 percent of the population, but about two-thirds of the jobs of the industrial firms which moved from 1945 to 1951 had concentrated there.

This achievement was a result of the fear of unemployment, the shortage of premises, and the government's determination to make the policy work. But, as the threat of unemployment subsided towards 1950, pressures began to mount for easing controls and for switching emphasis to providing industry for the New Towns. At the same time, the continuance of building controls in the Greater London area forced many new or expanding firms to consider other locations. Many of these firms were reluctant or unwilling to go to the North. Of necessity, they became more knowledgeable about and more interested in the privileged industrial sanctuaries of the New Towns and the expanded towns of the South. As a consequence, the 1950's witnessed a massive redirection of the industrial movement from Greater London to the rest of the South East instead of to the peripheral areas.[29]

"Between 1942 and 1960," Thomas Wilson observed, "the employment provided by new firms in the whole of Scotland—not merely in the Scottish development districts—was less than the expansion that took place in the seven new towns in the South-Eastern region of England, which was only a small part of the total expansion within a hundred miles of the center of London."[30] The problem for most of the Southern New Towns had, in effect, shifted from one of finding industries to one of selecting the most appropriate firms for their purposes. This change was not unwelcome for the New Towns in the South. But it did not dispel the strong reservations which prevailed in some quarters about the way in which the program was developing during the 1950's. Although there was still much skepticism about whether development could or should be diverted away from the South, others questioned whether enough of an effort and the right kind of an effort had been made to induce firms to locate in the less prosperous regions of the North.

One of the reasons that it was so difficult to change the pattern of development was the manner in which expansion took place in the South. It was concentrated in those industries (chemicals, production and assembly of vehicles) and those services (printing, food, drink, tobacco, and professional, scientific, and research activities) which either did not require new building or were sufficiently small so that industrial development certificates (I.d.c.'s) were not

126

needed. At the same time, the Board of Trade was loath to block expansions which required I.d.c.'s if the firms were able to show that they might have difficulty surviving outside of the London region. The Board, after all, was anxious to avoid the charge that "the growth prevented . . . would not be diverted elsewhere but would be lost to the national economy altogether."[31]

Unquestionably, the proportions of both types of expansions (the smaller ones beyond the purview of the Board and the larger ones exempted from location in the North) were quite high. Of the total increase in employment in manufacturing industries in Great Britain from 1950 to 1963,[32] the industries in the South East accounted for 53 percent. And, during this same period, employment in services and office employment in southeast England increased by approximately 615,000 persons; this was even more than the increase in manufacturing.[33]

One of the main justifications for changing the pattern of development was supposed to be the congestion in the South. But "almost two-thirds of the growth of employment in manufacturing took place outside the London conurbation . . . [and] almost four-fifths of the estimated additional employment resulting from building subject to control by I.d.c. was . . . in part of the Southeast where there [was] little evidence of congestion that [was] worse than in some of the industrial areas where growth [had] been slower and unemployment higher."[34] The same trends characterized the increase in nonindustrial activities. For example, office employment in Central London "accounted for not much more than one quarter of the increase in service employment in southeast England, so that service employment in total would still have risen rapidly even if the growth of office employment in Central London had been severely restrained."[35] In short, as Holmans has observed, unless direct transfer of firms was contemplated, which was most improbable, the expansion in the South was likely to continue.

These patterns of expansion—as well as the limited backing of these policies by the Conservative Government—help to explain the relative ineffectiveness of the government's efforts to promote growth in the North in the 1950's. Government reports estimated that, during the years 1962 to 1971, more than 200,000 additional jobs would be needed for Central Scotland and the North East alone. Yet, as Needleman and Scott have remarked, the government was able to provide only 200,000 net additional jobs for all of the less prosperous areas combined during the seventeen-year period from 1945 to 1963.[36] Their conclusion was that

> in terms of the impression made on regional differences in incomes, unemployment, emigration and growth of employment, very little [had] been accomplished. A comparison of the relative dispersion of earned income per head in the regions of Britain in 1948 and in 1959–60 show[ed] that the difference between regions [had] increased a little. . . . There [had] been a persistent net emigration out of the less prosperous regions, and far from having slowed down as a result of the Government's policy of bringing work to the workers, net emigration [had] actually increased recently from the regions with the heaviest losses over the last decade or so, in Scotland and the Northern region.
>
> But perhaps the most serious inadequacy of the Government's location of industry policy [was] its failure to increase employment opportunities significantly in the less prosperous regions of Britain. In four of these regions, over the decade 1952–1962, total employment increased by only 4 percent while in the rest of Britain the labour force increased by over 12 percent. But of the small increase in total employment in the less prosperous regions, almost three-quarters was accounted for by the increase in female employment. The male labour force in the regions increased by only 1.0 percent over the decade, compared with an increase of over 10 percent in the remainder of Britain. Scotland's increase was particularly small, only 1.6 percent over ten years. The four less prosperous regions, with 35 percent of Britain's male labour force in 1952, obtained only 8 percent of the increase in male employment over the next decade.[37]

The views expressed may appear somewhat strong considering that the unemployment rates in Britain's lagging regions (ranging from 1.3 to 9.3 percent during the period from 1954 to 1963), though generally about twice the national average, have been relatively low in comparison with those of North America, France, and Italy.[38] However, the unemployment rates of these regions do not fully mirror the regions' high sensitivity to unemployment in periods of stress or the problem of generating future jobs in relation to the probable size of the work force. Nor do the unemployment rates reflect the substantially lower participation of the population in the active labor force, the lower income per family, the more limited opportunities for secondary wage earners, and the steady loss through migration of some of the ablest elements of the population.[39] If the unemployment and activity rates of these regions were brought in line with those of the South, the national labor force might well be expanded by as much as 2 percent. Calculated at an average of more than £600 per annum per employee, the value of this output for the region and the nation would be substantial.[40]

There were at least three major choices open to the British planners. One was to abandon the existing policy. Another was to apply still tougher and more refined controls to deal with expansions of small and large firms in the South. The third was to devise more effective positive measures, if possible. Almost no one was prepared to recommend the first course. As for more refined administrative controls, higher taxes, or other penalties, there was no assurance that they would help the development areas. They might, in fact, eliminate some types of expansion and push a large part of the restricted activities into the outlying zones of the South.[41] In addition, the pressures still besetting the British economy to solve its balance of payment problems, to expand, and to become more efficient made it increasingly difficult to impose strong restrictions on the fastest growing regions in Britain—the areas surrounding the London metropolis—especially since the traditional argument of congestion was less relevant to growth in this part of the South.[42] Although tighter controls might nonetheless be required to draw the attention of firms to feasible locations which they otherwise might overlook, it was clear that major emphasis would have to be placed on the third solution—offering more attractive incentives.[43]

Government Responses, 1958–1969

In time, a more sensitive appreciation of these needs began to emerge. This was further sharpened by the economic setbacks in the late 1950's. The collapse of the boom in the traditional industries (coal and shipbuilding especially) and the general slowdown of the economy (due to sustained inflationary pressures and balance of payment problems) had a particularly severe impact on the North and revived the demand for strong measures to help these regions.

The first response of the Conservative Government in 1958 was to increase the number of Development Areas eligible for some assistance. Then, in 1960, new legislation did away with the cumbersome system of identification and extension of Development Areas by statute. In its place, the legislation created a system of administratively determined Development Districts characterized by persistent high unemployment (4.5 percent or over). The new Districts, based on Local Employment Exchange Areas, included most of the older Development Areas, plus a good many other smaller areas in almost all of the other regions of Great Britain, including the South East.[44]

In addition, the pressure to come to grips with the repeated economic crises led the Conservative Government to prepare a national economic plan and to create for this purpose a National Economic Development Office and a National Economic Development Council. A year later it established a new post: Secretary of State for Industry, Trade and Regional Development, "held in conjunction with the office of President of the Board of Trade. [This was] preceded in Scotland by the creation in 1962 of the Scottish Development Department . . . ."[45] The government also set up a Location of Offices Bureau to encourage the shift of office activities from congested Central London to suitable growth centers elsewhere, and it adopted a policy of moving appropriate government offices out of London and the South East. In addition, it decided to build a second generation of New Towns, located mainly in the North, larger in size than the first New Towns, and designed to serve as growth centers.

The government also began to provide more generous incentives for firms locating in the North. Before 1963 only a small proportion of the firms which received government help (only one-sixth to one-seventh between 1960 and 1963) had gotten direct grants. The government had assisted most firms by either renting them government factories for approximately 40 to 50 percent of the economic rents[46] or by providing loans at the market rates of interest that would have been "charged by a commercial lender to a first class commercial borrower for a well secured loan."[47] There had been many complaints about the inadequacy of this assistance and about the delays involved in obtaining it. Therefore, in 1963, the government agreed to provide clearer and more substantial incentives for firms locating in the Development Districts. A new system of depreciation allowances made it possible for these firms to write off against taxes all new investments in plant and machinery at any rate desired in the first year after purchase. This device, in addition to the standard investment allowances (tax remissions equivalent to 15 percent of expenditure on building and 30 percent of expenditure on equipment) permitted more rapid return on investment. The budget of 1963 also provided for so-called "standard grants" to businesses locating in Development Districts. These approximated 25 percent of building cost and 10 percent of the investment in plant and machinery. In addition, the government covered 85 percent of the costs for clearance and rehabilitation of derelict sites in Development Districts and provided special grants for employee training and improvement of infrastructure. These measures supplemented the provision of industrial space at subsidized rents and special loans which depended on the estimated number of jobs that might be created. There was also a less restrictive credit reserve applied by the central bank to the commercial banks in the less prosperous areas.[48] The net effect of this expanded assistance was to reduce the average capital outlay of firms in Development Districts to 75 percent of capital costs as compared to 87 percent in the rest of Britain and to reduce their outlay to 50 percent of expenditures for the first year as compared to 80 percent for firms elsewhere.[49]

When the Labor Party came to power in 1964, it was determined to go much further in advancing the interests of the North. The new government established a Department of Economic Affairs to help formulate the government's policies for economic planning.[50] It also set up regional economic planning boards, responsible for advising on and coordinating regional economic studies and plans for all of Britain.[51] Six regional boards were set up in England (there are now eight[52]), each chaired by a representative of the Department of Economic Affairs. One for Wales and Monmouthshire and another for Scotland were also established. Each board was staffed by senior civil servants representing the main government departments of the region. To represent the views of local authorities, universities, industry and commerce, trade unions, the social services, and other significant regional interests, the government created a series of advisory regional economic planning councils which prepared evaluations of the development problems of their regions and recommendations on desirable growth strategies.[53]

The government also took steps in 1964 to control the growth of offices in London.[54] Legislation was enacted the following year requiring office development permits for new office buildings in the London metropolitan region in excess of 3000 square feet and for changes in the use of existing buildings. The controls have since been extended to the areas where most of the new offices had been erected in the preceding decade: the South East, East Anglia, the West Midlands and the East Midlands.[55] The Labor Government also actively continued the policy of the Conservative Government of building more New Towns. As a result, Livingston (1962) and Irvine (1966) were authorized to serve Glasgow; Washington (1964) to serve Tyneside; and Dawley (1963) [expanded and now known as Telford (1968)] and Redditch (1964) to serve the West Midlands. There were also four towns planned for the Merseyside-Manchester complex in the North West: Runcorn (1964) in Cheshire; and Skelmersdale (1961), Warrington (1967), and Preston-Leyland-Chorley (1969) in Central Lancashire. In addition, three New Towns were designated for the London region: Milton Keynes (1966), Peterborough (1966), and Northampton (1968)[56] (see Figures 9 and 10).

Since these stepped-up planning efforts led to shortages of regional economists, planners, sociologists, and other professional specialists, there was a growing disposition to expand university training programs and to engage university staff and private consultants to assist civil servants in defining problems and strategies. The government also conceded, after years of pressure (and some significant changes of staff), that the ignorance on some of these matters related to planning was perhaps unnecessarily profound. It therefore authorized more research within the relevant ministries and helped to set up a national Center for Environmental Studies to provide grants and assistance for research.[57]

By the mid-1960's the system of territorial planning created in the late forties had also become the subject of widespread criticism. There were objections to the heavy emphasis of the five-year County Development Plans on the physical and regulatory aspects of planning, and there was much chagrin about the Plans' wrong assumptions on population trends, car ownership, and social standards.[58] Therefore, a major attempt was made to recast this system. The new approach stressed that a key function of the Plans was the mapping out of broad policies and development patterns which in turn would offer guidance for more detailed area and project plans. Changes along these lines were expected to spur growth and to simplify the planning process, thereby allowing more flexibility for creative designers and private developers and minimizing the oppressive administrative burdens resulting from appeals.[59]

When, in July 1965, the balance of payments crisis became acute, the government decided to introduce strong measures to curb investment and, at the same time, undertook to tighten the industrial building controls further, to modify the system of investment incentives, and to change the definition of Development Districts. The new regulations required permits for all new building and extensions of industrial plant of more than 1000 square feet in London, the South East, the Midlands, and the eastern region.[60] (This was later increased to 3000 square feet in 1966.) In the same year, the government added two complementary measures. One was the *Selective Employment Tax* (SET), a variable charge designed not only to tax payrolls but to exempt and "to subsidize" labor-intensive industrial employment and tourism in the Development Areas.[61] The other measure sought to promote capital investment and to spur further modernization and exports. It substituted cash grants for free depreciation, but the benefits were limited mainly to investments in new plant and machinery in manufacturing, construction, and extractive industries.[62]

A new administrative unit—the *Development Area*—was also devised to replace the Development District. The five Development Areas which were designated covered a far larger territory than that covered by the previous Development Districts. Encompassing almost half the area of the country and about one-fifth of the country's total working population, they included all of Scotland except the Edinburgh district, the whole of England north of York, Merseyside, almost all of Wales with the exception of the area around Cardiff, and most of Cornwall and North Devon[63] (see Figure 9).

Unemployment was no longer to be the major criterion for the selection of the areas; nor was estimated employment to be a major factor in determining the grants to firms. The normal grant

9. Great Britain: New Towns and Development Areas 1969

New Towns
- Existing, Authorized, or Under Construction
- Development Areas
- Special Development Areas
- Proposed Intermediate Areas
- Urban Areas
- ----- Economic Planning Region Boundaries

Miles
0   80

Kilometers
0   120

N

SCOTLAND

HIGHLANDS

Glenrothes
Cumbernauld
Glasgow   Edinburgh
East Kilbride   Livingston
Irvine

NORTHERN
IRELAND

Newcastle
Washington
Peterlee
NORTH   Aycliffe

IRISH   SEA

NORTH   YORKSHIRE
WEST   HUMBERSIDE

Central Lancashire   Leeds
Skelmersdale   Manchester
Liverpool
          Warrington
          Runcorn

EAST
MIDLANDS

Telford
Newtown
WEST   Birmingham   Peterborough
          Corby
          Redditch   Northampton   EAST
MIDLANDS   ANGLIA

WALES   Milton
                     Keynes   Stevenage
                  Welwyn   Harlow
Cwmbran   Hemel Hempstead   ESSEX
                  Hatfield
Bristol   London   Basildon
          Bracknell

KENT

SOUTH   WEST   SOUTH   EAST
                     Crawley
DEVON

CORNWALL

ENGLISH   CHANNEL

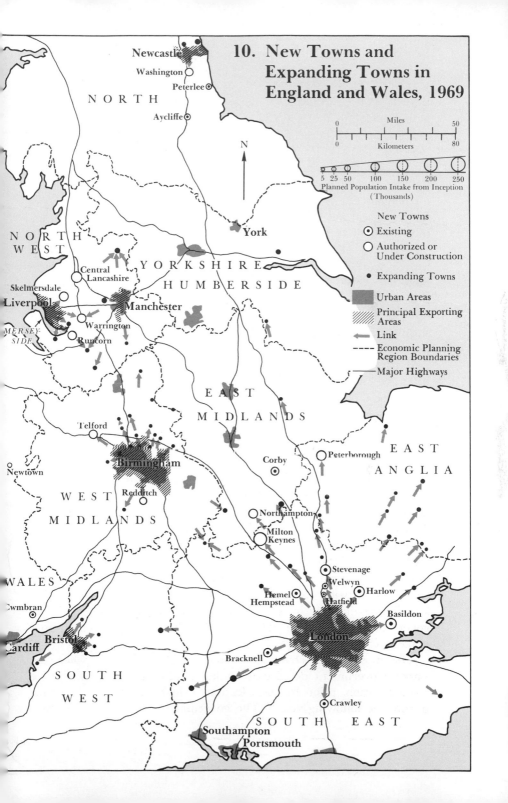

10. New Towns and Expanding Towns in England and Wales, 1969

Miles
0 ———————————— 50
0 ———————————— 80
Kilometers

5 25 50   100   150   200   250
Planned Population Intake from Inception
(Thousands)

New Towns
⊙ Existing
○ Authorized or
   Under Construction
• Expanding Towns
▨ Urban Areas
▨ Principal Exporting
   Areas
← Link
--- Economic Planning
    Region Boundaries
— Major Highways

NORTH

Newcastle
Washington
Peterlee
Aycliffe

N

NORTH
WEST

Skelmersdale
Liverpool
Central
Lancashire
Manchester
Warrington
Runcorn
MERSEY-
SIDE

YORKSHIRE
HUMBERSIDE

York

EAST
MIDLANDS

Telford
Birmingham
Newtown
Redditch
WEST
MIDLANDS

WALES

Cwmbran
Cardiff
Bristol

SOUTH
WEST

Corby

Peterborough

EAST
ANGLIA

Northampton
Milton
Keynes

Stevenage
Welwyn
Hemel
Hempstead
Hatfield
Harlow

Basildon

London

Bracknell

Crawley

Southampton
Portsmouth

SOUTH   EAST

was to be 20 percent of investment in plant and equipment (other than factory building) and twice that if the investment was made in a Development Area. (The rates were temporarily raised to 25 percent and 45 percent respectively for expenditure incurred between January 1, 1967 and December 31, 1968 inclusive.) Taking into account the corporation tax, firms would get back "about 67 percent of their investment [in Development Areas] compared with 55 percent elsewhere."[64] Other forms of assistance, such as grants for plant and machinery, for training, for clearing derelict land, for improvement of basic services and special loans and grants made on the recommendation of the Board of Trade Advisory Committee, were continued. In addition, firms renting Board of Trade factories would receive an initial rent-free period and firms establishing new branches in the Development Areas could, depending on the number of additional jobs they created, receive a supplementary building grant of 10 percent bringing the rate to 35 percent.[65]

Partly to increase the employment effects (since mainly capital-intensive enterprises were attracted by the new grants) and partly to reduce the gross cost of the subsidies by about £300 million,[66] the government also set up in mid-1967, for a period of seven years, a system of supplementary grants for each worker employed of 30s. per man per week. These *regional employment premiums* (REP) supplemented a premium of 7s. 6d. per man per week (in addition to a tax rebate) paid to manufacturers under the Selective Employment Tax machinery. The two premiums together lowered labor costs by roughly 8½ percent for firms in the Development Areas.[67] Although some criticisms were raised that corporate taxes would reduce these benefits substantially and that the costs per job created would be exorbitant, the government insisted that an unemployment rate in the Development Areas of roughly 4.4 percent, about twice the rate prevailing elsewhere, was intolerable socially, particularly in terms of Britain's manpower shortage. The government hoped that REP would reduce the differential to 1 percent or less.[68]

The most recent change occurred in October 1969 when the Labor Government decided to make its last major administrative reorganization prior to the elections which were to take place during the following year.[69] The government decided to shift most of the Board of Trade's powers over the distribution of industry and the functions of the Ministry of Power to the Ministry of Technology. In addition, it created a new department, the Department of Local Government and Regional Planning, which was to be responsible for housing, local government, transportation, and regional planning. However, the Ministry of Housing and Local Government and the Ministry of Transport continued as separate ministries within this new department. Headed by a Secretary of State, the department also acquired the regional boards and councils and the regional economic planning functions of the Department of Economic Affairs, which was then dismantled. (Most of the other functions of the Department of Economic Affairs were transferred either to the Cabinet Office, the Treasury, or the Ministry of Technology.) These changes were intended to make the structure of government more efficient, but industrial development was still divorced from regional development. Also, for political reasons, Scotland, Wales, and Northern Ireland did not come within the jurisdiction of the new regional super-department. So, although the new organization is more logical in some respects than the former set-up, its administrators still have to grapple with some formidable problems of coordination.

EVALUATION OF THE STRATEGY

After more than a generation and a half of groping efforts, the British appear to be on the verge of evolving an urban growth strategy. There is a clearer sense of the problems and a disposition to do something about them. The tools, too, have been steadily refined. Although it is a little too early to gauge with assurance the influence of recent legislation and ideas, there is enough evidence to evaluate the changes which have occurred and the progress to date.

Development Districts versus Development Areas

As noted earlier, repeated economic crises persuaded the Conservative Government in 1960 to substitute administratively determined Development Districts for legislatively determined Development Areas. The government felt that areas hard hit by unemployment had to be helped promptly and that the level of unemployment was a relatively objective, reliable, and flexible indicator of the location of these problem areas. Nonetheless, the new approach was soon sharply criticized because "the practice of cutting off aid as soon as the unemployment level seemed likely to fall below the 4.5 percent level prevented the industrialist from being certain of obtaining for a worthwhile period the benefits to be received by moving to a development district."[70] Moreover, the objections continued, instead of focussing assistance on significant growing points within the region, the new legislation dispersed aid "over wide and often remote areas lacking any economic advantages and maintain[ed] small communities in existence that had no social capital or amenities worth preserving, such as worked out mining villages."[71]

Gradually an alternative development strategy was evolved— one that emphasized the encouragement of urban growth centers. This new approach combined the strongest elements of the rival prescriptions for helping the less prosperous areas. Instead of assuming that jobs had to be brought directly to the workers or that workers had to leave their regions to obtain jobs, it suggested that there might be some places within each region where significant growth could be fostered.

To identify these growing points and to encourage new activities in these places consistent with the development plans for the regions' metropolitan areas and surrounding hinterlands, sophisticated intelligence mechanisms were needed. Unfortunately, all too little had been done in the past to analyze the resources of these areas, or to investigate systematically the types of firms which might be attracted in terms of either the incentives required or the location and character of existing or proposed infrastructure and other innovations. Moreover, to make such programs work, the support of the relevant national ministries, the nationalized industries, the Prime Minister's Office, and the Treasury was also required.[72] In addition, the fate of the less prosperous regions depended not only on the central government but "to a large degree on the attitudes adopted by the more prosperous regions and the way in which their growth [could] in some measure be steered toward the less prosperous."[73]

The Toothill Committee's Inquiry in 1961, which explored the ways growth could be fostered in Central Scotland, played a considerable role in refocussing national views on what needed to be done.[74] It influenced the two *White Papers* prepared in 1963 dealing with Central Scotland and the North East, and a series of subsequent regional studies for the South East, Wales, the North West, and the West Midlands.[75] The White Papers strongly endorsed the Toothill Committee's basic recommendation that reasonably comprehensive and coordinated government assistance should be made available to specified urban growth centers. In these centers one could concentrate the bulk of economic, social, and technical assistance; provide the infrastructure, training and other facilities essential for expanding and diversifying economic activities; and attract many able individuals from other areas who were seeking fresh opportunities in a different environment. After being adopted first in Scotland and the North East, this policy soon won strong adherents in the North and the South, for it appeared both reasonable and effective to focus efforts on a few promising urban centers of a region.

The reports on Scotland, which were prepared largely from the point of view of economic planners, explicitly identified the New Towns of East Kilbride, Cumbernauld, Livingston, and Glenrothes as major growth zones which could accommodate another quarter of a million people in addition to their present populations. The development of these communities was looked upon as an *economic weapon* to accelerate growth, to reduce unemployment and migration from Scotland, and to modernize not only the new Development Areas but the entire regional environment.[76]

Similarly, the study of the South East,[77] prepared largely by physical planners of the Ministry of Housing and Local Government, urged the fostering of growth centers in the form of three large New Towns (two of 150,000 and one of 250,000) near Southampton-Portsmouth, the expansion of three existing cities, and the building of two additional ones in Kent and Essex if the Channel tunnel and the third international airport were approved.[78] These measures were urged to spur the growth of the national economy and to reduce the staggering infrastructure costs entailed by the disproportionate increase of employment in industry and services in the outer areas of London.[79]

None of these reports pretended to be plans; nor did they take account of the effects of their proposals on other regions. But they did propose urban growth strategies for their regions which were remarkably attuned to felt needs. In fact, most of the regional economic councils soon adopted similar regional development views.

The Labor Government was only taking account of these new perspectives when it decided in 1965 to eliminate the Development Districts and substitute vastly enlarged Development Areas. The proposed changes, however, prompted *The Times* to protest that "by widening the districts to large regions, the whole idea of concentrating effort on 'growth points'—points that are showing signs of individual initiative and life—[was] frustrated."[80] This criticism, however, missed the essential point: the Development Districts were eliminated because they focussed on unemployment rather than on growth and because they were dispersed and small rather than linked to a general strategy for the development of a region. The new definition of Development Areas made the boundaries much broader than those of the growth centers. But there was nothing in the new policy or definition to prevent a focus on growing points while at the same time providing more choice for the entrepreneur and a more attractive regional policy to defend politically.

In the future, however, serious problems were to arise from the ambiguity of the growth center concept and the inflexibility of the arrangements for responding to the needs of areas which might require either more or less assistance. Soon, promotion of growth centers was to be advocated for far more areas than could be reasonably developed, and some regions would complain of being systematically disadvantaged because they lacked either the location, the economic structure, and other assets of the South or the incentive system that was serving the North.

Depreciation Allowances versus Cash Grants and Employment Premiums

One of the key incentives which the government deployed to encourage development in the North was the system of depreciation allowances set up in 1963. By permitting write-offs of new investments against taxes, it eased cash problems in the early period of transition and settling-in when costs were about one-third higher than later on.[81] Even though less depreciation could be claimed later, this was a significant subsidy. But it did not absorb all the risks or costs; and if sufficient profits were not obtained during the first year by the new firm or branch, the easing of its cash position was of limited value.

The vast majority of the firms which did locate in the North fared well. To be sure, there were some failures; the worst ones "occurred when a departure was made from the normal procedure and public money [was] used in a futile attempt to prevent an old and moribund firm from collapsing." [82] But, during the 1960's, the record became more favorable. Though the percentage of unemployment in the Development Districts was still greater than the national average, the number of unemployed in these areas had fallen over the last few years. This trend is of particular interest since the less prosperous regions had been the parts of the country mainly affected by unemployment arising from technological change and decline in demand for the products of the older industries.

The statistics on new employment furnish the basic evidence on these trends. [83] In 1964, the additional jobs estimated to arise from new industrial plants were 29,040 for the Northern region, 15,290 for Scotland, and 6,090 for Wales, as compared to 5,810 for the West Midlands and 18,890 for London and the South East. The trends between 1960 and 1964 are also of interest. There was a sharp and steady drop in additional jobs for the South East (from 44,200 to 18,900) and for Wales (from 16,700 to 6,100) and there was a lesser decline for the West Midlands (from 9,800 to 5,800). There were also significant increases for the Northern region (from 7,800 to 29,000). The trend for Scotland was upward but the figures fluctuated substantially from year to year. Thus, net additions to employment were 9,600 in 1959; 20,200 in 1960; 14,000 in 1961; and 10,100 in 1962. They then ranged between 15,000 to 28,000 over the following three years. These figures suggest that, for the first time, British policies brought about a situation in which a much higher proportion of new industrial jobs was arising in the less prosperous areas. However, the net figures apply as yet only to industrial employment, which is only a part, and a diminishing part, of total employment.

Despite the apparent success of this record and the rather favorable attitude of investors to the policy of free depreciation, the depreciation system became the subject of growing concern. Critics feared that the free depreciation formula was not as effective as intended. The firms that benefited most from it were those upon which its incentives operated least. Equivalent to an interest free loan, free depreciation tended to favor large established firms setting up new branches or existing firms engaging in new activities within the region.[84] However, these firms already possessed easy access to the capital market; and, if they were reluctant to shift their location, they could more easily ignore the offered concession. Moreover, the view persisted in many quarters that the real need was to help new or smaller firms to shift to the Development Areas and to cover the higher initial outlays and development costs for new branches located at a distance from a firm's headquarters.

The changes in the incentives established by the 1965 legislation tried to correct these defects. They made it possible to help capital intensive activities with investment and building grants, and to help labor intensive activities with regional employment premiums and the rebate on the Selective Employment Tax. According to T. Wilson, "the combined effect of the capital grants, Board of Trade Advisory Committee Assistance and the employment premium may be put at 5 percent of the total costs of a profitable firm. . . ."[85]

As might be expected, however, the new provisions stirred both applause and concern. Some critics favored varying the tax rates of corporations in Development Areas to encourage the more profitable firms. They charged that the REP's discouraged efforts to improve labor productivity and to introduce labor saving machinery and would provide a temporary and expensive crutch for many inefficient firms making questionable investments. The rejoinder, however, was that companies "still [had] to find 60 or 80 percent of the cost of a qualifying investment and no one [was] likely to invest in a company simply because the government was putting up most of the rest."[86]

One commentator dubbed it "grapeshot regionalism"[87] to provide indiscriminate and not particularly ample assistance to all manufacturing activities since many firms would locate or expand in these areas in any case. What was needed, he argued, was more analysis and guidance and more selective grants to promote diversification, growth industries, and the integration of appropriate industrial and employment complexes. Others urged more help in remedying inadequate services (schools, community facilities, and defective infrastructure such as roads and housing). The government's view, however, was that the new system of incentives offered an effective response to three persistent criticisms. First, firms could now assess beforehand the direct grants they were to receive; second, the grants would be particularly helpful in tiding many firms over the initial settling-in period; third, the costs were not only £300 million lower but the government had a clearer idea of what they would be.[88]

Some critics objected to the serious anomalies. At the very least, they contended, the aids ought to be extended to other important activities, particularly tourism which earned foreign exchange and was one of the main sources of support for such problem regions as the Highlands, the Lake District, North Wales, and Cornwall. SET, they charged, did just the opposite, for it imposed payroll taxes on tourism without providing any tax rebates, employment premiums, or investment incentives.[89] The government partially conceded the merit of this criticism by arranging in 1969 for loans and grants to reduce the costs of providing new hotel accommodations.[90]

Finally, there were those persons who argued that

> capital costs [were] still subsidized in development areas twice as heavily as labor costs . . . [This was] contrary to good sense in that it [meant] the concentration of capital-intensive industry where labour [was] relatively most plentiful leaving labour-intensive industry on the whole where labour [was] scarcest; it [made] investment grants expensive to the Exchequer in relation to the amount of unused labour absorbed into employment, and promot[ed] a geographical concentration of particular kinds of industry that [had] no obvious economic merit, even if it [was] not in some degree uneconomic in terms of transport costs or concentration of economic risk.[91]

The government has not chosen to do anything about this matter, however, in part because preliminary inquiries have not turned up any convincing "examples of mislocation of capital intensive projects."[92]

As yet, the actual experience with the new incentives established by the Labor Government is still too limited to draw firm inferences about their effectiveness. But the data that are available do disclose some favorable trends. During 1966 and 1967, years of recession and national economic difficulty, the Development Areas either maintained or improved their relative standing. Estimated employment for new industrial development was 19,250 for the Northern region, 18,230 for Scotland, and 17,475 for Wales, as compared to 16,070 for the South Eastern region and 6,730 for the West Midlands.[93] Specific projects qualifying for assistance rose sevenfold under the new legislation (from an annual average of 245 for 1960–64 to 1,700 for 1966–67), and gross financial outlays jumped eightfold (from a 1964–65 figure of about £33 million to a 1968–69 estimate of £260 million). The total sums involved are not large compared to the £300 million a year provided for agriculture or the even larger sums provided for transport.[94] Nonetheless, there can be no doubt that the government has now decided to attack the problems of the less prosperous regions on an entirely different scale than in past years.

Since July 1966 the Development Areas have also had less serious unemployment effects than either the South East or the Midlands despite drastic cutbacks in government investment. This was the first time the North has fared so well relative to the London region. Certainly one reason for this achievement is the Labor Government's insistence on maintaining investment incentives and employment premiums for the North regardless of the severity of Britain's exchange problems. Another reason may be the government's hesitance to accept officially the proposed development strategy for the South East because of the fear that it might "further tip the scales against the economic regeneration of the less fortunate regions of Britain and further strengthen the magnetism of the [South]."[95]

The record over the entire postwar period is of interest, too. According to the Board of Trade's study of the movement of industry, the Development Areas' share of the new employment resulting from moves between 1952–59 and 1960–65 rose from 29 percent to 55 percent. Similarly, the share of I.d.c. approvals for the periods between 1956–58 and 1965–67 "rose from 16 percent to 24 percent by number and from 22 percent to 53 percent in terms of estimated employment."[96]

Gavin McCrone has also shown that the major disparities in income, unemployment, and growth rates between the South and the different regions of the North had been substantially lowered by the mid-1950's, mainly due to three factors: the high level of domestic demand, the boom in the traditional industries, and the determination with which the industrial development controls and incentives were applied in the early years after the war. During the second half of the 1950's however, conditions in the North deteriorated substantially because of the ending of the boom and because of the measures necessitated by the chronic balance of payments crisis. There was also no vigorous effort to implement a regional development policy. When, starting in 1963, efforts were made to aid the North, "the regions did better than in the late 1950's though not well enough to narrow the gap between them and the rest of the United Kingdom to any substantial extent."[97] Although McCrone attributes this improvement to the regional policy, he also emphasizes that

> it would be a mistake to imagine that all development in the problem regions is the result of regional policy and that without these measures new developments would all be concentrated in other areas. One survey shows that around two-thirds of the growth in employment in Development Districts was accounted for by in-digent firms, who may perhaps have been encouraged by the offer of grants or tax allowances, but would be unlikely to transfer in any event to another region. Of the companies which moved into Development Districts, the same survey shows that between 10 and 20 percent of the employment created was by firms which would have chosen to move into a Development District location in any case. . . .
>
> During the period of the survey, it seems that the development which was steered to the problem areas by the legislation and would not have come otherwise amounted to rather less than a third of the development taking place in these areas. But even this may be an over-estimate, since in the absence of policy the shortage of labor and other resources which would have resulted in the congested regions might well have forced firms to consider locations elsewhere. Nonetheless, if all the development taking place in the problem regions was not a direct consequence of policy, policy still did ac-count for a significant proportion; without this, the state of the regions would have been much worse than it was.[98]

"Intermediate" versus Other Areas

Perhaps the most dramatic evidence of the effect of the regional assistance policies has been the emergence of a new issue. This is the problem of the intermediate or "grey areas." These areas—

located mainly in the North West, Yorkshire, and Humberside regions, either adjacent to or near the Development Areas—are not declining, nor do they have high unemployment. But wages there are low and the physical environments poor. As a result, these areas are experiencing persistent net outmigration and are finding it harder to attract new industries or to get existing industries to stay and expand, especially when the industries they seek can get a 40 percent investment grant in the Development Areas (as compared to a straight 20 percent elsewhere) plus labor employment premiums worth approximately £97 10 s. per annum for each adult male and £47 for each woman or boy. Since there is considerable anxiety that these areas might become the depressed regions of the future, pressures have mounted for corrective action. One observer has pointed out that

> the North-West Economic Planning Council, the Lancashire and Merseyside Industrial Development Association, and the regional leaders of the Confederation of British Industry have all gone on record with much the same argument: that other parts of the region are finding it more and more difficult to attract new investments because they remain at a serious disadvantage compared with the development areas. . . .
>
> No one has suggested that the special help for development areas was unnecessary or that it has not worked. The argument now is that the point has been reached at which if the government continues to pump aid into these areas at the present level, it will adversely affect other areas whose economic problems have been growing in recent years.[99]

This concern had become so widespread that in the fall of 1967, the government set up a special committee under Sir Joseph Hunt to explore the problem and to suggest changes in existing policies.[100]

Meanwhile, the Development Areas are under pressure from another quarter. For their growth depends also on what the government will do about the development proposals for the South East, a region which now has more than one-third of the population of England and Wales and close to one-half of the increase of new jobs. Further study—by the South East Economic Planning Council—has indicated that in addition to the population increase of 2.14 million expected by 1981, the region will grow by some 4 million persons between 1981 and 2000. This is projected natural growth since no further migration to the region is anticipated for this period.[101] To accommodate this expected population surge, the Council has advocated the fashioning of new city regions. Spaced beyond the greenbelt about 60 to 80 miles from London, they are to be connected to the capital by "growth sectors" along good roads or rail lines. For future planning purposes, the Council favors linking a number of towns "not as a continuous built-up area, but [as] a city region that can provide cultural, entertainment and shopping facilities that go some way to counterbalance the attractions of London.[102] Others, however, favor concentrated linear growth through the greenbelt on the grounds that urban centers should capitalize on the advantages of accessibility and investments in transportation. Still others fear that the development "of substantial new cities 80 or more miles from London inevitably requires a considerable switching of both industrial and office employment from the metropolitan region itself."[103]

These ideas, as well as other provocative studies and recommendations set forth by the Standing Conference on London and South East Regional Planning,[104] are now being reexamined in more detail by the South East Joint Planning Team. This group of technical planners is directed by the Chief Planner of the Ministry of Housing and Local Government and includes representatives of the Department of Economic Affairs, the Standing Conference, the Ministry of Transport, the South East Council, key local authorities, and other agencies. Its aim is to produce (probably in early 1970) a definitive guide for local authorities and the national government on appropriate social and economic policies for the South East region.

Clearly, the needs of the South East—plus those of the Midlands, the other major growth region—are enormous and are competitive with the claims of the North. It is equally clear that these regions contribute greatly to Britain's export industry; and they are also the most important seedbeds for nurturing growth industries for other regions including the New Towns and the expanding towns. From 1945 to the end of 1966, industrial movements from the South East involving a total of 427,000 jobs gave rise to 221,000 jobs in other regions, of which 175,000 were in the North.[105] Of the 122,000 "mobile" jobs that arose in the West

147

Midlands, an even higher proportion (75 percent) shifted to other regions.[106] The evident success in recent years in diverting jobs from the South East to other regions has prompted the South East Economic Planning Council to underscore the fact that the growth of employment in the South East and East Anglia has consistently fallen short in recent years of what would have been expected on the basis of national industrial trends. It has also reminded the Hunt Committee that, in terms of totals, the greatest unemployment is in the South East, not in the North or the grey areas where the percentages are higher. The Council fears that the increased assistance to grey and Development Areas will hurt the prospects of attracting industry to the new and expanding towns of the South East region, and it has requested equal opportunity for industries from these areas to get I.d.c's. The West Midlands Economic Council has voiced similar concern for towns in the Midlands. *The Times*, however, considers these "squeal[s] of pain ... a cheerful sign for the Government's regional policy" and has suggested that creating

> a no man's land of grey areas between the Development Areas and the more prosperous parts of the South-East and Midlands could give industrialists denied an I.d.c. in the south a soft option. Too few industrialists might choose Glasgow or Cornwall in preference to Milton Keynes, unless the differential in incentives was very considerable. . . .
>
> . . . It is far more difficult to conduct any flexible policy for economic growth when the first spurt of prosperity hits labour and other bottlenecks in the South-East and Midlands and the first whiff of recession plunges the Development Areas into socially intolerable and economically wasteful unemployment. . . .
>
> . . . The level of unemployment in the South-East as a whole is still lower than anywhere else in the country. The cure for unemployment in new towns of the South-East lies in a more rapid rate of growth in the country as a whole; but to this the disproportionately high level of employment in the South-East as a whole is a formidable obstacle. If, when this imbalance has been removed, the new and expanding towns of the South-East still have special difficulty in providing jobs, then and only then will there be a case for helping them, initially by even higher pressure on firms to move out of London and only as an absolutely last resort by easing the differentials against the South-East and Midlands as a whole.[107]

The issues have never been more explicit; nor have the pressures; and the outcome is still uncertain. The odds are that the development proposals for the South East will probably be implemented, perhaps less rapidly than would be desirable, but implemented nonetheless. Because of the extraordinary assets of the region, its jobs and population will continue to expand; and there appears to be no feasible alternative but to accommodate the minimum projected levels of growth and decentralization.

Meanwhile, the government is loath to cut back the subsidies it is pumping into the Development Areas. In cases of real urgency, it stands ready to increase the assistance even more. In late 1967, for example, 48 "Special Development Areas" were designated in those parts of the country affected by the accelerated closing of mines; and companies became eligible for even greater benefits (including inexpensive loans, building grants of 35 percent, and rent-free factories for five years) if they located in these areas[108] (see Figures 9 and 11).

The government's commitments leave very little room for maneuver. It could possibly establish an intermediate level of assistance for some areas under which grants would be made on a scale somewhere between the 40 percent of the Development Areas and the 20 percent available elsewhere; or it might limit assistance to renovations, infrastructure investments, and building grants. But these measures would be expensive. It might also tax congested areas and risk the violent outcry this would arouse.[109]

The Hunt Committee's report in April 1969 urged a set of compromise measures. The most important were freeing smaller firms from building controls, freely providing I.d.c's for the grey areas and planned "overspill" areas, and dropping Merseyside as a Development Area and then using the estimated savings for various public investments in growth zones in the grey areas (for trading estates, roads, and other essential infrastructure as well as for providing grants for industrial building, labor training, modernization, and physical renewal.[110] The report, however, was not unanimous, and the government decided to provide special assistance for seven Intermediate Areas (see Figures 9 and 11). But it ignored the Hunt Committee's most expensive recommendation (providing infrastructure investments) and its most controversial ones (descheduling Merseyside and relaxing controls for small

11. TIMETABLE OF PRINCIPAL MEASURES USED IN BRITISH POLICY FOR DEVELOPMENT AREAS

Legislation	Areas Scheduled	Special Assistance	Standard Grants		Tax Incentives	Controls	Other
			Buildings	Plant Machinery			
1934 Special Areas Act	Special Areas	Commissioner's Fund purposes limited			None		
1936		Loans	None	None			Trading estates started
1937 Special Areas (Amendment) Act		Loans			Contributions to rent, rates, tax. National Defense Tax exemption	None	
1945 Distribution of Industry Act	Development Areas	Loans and grants				Building licences	Industrial estates. Advance factories built till 1948
1947 Town and Country Planning Act			None	None	None	I.d.c. started	
1958 Distribution of Industry (Industrial Finance) Act	Development Areas and additional places	Aid extended to all trades					Advance factories restarted 1959
1960 Local Employment Act	Development Districts	Loans and grants	Cost value grant	None	None	I.d.c.	Industrial estates reorganized
1963 Local Employment Act, Finance Act			25% cost grant	10% cost grant	Accelerated depreciation		Advance factories program stepped up
1965 Control of Office and Industrial Development Act						I.d.c. limit lowered. ODP started	
1966 Industrial Development Act	New Development Areas		Raised to 35% in certain cases	40% investment grants	Discontinued		
1967	Special Development Areas added		Raised to 45% 1967/8		REP started. SET rebate		
1969 (Proposed legislation)	Intermediate Areas proposed		25% cost grant	None	None	Relaxing I.d.c. controls	Advance factories. Reclamation and training assistance

firms). It also decided not to provide loans and grants for general purposes and chose to finance the rest of the program (mainly building grants and providing factories in advance of requirements) by withdrawing the SET tax premium repaid the employers of labor in Development Areas. As might be expected, the decision was promptly denounced either for going too far or for not going far enough.[111]

The Relocation of Offices

As for the policy on office relocation, five years of experience has established that expansion and economy are the main reasons for the moves of private firms and that most of these moves are to the south and the west. To date, the least successful experience of the *Location of Offices Bureau* (LOB) has been with firms in professional and scientific services, banking and finance, painting and publishing, paper, and miscellaneous services. The most promising candidates, LOB has found, are the insurance companies, the distributive trades, marketing boards, nationalized industries, and large national and international firms. Several research efforts have been initiated to explore these questions further.

Most of the small firms (25 jobs or less) are not yet willing to locate much beyond the suburbs, and the larger firms (those with 100 or more jobs) want to remain within the Greater London area. Nonetheless, 20 percent of the jobs relocated in the period from 1963 to 1967 have been "to places more than 60 miles from London."[112] If the moves are to be successful, they must be made to acceptable locations offering "office accommodations, housing, postal services, telephones, closed circuit television with London, fast train services, motorways, international air communications, secretarial and clerical training. . . ."[113] However, there is always the danger that "if the net gain in trading profit appears likely to be small in relation to the risk of loss of efficiency, or sales, or prestige, then the firm will remain in London. Any reduction in the cost differential between London and decentralized locations will make LOB's work more difficult."[114]

On the basis of its opinion surveys and experience, LOB thought it could get 15,000 to 20,000 office jobs a year shifted out of central London and thus stabilize the current office population which has been increasing at approximately this rate during the past decade. For the year ending March 31, 1967, it claimed credit for moving close to 12,000 jobs. Since tight controls on new office building, a steady rise in space standards, and a large projected growth seemed certain to exhaust London's supply of office space and produce overspill in the future, LOB's target appeared feasible. By January 1968, however, these aims seemed overly optimistic. LOB discovered that it could encourage a high level of office moves only if there was sustained economic growth plus suitable premises for the relocated offices and an economic justification for the move.

Current policies, however, have been working against these criteria. The Selective Employment Tax penalizes office employment. The restrictions on office building in the South East are discouraging office relocation. And there are as yet no significant incentives for moving existing offices to the Development Areas. The government's efforts to increase the number of industrial jobs and to increase the supply of labor to fill these jobs in the Development Areas have tended, with few exceptions, to penalize tertiary employment. As of 1968, the number of office moves have begun to decline. Inquiries at LOB have also dropped drastically, while rents have begun to rise in suburban locations, thus adding another inhibiting factor to relocation.

Meanwhile, there have been increasing efforts to disperse government offices. Between 1963 and August 1969, about 16,000 jobs were moved from London and the South East. Another 22,000 are to leave within "the next few years" with approximately 13,000 scheduled to go to Scotland, Wales, and the English Development Areas. An additional 22,500 jobs arising from new government work are also expected to be diverted to these same areas.[115]

In general, British policy on these matters is still groping and uncertain. The government regards tertiary employment narrowly, as something to be discouraged in the South and to be diverted elsewhere. Unlike French policy, service activities (with the exception of tourism) are not regarded as appropriate tools, let alone *critical* ones, for the stimulation of lagging regions. Yet, one of the reasons British firms are reluctant to locate in the Development Areas is the inadequacy of existing services. Surely, it will only be a matter of time before current British policy on offices is reviewed and significantly overhauled.

The Prospects for the Future

H. G. Wells anticipated that the London citizen of 2000 A.D. would consider "nearly all of England . . . south of Nottingham, and east of Exeter as his suburb.[116] But what is more likely is that by the twenty-first century, the whole of Britain will have become one great metropolitan center. Already, planes which can travel at 2,000 to 3,000 miles an hour are on the drafting board. In several countries throughout the world, high speed trains, air cushion boats, and cargo plane flights are even now a reality. By 2000 A.D. and probably earlier, England and Scotland will form for all practical purposes a linear megalopolitan complex with London, the central metropolitan city, closely linked to Birmingham, Liverpool, Manchester, and Glasgow. These urban regions will be fringed by extensive greenbelt zones reserved for agriculture, recreation, and other rural and leisure purpose activities. Interspersed between these urban areas will be a number of key satellites threaded together along high speed transportation corridors. It will be surprising, indeed, if London then were more than half an hour distance by plane and more than two hours distance by train from all key British, not to mention European, population centers.[117]

If this is the prospect, one can predict some significant reversals in future attitudes. For it is likely that the North, like the South, will develop the same passion for space and the same hostility to overconcentration. Therefore, future debates will center upon the question of which areas in the North and the South should be opened for major urban development, which should be preserved for recreational and other purposes, and which should be set aside for accommodating overspill population.

Inklings of these difficulties are already on the horizon. Some fifteen to twenty million people will be added to the population of the United Kingdom between 1965 and 2000 and many millions more will have to be relocated because of higher space standards. Where and how this population will be located is already under discussion. The chances are that migrants will be progressively less welcome in the North as the Northern urban regions manage to compete with those of the South East. There are already signs of resistance to growth in Devonshire, in Hull, and elsewhere. Indeed, in 1966 the first five year plan for the Scottish economy predicted that the population may increase by 1½ million by 1980 and another 1¾ to 2 million by the year 2000. Soon, the plan observed, it would be necessary to consider "the substantial calls on the space available *throughout Scotland.*"[118]

Whether these prospects do or do not materialize as soon (or as late) as 2000 A.D., they eventually will have to be faced. To facilitate the inevitable process of adjustment, a number of steps can probably be taken within the next few years. For example, there is already a need for alternative urban growth models to indicate, by stages up to the year 2000, the scale and characteristics of the urban systems, administrative mechanisms, and living patterns which might be feasible within and between the various urban regions of the nation. There is an equal need for studies of probable changes in living standards, recreational patterns, and travel characteristics. The first models are likely to be as crude as were the first national models of the economic system. But even crude interregional models may help to clarify some of the critical elements and provide more explicit ideas on complementary relationships and orders of magnitude.[119]

One of the characteristics of the past was that urban (and transportational) systems merely accommodated themselves to existing trends of growth, sometimes all too belatedly. They anticipated and served no definite urban growth policy for the nation. But now radical changes in technology and in analytical and planning methods may make significant changes in the urban system not only feasible, but to some extent manipulable.

The current urban growth strategy in Britain does not yet address these issues explicitly: the essence of the effort at present is to channel the decentralization and growth of the more prosperous regions and to foster new planned cities in the North by spurring the growth and redevelopment of the lagging regions and by fostering new large urban centers in the Midlands and the South East. To accomplish these ends, the government serves as the balance wheel, offsetting the market and the other social and institutional advantages of the South with controls and incentives favoring the North. The strategy in other respects is permissive since each region sets its own urban patterns. The government has as yet devised mechanisms only to help organize the flow of activity and population from the central city to urban growth zones in the outer areas and from the South to urban growth poles in the North;[120] and it is just beginning, through the Interdepartmental Population Committee, to examine the conflicts in the assumptions and plans of the different regions and to ponder whether national strategies can be fashioned to deal with these problems.[121] There is still no policy on the urban growth pattern of the nation as a whole; no effort to relate the growth of London, Birmingham, Liverpool, Manchester, and other urban regions into an overall complex; no evaluation of the desirability of influencing one way or another the physical form or direction of development in these urban regions. To take on such responsibilities will not be an easy task. But it will be surprising if these questions do not soon rank among the most challenging policy problems on urban growth to confront the British nation.

Equilibrium Metropolises versus Paris: The Experience of France

For a developed nation, France had remarkably gradual rates of population and industrial growth in the century and a half before World War II. Still another exceptional aspect of French development during this period was the overwhelming dominance of Paris and the lack of any significant urban competitors even on a secondary level, features often associated with underdeveloped economies. In one respect, however, the pattern of French growth was similar to the experiences of both developed and underdeveloped economies. This was the increasingly visible disparity between regions, especially between the dominant capital city and the less prosperous regions in the West, the Massif Central, and the Southwest. Conservative cultural and political traditions in the less prosperous regions extending back almost a thousand years reinforced this pattern. So did the highly centralized administrative tradition dating back at least to Louis XIV, which had been intensified during the Revolutionary and Napoleonic periods.

In coping with these problems, little help had come from the French intellectuals. Perhaps in France more than in almost any other nation, the capital was associated with the avant-garde in all aspects of high culture, and the provinces with backwardness and parochialism. By the 1930's a highly refined heritage in urban design for a limited social elite had degenerated into an extremely narrow program of "urbanism," one which emphasized aesthetics almost to the exclusion of the most significant aspects of urban and regional development. Because economists did not traditionally concern themselves with the problems of urban or regional development, they, too, contributed little to the reversal of these trends. The same held true for other social scientists. The French geographers constituted the sole exception, but their awareness alone could hardly stem the tide.

After World War II, new intellectual currents emerged, stimulated in part by the upsurge of population and of economic activity. During this period, there was intense dissatisfaction with existing institutions and with prevailing patterns of urban growth, and there were a number of significant innovations in regional and national planning. The changes attracted considerable attention. The British, in particular, in the early sixties, began to show interest in and even envy of the French efforts. In part, of course, it was a case of the grass appearing greener on the other side of the fence. (One could point to equally envious references to the British experience by French planners and French publications.) In part, also, the interest was more avid than usual because the British and French policies were responses to roughly similar problems on a somewhat comparable scale. For, while the British were producing their First National Plan in September 1965, the French were already completing their Fifth Plan. And, while the British discussion of regional development was still largely in the realm of generalities, the French had developed an advisory and administrative organization to formulate the regional portions of the National Plan, as well as a reporting system for regional capital investments and expenditures, and they were soon to begin implementing regional plans within this framework.

Yet, on urban and regional strategy, the British and French planners were poles apart. The British were not especially attracted to the French notion of accelerating the growth of eight existing regional metropolises to offset and compete with Paris. Top British planners considered their big cities too big and they wanted to slow down and change the form of their growth. The French planners, on the other hand, strongly felt that their country didn't have enough large cities and that only large, regional cities would be able to offset the growth of Paris. What the French admired most about the British were not their ideas about new cities but their ability to get them built. Their own system, elegant enough in principle, seemed as yet to lack operational effectiveness in many aspects of regional physical development.

The misgivings of the French planners were not altogether without foundation. Although France was ahead in certain aspects of regional planning, it had still not passed the fumbling phases in many other respects. The basic regional planning legislation in France had been developed only within the last five to ten years; it was not till 1964 that a national strategy for urban growth was formulated and became official policy. Nevertheless, some fresh ideas were animating French urban and regional planning. Although still fairly abstract, these concepts were suggestive enough to arouse new expectations and to generate a fresh approach to traditional issues. To appreciate their significance, however, they must be seen in relation to long-term trends of urban and regional development and the range of measures devised to grapple with them.

Growth Trends and Urban Policy Issues, 1800–1962

Atypical Development Features

Most difficulties of urban growth are associated with surging population, rapid industrialization, and an immature system of cities. What makes the French experience so special is that the problems of urban concentration and lagging regions began to cumulate even in the absence of these three characteristic conditions.

158

French population trends were quite unusual. In 1850 there were approximately 36 million inhabitants in France, 35 million in Germany, 24 million in Italy, and almost 21 million in Great Britain. While, in the century that followed, the populations of Britain, Germany, and Italy approximately doubled, France's population increased by only 14 percent. The reason for this population lag was the simultaneous decline in France's birth and death rates during the nineteenth century.[1] In the three other countries, the birth rate did not decline until much later.

These trends can be traced more specifically. In the period from 1801 to 1861 the average increase of France's population was only $^6/_{10}$ of one percent per annum. The rate dropped to $^1/_{10}$ of one percent over the next fifty years, and then rose to $^2/_{10}$ of one percent until 1936. In terms of total population, France experienced an increase of 37 percent from 1801 to 1861, an increase of 12 percent over the next seventy-five years, and then an absolute decrease of 3 percent from 1936 to 1946. Were it not for immigration and lengthening lifespans, the population decline would have occurred much earlier because France's population often did not reproduce itself. However, a significant reversal occurred after World War II. Population rose 23.5 percent between 1946 and 1968, an average per annum increase of 1 percent.[2]

Industrialization was the second major atypical trend in France. It, too, proceeded very gradually.[3] Throughout the nineteenth century, the industrial labor force expanded slowly: between 1860 and 1936 only 15 percent of the two million additional persons in the nonagricultural labor force went into industry.[4] Moreover, most persons in France did not work in large establishments. In 1896 the average French industrial firm contained 5.5 employees; in 1950 the average was 5 employees.[5] About 75 percent of the industrial establishments in 1954 employed under six salaried workers.[6] The result was "a slow shifting of [France's] economic centers of gravity from the side of agriculture to that of industry, and a slow change in the methods of industrial organization."[7]

The principal expanding sectors of the economy were textiles, silk, wool, food products, steel, automobiles, and chemical and engineering products. The expansion of these sectors prompted sizable increases in the populations of St. Étienne, Lille, Roubaix,

Tourcoing, Nantes, Bordeaux, and Toulouse in the first part of the nineteenth century and similar increases for Dijon, Reims, Grenoble, and Clermont-Ferrand in the second half of the century[8] (see Figure 13). The bulk of the nation's economic activities, however, remained concentrated in Paris, Lyon, and Marseille, the three largest cities.

France's urban pattern was also uncommon. It was shaped by France's well developed railroad and road systems. Often based on Roman routes, the roads left "scarcely a corner of the country, however remote, really inaccessible."[9] They linked together a great number of urban settlements, most of which had existed since the Middle Ages or earlier. This is not to say that the pattern of urban development was uniform in France, but "real isolation [was] very rare ... [R]ight across such seeming obstacles as the Vosges and the Cévennes [there spread] a continuous, though attenuated sheet of settlement."[10]

Growth Trends and Migration

Although French settlements were numerous and widespread, most of the thriving industrial activities were located in the East where superior resources, transportation, and markets were readily available. Traditionally, the dividing line has been drawn from the mouth of the Seine (Le Havre) to the mouth of the Saône-Rhône river basins (Marseille) (see Figure 13). Most industries tended to concentrate in a few départements to the east of this boundary: Seine, Nord, Loire, Bouches du Rhône, Seine Maritime, and Isère.

Some industrial activities developed elsewhere, of course. Bordeaux, for example, was an important center in the Southwest for agricultural processing, shipbuilding, and other miscellaneous activities; and Toulouse, besides being an important provincial railroad and administrative center, contained chemical, aircraft, and some light industries. Clermont-Ferrand in the Massif Central and Nantes in Bretagne also attracted industrial development. But these urban centers never burgeoned into more than minor growth complexes. Excluding Paris, cities of 100,000 or more west of the Le Havre–Marseille diagonal had about half the population of equivalent cities on the other side of the line; with the inclusion of Paris, the ratio dropped to one to six.[11]

The main urban settlements were concentrated in the North, on the Mediterranean, in the Saône-Rhône valley, and in the Seine Basin. The North, the first of these areas of high urban density, owed its development to its basic resource endowment: its coal and ore fields, its rich agricultural hinterland, and the harbor facilities of Le Havre and Rouen. These resources had greatly influenced the initial location and subsequent growth of the textile industry in French Flanders, Lorraine, and La Basse Seine; the emergence of the steel and other resource-based activities in Nord, Pas-de-Calais, and Lorraine; and the development of other activities such as chemicals in La Basse Seine. The fact that these activities were readily accessible to the principal concentrations of population, capital, purchasing power, and centers of decision-making—in western Europe as well as in France—had further weighted the balance in favor of development in the North.

The Mediterranean region, too, and Provence and Côte d'Azur in particular, had experienced substantial growth, especially since 1880. Favored by an extraordinary climate, the region was well adapted to tourist development in all seasons. Closeness to Alpine sources of power and the bauxite deposits of the Southeast had spurred its aluminium and chemical industries. Oil, sugar, and chemical products possessed easy access to the internal market and, via Marseille, to the markets of the Mediterranean. The growth of the economy of southern Europe and colonial Africa had also contributed to the expansion of the port of Marseille and its ancillary activities and was likely to play an even more important role in the future.

The Saône-Rhône valley was still another significant growth zone. Its importance was derived only in part from its vineyards and other agricultural activities, for the Saône-Rhône valley was the principal link between the economies of the North, East, South, and Paris. Within this region, Dijon and Grenoble were firmly established as important crossroads and sub-regional marketing and tourist centers with minor industrial functions (aluminum, food production, and gloves). But Lyon, with its flourishing industries based on silk and silk synthetics and its ready access to both the coal fields of the upper Loire and the hydroelectric power of the Alps, was unquestionably the dominant center. The growth in these areas, however, was dwarfed by the burgeoning of the Paris region within the Seine Basin. In 1861 this region had accounted for one out of every thirteen persons in France; by 1962 it contained one out of every 5.5 Frenchmen.[12] During this same period, the population of France grew by less than 19 percent whereas the population of the Paris region almost tripled.[13] In retrospect, this growth seems almost to have been inevitable, for the Paris region was favored in nearly every respect. It was the center of the principal river basins of France, the focal point of a highly centralized political and administrative system, and the seat of the nation's most important commercial, industrial, cultural, and social activities.[14] These advantages were buttressed by a radially-designed, Paris-centered railroad system deliberately planned as such by the July Monarchy. They were further reinforced by the civic design policy of the Second Empire which enhanced the attractiveness of Paris, drew rural migrant labor from many surrounding regions, and induced additional infrastructure investments.

For more than a century, the dominance of the Paris region resulted in increasingly substantial population losses for the rest of the nation. By the end of World War II, the vast majority of the eighty-nine départements in metropolitan France were experiencing a decided decline in population. This marked the culmination of a century-old trend: from 1831 to 1862, the number of such départements had risen from 0 to 33; by 1901, the number had risen to 45; and by 1946 it had reached 71.[15] The migrants, of course, wound up in the cities, most of them eventually in or near the region of Paris.[16] But the main sources of the migration to Paris varied. In the second half of the nineteenth century the migrants came from the neighboring small towns and agricultural regions, the départements east of the Paris Basin, and the départements of the Center. After the end of the century, significant additions flowed in from the regions of Normandie, Bretagne, Nord, Lyon, the Massif Central, and abroad. With improvements in transportation and communications, long distance moves were made easier. In 1962 two out of every three residents of Paris had been born elsewhere; of these migrants, more than two out of three had come from distant regions or other countries.[17]

The specific reasons for the population movements also varied. In some regions, such as Nord or St. Étienne, structural unemployment or declining economic activities provided the impetus. In others, such as the Saône-Rhône valley, it was excessive parcellization of land.[18] In Bretagne, it was the relatively high birth rate. But, the main causes of migrations to the Paris region were disparities in employment opportunities, in living conditions, and in incomes.[19]

The regions of the West and Southwest constituted a special problem. Most of the economic activities in these regions were declining and employment was stagnating or diminishing. Although they contained 37 percent of the population, all of their industrial sectors lagged behind the national average growth rate.[20] Their economic activities were relatively insensitive to growth and innovations elsewhere, and their agricultural hinterlands were disadvantaged because of the absence of metropolitan markets. It was estimated that if employment were to increase in France by 16 percent, the increase on the average would be "29% in the Paris region, 18% in the East and only 7% in the West."[21] Moreover, a 1958 survey disclosed that in the six regions of the West and Southwest (Bretagne, Poitou-Charentes, Limousin, Midi-Pyrénées, Aquitaine, Pays de la Loire) average income was approximately 50 percent less than in the Paris region and about 30 percent less than in four other regions (Haute Normandie, Nord, Rhône-Alpes, Lorraine). The same six regions ranked lowest, on the basis of 1963 data, in salaries of white and blue collar workers and highest in the percentage of wage earners earning less than 5000 F per year.[22] It is not surprising then that many of the residents of these regions decided to take advantage of opportunities available elsewhere, particularly since French policy makers did little to arrest these trends, however painful the process of migration was for the migrant or for the region losing its population.

And the situation threatened to get worse. Paris was still expanding, even in the sixties. Its rise in employment, 10.8 percent between 1954 and 1962, was the highest of all regions of France.[23] Moreover, Paris had most of the fast growing science-based industries, and the development of the European Economic Community also appeared likely to favor the growth of services in the Paris region.

The dominance of Paris was only one of the problems of French urban development. A second and related difficulty, particularly emphasized by French geographers and urbanists, was the scarcity of other large metropolises. There were only three major urban agglomerations in France—Paris, Lyon, and Marseille—whereas in the rest of western Europe, the situation was quite different. West Germany, for example, had eleven such metropolises with populations exceeding half a million, the United Kingdom seven, and Italy six. None of France's other metropolises were even close to Paris either in size or significance, and the gap seemed to be widening. In 1891, Paris was almost six times the size of Lyon; by 1961 it had grown to almost eight times the size.[24] Rouen, Le Havre, and Reims were the only cities with more than 100,000 persons within 200 km. of Paris. Although there were some smaller cities at the perimeter of the region, such as Orléans and Amiens, which retained their regional trading and administrative functions, these cities had almost no expanding activities and few new ones.[25]

Prominent Frenchmen began to believe that the growth of Paris had resulted in the stunting of the development of the rest of urban France. Even astute foreign observers shared this view. Kindleberger, for example, pointed out that

the dominance of Paris and the small size of most communities outside it bred defeatism at the local level. ... Moreover, with ... the exception of Lyon, which had both large size and an independent tradition, there was something wrong with each substantial city. In Rouen the inferiority complex vis-à-vis Britain was at its most acute; it was the home of protectionism. Marseille, an enormous agglomeration, lacked ties to its region, though it served the hinterland of all France as a military and colonial port. Bordeaux was purely commercial, hurt by the loss of colonial trade in sugar and too far from the center to attract manufacturing. Lille-Roubaix-Tourcoing had a strong commercial and financial tradition in Lille, but for the rest consisted of overgrown villages swamped by industrial expansion, with little tradition or individuality. Paris was not only comparable to New York and Washington, as was London, but also to Chicago in transport, Detroit and Cincinnati in manufacturing, and Boston in letters and education.[26]

Not all of France's urbanization characteristics were atypical or unsatisfactory, however. The proportion of persons working in industry was "about the same in Paris as in other western European capitals."[27] And, because of the fertility of its hinterland and the large market which the Paris region provided for agricultural products, its surrounding agricultural regions did not experience any larger movement off the land than did other more peripheral regions such as Bretagne or Basse Normandie.[28]

Nor was the exodus from other regions altogether undesirable. Major shifts of population to areas providing greater opportunity resulted in a steady improvement in living conditions throughout France. Moreover, migration to urban areas actually occurred more slowly and at a later date in France than in other western European countries. France became more urban than rural in population only "towards 1930, 100 years after England, 50 years after Germany."[29] In fact, one of France's problems was its lack of enough people to make these shifts. To obtain a sufficient labor force, the government had found it necessary to keep its doors open to immigrants; nevertheless, the shortage remained sufficiently severe to persuade some economists that France's economic growth may have been retarded because of it.[30] It is not surprising then that many French policy makers hesitated to reverse the growth trends of Paris for fear of possibly jeopardizing French economic development.

Emergence of Policy Issues

Two factors provoked a decisive change of attitude toward migration and urban development. The first was the likelihood of further massive inundations of new activities and population in the Paris region. The second was the growing conviction that, through a combination of national, regional, and urban growth strategies, far more effective solutions might be feasible for Paris and the lagging regions. The essence of the new approach was to encourage development elsewhere, especially in the lagging regions, and to reduce the pressures on Paris. A major limitation, however, continued to operate: the new policy could not be more than a constraint on an even more overriding national objective, the promotion of the economy's maximum growth and the enhancement of its competitive potentials, especially within the European Common Market. Unfortunately for the lagging regions, satisfying the growth objective implied making or encouraging a wide range of investments in the more prosperous regions.

Paris, for example, required tremendous investments in its outlying areas for housing, schools, roads, and other services, and major rehabilitation measures within the city to relieve the congestion and decay that were crippling its activities.[31] Though for a while an effort was made to underequip Paris in the hope of limiting its growth, this policy was steadily whittled away under pressure. As significant growing points competitive with Paris, the cities of Strasbourg, Lyon, Grenoble, Annecy, Chambéry, Nice, and Marseille, too, could make strong claims for extensive infrastructure investments to maintain or improve their relative positions.

In addition, a number of intermediate regions had special problems which also required financial attention. In Nord, traditional textile, ore, and coal industries were declining. Future employment and growth prospects were especially poor and there were strong pressures to introduce some expanding economic activities to diversify the economy. In Alsace, a number of traditional industries, such as shoes, textiles, and furniture, required more modernized equipment and more rationalized production processes. As for Lorraine, which had experienced impressive growth since 1950, it faced the prospect of rising unemployment. This situation had been brought about after 1962 as a result of the increasingly severe competition confronting its iron ore, coal, and textile industries and the probable stabilization of production at its steel plants. Given Lorraine's strategic position at the frontier of the Common Market and its special position in contemporary French history, the government felt obliged to try to reverse these trends—largely by promoting metallurgical industries linked to the existing steel complex.

Elsewhere there were still other pressures: to improve communication facilities; to equip the country with a national network of superhighways; to transform obsolete agricultural patterns of many regions; to link the Mediterranean to the North Sea through an ambitious program of canal, highway, rail, and other infrastructure investments; to provide the housing and urban facilities so urgently required in the major metropolitan areas; to expand and rehabilitate the existing plant and services for education and scientific research; to promote essential facilities for tourism, recreation, and the leisure needs of the future. These were only a few of the vast range of projects and programs that competed for the scarce resources available.

Providing help everywhere through a "general sprinkling"[32] of investments in all regions was considered wasteful and, even worse, ineffectual. On the other hand, providing help only in the most productive regions would widen the gap between the growing and lagging regions and exacerbate the problems of Paris. The only acceptable technical and political solution was to steer a course between these two alternatives. But this presupposed the establishment of criteria which would enable planners to provide reasonably effective help for the poorer regions without arresting the progress of the growing ones and to provide jobs and other opportunities in the lagging regions without producing labor shortages in those that were expanding. It also presupposed the creation of staffs and administrative mechanisms to devise and carry out the necessary development measures. Attempts to solve these problems exposed the inadequacies of sectoral analysis of national development problems and ultimately compelled the French planners to regard urban and regional planning as an indispensable territorial expression of national economic planning.

The Precursors

A number of measures were explored before a national strategy for urban and regional development was consciously formulated. The initial impetus for such experimentation came from a research team, composed mainly of geographers, which was working during the war at the Délégation Générale à l'Équipement National. Anticipating some of the problems of the postwar period, the researchers documented some of the disparities of French regional development and some of the possible remedies. Subsequent postwar planning and reconstruction problems kept the discussion alive and the social environment receptive. Then, in 1947 a book appeared which transformed the technical discussions into a major public issue. Prepared initially as a report for the Minister of Reconstruction and Urbanism, this study, *Paris et le Désert Français*, by J. F. Gravier, a geographer, aroused enormous interest in the national effects of excessive centralization and the growth of Paris.[33] Its simple and timely presentation touched off reverberations among policy makers and the literate public comparable to those produced in Britain by the Barlow Commission report.

Three years later, Eugène Claudius-Petit, the Minister of Reconstruction and Urbanism, enunciated a significant policy. "A declaration of intentions rather than a definite program,"[34] it was an ardent plea for a national plan to improve the distribution of the population of the country in relation to its resources.[35] It called for, first, the decentralization of new or expanding industries in centers lending themselves to industrial development or requiring diversification; second, the consolidation and modernization of agricultural holdings; third, the expansion and promotion of tourist facilities in all regions; and fourth, the decentralization of universities, museums, and other artistic and intellectual facilities. To be effective, Claudius-Petit insisted, the program would have to be governed by the broad welfare needs of the nation and not simply by economic considerations; furthermore, it would have to be based on a penetrating series of studies on the role of cities in relation to their regions and the role of regions in relation to the country.

Though not then immediately apparent, the Gravier study and the Claudius-Petit declaration marked the first reversal in official thinking on a national policy for urban and regional development. A lead had been furnished for the orientation of national energies, a lead that responded to deeply felt needs. In the years to come, policies would be adopted and measures undertaken on a large enough scale so that the issue of urban growth policy would become impressed upon the national consciousness.

Fashioning the Controls, Plans, and Incentives

In the early postwar period, the instruments for government action in France were even more limited than those that the British had possessed at the time of the Barlow report. A 1945 ordinance gave the government some vague power to revoke construction permits for buildings in Paris which threatened the public health and safety. Another law, passed in 1953, gave local authorities the right to expropriate land intended for housing or industrial purposes in cases of bankruptcy or persistent misuse. Other decrees permitted the Minister of Construction to exercise more explicit power over all new industrial construction or extension of existing structures involving the addition of more than 500 square meters or in which more than 50 persons were employed. In 1958 this power was extended to all government agencies, to scientific and technical establishments, and to private office buildings of more than 1000 square meters. In addition, a permanent committee was formed to make an inventory of all agencies which might be moved to other regions and to advise the government on the creation or extension of all new public or quasi-public establishments in the Paris region. The main reasons for its establishment were to relieve the congestion in Paris and to create some additional employment elsewhere. However, another objective was to undercut the argument of various firms that they had to be in Paris to maintain close connections with various ministries.[36]

Then, in 1958, a group within the Ministry of Construction began a new land use plan for the Paris region. Drawn up quickly with limited resources, the *Plan d'Aménagement et d'Organisation Générale de la Région Parisienne* (PADOG) dealt with general principles and policy and provided no details on costs and staging. It proposed to reduce migration to Paris to 50,000 a year (a cut of approximately 50,000 to 80,000 of the annual volume of migration for the 1955–1960 period). This would limit the growth of Paris to 100,000 a year and keep the total 1970 population of the region at 9.4 million.[37] To curb the extension of Paris, PADOG also recommended equipping the suburban dormitory areas with the essential community services and facilities that they lacked. This would relieve the pressures on the central areas and would provide the suburbs with more social amenities.

Finally, in 1960 the region of Paris was divided into zones. Within these zones a range of taxes was imposed on new buildings and a range of premiums provided to encourage new uses of existing industrial and commercial buildings. Through this combination of efforts, the government hoped to influence land use patterns throughout the Paris region.

The land use plan for the Paris region and the building controls were not the only tools devised by the government. It also designed a wide assortment of relocation incentives. These emphasized the setting up of industrial areas in various regions outside of Paris and the provision of subsidies to attract industries. Among the subsidies offered were: exemption from several taxes, special rates for power and transportation, arrangements in certain cases for low interest loans, and grants for modernization of industrial equipment and retraining of employees. Here again, the aim was to reduce migration and to encourage new firms or firms contemplating expansion, decentralization, or transformation of their operations to shift to an appropriate zone outside of Paris.

The Creation of New Institutions

Several institutional innovations were necessary to support these policies. The first of these, the *Société d'Économie Mixte* (SEM), was promulgated after 1948. The regulations made it possible for communes, départements, cities, and regions, in association with private organizations such as chambers of commerce, to set up joint ventures for public development purposes. As quasi-public development corporations, these societies were not subject to the restrictions usually placed on public agencies, especially in regard to recruitment and decision-making and in being able to borrow and spend funds.[38] The character of these organizations varied. Some, like the Compagnie Nationale d'Aménagement de la Région du Bas-Rhône et du Languedoc (CNARBRL), were relatively well-staffed and functioned fairly independently over a vast region. More typical, however, were the small joint enterprises which were set up to acquire and equip land for industrial and commercial areas, for high priority "urbanizations," and for urban renewal.

To help these societies and the local authorities, the government in 1950 created the *Fonds National d'Aménagement du Territoire*. (In 1965 FNAT was transformed into the Fonds National d'Aménagement Foncier et d'Urbanisme—FNAFU.) FNAT was given the power to make short-term, low-interest loans to these societies at 2½ percent for two years. But the funds available were

modest, and after 1954 the loans were restricted primarily to organizations concerned with residential development. However, the
activities of the societies received further encouragement in 1954
by the creation of the Société Centrale pour l'Équipement du
Territoire (SCET). This new agency was established to help the
local societies prepare their financial and development plans and
to set up similar societies elsewhere.[39] The societies were also
helped by the creation of the ZUP program (Zone à Urbaniser par
Priorité), which sought to expedite the building of large-scale
residential projects.

In addition to FNAT, the government created a number of
other funds from 1948 to 1955. These were designed to promote
decentralization, reconversion, increased productivity, and the
modernization of equipment. But this proliferation of agencies con-
fused clients and weakened the management of public investment
capital. Few requests for assistance involved only one of these
organizations, and squabbles developed over the question of jurisdiction. Therefore, in 1955, all of these funds were put into a new
organization, the *Fonds de Développement Économique et Social* (FDES)
under the direction of the Minister of Finance and a number of
other key ministers and administrators including the Commissaire
Général of the national plan. FDES became a source of funds
which the joint societies and private firms could tap if funds were
not procurable elsewhere or if market rates were significantly
higher than those of the state. But such assistance was fairly exceptional. The general policy was to intervene only in rare cases and
to let specialized financial organizations handle these matters. The
real influence of FDES was derived from the power of its special
committees. They were required to approve all government financial assistance to private firms and local societies for decentralization, regional development, and other purposes.[40]

The *Sociétés de Développement Régional* (SDR) were still another
innovation. Begun in 1955, they were really regional investment
banks whose functions were to mobilize more local and outside
resources to promote trade and industry in regions of high unemployment or underdevelopment. These new institutions could take
up capital subscriptions, but their investments could not exceed
more than 35 percent of the capital of any one enterprise and
more than 25 percent of their subscribed capital. They could also

make short and long-term loans, furnish technical advice in preparing financial plans, and provide management assistance. Most of their funds were supposed to come from local sources. They could, however, generate additional funds by joining with other societies in issuing debentures guaranteed by the state.[41]

The Evolution of a National Policy on Regional Development

The burgeoning of these measures for encouraging regional development occurred during the same period that France's national planning system was being evolved, but, in general, these institutional innovations and the National Plans developed independently of each other. The plans focussed primarily on economic sectors and tried to encourage general economic growth; they had little to say on the problems of regional development. Not till the Fourth Plan was there some convergence of these two efforts.

The First Plan (1948–52) dealt with reconstruction in several critical sectors (coal, electricity, steel, transport, cement, fertilizers, and agricultural machinery). The Second Plan (1954–1957) stressed a series of basic reforms: in agricultural production, industrial specialization, commercial and agricultural marketing, training programs, and scientific and technical research. It also emphasized the importance of resource development programs and the need to encourage expanding industries to locate their new or branch plants in depressed regions.[42] The Third Plan (1958–61) was designed to take account of a number of problems resulting from unbalanced growth.[43] Its principal emphasis was on exchange and fiscal problems, but other matters were also reviewed, including the congestion of Paris and the need to shift industries, government agencies, scientific laboratories, and banking and credit institutions to the South and West.[44]

On the whole, the National Plans were highly successful. By the end of the Third Plan, the economy's productivity had been increased, the growth rate during the fifties had reached an average of 4.5 percent per annum, and the desired exchange balances and output targets had been achieved. The accomplishments were all the more remarkable considering the political turmoil in France during this period, especially in the years immediately preceding and following the establishment of the Fifth Republic.[45] However, even by the start of the sixties the Plans still lacked a systematic regional focus. They did not examine the regional components of the national planning programs; nor did they deal with the development needs or potentials of the different regions or even with the regional effects of sector investment plans. The main reasons for this neglect were limited resources, "higher priorities," inadequate training of economists on these matters, and lack of any clear sense of how to proceed. But as Paris continued to grow, and as regional problems persisted and even threatened to become aggravated by the "open competition" of the Common Market, the need for remedying these deficiencies won increasing recognition.

The mushrooming during this period of a large number of regional development committees and of some regional missions and programs spurred this change of attitude. The committees varied considerably in character. Some were formed largely as a result of local initiative. Others were stimulated by the government, particularly the Ministry of Construction. Many concerned themselves only with the problems of a département or a group of départements, others with the area affected by the development of a river basin or a major development project. As a rule, the committees included representatives of local communities and of private organizations representing banking, industry, commerce, and agriculture. The organizations functioned ostensibly as local study and advisory groups on regional development, but they were adroit in drawing attention to regional problems and in promoting measures for regional development. Before long, the government decided to tap the energies these organizations had demonstrated by formally recognizing in 1954 the existence of the *Comités d'Expansion Économique* (CEE).[46] The government hoped that these committees would help local officials evaluate and cope with their regional problems. By giving them official status, the government sought to stimulate the formation of committees in regions where they had not as yet been formed.

The economic recession and the Poujadist movement in 1954 and 1955 made the country even more attentive to some of the grievances of the provinces. When, in April 1955 (at the height of the Vietnam crisis in France), Premier Mendès-France was accorded special powers to govern for one year by decree, the Parlement also emphasized its desire to see the government deploy all necessary measures to favor the development of regions suffering

173

from or soon likely to suffer from unemployment or underdevelopment.[47] These areas were subsequently defined as *critical zones*. To these lagging regions, additional government subsidies, tax exemptions, and special allowances would be made available beyond those normally provided for encouraging decentralization or regional development.

At the same time (1955), the government made the *Commissariat Général du Plan* (CGP) responsible for the preparation of regional development plans for each region.[48] After a lengthy series of studies and reviews, twenty plans were produced.[49] They dealt with population trends, major land uses, communications, and infrastructure. Although weak, the studies yielded some useful information. They brought to light the difficulties of getting effective help from the regional public services because of the hierarchical channels of French public administration. They also revealed the need for more sophisticated economic analyses, more adequate physical plans, more thorough examinations of urban and rural problems, and more specific project proposals, including evaluations of cost, staging, and feasibility.

In some cases, the CGP studies overlapped Ministry of Construction plans for land use and physical development.[50] The differences in views led to jurisdictional frictions. Suspicion in some quarters that the action phase of regional development would be retarded unless physical planning studies also received support prompted the enactment of legislation in 1957 providing for the preparation by the Ministry of Construction of land use plans for the regions. This legislation, in turn, produced concern that none of these regional plans would be effectively integrated with the National Plan and that the existing procedures would lead to divergent as well as overlapping results. Therefore, in December 1958 the government decided to merge the regional programs of CGP with the physical development plans of the Ministry of Construction.[51]

Meanwhile, dissatisfaction mounted with the critical zones program, the program for helping areas of high unemployment or underdevelopment. Thirty-four areas had been so designated. This large number of critical zones had forced a dispersion of efforts and had limited the program's effectiveness. It had also resulted in a blurring of the distinctions between the needs of one area and another. This was particularly unfortunate, for the areas frequently differed greatly from each other. Some were underdeveloped or only in temporary difficulties. Others, although already possessing fairly developed infrastructure facilities, skilled labor, relatively attractive locations, physical resources, and substantial populations, were experiencing basic structural changes in their economies. In 1959 the government sought to make this program more flexible by pinpointing within the critical zones a small number of "conversion zones," or growth points. Initially, seven areas received this new designation.[52] Higher subsidies were provided (ranging from 15 percent to 20 percent of total investments) and special arrangements were made to simplify and facilitate the granting of assistance in these zones.

What appeared to be a decisive shift in policy from dispersed assistance to concentration on a few effective growing points was offset in large measure by the almost simultaneous adoption of a *coup par coup* (blow-for-blow) policy. The recognition that changes in demand or other contingencies might create serious unemployment problems in other areas led to the decision to extend the increased benefits available in conversion zones to all areas in which such problems might exist. As Prof. Lajugie observed,

> the arrangements had the merit of being more supple than the preceding measures. They provided a more manageable instrument to fight against the recession which menaced in this period important sectors of the French economy. It marked, nonetheless, an irritating return and aggravation of the policy of dispersal of investments. . . .[53]

In 1960 the details of the system were revamped without modifying the basic policies. The benefits of the program, which previously had been available only to industries,[54] were subsequently extended to scientific and research establishments, and then to commercial, service, and other activities.

The regional programs and policies that were evolving catalyzed some further institutional innovations. Ever since de Tocqueville, criticisms had been leveled at the highly centralized départemental administrative system and its inability to adapt to the problems of different regions.[55] To this worsening situation, the growth of cities had added the anomalies of outmoded, multiple, and overlapping local jurisdictions and inadequate staff and financial resources. But the reorganization of local government was too hazardous and complicated an enterprise to be undertaken, especially in a turbulent decade like the fifties. Manipulation of the administrative apparatus of the central government had its pitfalls, too, but it seemed the only feasible approach at the time.

The problems which emerged in the preparation of the regional plans and the activities of the CEE lent new force to the pressures to reduce the conflicting regional boundaries of ministerial subdivisions and to establish some broader jurisdiction than the département for purposes of regional programming and implementation. There already existed some precedents for such experimentation with regional organization. Under the Vichy regime, superprefects had been appointed to cope with the problems of the occupation, and, after the liberation, a new institution of superprefects had been created to police and coordinate civil administration in the military regions. The départements, however, resisted restraints. In actuality, the innovations hardly changed the system at all and they were officially abolished in 1946. Then, in 1959, after studying for four years the problem of boundaries, the government agreed to set up twenty-one *program regions* of varying sizes. Each contained two to eight départements and an average population of about two million persons. (Paris, of course, was an exception, for its population was already more than eight million.)

The definition of the regional boundaries required agility and the ability to compromise. The boundaries had to take account of geographic, historical, employment, and demographic considerations and had to fit the perimeters of the départements and the zones of influence of large communities. As might be expected, no one was altogether satisfied with the results.[56] The boundaries clashed with existing administrative interests; they were not especially appropriate for analytical purposes; and they threatened to subordinate the regional staffs of ministries to the authority of the coordinating regional prefect. Because of this dissatisfaction, ministerial regional subdivisions were not adjusted along the lines of these new boundaries until the government passed a general decree of principle in 1959 and followed this by a sterner decree enjoining the prompt application of these boundaries by June 1960 for approximately thirty government agencies.[57]

Evaluation of Changes

By the end of the 1950's, the principal directions of the government's policies were clear. There was a genuine recognition of the need for regional planning to complement national sector planning and for changes in the administrative system to serve these ends. The growth of Paris was to be restrained; and an elaborate incentive system had been devised to induce industrial development in other regions, particularly in the less prosperous areas. Each of the measures undertaken had been originally introduced as an ad hoc effort to relieve the congestion of Paris and to encourage growth elsewhere. But the obvious relevance of such measures to France's sectoral plans and policies and the prospect that a dual system of area planning might grow up along side the sectoral planning system had made it essential for a series of corrective mechanisms to be invented and grafted onto the national planning institution.

This revised planning system won credit for curbing some development in Paris and for encouraging some relocation elsewhere. Because building permits between 1956 and 1960 were about 40 percent of those granted during the period from 1951 to 1955,[58] the rate of increase of large new industrial establishments and expansions in the Paris region appeared to be on the decline. However, as indicated by the experience of Britain and the United States, much of this decentralization would have occurred even without government controls and special assistance. This is what actually happened in France, for studies showed that "only 14% of the 1000 operations of decentralization realized from 1950 to 1961 had benefited from the special equipment premiums."[59]

The decongestion measures soon revealed other serious failings. The growth rate of Paris was not really reduced. Between 1954 and 1962 Paris grew at about the same or a slightly greater rate than the rest of the country. In part, this was because the controls in the Paris region exercised by the *Commission Interministérielle de Décentralisation* (CID) were very flexible and had large loopholes. Small and average-sized enterprises were exempt from its power. So were extensions of less than 10 percent. Moreover, CID tended to follow a policy that favored the expansion of Paris during this period.[60] Almost three times as much new floor space was au-

177

thorized in the Paris region for office or industrial purposes (1,400,000 square meters) as was destroyed or converted to other uses (523,000 square meters).[61] Although more than 235,000 jobs were moved outside of the Paris region between 1950 and 1961, the areas which benefitted the most from these moves were located within 70 to 200 km. of Paris.[62] As for the decentralization of government offices, the progress was generally conceded to be even less satisfactory than was the case in the private sector.[63]

There was also some question about whether the new agencies were proving equal to the task. FNAFU was charged with dispensing its limited funds "with too little concern for the type of operation being financed and their relation to the objectives of the plan."[64] The local joint venture societies flourished but tended to be distributed unevenly. They did not exist at all in many of the underdeveloped regions, and there were sometimes a half dozen or more in other départements or metropolitan areas. This resulted in a dispersion of efforts, higher costs and poor coordination.[65]

As for the Regional Development Societies, they undoubtedly provided a useful service for some small and medium-sized firms in the expanding regions, but they were least effective in the regions requiring the most assistance. This was inescapable since they had no mandate to function otherwise. They had to adhere more or less rigorously to the conventional banking criteria imposed by the big Parisian banks which were their principal sponsors. Furthermore, they operated on a very modest scale. The total combined capital of the fifteen societies in existence by the end of 1964 was less than 98.7 million NF ($20 million) and the total sum raised and loaned was only a little more than 661.5 million NF ($132 million).* The societies aided only 703 undertakings between 1957 and 1964 or an average of about 100 firms a year. FDES was the one agency which focussed its efforts on the lagging regions. The evidence showed, however, that its procedures were cumbersome, its interest rates high and its collateral excessive. All told, its assistance was "simply not sufficient to offset the advantages of external economies available in more advanced regions."[66]

Another serious concern involved the issue of concentration versus dispersion. There were numerous complaints that SCET

*Translations from francs to dollars are based on the assumption of 5 francs being roughly equivalent to 1 dollar.

and FNAT were in fact dispersing resources by sprinkling a large number of investments throughout the country. The adoption of the *coup par coup* policy reinforced these suspicions. The problem was particularly vexatious because of the government's ambivalent attitudes. It desired to help areas and communities in difficulties. But it sought, also, to increase the economic growth of the country and to speed up the modernization of France's economy and administrative procedures in anticipation of the competition as well as the benefits resulting from membership in the Common Market.

Almost needless to say, lack of staff and resources precluded systematic, long-term studies of the problems and development opportunities in different regions. The regional plans that had been produced were inventories rather than adequate analyses of problems and possibilities, and the physical plans were poorly related, if at all, to economic and social studies. Moreover, none of these plans contained any provisions for financing or implementation. A nagging suspicion remained that these inadequacies not only weakened what was done but also held up the creation of an effective national strategy for urban and regional development.

The Emergence of a National Urban Growth Strategy, 1960–1969

Innovations in Urban and Regional Organization

As a result of these criticisms, major efforts were made in the sixties to integrate area and national planning. These met with varying degrees of success. One change was in the procedure for preparing and reviewing local plans. Special teams or firms were employed to prepare these plans under the guidance of the départemental prefect and the mayors of the communities concerned. When completed they were reviewed by local officials, members of the chambers of commerce, and other interested public groups. Unlike earlier planning efforts,[67] the final versions of these plans included recommendations on priorities and timing of investments. These were then submitted to the appropriate committee of FDES. Its approval of the plans did not guarantee that they would in fact be carried out. But it did assure a more cooperative attitude on the part of the ministries and such financial agencies as FNAFU, and it enhanced the prospect of specific projects being included in the future public investment program budgets.[68]

Another change was the creation of the *Commissions Départementales d'Équipement* (CDE). These commissions, presided over by a prefect, included the head of the local council, one or several mayors of the département, and the départemental chiefs of various state agencies. Their main functions were to help local and state officials coordinate the various programs for community facilities within each département. They decided in effect which areas to "urbanize," where to build housing, and what schools and hospitals to construct. They also provided information and suggestions about these local programs when regional plans were being prepared by the regional prefect and the other organizations established for this purpose.[69]

Even more substantial changes occurred in the method of preparing regional plans.[70] The establishment of twenty-one program regions meant that development programs had to be worked out for all of these areas. This required the preparation of the National Plan with regional divisons *(tranches opératoires)* as well as with sectoral divisions. Moreover, to make the Plans operational, it was necessary to create mechanisms to program, to advise, to coordinate, and to implement them at the regional level. These needs led to several significant administrative innovations.

The first of these was the Conférence Interdépartementale. This body was set up in 1959 as a coordinating and implementing device for each of the various regional development programs. Subsequent decrees in 1960, 1961, and 1964 adapted the mechanism to the new programming role set for it by the Fourth Plan. Each regional branch of the *Conférence Administrative Régionale* (CAR), as it came to be called, included all of the prefects of the region, regional representatives of all the relevant national ministries, and the chairmen or directors of all public and quasi-public agencies in the region. The coordinating prefect (later known as the *Préfet de Région)* was the prefect of the département containing the capital city of the region. He served as the chairman and was specifically entrusted with coordinating and watchdog responsibilities for all interdépartemental matters. CAR had three specific functions: to prepare the prescribed studies of the regions, including the regional portions of the National Plan; to evaluate and recommend proposed public investment budgets for the region; and to provide progress reports each year on the execution of the Plan.[71]

Although representatives of the private sector could be invited to join the deliberations of CAR on a consultative basis, the Comités d'Expansion Economique seemed even more appropriate vehicles for such soundings. Their consultative role, therefore, was spelled out in a government circular and decree in 1961. But the amount of aid rendered by these committees proved to be quite uneven. In some cases, they "contributed valuable studies, pertinent observations and well founded suggestions."[72] In others, they did little more than act as difficult critics or obstreperous claimants. There was also concern about the representativeness of their membership. As a result, in 1964 a new regional consultative body, the *Commission de Développement Économique Régional* (CODER) was established.[73] Three-quarters of its members were nominated by the local councils of the region, by chambers of commerce, and by agricultural, union, and various professional organizations. The remainder, usually prominent citizens, were nominated by the Premier.[74]

The actual preparation of the regional portions of the National Plan came under the supervision of CGP, through its *Comité de Régionalisation du Plan* (CRP) (formerly known as Comité des Plans Régionaux) (see Figure 12). It furnished the Préfet de Région, CAR, and CODER with the text of the National Plan, the results of the manpower studies, and the regional capital investment budget. In turn, the Préfet de Région drew up a draft of the regional portion of the Plan, including estimates of costs and financing arrangements and recommendations for investment priorities and linkages. (He was helped in this task by the Commission Départementale d'Équipement [CDE] which, since 1965, was organized on a regional basis.) The Préfet's reports and those of CAR were then forwarded to Paris. Here the conflicts were arbitrated and the reports cast in final form by CRP, the relevant ministries, and ultimately the Comité Interministériel Pour les Problèmes d'Action Régionale et d'Aménagement du Territoire (CIPARAT). The latter, set up in 1960, was the equivalent at the national level of CAR at the regional level. Meeting every month, it dealt alternately with the regional problems of the nation and those of the Paris region.[75]

12. French Regional Planning Organization Chart
National, Regional, and Local Levels

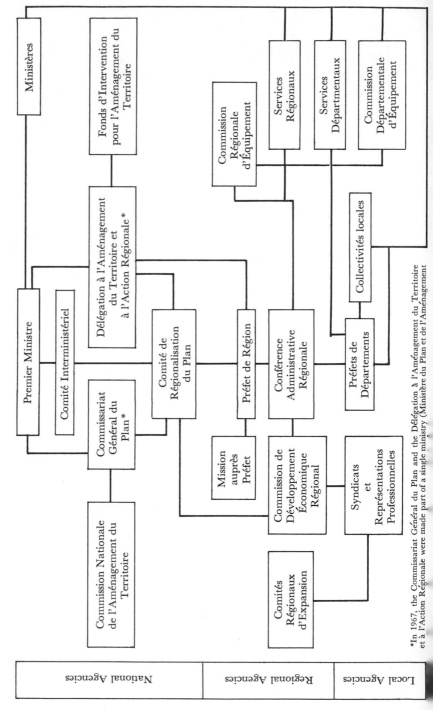

*In 1967, the Commissariat Général du Plan and the Délégation à l'Aménagement du Territoire et à l'Action Régionale were made part of a single ministry (Ministère du Plan et de l'Aménagement

Since neither CAR nor CODER could actually prepare the first drafts of the regional portions of the National Plan, the responsibility was formally assigned in 1964 to the Préfet de Région. For this purpose, he was given a special technical staff working in close liaison with regional representatives of the Ministry of Finance and of other ministries. To provide a direct link with the national planning system, the Premier appointed the Préfet de Région directly (other départemental prefects were appointed by the Minister of the Interior). Without doubt, the Préfet de Région was becoming a critical hinge in France's regional planning process.

Once the National Plan was approved, each Préfet de Région played a decisive executive role. He was kept informed by the national agencies of all proposed credits and projects for his region. Prefects within his region reported to him on the progress of all projects within their départements. In turn, he was expected, after consulting with CAR, to brief ministers on the status of their programs in his region and to exercise some discretion in the use of nonearmarked funds. Beyond these formal responsibilities, however, much depended on his personality and his conception of his role. For the future of the region was not assured; it was an ambiguous and rather arbitrary division, not a separate legal or corporate entity. What was accomplished by its head was to a very large extent a reflection of his zeal and charisma and his ability to get départemental prefects, other public officials, and key businessmen to accept the logic of and the need for the new administrative system.[76]

These administrative innovations fixed the basic pattern for regional programming in France. The new machinery set the procedures for periodic evaluations of the problems and development possibilities of the different regions. It provided for representation of different interests in the preparation of regional proposals. It also made possible the adaptation of national policies and programs to the differing requirements of regions and the arbitration of regional claims. But, what these innovations failed to do was to provide some mechanisms at the national level to formulate a unified strategy for regional development. In addition, there remained a need for an organization to help augment the staff of the Préfet de Région, to coordinate the regional programs of the various ministries at the national level, and to serve as a gadfly to stimulate action along desired lines. A similar mechanism appeared essential for the Paris region, too, since Paris figured so prominently in both national and regional development plans.

Innovations in National Organization

Largely to meet these requirements, the government in 1963 formed a parallel complex of organizations at the national level. By a not altogether surprising coincidence, the still inadequate coordination of physical and economic planning played a role in sparking these changes.

In 1962, at about the time that CGP was presenting the proposals later elaborated in the Fourth Plan to Parlement for discussion, the Conseil Supérieur of the Ministry of Construction proposed a twenty-year national program for urban and regional development.[77] Dealing with important and neglected aspects of national planning and emphasizing the country's major growth poles and axes, the study in substance was an elaboration of some of the ideas Claudius-Petit had propounded more than a decade earlier. It set forth desirable objectives and priorities for a more balanced system of cities and regions and the steps necessary to achieve these goals. Its recommendations were long-term and dealt primarily with urban and regional, rather than economic and social, development.

These proposals acutely embarrassed and vexed CGP. Its own activities in this area, despite a special effort to introduce regional dimensions into the Fourth Plan, were less sophisticated than the work of the Conseil Supérieur and its failure was mocked in Parlement.[78] CGP, thereupon, insisted on having responsibility for all basic long and medium-term studies and plans involving physical, economic, and social planning.[79] The government agreed. It promptly set up (in 1963) the *Commission Nationale de l'Aménagement du Territoire* (CNAT) to help CGP formulate a long-term strategy for urban and regional development and then simply transferred the Conseil Supérieur to CGP.[80] This decision balked once again the initiative of the Ministry of Construction and marked a further shift in power over development matters to CGP. On the other hand, CGP, to preserve its influence and authority, was literally forced to take more account of the long-range requirements and perspectives of urban and regional development.

During this period, to ensure better coordination and implementation, the government set up two new organizations to work with CGP under the direct authority of the Premier. One was the *Délégation à l'Aménagement du Territoire et à l'Action Régionale* (DATAR), which was established in February 1963. The other, created in August 1961, was the *Délégation au District de la Région de Paris* (DDRP) (see Figure 12).

DATAR was a coordination and expediting mechanism. Until 1967, its head was responsible directly to the Premier. DATAR's functions touched on almost every aspect of regional development. It promoted and maintained liaison with the regional agencies. It participated in the preparation of the National Plan, in the preparation of the regional public investment budgets, and in the evaluation of modifications proposed by the regional and national advisory councils. It presided over and provided secretariat services for the Groupe Central de Planification Urbaine (GCPU), an inter-ministerial committee of representatives of different ministries created in 1964 to deal with the problems of the principal metropolitan regions. It also provided similar services to CIPARAT, another key government committee responsible for formulating basic government policy on geographic issues.

DATAR was also responsible for the management of the *Fonds d'Intervention pour l'Aménagement du Territoire* (FIAT). The purpose of this fund, amounting to 1½ percent of the public investment budget (equivalent to about $40 million annually) was to help programs get underway or to overcome critical obstacles. Often it succeeded in promoting studies and projects in high priority development areas which might otherwise have been neglected.[81] DATAR had a small staff, but it could, if necessary, obtain assistance from other ministries and government agencies as well as from private consultant firms. The head of DATAR, the Délégué (or key members of his staff), was also a member of, or provided services for, several powerful interministerial committees or missions, including the powerful FDES. This enabled the Délégué to have a voice in all key decisions affecting regional development. These ranged from participation in regional development programs to the review of applications of firms seeking financial benefits for industrial decentralization and the shaping of policies governing the decentralization of various government, state-influenced, and private organizations. According to the text of the decrees which established DATAR, the Délégué only coordinated and expedited, but the text was vague and there were many officials who believed that the power which CGP had gained vis-à-vis the Ministry of Construction had been lost to DATAR.[82]

The office of the Délégué Général au District de la Région de Paris (DGDRP) was also new. The District[83] had been established in 1961 for the purpose of planning regional facilities until the three existing départements of the region were replaced by eight new départements. The Délégué Général, who was appointed by the Premier, was responsible for the relevant studies and development plans undertaken for this purpose. He also coordinated development in the region and administered programs. The district was governed by a board of twenty-eight (later increased to fifty-four) members, but the Délégué Général was the executive officer of this board.

In 1968 the eight départements were established, and the Délégué was also appointed Préfet of the Paris region.[84] As Préfet, although not in charge of a département, he was responsible for administering the economic development and territorial planning policies for the region. He helped to formulate the public investment program, to devise policies for transportation and urban development, and to coordinate public services. And, he was also in charge of the regional civil service, except for the departments of justice, police, and public education.

The powers of all these new organizations and offices were enhanced by the personal influence of their chiefs and the extensive use of the device of interlocking directorates. The first persons to direct DATAR and DDRP were close associates of the President of the Republic or the Premier. They spoke with the support of many influential associates who were members of their advisory committees. These factors—partly accidental, partly deliberate—strengthened the capacity of the new regional organisms to gain a hearing for their views in their confrontations with some of the older, more powerful ministries. But all of the new administrative machinery and personal influence would have been of little value if there had been no significant ideas to coordinate and implement. The provision of such ideas and strategies was to be the role of the Fourth and Fifth Plans and the Schéma Directeurs for Paris and other metropolitan areas.

Urban and Regional Policies of the Fourth Plan (1962–1965)

In contrast to previous Plans, the Fourth Plan tried to devise appropriate policies for all of the regions of France. This emphasis on comprehensiveness was a political necessity, but it also reflected the need to explore systematically the regional effects of national economic and development policies and of France's membership in the Common Market.

For purposes of simplification, a broad distinction was made between the growing and the less prosperous regions. For the growing regions, the Fourth Plan proposed complementary policies *(politique d'accompagnement)*. These were aimed at reinforcing desirable aspects of growth, curbing excesses or diseconomies, and correcting maladjustments caused by declining industries. For the less prosperous regions, the emphasis was on propulsive measures *(politique d'entraînement)*. These focussed on employment opportunities, which were closely related to disparities in levels of investment, cultural facilities, income, and migration patterns. The planners conceded that in some regions, such as those along the Atlantic coast or in the Southwest, there was an unsatisfactory equilibrium between employment needs and opportunities which was rooted in unacceptable levels of living. But they preferred to defer these special and difficult problems until the more detailed regional studies could give them a better idea of how to handle them. The Plan also made clear that the government did not intend to arrest the growth of the Paris region or to provide enough jobs in the lagging regions to curb the outflow of population. The aim rather was to slow down the "excessive" growth of Paris and the "excessive" migration of population from the provinces.[85]

Several means were counted upon to realize these objectives. Two of the most important of these were maximum "localization" of public investment (nearly half of the total investment was directly controlled by the Government) and the guidance of private investment through the location of infrastructure and the manipulation of incentive and control mechanisms. Other measures included clearer formulation of goals, technical studies, modifications of statistical reporting, relocation of government offices, and the working out of agreements with the Common Market countries.[86]

The Plan sketched out some of the specific kinds of policies and programs contemplated for the different regions. For Paris, it stressed the need for modernization and for decentralization of existing industries to the north and west, and also to the east, to Champagne in particular. There were also programs to develop university and cultural facilities and to shift certain government agencies to the ring of cities surrounding Paris: Amiens, Rouen, Le Mans, Orléans, Tours, Reims, and Troyes[87] (see Figure 13). Hoping to draw new industries to the North and extend the zone of influence of Dunkerque's new integrated steel development, the Plan pressed for the rapid completion of the Dunkerque-Valenciennes and Bauvin-Lille canals. In Bretagne, to encourage the further extension of the electronic and mechanical industries, new technical lycées and agricultural schools were planned as well as the creation of two new airlines connecting Brest and Lorient to Paris and Strasbourg and linking Nantes to Lyon and Marseille. The discovery of oil and natural gas deposits in the Pyrénées and the Aquitaine region and the decision to establish aerospace complexes there made Toulouse and Bordeaux logical centers for industrial and educational centers.

Two of the most dramatic regional improvement schemes involved river basins. One was the Lower Rhône-Languedoc program. Officially initiated in 1955 after much study, the principal aim was to tap water from the Rhône for a vast irrigation network which would free the region from a precarious vine culture suffering from the overproduction of a mediocre product. The agency created for this specific purpose was also authorized to help develop the entire region in general. It soon embarked on a vast range of studies and programs concerned with the improvement of the soil, the encouragement of fruit and vegetable production, the acquisition of land to remedy the problems of parcellization, the improvement of marketing facilities, and even the promotion of rural and urban-based industries.[88]

The other scheme was equally daring and far more controversial. It proposed to connect the Mediterranean to the North Sea through a system of canals linking the Rhine to the Rhône through Alsace and the Rhine to the Moselle through Lorraine. Similar canals were planned for the South. Subsequent studies disclosed the need for more adequate rail and highway facilities to parallel the canals. It was clear, however, that these investments, even if justified, would never receive the necessary support unless there were proposals for the Atlantic coastal regions and for the regions of the Center. As a result, plans were made to develop three transversal axes connecting the West with the East: in the South, the Center, and the North of France.[89]

These initial proposals were endorsed by the European Economic Community. But they produced divided reactions among differing ministries and within the Boulloche Commission which had been appointed to examine the ideas. The key issue was whether the probable traffic and even the future induced investments would support the costs. It was argued that other countries, such as Belgium and the United States, had encouraged decentralization by means of canals and improved transportation and that only by such bold policies could France loosen the stranglehold of Paris and improve the links between the eastern regions of the country and the economic centers of Europe. The government agreed that the improvements were desirable, but noted that there were other activities which also required support. Therefore, it decided to undertake the improvements segment by segment, as and when the economic justification of each stage became manifest.[90]

Subsequent Programming Innovations

Until the regional programs were worked out in detail, the planners could do little more than allude generally to the various things which might be done in the different regions and indicate how they fitted into a grand design of inducing or complementing growth throughout the nation. But wrestling with the problem of "regionalizing" the Plan prompted the improvement of the information system and the regionalization of the investment budget. It also led to some ingenious research tactics.

The most immediate need was for the organization of systematic background studies for the regional portions of the Plan. But the meager data and small size of the regions precluded any sophisticated economic analyses of the regions and so the studies dealt mainly with manpower and migration issues: with changes in the growth and composition of the population and labor; with the growth and decline of the main economic activities in rural and urban areas; and with the needed changes in policies and investments.[91]

However, to be made an integral part of the National Plan, the recommendations had to be converted into staged programs with estimated costs and investments for the different regions. The initial attempts to do this took place during the preparation of the Fifth Plan. The regionalization of the investment budget made it possible to raise questions concerning the balance of public investments within and between regions and to collect systematic information and indicators on regional development. Heretofore, budgets for the various state agencies had been examined in terms of a variety of criteria — scale, general programs, relative importance in relation to other programs — but never systematically for consistency or adequacy in terms of regional development.[92] Each ministry had pursued its own policy for regional allocations. But this was now at an end.

To be sure, regional budgeting was still crude and imperfect as an instrument for helping to weigh public investments. Many types of investments or credits could not be localized. Others were regionalized which should have been localized.[93] Criteria for the choice of investments among regions still varied from ministry to ministry and were somewhat vague and general. Often comparisons were not possible or easy to make because regional budget plans were based on the nomenclature of the National Plan, whereas the reports on execution followed standard budget classifications. In addition, although many ministries had only partially or recently regionalized their investment plans, the reports of others covered several years of operation.[94] Nonetheless, the staffs of CGP and DATAR were confident that the data would be sufficiently improved in the future so that Parlement, the ministries, and the planners would be able to evaluate the relative coherence and consistency of regional investments.[95]

An important feature of the new regional programs was the recognition that they would require a considerable investment in research. Fortunately, several organizations could be of assistance in this area. For more than a decade, the government had adopted a policy of encouraging the formation of public or quasi-public, fact-gathering research organizations such as the Institut National de la Statistique et des Études Économiques (INSEE), the Services des Études Économiques et Financières (SEEF), and the Centre de Recherche et de Documentation sur la Consommation (CREDOC). Faced with growing research needs, CGP and DATAR would simply farm out the necessary studies to some of these agencies. This was the procedure followed to obtain general data on population and migration trends. It was also employed to investigate a wide range of specialized topics: the structure and hierarchy of cities, urban-rural relationships in the different regions, and the implications for urban development which could be drawn from the reports submitted by the different Préfets des Régions.[96]

One of the most influential of these efforts was the long-term perspective study. This tool soon proved to be an indispensable means of checking and coordinating regional projections and policies for the nation and of setting targets for the growth of population and industry in Paris and the West. The methodology was relatively simple. First, the studies sketched the implications for three macro-sectors (industry, agriculture, and services) and for three macro-regions (the ten regions of the East, the ten regions of the West, and Paris). The regional distributions were derived from a projected total population of 60 million and a doubling of consumption. Although the studies proceeded initially on the basis of these crude, highly simplified categories, they were later refined for 28 sectors and then for 100 sectors. The aim in part was to arrive at more consistent projections of population for different regions by exploring the implications of explicit assumptions concerning the localization of economic activities, manpower requirements, and migration trends.

In the case of Paris, to cite one example, it was estimated that the population would increase from 8.5 million in the mid-sixties to 13 million by 1985. This was based on a population growth of 150,000 per year over the previous twenty years and of 135,000 per year between 1954 and 1962. Of this 135,000, approximately 50,000 represented natural increase and 85,000 in-migration. Even if in-migration were completely stopped, the population of Paris would still reach 11 million by 1985 based on these assumptions. It appeared unlikely, however, that such migration could be arrested entirely. This was clear from the studies of industrialization. The ten regions of the West had an estimated 25 percent of the existing industrial jobs in 1965. To stop the migration of its population over the next twenty years, the region would have to receive at least 60 percent of all new industrial jobs. This was simply not feasible, despite plans of the government to promote aeronautic activities in Toulouse, space industries in Bordeaux, and automobile, electrical, and electronics industries in Nantes-Saint Nazaire. Based on this information, it was decided that, for the five-year period of the Fifth Plan (1965-1969), the aim would be to induce at least 35 percent of the new industrial jobs to the West. This was expected to reduce migration by two-thirds. The target population for Paris was then adjusted to a minimum of 11.6 million with the likelihood that it might increase to 13 million or more if the effort to promote new jobs and development in other regions was not too successful.[97]

Meanwhile, a new Schéma Directeur for the region of Paris was prepared by the staff of the Délégué Général au District de la Région de Paris. The planners' studies had suggested that even if the Paris population did not exceed 11.6 million by 1985, there would still be a threefold increase in the requirements for space, housing, roads, parks, and other facilities in the region. Moreover, by the year 2000 the population might well be between 14 to 16 million, the actual figure depending in large measure on the government's success in reducing migration.[98] It was this anticipated need not only to decongest Paris but to accommodate an increase of about five to seven million inhabitants that led the technical staff to prepare the new Schéma Directeur. Published in June 1965, it proposed a variety of innovations for the Paris region: three regional railway express lines, ten principal radial highways plus secondary auto routes, three ring roads, the provision of essential utilities and community services in the outer areas, and a major effort to change the form of the city by stressing east-west linear travel networks and growth patterns to reduce the traffic bottlenecks created by the older system. The plan sought to relieve population pressures by accommodating families in the outer cities and in eight self-contained new towns, each serving about 300,000 to 500,000 people. The bulk of these ideas were incorporated in the Fifth Plan.[99]

The Schéma Directeur did not spell out costs, priorities, or means. But one measure of the staggering sums involved was that the estimated cost for the building of métros and highways alone ranged from 20 million to 100 million francs ($5 million to $20 million) per kilometer. Yet Paris had had no major improvements since 1929 and it was tremendously in arrears in comparison with other European capitals in providing for the needs of its population. Further delay, it was felt, would not make the costs any less expensive.[100]

Meanwhile in the North, the Northeast, and the Southeast of France, there were equally explosive pressures to provide housing, roads, industry, schools, and other urban facilities. Further studies indicated that these regions would require a wide range of essential infrastructure investments, only a small portion of which could actually be satisfied. This intensified the search for additional criteria to guide the location and priorities for those investments where the conventional indices and the play of politics still left some possibility of choice. Technical tools, such as input-output and cost benefit studies, were experimented with to explore complementary relationships and to gauge the comparative advantages of alternative investment possibilities. But these tools were hardly able to cope with many of the broader issues, let alone the more specific questions concerning the location of strategic transportation networks, the encouragement of industrial development in specific growth poles, investments in cultural and university facilities, and the selection of centers for the decentralization of government offices.[101]

Urban Growth Strategy of the Fifth Plan (1966–1969)

To confront these problems required more than a consensus on the vague development aims and sectoral priorities that were articulated in the Fourth Plan.[102] What was needed was a strategy for carrying out these programs in particular regions. The proposals of the Conseil Supérieur of the Ministry of Construction furnished some clues for such a strategy. Influenced by the notion of an ideal urban "armature," or hierarchy of cities, the Conseil suggested that the most effective way to handle France's regional growth problems was to build up *equilibrium metropolises* throughout France to balance the influence of the Paris region.[103] This answer appealed to key advisors and officials of DATAR and CGP, and they promptly embraced the doctrine officially in the Fifth Plan.

Although the idea of *métropoles d'équilibre* (equilibrium metropolises), was intriguing, it contained little that was actually new or surprising. The concern about the dominance of Paris and dearth of large cities in France in comparison with other European countries, and the emphasis on the encouragement of growth in other cities and regions to offset this dominance and to spur more effective industrialization and development elsewhere, were snippets of ideas that had been bruited about since the end of the war and even earlier. The real significance of the *métropoles d'équilibre* policy lay in its timing and its use, not in its originality. This was the first time that ideas on urban hierarchy were operationally linked to a national policy. And, it was the first time that the nature of the problems and the way the ideas were formulated made it possible for administrators and planners to sense how they could be used to guide resource allocation and to influence some of the most critical economic, social, and physical determinants of national development.

The first sharp articulation of the *métropole d'équilibre* idea was Hautreux and Rochefort's study of urban structure in 1964.[104] As its starting point it took the view of the French geographer, Pierre George, that in the past regions made cities but today cities made regions. The main concern of this study was to identify the principal metropolitan areas whose growth could be encouraged to offset the dominance of Paris. This was a refreshing change from the essentially fruitless inquiries of the past seeking to determine the optimum size of a city.[105] Hautreux and Rochefort took for granted that a large city offered numerous advantages and that it would be useful to devise a pragmatic measure of the most significant French cities and the potential areas of their influence. Four basic criteria were used for their selection: the size of the cities, the services they had evolved for economic activities; the special services or functions performed by the cities; and their zones of influence. Twenty or more indicators were employed to identify and to weigh these factors.[106]

Eight leading cities passed this screen: Marseille, Lyon, Toulouse, Bordeaux, Nantes, Nancy, Strasbourg, and Lille-Roubaix-Tourcoing (see Figure 13). The leading metropolises differed in size, in function, in physical form, in their needs, and in their range of influence. Some, like Marseille and Lyon, exercised extensive influence in their regions and on important secondary cities, such as Grenoble in the case of Lyon, and Nice and Montpellier in the case of Marseille. Other dominant cities, such as Toulouse and Bordeaux in the Southwest and Nantes in Bretagne, exerted their influence imperfectly, presumably because of inadequate facilities, services, and communication linkages within and outside the region. It was taken for granted that more extensive and detailed studies would be required to evaluate the varied problems and potentials of these metropolises. What Hautreux and Rochefort hoped, however, was that their investigations would provide the lead and the emphasis needed to guide national strategy for metropolitan and regional development. They hoped to bring about a concentration of effort to utilize most effectively the French government's limited resources. It was from these metropolitan areas, they argued, that a major influence could be exerted on their surrounding regions. Therefore, it was in these metropolitan areas and in their hinterlands that France's major studies and programs should be concentrated.[107]

The lucidity and simplicity with which the ideas were presented contributed to their appeal. The argument held out the possibility of developing a national strategy based on the needs of other regions while contributing to the solution of the problems facing Paris. It embraced all of France, yet suggested a limited number of metropolitan areas where action could be initiated with effects that would penetrate whole regions. The basic idea was easy to explain and to popularize and it was sufficiently general (and vague) to permit flexibility in adapting to criticisms or practical requirements. It satisfied all essential points: one could emphasize its "scientific" origins and its national, regional, urban, and rural dimensions. It provided a rationale for stress and sacrifice in resource allocation. It also satisfied diverse claims: the idea appealed to the provinces; it served Paris; it was presumably consistent with future urbanization trends; and, perhaps most important of all, it squared with what intellectuals and decision-makers in

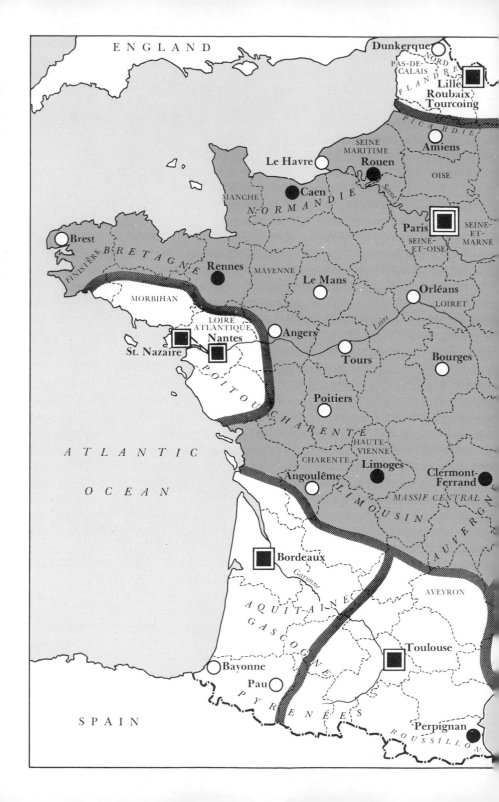

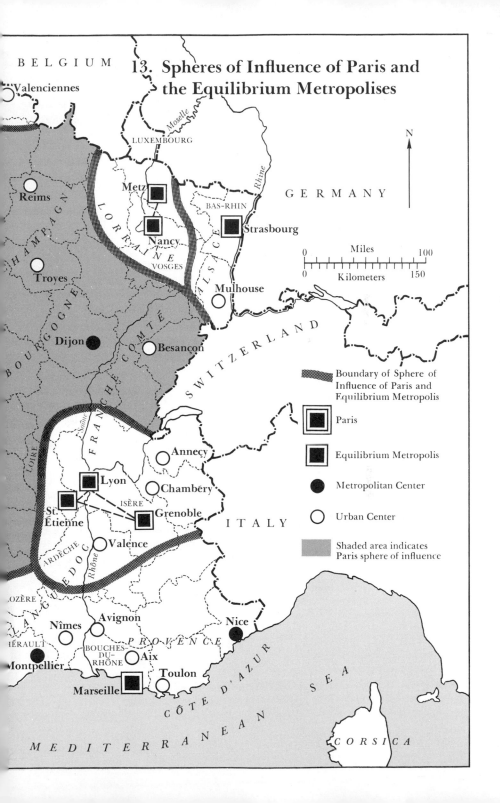

13. Spheres of Influence of Paris and the Equilibrium Metropolises

BELGIUM

Valenciennes

LUXEMBOURG

Moselle

GERMANY

N

Reims

CHAMPAGNE

LORRAINE

Metz

Nancy

Rhine

BAS-RHIN

Strasbourg

ALSACE

V O S G E S

Troyes

B O U R G O G N E

Mulhouse

0   Miles   100
├┼┼┼┼┼┼┼┼┼┼┤
0   Kilometers   150

Dijon

F R A N C H E   C O M T É

Besançon

S W I T Z E R L A N D

Saône

L O I R E

Annecy

Lyon

Chambéry

ISÈRE

St. Étienne

Grenoble

ITALY

A R D È C H E

L A N G U E D O C

Valence

Rhône

Boundary of Sphere of Influence of Paris and Equilibrium Metropolis

Paris

Equilibrium Metropolis

Metropolitan Center

Urban Center

Shaded area indicates Paris sphere of influence

LOZÈRE

Nîmes

Avignon

Nice

P R O V E N C E

HÉRAULT

Montpellier

BOUCHES-DU-RHÔNE

Aix

Toulon

C Ô T E   D' A Z U R

Marseille

S E A

M E D I T E R R A N E A N

C O R S I C A

Paris and the provinces thought the provinces required. It was not surprising, therefore, that the idea of *métropoles d'équilibre* was picked up by the administrative bodies and, with minor adjustments, adopted as the basic urban and regional strategy endorsed by the Fifth Plan.

The new doctrine furnished some fresh rhetoric for national planning and some new leads for regional programming. The basic territorial problem, the Fifth Plan emphasized, was the appropriate distribution of activities between Paris and the other urban agglomerations. Industrialization of the West was now to be encouraged principally in three major equilibrium metropolises: Nantes-Saint Nazaire, Bordeaux, and Toulouse. It was in these metropolises that general physical development proposals (Schéma Directeurs) were to be prepared; universities, government research establishments, and technical training institutes established or extended; and highway and air activity encouraged. It was in the hinterlands of these urban areas that major agricultural modernization and irrigation schemes were to be undertaken and major regional parks and recreational zones established. An equally impressive list of infrastructure improvements — roads, canals, port facilities, educational establishments, and urban renewal plans — were outlined for the East, in particular for the urban regions of Lille-Roubaix-Tourcoing, Strasbourg, Nancy-Metz, Lyon, and Marseille.

Since the Paris region was the most important growth pole, its needs for general modernization — for roads, schools, and housing and for the economic and social development of the existing and new cities within the region — were also sketched in as part of the Fifth Plan's efforts to deal with urban growth requirements.[108] But it was emphasized that one of the tasks of planning was to assess and impose true long-run social costs and to see that they were reflected in a more equitable price and tax policy which would discourage unnecessary location of families and firms in the Paris region. Some tentative targets were set to indicate the reversal of trends that was sought. Despite problems of housing, by 1970 the proportion of housing financed in the Paris region was to be less than the 27 percent of the total budgetary allocation for housing set in the Fourth Plan for 1965. Similarly, the proportion of total university students who would be admitted to the University of

Paris was to be reduced still further, from 33 percent in 1964 to 26.5 percent in 1973. The same policy applied to state investment in research. Under the Fourth Plan, 58 percent of the state's total investment in research went into the Paris region and Orléans, 22 percent into the ten next largest agglomerations, and 20 percent into the other larger cities. Under the Fifth Plan the aim was to change these proportions to 35–40 percent, 50–55 percent, and 10–15 percent respectively.[109]

Subsequent studies of urban growth targets tended to strengthen these resolves. By the year 2000, it was expected that the French population would increase by about 40 to 50 percent (from 46.2 million in 1962 to 65–70 million) and that the urban population would increase from 62 percent of France's population in 1962 to 75 to 80 percent of its population (from 28.7 million to 50–55 million). If so, the planners hoped that with their revised strategy the population of Paris might be limited to 14 million. This would be an increase of approximately 71 percent from its 1962 population of 8.2 million. They also hoped to increase the population of the equilibrium metropolises by more than 10 million (from 6.3 million to 16.5 million). In other words, the planners not only expected Paris to increase its population but to experience a percentage increase (from 18 percent to 20–22 percent) of its proportion of the total population. They did not consider it feasible to do more than to reduce the proportion of the population of Paris to the total urban population by about 1 to 3 percent. Even this effort, it was argued, would be a considerable achievement since it would involve a 162-percent-increase in the population of the equilibrium metropolises.[110]

Subsequent Legislative Innovations

But the revised strategy soon confronted the planners with a number of additional problems. Two obvious ones were how to expand local government boundaries and how to reduce land costs. Other, even more basic issues, such as the reform of local government and finance and the establishment of more local and regional autonomy, loomed on the horizon. None of these problems could be evaded for very long if the programs of the Fifth Plan were to be successfully implemented.

To deal with the problem of local government boundaries, the national government in 1966 passed a law to facilitate the enlargement of the jurisdictions of four of the metropolises: Lille, Lyon, Bordeaux, and Strasbourg.[111] Under this legislation, the older administrative units remained intact. The new boundaries simply enabled the urban communities to deal with the problems confronting the entire agglomeration (development plans, land reserves, urban transport, water, health, markets, lycées and colleges). The new boundaries could be established formally by decree if all the communities concerned approved of the proposed unification. Since this was most unlikely, the legislation provided that such a decree could also be passed by the national government in cases where two-thirds of the interested municipal councils representing at least half the population (or at least half the municipal councils representing at least two-thirds of the population) make a request for such a consolidation of boundaries. The methods prescribed could also be applied to other cities of 100,000 or more. In general, the proposal was greeted in many quarters as an important reform. Others, of course, denounced it either as a devious effort to undermine local self-government or as a dangerous instrument destined to change the power relationships of communities within the region. But, by September 1, 1969, Bordeaux, Lille, Strasbourg and Lyon had obtained the necessary approvals.[112]

At the end of 1967, the government also passed major legislation dealing with land policy. It required cities with populations of 50,000 or more[113] to arrange for multidisciplinary teams to prepare two types of urban plans: long-term Schéma Directeurs and land use plans. The Schéma Directeurs would be prepared by 1970 and would spell out for each of these cities basic goals, land use policies, major lines of physical development, and the staging of infrastructure investments. Following approval of these Schémas, the cities would prepare land use plans to implement these ideas. These had to be completed by 1971, for they would provide the legal authority for opposing any developments contrary to the agreed upon Schémas. The legislation also authorized municipal land reserves and arrangements for publicly financed research organizations to help prepare the plans. It changed the system of land taxation[114] and set new rules concerning commercial leasing and the rights and obligations of land owners and developers. Finally, the legislation placed heavy taxes on developments of excessive density and limitations on the sale of buildings belonging to local authorities and public agencies. As a result of this new legislation, some new revenue and development possibilities for cities were opened. Although, in the early years of implementation, action was sure to be blocked by shortages of technical staff, nonetheless, the legislation, if vigorously administered, could spur major changes in land use planning.

SOME UNRESOLVED PROBLEMS

It took more than a generation after the evolution of the national system of planning in France to evolve a parallel system for territorial planning with explicit policies for urban and regional development. By 1967, the interrelationships of the two programs had become so clear that both were made part of a single ministry, the *Ministère du Plan et de l'Aménagement du Territoire*, under a new head, the Ministre Délégué. By the mid-sixties, as well, the principal development aims had been articulated. In substance they called for: the decentralization of Paris, the industrialization of the West, the integration of regional and national planning, and the encouragement of modernization and new development through an increased focus on growth poles in the major metropolitan areas in the East, West, and around Paris.

Popular Acceptance?

Although the goals of the programs still left much to be desired, opposition was desultory. During the election campaigns of 1965 and 1966 and again during the summer of 1968, when the government's other major policies and programs were raked fore and aft, few objections were raised about its general goals of territorial development. This lack of criticism was not because the issues were regarded as unimportant. By the mid-sixties, interest in regional and metropolitan development had reached a high pitch. Articles on these matters filled the journals. Studies of urban and regional planning filled the bookstores. Urban and regional questions were constantly being debated by highly visible political figures ranging from the Premier to the local mayors, and councils. The issues evidently aroused concern but the debate focused mainly on inadequacies of execution.

One of the reasons for this apparent consensus was the absence of an acceptable set of alternative goals. Of the hypothetical alternative strategies, none appeared particularly feasible or attractive. One might favor, as some persons did, eliminating the restraints on Paris or paying less attention to the problems of the lagging regions.[115] But Parisians and non-Parisians alike felt that Paris had grown much too big. One might have gotten an attentive but limited hearing by urging that efforts be concentrated primarily on the lagging regions. But this would have implied penalizing the most populous and dynamic areas and inhibiting the competitive potentials and economic progress of the entire country (or drastically reducing the budget for military expenditures), and no responsible group was prepared to argue in these terms. Since most Frenchmen disliked big cities,[116] one might have pressed for goals stressing smaller urban centers. But small cities appeared incapable of competing with Paris for jobs or of providing the range and quality of services, cultural opportunities, and employment which the different regions desired. One might have argued in favor of a more flexible policy favoring medium as well as large cities and growing as well as lagging regions. But with France's limited resources this would have been tantamount to a return to no policy at all. Finally, one might have supported the development of only three or four key metropolises on the grounds that limited resources made it impossible to take on larger commitments. But this, too, was not feasible politically. Indeed, at the very outset of the program, the decision to promote only seven *métropoles d'équilibre* was upset by pressures which compelled the addition of Strasbourg. Even this judicious distribution of equilibrium metropolises to the appropriate corners and interior of France's vaunted "hexagon" was being beset by additional pressures to aid other growth poles such as Rennes, Rouen, Dunkerque and Grenoble.

Shortages and Conflicts

But if, in retrospect, the course taken seems to have been inevitable, so too do some of the problems encountered. Inescapably, there were the usual shortages of staff and of funds. There were simply not enough professionally trained specialists, particularly economists, urbanists, and urban sociologists, to deal with the new responsibilities. General engineers, architects, and social scientists were called upon to handle specialized assignments for which they were ill equipped on the basis of their professional training. The Institut d'Urbanisme had the only professional program for urbanism in all of France, and even this program hardly provided more than some finishing school training for architects in urban design. Despite some pioneering work by a few specialists, regional economics and urban sociology were in their infancy. Only in 1965 was a chair in "urbanisme" created at the Sorbonne.[117]

The problems of remedying the shortages were further exacerbated by bitter conflicts over professional status. Civil engineers occupied most of the urban and regional planning positions, and because of their limited qualifications, they were resented in many quarters. The political scientists, administrators, economists, and other social scientists responsible for developing and guiding the new policies in CGP and DATAR could barely conceal their contempt for the École des Beaux Arts and the Institut d'Urbanisme and for the architects and engineers in the Ministry of Construction and in the local communities.

Overlapping staffs and poor organization added to these difficulties. Some improvement occurred in 1966 and 1967 with the establishment of the Ministry of Equipment (which combined several government organizations including the former Ministry of Construction and the Ministry of Public Works) and with the linkage of DATAR and CGP. But the Ministry of the Interior still had some responsibilities for roads, water, sanitation, and maintenance as well as for a bureau for general urban studies and for urban equipment, all of which duplicated more or less similar functions in the Ministry of Equipment. There were also problems associated with the distribution of coordinating responsibilities among other ministries and agencies. In principle, CGP had overall responsibility for coordinating physical, economic, and social planning and for conducting medium and long-term urban and regional studies; DATAR was responsible for coordinating and expediting urban and regional projects throughout the relevant ministries; and the Ministry of Equipment was in charge of coordinating urban plans, land policy, and construction. In addition, there were many other ministries (Economics and Finance, Industry, Education, Health, and Interior) which had their own special interests and concerns with aspects of urban and regional development. One government seminar, after contrasting the administrative experience on these matters with the formal assignment of functions, concluded that although "apparently well defined, in reality the responsibilities [were] very tangled: duplications [were] frequent and [led] to numerous contradictions."[118]

The shortages and conflicts were not novel, but they took their toll. Because of shortages, the Bureau of Urban Development of the Ministry of Construction neglected its socio-economic studies of urban complexes and used its limited staff for more routine and immediate tasks relating to industrial zones. Because of shortages, the reports of the regional prefects betrayed serious uncertainties and gaps in basic information about their regions.[119] Again, because of shortages, many other elementary and essential technical studies were not conducted. Inadequate resources made it difficult in most cases to carry out effectively the studies in depth for cities and regions that Claudius-Petit had called for in 1950. This was even true for the Schéma Directeur of the region of Paris which was roundly criticized because it lacked really adequate economic and social studies of the region. By September 1969, however, many research organizations had been created or strengthened in order to assist the programs directed by DATAR, CGP, the Ministry of Equipment, and the more important metropolitan areas.[120] Nonetheless, there were still far too many neglected evaluations: of the aid available to firms moving to critical conversion zones compared to the actual costs entailed in making such moves; of the experience of firms that did move to these zones;[121] of the economic impact of past investments; of the types of activities that produced significant multiplier effects and of the conditions necessary to produce those effects—to cite only a few of the studies that were needed.

The shortage of resources also seriously hobbled efforts to limit and to reorganize the pattern of growth of Paris. Officials were loathe to bar development in Paris until alternative development areas were equipped with the necessary facilities and services. So, despite the Schéma Directeur, Paris as of September 1969 was still proceeding, as one top official sadly put it, as though there were no plan.

Other problems dogged the equilibrium metropolises. At the outset, as one might expect, there was controversy about the selection of equilibrium metropolises and about the relationships of these favored areas to others within the region. Almost any of the decisions taken were bound to embitter urban relationships; and indeed, in most of these areas, they did. The choice of Lyon, it was charged, favored the dominant city of the region to the disadvantage of several other fairly autonomous growing points: Annecy, St. Étienne, Chambéry, and particularly Grenoble. The resentment was moderated somewhat by including Grenoble and St. Étienne as key centers within the *métropole*. But as long as decisions were based on regional allocations and development strategy, such sensitive problems were inevitable.[122]

The same issue in different guise cropped up in the case of Nancy-Metz. Here, the initial notion was that because these two cities were within 50 kilometers of each other, they could and should be linked to from a major metropolitan complex with some basic common services and facilities. But for a long time the plausibility of the proposition was impaled by the facts. The local officials of these communities, proud of their independence and concerned with substantially different economic and political interests, were intransigently hostile to infringements of their authority and in no way wished to reverse the current tendency of the two cities to grow in opposite directions. Though frustrated by the conflict between Nancy and Metz and between these cities and the neighboring communities, the central authorities were reluctant to concede failure. After a series of reconnaissance studies, DATAR decided not to oppose the divergent growth trends. Instead, it agreed to help finance a Schéma Directeur to develop the basic policies for those joint needs on which there was a consensus, such as an airport, major industrial areas, and major infrastructure improvements including regular rail service between the two communities.[123]

There were other difficulties as well. The delay of several years in organizing missions for the other equilibrium metropolises caused much apprehension because Paris, despite its problems, was ahead in its plans and project proposals and inescapably had the advantage in the bidding for future resources.[124] In some quarters, there was also concern that too much emphasis was being placed on the programming of service and cultural activities and not enough on the analysis of the region's economy and on identification of the most appropriate propulsive activities. Still others were troubled by the prospects of success: some because of their objections to big cities; others because of their fears that communities and regions surrounding the equilibrium metropolises were destined to become "deserts" like the area around Paris.[125]

Decentralization

Another serious practical problem, growing out of inadequate resources, was the allocation of infrastructure investments. The aim was to avoid the frittering away of investments by focussing development on growth poles. But the large number of growth poles and the wide range of possible investments in and among the growth poles (not to mention outside of them) tended to produce a sprinkling effect nonetheless. Thus, the effort to provide some superhighways to extend routes of neighboring countries, to facilitate tourism, to connect major regions, and to relieve political pressures as well as the problems of metropolitan congestion led in fact to the building of small segments of highways in each region.[126] None extended very far within the region. None achieved significant interregional connections. None were likely to do so for some years at the current rate of highway development. Therefore, the impact of the investment, especially in the West, was necessarily marginal. The same failings characterized programs for industrial areas where the *coup par coup* policy effectively offset the policy of concentration. Inescapably, housing, community facilities, and other derivative programs took on a similar hue.

Somewhat the same problem appeared in relation to educational facilities. The stated objective was to draw such facilities to the regions because of their role in stimulating development and decentralization. The initial suggestion to shift about a dozen different schools to different universities in the provinces aroused serious controversy,[127] and a compromise was reached to curb the expansion of these schools in Paris and to finance expansions or new programs in other regions. The boldness of the original proposals and even that of the compromise was impressive. But effective teaching and research required close linkages of basic disciplines. It was far from certain that the desired quality could be ensured by strengthening one or two disciplines if the other fields were inadequate in quality and underfinanced.[128]

The industrial decentralization policy for Paris and for the lagging regions also wobbled along unevenly. The whole system of incentives had become fairly complex since the appearance of the first decree on this subject in 1954. The changes (in 1960, 1964, 1966, and 1967) were mainly in the rates and the flexibility of the system. Industrial development and industrial adaptation grants were substituted for the special equipment grants. The system of zones was also modified. But the basic methods of the system remained unchanged. The incentives varied according to the zone, the number of new jobs created, and whether a new or expanding firm was involved. The zones eligible for the most assistance were areas of high employment and areas which contained declining industries facing the threat of impending unemployment. The other zones were defined by the lack industralization, by the inadequate industrial diversification, and by the role of the region in relation to the effort to decongest Paris. The assistance ranged from direct subsidies (based on standard percentages of the invest ment) to allowances for removal expenses, for demolition of premises, and for vocational training. In appropriate cases, it was also possible to obtain direct loans with interest rate subsidies and first-year depreciation allowances of 25 percent. There might also be exemptions from business licenses; reductions of the cost of land, electricity, and utilities; lower transfer duties; allowance of the capital gains from the disposal of building; some limited assistance in obtaining housing for employees; and a variety of privileged financing procedures.[129]

Despite the changes, the performance of the system was still far from satisfactory. True, some progress was made. Between 1961 and 1966 the proportion of permits to build or expand industrial establishments in the Paris region dropped to 10 percent of the total permits compared to the 1955–1960 period when it was 23 percent. Somewhat similar proportions held for floor space and for estimated jobs created. This reduction appeared all the more significant because the rate of new industrial construction or expansion during this six-year period was more than double the rate prevailing during the previous decades. Also, the subsidies for decentralization provided during 1964 and 1965 rose from $15 million (76 million NF) to $18 million (91 million NF).

On the other hand, the number of subsidized decentralization operations from Paris dropped from an average of 270 since 1959 to 41 in 1964 to 16 in 1965; and the number of new subsidized enterprises in the provinces also dropped from 77 to 60. The result of all of this was the halving of new jobs in the provinces created by decentralization, a reduction from an average of 62,300 jobs per year for the years 1959 to 1963 to 37,500 jobs in 1964 and 26,500 in 1965. The blame for this drastic decline was rightly placed on the recession of 1964–65 induced by the government's stabilization measures, which had also produced industrial unemployment in Paris. There were even claims that the government was loathe to see the growth of Paris significantly arrested. But although these factors aggravated the situation, the fact remains that attractive subsidies were not provided.[130] From 1960 through 1967, the scale of annual subsidies for decentralization operations (covering industrial equipment costs until 1964 and industrial development and industrial adaptation grants after 1964) ranged from roughly $10 million (53 million NF) to $18 million (90 million NF). Direct FDES loans from 1961 through 1966 ranged from $360 thousand (1.8 million NF) to $12 million (60 million NF). Even taking into account other government subsidies, the sums spent on decentralization incentives were paltry.

To reverse these trends, the Minister of Economics proposed in mid-1966 to increase the amount of government-built factories available on a long-term lease, enlarge the role of the Regional Development Societies, enlist the help of national and private enterprises, and increase sixfold the amount of grant per employee and tenfold the amount of loans provided by FDES. But the political and economic crises in the next two years made it unlikely that these efforts would prove successful, at least in the short run. Available evidence in 1969 appeared to bear out this view.

Although the number of subsidized enterprises rose to 240 in 1966, 250 in 1967, and 340 in 1968, the number of new jobs was still very low, approximating 28,500, in 1968.[131] These discouraging trends, and the fact that the amount of aid provided by France was much lower than government aid in Britain or Italy,[132] led DATAR to discuss the need for more generous assistance.

The growth trends of tertiary activities also exceeded plans and expectations. Of approximately 8 million tertiary jobs in France in 1962, more than 2 million, or approximately 27 percent, were in the Paris region. According to the Fifth Plan, this proportion was supposed to increase only slightly by 1970, by about 1 percent. But the latest data indicated that 35 percent of the new tertiary jobs created between 1962 and 1970 would be in the region of Paris. This was not only because of inadequacies in the communications system and in facilities elsewhere, but because of the needs and attractions of Paris and because of defects in the system of controls and incentives. The government decided, therefore, to tighten the regulations on expansion of tertiary activities in Paris and to provide some incentives to encourage the location of research and similar activities in the *métropoles d'équilibre.* It is much too early to judge the effects of these measures however.[133]

The only consolation those responsible for the decentralization policy could draw from the data was that, without efforts to encourage location elsewhere, there would have been even more "spontaneous growth" in the Paris region. But the hard fact was that "in 1954, 17% of the French population was concentrated in the Paris region, in 1967, 19%."[134] This was another reason why in October 1967 the government decided to impose strict controls, including tax penalties, on all new or expanded building of more than 3000 square meters in the region of Paris. It also decided to provide grants ranging from 5 percent to 15 percent, and even 20 percent in exceptional cases, of the total investment in plant and equipment to firms, or branches of firms, locating in designated areas in the provinces.[135] The designated areas included the eight equilibrium metropolises, the cities of Brest and Aix-en-Province, and the seven capital cities outside the Paris basin (Limoges, Poitiers, Clermont-Ferrand, Dijon, Besançon, Rennes, and Montpellier), plus some of their surrounding areas. But the grants did not in any way favor the lagging regions in relation to the expanding regional metropolises in the East. Given the way the grants were made available, moreover, there was a real danger that the bulk of assistance would go to marginal firms or to those which would have expanded anyway in the designated areas.

About a year later, however, a different trend appeared in the offing. Provisional results of the census taken early in 1968 indicated that the population of Paris was then 9,240,000, a growth of 770,000 persons since 1962.[136] This was about one-third less than the 1,150,000 increase expected for the period. The figures pleased but puzzled the planners, for they were uncertain whether the smaller increase was due to a reduction in migration from the provinces, an outmigration of some of the foreign population living on the outskirts of Paris, or simply errors in estimating the "floating" population.

CONCLUDING OBSERVATIONS

1. Many misgivings have arisen over the new regional institutions. The Fourth Plan, it will be recalled, stressed the importance of drawing up adequate programs for all of the regions of the country, not just the lagging ones. The creation of twenty-one program regions for the National Plan and the reorganization of the territorial subdivisions of the ministries and other government agencies presumably consolidated this new perspective. Nonetheless, after ten years of operation, the new program regions have not increased their power. Despite the vast reorganization which this reform has brought about, many persons are convinced that the current regional boundaries are unsatisfactory and may have to be changed again. Local leaders feel little or no loyalty to their program region; neither do the members of CODER who charge that Paris is simply consulting with its regional representative, the Préfet de Région. And, with the exception of the imaginative Schéma Directeur for the lower Seine and some current plans for Nord and Marseille, few truly regional projects have yet emerged. Loyalty to the département remains strong and perhaps has even been intensified, and the interests of the département continue to shape basic attitudes. Change is always a threat to

existing interests, but the threat in this case has been reinforced by the special status of the key figure, the Préfet de
Région, who is identified with "the central power" and with
the interests of the region's capital city, rather than with the
public interest of the entire region. In the future, the Préfet de
Région might be disassociated from a particular département
as has been done in Paris. But there is a widespread conviction
that a Préfet without a département might be a Préfet without
power, unless the functions of the départements and regions
were drastically reorganized.[137]

Attitudes might change radically if the regions and key
groups within the region were given real power: if, for example, the people of the region or the urban and rural authorities were permitted to elect the councils of the region and
if the councils had significant planning, development, and
revenue-raising powers. Such a reform was urged for several
years by the Gaullist opposition, but met with only lukewarm
or negative responses prior to the revolutionary disturbances of
May 27, 1968.[138]

After June of that year, however, the widespread support of
the idea of more participation persuaded the government to
propose a major regional reform involving the creation of
regional assemblies to decide on programs and budgets for
development within their regions. The government's proposal,
however, provided for very limited autonomy, at least at the
outset. The Préfet de Region would no longer be limited to a
département, but he would be an executive officer. Revenues
would come mainly from loans or central government grants.
And the members of the assemblies would include elected
representatives to Parlement plus delegates nominated by various labor, business, agricultural, and professional organizations,
and representatives elected by municipal and départemental
councils. But this proposal was coupled with a less popular
reform measure, the elimination of the Senate as the upper
house of Parlement and the creation of a new national council,
consisting of representatives of the regional assemblies. The
new council was to have only consultative functions and would
deal only with economic and social questions. The two
proposals had to be accepted or rejected by a single vote in the

211

referendum held in April 1969. Although they were rejected, it is generally believed that the former—with all its limitations—might well have been approved if it were voted on alone. Be that as it may, the negative vote led the De Gaulle government to resign. However, the new government which was elected in May 1969 asserted that the regional autonomy measure would be reintroduced as soon as conditions appeared "appropriate" for such action.

But if such a change occurs in the future, as appears likely, then some account may have to be taken of the fact that the program region is really too small for analytical purposes[139] and not effectively integrated with the basic development strategy. Some of the program regions have already begun to cooperate for analytical and other purposes. The difficulties have betrayed themselves, also, in the frequent resort to different regional groupings. Thus, for the statistical purposes of the European Economic Community, there are nine socio-economic regions; for general economic discussions the emphasis is usually on three regions (East, West, and Paris or growth regions, lagging regions, and zones of renovation and expansion); and from the point of view of the equilibrium metropolises, there are nine regions. Still other regional subdivisions are required for specific resource development programs such as the North-South internal waterways axis or the Languedoc-Rousillon agricultural and littoral improvement schemes. In one sense, the issue is inherently frustrating because no single set of boundaries is likely to serve all the different interests or programs. But few persons now have any doubt that, for programming purposes, the number of regions can be substantially reduced and yet serve more effectively the needs of analysis and ensure a higher quality of regional staff members.

2. A smaller number of regions, however, would not necessarily cure the growing discrepancies between the avowed growth strategies. It has been virtually impossible to finance at the same time the new towns proposed for Paris in its Schéma Directeur, the expansion of cities in the Paris Basin advocated

by the inter-ministerial group concerned with the problems of this region (GIABP), and the growth of eight equilibrium metropolises—not to mention the secondary cities within these agglomerations or other growing points such as Rennes and Dunkerque—proposed in the Fifth Plan. It is not surprising, therefore, that despite efforts to redress the regional balance, the Paris region will have absorbed "half of the [investment] for national urban equipment during the period of the Fifth Plan." [140] And, while the Paris region may have begun to "free itself of its state of underequipment," [141] it appears to be doing so at the price of a "sprinkling effect" in most of the other regions.

3. One of the more complex issues of the future is how to deal with the effects of the Common Market on the various urban regions. Those near Switzerland, the Low Countries, and Germany are competing with cities in these other countries for the location of branch plants. Some of them also face increasingly acute jurisdictional problems growing out of population movements and the provision of essential public services (water, sewage facilities, transportation, and housing). A number of these issues have already engaged the attention of the European Economic Community. In addition, membership in the Common Market has increased the tendencies of the French government to regard Paris as the political center of the European community and the leading location for headquarter firms from Europe and the United States. It has therefore felt obliged to support vigorous measures to correct the congestion as well as the inadequate and obsolete facilities of the Paris region.

At the same time, the metropolitan areas of the West and the South have been especially disadvantaged by the relative growth of and competition from the more favored regions (including those in other countries) and by the absence of adequate highway, railway, and waterway connections with other regions. This is all the more serious because these lagging regions are the regions most distant from the principal concentrations of population and income. Unfortunately, the em-

213

phasis of the French government on a policy of proceeding only with "economic" investments in effect has consigned many of the proposed infrastructure developments for the West to the end of the queue.[142]

In the short run, it appears that efforts to reduce the lag between the advanced and the poorer regions will have to contend with the Common Market as a new and powerful obstacle. The problem is of concern to all of the Common Market countries and there is a clear need to do something about it. Largely for this reason, the European Economic Community took the initiative in organizing a conference on regional economies in December 1961. The conclusion of this conference was that a regional development policy was essential for the balanced growth of western Europe.[143] But as of September 1969, little has been done at a European level to formulate or carry out such a policy.

4. Though the boat, as one official put it, is not yet moving in the right direction, it is definitely turning. Despite problems and inadequacies, available indices — tax returns, holdings of savings, energy consumption, migration trends, construction permits, new industrial jobs — do indicate a relative improvement in the West. Standards of living and number of industrial jobs have risen in the West in comparison to the rest of France, particularly during the period from 1960 to 1968.[144]

Surely some credit for this improvement is due to the fact that in France, more than in any other western country, the planners have faced up frankly to the need for linking economic and urban planning on the national scale. They have experimented with new approaches and new institutions and they have made many innovations during the past generation. The basic area development policies have progressed from a focus on physical planning, decentralization, and ad hoc regional programs to a national system of economic, social, and regional planning.[145] Leadership has shifted from a sector agency, the Ministry of Construction, to three national development agencies (DATAR, CGP, and FDES). This is a reflection of the broadened conception and scope of urban and regional development in France and of the direct intervention of the Premier's office and administrative organs.

The French planners have gone beyond decentralization and are experimenting with an explicit national strategy for urban development. To be sure, they are still seeking to promote the development of the peripheral areas by such traditional means as encouraging the movement of industry and tertiary activities, particularly the transfer of different government agencies and selected professional, technical, and vocational schools to key metropolitan areas in the provinces. But they are also improving communications between and within these regions and are organizing intelligence services for guiding the growth of these areas. And they are seeking to modernize the agricultural hinterlands, partly by extending the range of urban effects throughout entire regions.

Still other mechanisms, in addition to incentives, controls and infrastructure allocations, are being adapted to serve these objectives. French planners have pioneered in the regionalization of budget planning and reporting of their public investment programs.[146] They have had some success in changing the approach to land use planning and in extending the boundaries of several major metropolitan areas. The government has created (and is still creating) new organizations to modernize information and research systems in order to carry out necessary urban and regional programs. It is making strenuous efforts to modernize the system of education for professional specialists in the field.[147] The planners have also persuaded the government in 1969 to try to counter the influence of Paris by authorizing DATAR to coordinate and to integrate the major regional development programs and policies for the rest of France in the form of a Schéma Directeur.[148] Moreover, the current ideas and machinery are still regarded as provisional hypotheses which are likely to be improved over time. These, surely, are no small accomplishments.

5. Nonetheless, the basic strategy seems unlikely to be successful, or far less likely to be successful, because of the extraordinary centralization of French society which in turn is reinforced by the concentration of both the political and social capital and the dominant economic center in the same region. These relationships will not be changed easily. Indeed, the prospects for change would appear even more unattractive were it not for

the ironical fact that "the central power" now appears to have decided to confront the problem of "the central power." Recognizing the difficulties created by its own influence, France's national government has deliberately campaigned to establish more autonomous regional authorities. If this innovation in France's institutional system comes to pass, it will doubtless contribute to more local initiative and more strongly supported regional development programs. But even relatively autonomous regions cannot do more than slow down or arrest centralizing tendencies, as the experience of the United States has suggested.

In these circumstances, what may be needed is a decisive as well as symbolic reinforcement of the government's efforts to decentralize its power. Unfortunately, the most obvious and daring possibility, a shift in the location of the capital, is the least likely to occur. It is the most obvious measure because the central government is the one "industry" that could draw a large portion of the elite from Paris; and it is the one major growth industry which could be located in the Center, the South, or the West and not be disadvantaged vis-à-vis the Common Market. Paris would still remain the leading metropolis of France and might eventually become the capital of the European Union. This move, coupled with more local and regional autonomy and fiscal reforms such as block grants to cities and regions, would lend credence to the ideal to which everyone in power now gives lip service: the need to provide the nation with more opportunities to participate in basic decisions.

One could go on exploring in more detail all sorts of intriguing nuances and implications if such a possibility were at all practicable. But to mention such a move, even as a remote hypothetical possibility, sounds too absurd, too much like the kind of suggestion only someone alien to the traditions and attitudes of the country would presume to propose. And, this being so, the French nation seems condemned to roll its stone uphill for a long time to come.

The Quest to Save the
Central City: The Experience
of the United States

A century ago, the cities of New England and the Middle Atlantic states formed the dominant urban hierarchy in the United States. Today, the country has four widely dispersed urban regions concentrated in urban axes along the coastal perimeter of the country[1] (see Figure 14). Each of these vast agglomerations of population and economic activity—now popularly known as megalopolis—extends hundreds of miles in length and encompasses loosely linked metropolitan areas containing aggregate populations of 5 to 45 million people. Although the United States, unlike Britain and France, has made no effort to curb this growth, in recent years two facets of this development pattern have provoked concern and remedial measures on a national scale. One was the emergence of depressed areas outside of the urban regions, especially in the South. The other was the plight of the central cities within the metropolitan regions. Both types of areas had high fertility rates and relatively low per capita incomes. Both had high rates of unemployment and underemployment. Both were experiencing net losses of jobs and population, and both suffered from limited skills, lack of capital, and difficulties of adaptation.

As was the case in France and Britain, few persons at first saw the interdependence of these problems or their solutions. Two autonomous federal programs were created in the decades following World War II. One, labeled *area development*, tried to help almost any and all hard pressed localities to devise economic development proposals and training projects to cope with unemployment. The other, called *urban redevelopment*, sought to reduce the costs of acquiring and clearing blighted areas of the central city. Both hoped to stem the outmigration of, and to attract, revenue-producing activities. But before long it became clear that the area development policies were ineffectual, especially in providing jobs and other opportunities for substantial proportions of the black population in the South; and it became equally obvious that the brunt of the burden of the urban redevelopment programs was falling on the low-income, nonwhite families which were increasing substantially as a result of migration from the South.

Mounting criticisms led to changes in policies. Instead of scattering assistance among a great many communities, the government decided to encourage economic growth in a few designated urban growth centers in the lagging regions. But this approach could obtain only limited backing, for in the United States, perhaps more than anywhere else, decisive votes might hang in the balance if subsidies and other assistance were not distributed liberally. Meanwhile, in the metropolitan areas, growing resistance made the high-handed, bulldozer tactics of urban redevelopment less practicable. The rediscovery of the poor in the 1960's also contributed to a change in tactics. Some policy makers began to put more emphasis on rehabilitation than on slum clearance. Others began to view the needs of the poor in a different way, worrying more about jobs and better education and welfare programs and less about improvements in physical conditions. Still other officials, troubled by the financial and growth problems faced by the suburbs, thought the solution lay in metropolitan planning and controls; and so legislation was passed providing federal help to finance extensive public works and other facilities needed by suburban communities.

Throughout this period, black migration which was mainly to the central cities of the North and West, dropped steadily—from 160,000 a year in the forties to 95,000 a year from 1960 to 1965, to 80,000 a year in the next two years; and census officials believed that statistics for 1967 and 1968 would reveal an even sharper drop. However, more than half the black population of 12 million persons still lived in the South, so that the potential for the renewal of migration was still substantial.

At the same time, largely because of crime and riots as well as higher costs and other problems, the movement of the white population out of the central cities accelerated sharply, rising from 140,000 a year before 1966 to a half million a year between 1966 and 1968.[2] An equally significant movement was the increasing number of jobs being located in the outer areas of the metropolis, a trend that was likely to continue for some time to come. It was predicted that most of the growth in employment during the next generation would occur in suburbs outside the central city, raising the outer areas' share of total metropolitan employment to three-fourths. These trends—plus the growth and concentration of the nonwhite population in poverty neighborhoods in central cities and the restrictions on their settlement in the surrounding suburbs—created enormous problems for the cities and their underprivileged residents.

This movement of firms and families out of the central city is now proceeding on such a scale that the problem has become, depending on whether the point of view is urban redevelopment or area development, either how to get them to stay or how to get them to move to more socially desirable locations. On their own, the lagging regions are scarcely able to entice them; and the central cities, hobbled by meager revenues, mounting welfare and social problems, rising costs, and higher tax rates, cannot keep them.

This evolution of events has made the urban problem the most important issue in the United States—next to war and peace. Any reservations on this score were decisively dispelled by the explosions of discontent of the black population in the mid-sixties which cast doubt on all the customary "solutions" and underlined

219

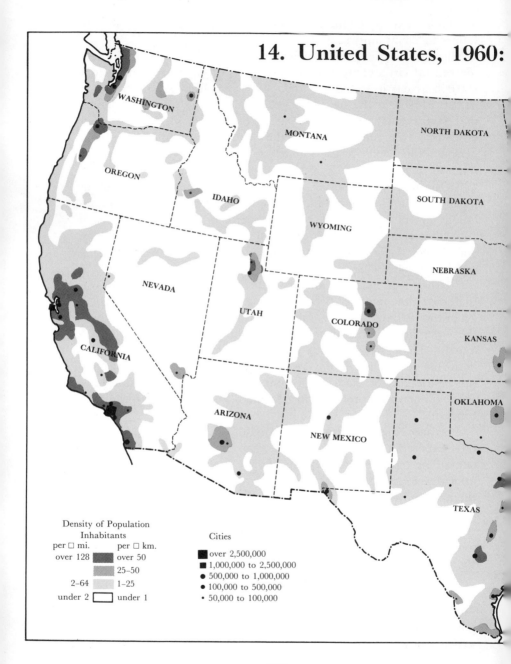

14. United States, 1960:

Density of Population
Inhabitants
per □ mi.   per □ km.
over 128   over 50
   25–50
2–64   1–25
under 2 □   under 1

Cities
■ over 2,500,000
■ 1,000,000 to 2,500,000
● 500,000 to 1,000,000
● 100,000 to 500,000
• 50,000 to 100,000

Density of Population and Cities Over 50,000

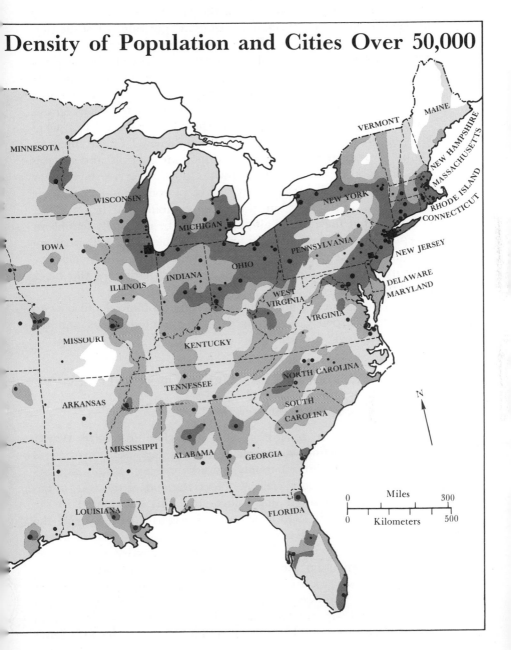

MINNESOTA

VERMONT · MAINE

NEW HAMPSHIRE

MASSACHUSETTS

WISCONSIN

NEW YORK

RHODE ISLAND

CONNECTICUT

MICHIGAN

IOWA

NEW JERSEY

OHIO

PENNSYLVANIA

ILLINOIS · INDIANA

DELAWARE

WEST VIRGINIA

MARYLAND

VIRGINIA

MISSOURI

KENTUCKY

NORTH CAROLINA

TENNESSEE

ARKANSAS

SOUTH CAROLINA

MISSISSIPPI · ALABAMA · GEORGIA

N

LOUISIANA

FLORIDA

0	Miles	300
0	Kilometers	500

the fact that the most ominous of the lagging regions was indeed the central city. The "shock of recognition" growing out of the riots has forced a reappraisal of the assumptions underlying current policies. Clearly, the role of Washington is critical, for only the federal government has the necessary leverage via its grants for housing, transportation, welfare, education, community facilities, and public works, not to mention the unrestricted block grants which it is on the verge of giving to the cities or states.[3] But, what kind of strategy should these grants implement? Ought they attempt to weaken resistance to metropolitan controls and services and pry suburbs open for the nonwhite population, or should they try to transform the central city? Most persons would favor some combination of the two; but, if so, what combination? It is possible, of course, that none of the alternatives will be politically feasible or acceptable. And, even if they are practicable, they still may not accomplish their purposes unless they are accompanied by effective measures to stem the inundation of central cities by the black population.

With these issues in mind, let us examine in more detail how an urban growth policy has evolved in the United States and the options which lie ahead.

DEPRESSED AREAS AND URBAN GROWTH POLICY

Prelude to Area Development Legislation

It was almost a generation after the close of World War II before decisive action was taken to aid the depressed areas. Until 1960, the problem attracted only sporadic interest, usually as a by-product of some greater concern. Near the end of the war, attention became riveted on unemployment. This culminated in the Employment Act of 1946 which established as a national goal the policy of creating full employment. The continued rise of unemployment in specific areas prompted proposals such as the Economic Expansion Act of 1949 to help retrain and relocate unemployed workers and to promote preferential policies and other assistance for depressed areas. But interest in the subject, having been sparked by the recession of the forties, dwindled with economic recovery in 1950. Even as late as 1955, the President's

Council of Economic Advisors shunned action on the grounds that these problems had to be dealt with locally.[4]

In 1954 the Democratic Party captured control of Congress. Their leaders quickly opened fire on the Council's attitude. Senator Douglas, Chairman of the Joint Economic Committee, advocated the adoption of several measures: the establishment of a building program to improve the infrastructure and public services of communities with high unemployment; the creation of a federally supported industrial development corporation to supply inexpensive long-term credit to firms locating or expanding in these areas; the expansion of unemployment insurance coupled with measures for occupational retraining; and federal technical assistance for community planning of remedial measures. A bill incorporating these ideas was drafted in 1955 by Senator Douglas and others. To gain additional political support, the bill also extended aid to low-income rural areas.[5]

Despite this maneuver, the prospects for this legislation were dim. For, during periods of prosperity, there was little interest in the problem; and when unemployment was widespread, there was reluctance to allocate special resources for the poorest areas. Opponents felt these "bleeding heart" measures would simply shore up marginal economies and marginal firms and draw jobs away from other areas; instead, they preferred retraining measures and subsistence allowances to bring workers to new jobs.

Then, in 1956, largely because of increases in the already high levels of chronic unemployment in the depressed areas, the Council of Economic Advisors changed its position. Shortly thereafter, the Eisenhower administration introduced a bill which provided for a 50 million dollar revolving loan fund to assist new or expanding firms in depressed areas. But both this bill and the one introduced by Senator Douglas were killed by the House Rules Committee. The same legislation came before Congress in 1957. Again, the bills were unable to muster support. With the recession of 1957, however, interest in combating general unemployment was renewed. But, to the dismay of those who favored emphasizing the needs of the depressed areas, an attempt was made to substitute for their legislation a measure providing 2 billion dollars for the construction of community facilities *throughout* the country. After prolonged efforts and much maneuvering, the supporters of the

Douglas bill were finally able to get their proposals through Congress—only to have the legislation vetoed. The features of the bill that President Eisenhower most objected to were: the 100 percent grants for public facilities, the loosely drawn eligibility criteria, the provision of assistance for rural areas, the failure to require adequate local participation for industrial and commercial loans, and the assignment of the program to the Housing and Home Finance Agency (HHFA) instead of to the more conservative Department of Commerce.

This veto became a major issue in the 1958 Congressional campaign. It was even partly responsible for the subsequent Democratic landslide, since there were mainly Democratic victories in the depressed areas. Legislation was reintroduced at the next session of Congress, but, although trimmed down substantially in the scale of assistance offered, it was blocked once again by a Presidential veto on the same grounds as before.

By 1960, the issue had become prominent enough to play a role in the election of John F. Kennedy. The new President had long been a firm supporter of aid to depressed areas. In 1956 he had steered the original Douglas bill through the Senate. In 1955 he had sponsored a version of the Trade Adjustment Act which contained some of the provisions of the bill Senator Douglas had introduced toward the closing days of the 84th Congress. Kennedy was familiar with the depressed areas of Massachusetts, and the crucial primary campaign waged throughout West Virginia—one of the poorest states in the country—had profoundly sensitized him to the plight of families trapped in such environments. During the campaign, Kennedy pledged that, if elected, aid for depressed areas would receive first priority. Such legislation was, in fact, the first recommendation he submitted to the new Congress. It was quickly passed in 1961 and differed from the original Douglas bill in only one major respect. The program was assigned to a new agency, the *Area Redevelopment Administration* (ARA), within the Department of Commerce, with the expectation that both the Administrator of the program and the new Secretary of Commerce could be counted on to back it vigorously.

It had been a long struggle, lasting over five years, but now a bill to help the depressed areas had been enacted. Unfortunately, during that five-year period, the economic conditions that the bill was supposed to ameliorate had not stood still.

> When the Senate approved the Douglas bill in 1956, 21 of the nation's 149 labor-market areas averaged an unemployment rate in excess of 6 percent, which the Department of Labor classifies as 'substantial labor-surplus' areas. In 1958, the . . . number of substantial labor surplus areas rose to 69. . . . When Congress finally approved the bill during the recession of 1961, two out of every three labor-market areas had unemployment above 6 per cent.[6]

Surely, the ARA would have its job cut out for it.

The Initial Area Redevelopment Policy

ARA was made responsible for deciding on area designations and grants of loans and subsidies and for administrating all redevelopment programs. But the budget and the legislation kept the size of ARA's staff small. Whenever practicable, therefore, ARA delegated key responsibilities to other agencies, such as the Department of Agriculture, the Community Facilities Administration of HHFA, the Small Business Administration, the Department of Labor, the Department of Health, Education and Welfare, and the Office of Indian Affairs.

The new agency was given 150 million dollars for inexpensive business loans.[7] These could be used to assist any businesses that ARA wished, provided that there was a reasonable assurance of repayment. To avoid charges of "pirating," the legislation limited the loans that could be made available to firms which were not relocating from other areas or to firms whose expansion would not increase "unemployment in the area of original location or in any other area where such entity conducts business operations"[8] These provisions restricted the loans largely to new activities or to firms establishing branch plants and to industries which were not operating below capacity or likely to operate below capacity because of growth prospects.

ARA was also given funds for the construction of public facilities: 100 million dollars for loans and 75 million dollars for grants. The grants could range up to 100 percent of cost. ARA had to be satisfied, however, that the projects could not be carried out without such assistance and that the communities involved were contributing to the cost to the extent that they were able to do so.[9] The legislation required the communities to assess their future prospects, partly because the public facilities and training programs were supposed to be evaluated on the basis of these analyses. These assessments would be used in the preparation of an Overall Economic Development Program (OEDP), describing the main activities and trends of the area and its opportunities and problems. ARA was also allocated about 7 million dollars for technical assistance. Some of this money was used for studies and plans of regions such as the Upper Peninsular area of Michigan and Appalachia.[10] But most of the funds were spent on feasibility studies.

In 1962 ARA acquired responsibility for administering the Public Works Acceleration Act.[11] This was a short-term, anti-recession measure, effective until June 30, 1964. It provided 900 million dollars for public works. Grants were limited to 75 percent of project costs and no more than 10 percent of the funds could be spent in any one state. The main aim of this measure was speedy generation of the maximum number of jobs in the greatest number of areas suffering from unemployment. More than 900 areas obtained projects; three-fourths of these were already ARA areas.

The new program betrayed many weaknesses. Some were teething difficulties such as getting experienced staff, working out relationships with other departments and agencies, defining the areas and activities to be assisted, developing techniques for economic background studies, and starting useful backup research programs. But there were more serious limitations as well. These were the result not only of a superficial grasp of the problems confronting ARA, but of the difficulties involved in attempting to serve a large number of poor communities without a clear strategy.

When the legislation was first introduced, about 19 major labor market areas and 50 smaller industrial areas were intended to benefit from the program. President Kennedy, however, thought the bill should also provide assistance for some 200 communities with stagnating economies. As part of the general effort to generate Congressional support, the criteria for eligibility were further relaxed.[12] Eventually, the final version of the bill contained a clause which requested ARA "to distribute the projects widely among the several States . . . in order that actual experience with this program may be had in as many States and in as many areas and under as many circumstances as possible."[13] Congress wanted to provide assistance for as many of the poorer communities with surplus labor as possible, not just the neediest; and ARA wanted Congressional support. Therefore, all of the designated areas were made equally eligible. After two years of operation, the number of eligible areas exceeded 1,000, and these areas were distributed throughout the United States.

The result was a scattering of resources over a large number of relatively small projects. Only 40 percent of total loan funds during the early years "were invested in areas with unemployment double or more the national average in 1961";[14] more than 25 percent of loan funds went to areas "where the unemployment rates were less than 1.5 times the national average . . . and where the median income was at least 80 percent of the national average."[15] During the first two years, about six out of every 10 loans were below $350,000. One out of every eight designated areas received an ARA business loan, and, of these, almost two out of three were smaller areas with labor forces of less than 15,000.[16] Roughly the same proportions held for loans and grants made for public facilities. About two-thirds of the projects and investments made were allocated to smaller urban areas and rural communities with populations of less than 50,000.[17]

In other ways, too, the policy of scatter made a mockery of the aim of strengthening the local economy instead of merely adding another marginal firm or two to the list of local activities. Presumably, the purpose of compiling an OEDP was to attract firms which could capitalize on the resources and location of the community. But most of the communities lacked the necessary knowledge and experience, not to mention faith in the outcome of such exercises. They required help if their OEDP's were not to degenerate into a routine filling out of forms to satisfy the federal "bureaucrats." However, ARA's staff was small, overburdened, and often unfamiliar with the problems of all these local communities. They were in no position to help in the preparation of these analyses or to monitor carefully the contents. ARA could not even object to flagrantly inadequate documents without raising a

227

hornet's nest. In some cases, other organizations, such as state planning agencies, provided some assistance. But in general, communities had to work out their own programs, sometimes with the aid of private consultants.[18]

The Public Works and Economic Development Act of 1965

Despite the difficulties which were besetting the fledgling program, ARA's main aims were in line with the goals set by President Johnson for his administration. Therefore, rather than eliminating the program, an attempt was made to modify the workings of ARA through the passage of the *Public Works and Economic Development Act* in August 1965. As an expression of administrative confidence, appropriations for ARA were more than doubled and its staff was increased by 150 percent. In addition, ARA was given a new name — the *Economic Development Administration* (EDA).[19]

The most important legislative changes in relation to urban growth policy were in the definition and organization of the areas which might receive assistance. The new act set up larger districts and regions and reduced the number of designated areas. Equally significant was the conscious attempt to devise a general development strategy. The administrators tried to persuade Congress that economic assistance was most effective "in areas which [were] in relatively better economic health."[20] A strategy based on a comparatively small number of urban growth centers was considered the key to spurring desired effects throughout an entire region.

The smallest planning unit under the 1965 Act was still the *redevelopment area.* There had to be at least one such area in each state.[21] To be eligible for assistance, an area had to have substantial and persistent unemployment and either median family incomes not greater than 40 percent of the national median or a substantial loss of population due to lack of employment opportunities.[22] An area might also qualify for aid if it was experiencing severe economic distress (for example, an Indian reservation) or an unusual and abrupt rise in unemployment (approximately 50 percent above the national rate) because of the closing or threatened closing of a major employment source. Finally, areas with substantial unemployment, averaging 6 percent or more during the preceding calendar year, could also receive help even if not otherwise qualified.[23]

The multi-county *Economic Development District* (EDD) was the intermediate unit in this system (see Figure 15). A micro-regional organization, EDD was to serve as the basic unit for planning the growth of a lagging area within a state. Like the redevelopment area, it was responsible for preparing an OEDP and it could obtain financial assistance from EDA for planning, organization, and staff. Each EDD had to include at least two redevelopment areas and an urban center of less than 250,000 people. The choice of an urban center was critical. For it

> had to have sufficient population, resources, public facilities, industry and commercial services to ensure that its development [could] become relatively self-sustaining [and] . . . that its growth [would] help alleviate distress in the redevelopment areas.[24]

To supplement these smaller units, the 1965 legislation also provided for the establishment of *regional planning commissions* for redevelopment regions involving several states. In addition to the regional commission for Appalachia which was set up under separate legislation (the Appalachian Regional Development Act of 1965), regional commissions were established for the Ozarks, the Four Corners area of the Southwest, the upper Great Lakes, New England, and Alaska.[25] The jurisdictions of the commissions were larger than those of the other administrative units but the jobs were essentially the same: to evaluate the best investment and implementation strategies for their regions,[26] and to utilize effectively the technical assistance and economic studies made available to them through EDA.[27]

Although EDA's dominant concern remained the depressed region, nonetheless, spurred by the Watts riot in 1965, it also began to deal with poverty areas in the big cities. It undertook an experiment in Oakland, California to provide 3,250 jobs for the hard-core unemployed. EDA furnished approximately 9 million dollars in loans and 14 million dollars in grants to the port and city of Oakland to assist in the construction of a marine terminal, new hangar facilities at the airport, a thirty-acre industrial park,

15. Regions, Districts and Redevelopment Areas

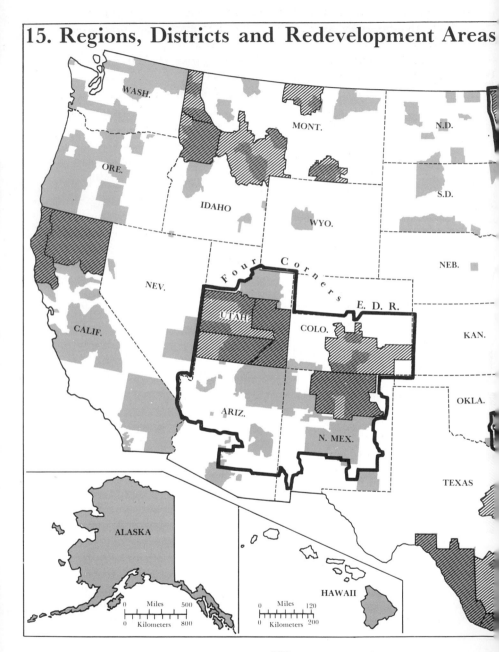

of the Economic Development Administration, 1968

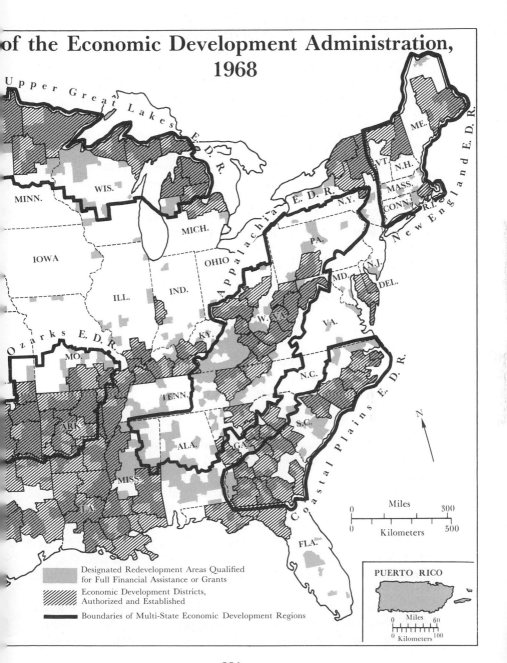

Designated Redevelopment Areas Qualified for Full Financial Assistance or Grants

Economic Development Districts, Authorized and Established

Boundaries of Multi-State Economic Development Regions

PUERTO RICO

and a four-lane highway. Employers who received EDA business loans or who leased or acquired property developed with EDA loans or grants were asked to specify how they proposed to provide "employment opportunities for the long term unemployed in Oakland, with training where needed."[28] EDA also worked with the Departments of Labor and of Health, Education, and Welfare to set up a job training program.[29]

EDA soon discovered — as did similar government agencies in other countries which had to grapple with these problems — that there were few experts in the field of area development. EDA, therefore, tried to encourage the training of area specialists, and it financed some research on job creation strategies and ways in which federal policy could help lagging areas. It also urged its regional commissions to press for more federal spending in their regions and to recommend the most effective deployment of federal expenditures made available to them. It began to raise some timid questions, such as "why the federal government [had] not developed criteria for the geographic distribution of its investment expenditure. . . ." or why the "impact on regional economic development [was] not a major consideration in many grant-in-aid programs."[30] Finally, it not only examined appropriate national policies for regional development, it even began to discuss building new cities or expanding existing ones.

Evaluation of ARA–EDA's Progress

ARA–EDA learned some elementary lessons quickly. The inability to deal effectively with depressed areas on a county basis had led in a relatively short time to the creation of larger planning jurisdictions: the multicounty district and the multistate region. The central city had been identified as a lagging region for which the tools of the 1965 act might be used. In addition, ARA–EDA had begun to accumulate evidence designed to persuade Congress that "separate and unrelated projects" did not work and that jobs could not "be brought to every village and hamlet in the United States."[31]

Nonetheless, the operations of ARA–EDA were less effective than they might have been. Benefit cost studies showed returns ranging from 12 dollars to 24 dollars for each dollar invested in

ARA–EDA's loan program.[32] Preliminary surveys also indicated that 182 jobs were created for each million dollars of loan assistance, or about 36,000 jobs on approximately 200 million dollars in loans. This proportion would be respectable enough were it not offset by evidence that a substantial proportion of the labor force in assisted firms was not really the "disadvantaged" target population. In addition, the scale of the program was still trivial in relation to need.

There were similar failings in the training programs. From 1961 to 1968, the average annual enrollment in training programs was only about 170,000.[33] The training, . . . left much to be desired. Most of the emphasis was still too local: "It train[ed] people for jobs in their areas where jobs [were] short and low skilled and low paying."[34] In addition, efforts to design appropriate training courses were hampered because of too few surveys and projections of desirable jobs and skills. Weaknesses in this aspect of ARA–EDA's program were particularly unfortunate, for benefit cost ratios suggested that the social returns from training projects were high, perhaps on the order of 10 dollars to 12 dollars for every dollar invested.

Nor did the new approach of EDA prove a smashing success. Although the strategy required the concentration of private and public investments, technical assistance, and training programs either in significant growth centers or within their zones of influence,[35] the pressures favoring dispersal of investments were still strong and there was also much support for a "worst-first" emphasis. The forceful application of the urban growth center concept was also weakened by the ambiguity of the notion of growth centers and of the criteria for their selection. As of March 31, 1969, 68 EDD's with about 88 growth centers had been established; their median populations were small: 181,000 for the EDD's and 38,000 for the growth centers (see Figure 15). It was obvious that the policy of scatter still ruled. Additional evidence of this was the fact that

> . . . 125 loans approved by EDA through June 30, 1967 [had] been dispersed to 104 counties. The only instance in which individual loans appear[ed] to have been geographically coordinated to any substantial degree was in the unique case of Oakland, California where seven individual projects [had] been approved.[36]

233

And, as of February 1, 1969, there were over 828 designated and funded redevelopment areas, although EDA believed that it could effectively help only 300 to 400 each year[37] (see Figure 15).

Another problem was the poorly defined relationships between planning and implementation mechanisms. The jurisdiction of the redevelopment areas, the EDD's, and the regional commissions overlapped, and the basis for resolving conflicts in development policies was obscure. The various limitations placed on the organizations made them better able to discuss problems than to act on them. The redevelopment areas had to show evidence of broad community agreement on what was to be done. The policy or advisory committees of the EDD's had to contain elected officials from every major city in the district and all major interests including business, labor, agriculture, and minority groups. Before the regional commissions could take any actions, they needed the approval of a majority of the Governors and of the co-chairman appointed by the President. Even if imaginative plans were agreed upon, there were no adequate instruments, either public or private, to organize and promote development in the proposed growth poles. Neither the EDD's nor the regional planning commissions could substitute for the vigorous, aggressive, public or private corporations needed to carry out these programs.

Perhaps the most serious difficulty of all was the inability of policy makers to attack the problems of the most critical areas— the metropolitan regions. EDA was unable to extend aid to more than a handful of cities because the definition of a redevelopment area was still based on the existence of high unemployment *throughout* a city or county; this definition "unfortunately excluded most cities, where high employment in the business and industrial districts balanced low employment in the ghettos."[38] Oakland, which had a high unemployment rate for the whole city, was one of the few exceptions.

Nor was EDA able to come to grips with the issues raised by the migration of the black population from the South and the growth of ghettoes in the central cities. The failure to stress the interdependence of these issues led to EDA's neglect of what might have been one of its most important responsibilities, the transformation of the economy of the nation's most critical lagging region—the deep South. It was the South's lack of attractive prospects for the black worker—in agriculture and in the southern cities—which accounted for the black inundation into Washington, D. C., Cleveland, Chicago's South Side, Watts, Oakland, Harlem, and elsewhere. For, although southern cities offered opportunities to the whites who left rural areas during the 1950's, "Negroes concentrated in the slowest growing and most discriminatory states of the deep South showed no major gains to offset the almost 400 thousand jobs lost in agriculture." [39]

Some 3.7 million nonwhites left the South between 1940 and 1966. As a result of this migration, by the end of the sixties there were about 14.2 million nonwhites living in non-southern cities of 250,000 to one million, and another 2½ million in cities of one million or larger. In comparison with 1940, the number of blacks living in the South had been reduced by one-third; in the North, the number of blacks had almost doubled; and in the West (which had had only one percent of the total black population in 1940), the increase had been eightfold. [40] Yet, despite this vast migration, about 12 million nonwhites or 53 percent of the total black population still lived in the South, half of them in non-metropolitan areas, and three-fifths of these families in poverty or near-poverty conditions. The bulk of the migrants to the metropolitan areas of the North and West moved into the poverty neighborhoods of the central cities, neighborhoods which contained one-fifth of the nation's unemployed and two million of its underemployed (laborers either working full time, but receiving a poverty wage, or involuntarily working part-time). [41]

Only a national development strategy—one designed to create new economic and social opportunities for the nonwhite population in growth centers in the South as well as in the central city ghettoes of the North and the West—could hope to cope with this situation. But, as the experience of ARA–EDA illustrated, the prospects for a well designed strategy were hardly encouraging.

HOUSING AND URBAN GROWTH POLICY

Broadening Housing Perspectives

If the recognition of the need to concentrate efforts on urban growth centers marked a major step forward for ARA–EDA, an equally decisive broadening of perspectives occurred in the evolution of U.S. urban policies. During the 1930's, when New Dealers were exploring all sorts of direct and indirect ways to provide jobs and to solve problems of economic insecurity, almost nothing was done in the field of urban policy. The National Resources Planning Board came closest to the subject by publishing some perceptive studies.[42] The first of these, *Regional Factors in National Planning,* appeared in 1935 and was followed in 1937 by *Our Cities,* the first synoptic view of national urban trends, and in 1939 by *Urban Planning and Land Policies.* These studies, although reflecting slight shifts in doctrinal currents, were essentially pulse-taking essays. No changes in *national* urban policies or programs resulted from them; nor did their recommendations deflect any of the existing programs of the central government in the direction of a national policy for urban development.

To be sure, some tangential legislation and some activities in the 1930's significantly affected urban physical development. The Home Loan Bank System (HLBS), a mortgage credit reserve modeled on the Federal Reserve System, was created in 1932 to back up savings and loan institutions. Then, in 1934, the government set up the Federal Housing Administration, (FHA) an agency which insured loans on homes made by savings and commercial banks and insurance companies. Despite some inconsistencies and conflicts, these two legislative innovations provided powerful support for the building of homes for middle-income families, especially suburban tract developments of single-family houses by large builders. A low-rent public housing program was also initiated which made it possible to serve a minuscule number of poor families. But none of these efforts (including the related road building and public works programs) had an urban focus, though some were destined to add greatly to the complicated problems of the city. There were also some quasi-utopian experiments involving subsistence homesteads and three experimental greenbelt towns. But these activities, too, left little or no direct trace on subsequent policy.

In the thirties, the critical question was how to put idle resources to work. Aside from manipulating fiscal and tax policies, the remedies were to build housing, parks, roads, and other public works. To the extent that there was any thinking about the city as a whole, the emphasis was on fiscal problems and on economical operation rather than on development. Urban questions were of marginal interest then, except perhaps to a small number of professional specialists.

The first major proposal for national action on urban development was made in 1941.[43] It called for the central government to help cities buy and redevelop the blighted portions of their central areas. At the time, little appeared likely to come of the idea, for the country's energies were focussed elsewhere. But the war was bringing about a radical change in perspectives. Suddenly, the question was how to use to the utmost the existing resources of the local community: to achieve the most intensive utilization of the existing stock of housing for families of all income levels; to take maximum advantage of the transportation system; and to program the minimum amount of new public and private housing and community facilities to sustain the defense effort. At the war's end, when new policies and programs came up for consideration, it was these problems which led administrators to think naturally in terms of more comprehensive approaches to housing and urban redevelopment.

The new ideas appeared reasonable enough. The aim was to have a single agency for housing and home finance, not a medley of independent programs. It seemed sensible to look at the total housing market and to determine which segments could be effectively served by private builders and which could not be served (or served adequately) unless there were special inducements or direct building by the government. This was substantially the way local and national analyses of housing needs had been handled during the war years.

Soon after the testimony of the top administrators of the National Housing Agency to the Senate's Subcommittee on Housing and Urban Redevelopment in 1945, the administration introduced omnibus legislation designed to meet the varying housing requirements of middle, moderate, and low-income families. There were provisions for farm housing, for housing research, and for improvements in the system of mortgage credit and in the system of insurance of housing loans made by finance institutions. There was even a version of the 1941 proposal to encourage the redevelopment of central areas which called for loans and grants to reduce the high costs of land in blighted areas to feasible reuse values. Unfortunately, these apparently bland legislative proposals, initially sponsored on a bipartisan basis by Senators Wagner, Ellender, and Taft, resulted in virulent controversy which ended only with the enactment of the 1949 Housing Act four years later.

Perhaps the most striking aspect of the struggle was its narrow focus on the issue of housing. One reason for this exceptional interest was the postwar housing shortage. Another was the intense opposition to the public housing features of the legislation and to the establishment of a permanent national housing agency which would incorporate two previously independent and competitive agencies, the Federal Housing Administration and the Home Loan Bank System.[44] But on the question of urban redevelopment, attitudes had not yet hardened. There were some technical questions, some skepticism in some quarters, and some anticipation elsewhere, but little serious opposition. On the whole, the disposition of Congress was to try out the new ideas on urban redevelopment, provided that the program took account of planning considerations and of the relocation requirements of displaced families. As for the proponents of public housing, they tended to regard urban redevelopment as a "sweetener," as a means of reducing some of the opposition to public housing or to a unified housing agency.

Despite the furor raised by the omnibus legislation, one has only to think in terms of the city—or in terms of employment, education, transportation, and welfare—to see how limited, in fact, the comprehensive approach was. Even from a housing perspective, powers were limited. The administrator of the new Housing and Home Finance Agency (HHFA) could only coordinate the constituent agencies (FHA, PHA, URA, and HLBS), which were still, to a considerable extent, independent. The legislation, moreover, put its emphasis primarily on new housing and on clearance and rebuilding in central areas, not on ways and means of improving the existing stock of housing or on more efficient or attractive patterns of growth in the suburbs.

Even the urban redevelopment program was restricted in several ways. The program was confined to areas involving either predominantly residential land uses before redevelopment or land uses which were to be developed or redeveloped for predominantly residential purposes. Advocates of the redevelopment program opposed this restriction. But strong objections to their views were voiced by powerful backers of the legislation—especially Senator

Taft, who was willing to support legislation assisting housing and relieving poverty, but only to the extent that it served these aims and not the economic or aesthetic betterment of cities. HHFA could not even take advantage of an apparent loophole which authorized the development of projects on open land for predominantly residential uses necessary for sound community growth. Although the language of the legislation in effect permitted the building of New Towns, satellite communities, and even public housing, HHFA felt constrained by the Congressional debates and agreements during the passage of the act to limit this provision only to housing programmed "as an adjunct to slum clearance projects in the community."[45]

The New Urban Emphasis

Over the next two decades, however, the focus shifted from housing to the problems of the central city, and then to the relationships between the central city and the suburbs, and finally to the seething resentment of the ghettoes which involved all of these issues and more. The transformation came about gradually, but in retrospect it was a striking one.

What largely generated the shift in issues was the movement of firms and families to the suburbs. Though most economic activities were moored to the metropolis because of the markets and diverse resources and facilities available, the outer areas offered distinct advantages: modern buildings, more space, reduced taxes, and less congestion. The mushrooming of defense and war plants during the forties was only the prelude of what was to come. The sustained growth of the economy after the war, coupled with increasing obstacles to expansion in the central areas, simply accelerated these trends.[46]

Family movements followed the same patterns, partly in response to the relocation of jobs and partly because of the new forces influencing the building of homes. *Unintentionally*, the reforms of the thirties had created powerful national pressures favoring suburban development. The creation of a national home mortgage system and the insurance of the residential loans of financial institutions had revolutionized mortgage financing. The effects were not felt in the thirties, a period of depression and insecurity, in which the desire (and ability) to marry, to invest, to buy, and to build were all inhibited. But when the economy surged ahead in the 1940's, incomes rose, marriages increased, and families sought more space. The effect of these trends on housing was compounded by ingenious changes in financing terms: negligible down payments, and low monthly outlays due to lengthy amortization periods and low interest rates. Housing shortages transformed the slump in real estate into a seller's market. Attitudes toward building and investment changed; and these changes soon disclosed the extraordinary expansionary potentials of the new institutions. The alluring prospects attracted new firms into the field and also led the Levitt's and the Rouse's and many other house-builders to expand their organizations and to specialize in large-tract development at the outskirts of the built-up areas of the city. The upsurge of building activity eventually blunted the edge of the housing shortage for middle-income families and made it easy for them to move from the central cities to the outer areas of the metropolis.

But the reforms of the thirties did not solve the housing problems of low and moderate-income families, especially those of the nonwhite population. Private builders were not interested in serving them; and public housing was too insignificant in amount, too forbidding in appearance, and too hemmed in with legislative, physical, and social limitations to be of much utility. Most of the suburban communities did not want poor, and especially nonwhite, families; they blocked their entry, directly or indirectly, with zoning and other restrictions. Yet, more than 70 percent of the families displaced by urban redevelopment projects were nonwhite.[47] Fortunately, housing conditions in the inner city did improve for some of these families because, with the steady exodus to the suburbs, more and more apartments and homes became available. There was also a significant improvement in the quality of the stock of existing housing because higher incomes during the decade from 1950 to 1960 and in the years that followed enabled owners to make long-needed repairs. But population was increasing and so was the migration of the nonwhite population to the city. Thus, there were more nonwhite families in absolute numbers occupying more of the inner areas; and a good deal of the older, good-quality houses were either barred to nonwhite families or, for price and other reasons, were not especially suitable for them.[48]

What it all added up to was that the central cities, and the surrounding areas in the inner core, faced competitive disadvantages in relation to the outer areas. As a result, the central cities were losing a significant segment of their economic base and a large proportion of their upper and middle-income families. They were becoming the habitat largely of "contact-oriented firms," certain specialized business and consumer services, a variety of small industries getting their start, single persons, young families without children, older families, the very rich, and the very poor. Their costs in general and their burden of social services in particular were soaring. Their tax rates were rising and their capacity to raise funds was hemmed in by their limited tax powers and their constricted boundaries. And their deteriorating physical environments jeopardized their principal source of revenue, the property tax.[49] It was these cumulative, aggravating, self-reinforcing trends that caused the deflection of national policy away from the issue of housing—both generally and for middle-income families—to a concern for central cities and the population within these cities.

Urban Redevelopment

There were a number of ways the federal government could react to the problems facing the central city. It could do nothing and simply let the trends work themselves out. It could try fiscal reform, such as supplementing the local revenue system through federal collection and distribution of taxes on the basis of some agreed upon formula. It could attempt to improve public services: schools, transportation, recreation and community facilities, as well as housing. Or it could try to raise income by such transfer payments as a negative income tax, family allowances, or rent subsidies. It could also adopt some combination of these remedies.

To do nothing was impossible; the mood of the nation dictated some "positive" action. But only one or two of the possible approaches received serious consideration in the decade following the end of the war. The others were ignored, for reasons that we can only guess at in retrospect. Fiscal reform was considered too difficult. Family allowances and the negative income tax were not in vogue and not immediately relevant to the problem as it was then described. Rent subsidies, it was feared, would line the pockets of slum landlords and create inflationary and racial pressures. Improved schools and transportation were either not considered or did not appear to be critical variables—let alone systems that could be easily or appropriately manipulated to serve these ends. One must also recall that though the urban problem had been "sighted," it had not as yet acquired vast public significance. Under these circumstances, a complete national commitment to radical reform of the central city would have been surprising, indeed.

But just how narrow the approach selected actually was can best be seen by an examination of the "comprehensive" housing legislation of 1949. Its main concern was how to improve the competitive position of the central city and its basic answer was physical redevelopment. The immediate objective was to clear large areas of slums and blight, using the eminent domain power in accordance with some general land use plan. Federal short-term loans were to finance the undertaking; and capital grants (two-thirds federal and one-third local[50]) were to reduce the high land values to levels justified by the new uses. Redevelopment areas would have to be large enough to maintain their character and to produce a physical setting appealing enough to attract suburban families or those that were contemplating leaving the city. Although non-residential activities might be introduced into the area, the intent of Congress was that these areas should be predominantly residential before clearance, or at least afterwards.

Narrow as it may now appear, this urban redevelopment section of the 1949 housing legislation was the first national policy to deal explicitly with the city. And, it was the first major piece of legislation to take a position in favor of the central city. But there was no effort made to relate it to, or to modify, any of the other federal programs, such as FHA insurance, which implicitly favored the suburbs. Moreover, in the process of implementation, the new policy soon disclosed a number of flaws.[51] Most cities had no general land use plans or very inadequate ones. Knowledge of new uses to replace the old ones was skimpy. There was a shortage of competent city planners. Clearance of a few small areas merely created little oases in an ocean of blight. There were few multiplier or demonstration effects in other areas. Most serious of all, the clearance programs reduced the already inadequate supply of low and moderate-rent housing and substituted in its place relatively high-rent units or buildings for altogether new uses. Not enough equivalent accommodations were provided; and the pressures on poor families were intensified by the shortage of inexpensive housing to serve the additional low-income population resulting from natural increase and migration. Worse still, the clearance programs often rooted out minorities, particularly black families, who had the greatest difficulty in finding other places to live. In some localities, the tools of the program were used intentionally to serve these disreputable purposes.

The Shift to Urban Renewal

The gaps and limitations of the 1949 Housing Act led to corrective efforts. The first important legislative change came in 1954 and was based on the recommendations of President Eisenhower's Advisory Committee on Government Housing Policies and Programs. The new legislation was aimed at broadening the scope of redevelopment by getting private enterprise and local authorities to do more about improving the *existing stock of housing*. Of course, a few clearance programs would continue in the worst parts of the city or in areas where it was possible to achieve especially significant effects. But the new goals sought primarily to conserve good areas, to arrest decline by rehabilitation, and to upgrade generally the quality of the older areas of the city.[52]

To ensure the realization of these aims, the legislation required localities to establish "workable programs." These involved the preparation of neighborhood studies, long-range land use plans, and financial and administrative programs for implementation. The localities also had to spell out their plans for code enforcement, the housing of displaced families, and the participation of their citizens in decision-making. Congress also authorized FHA (in Section 221 of the legislation) to insure loans for moderate rental housing either on or off the renewal site to serve families displaced from redevelopment areas. Another clause (Section 220) permitted FHA to insure any other appropriate housing on the renewal site.[53] These were the first explicit attempts to extend FHA help to families in the central city.[54] The 1954 act also allowed 10 percent of the total grant to the locality to be used for redevelopment areas which were not predominantly residential in character and were not to be redeveloped for predominantly residential uses. This proportion was later increased to 35 percent.[55]

In substance, the new legislation shifted the emphasis from specific redevelopment projects to efforts to improve residential areas throughout the city. It tried to solidify the effects of the assistance provided by requiring careful studies and specific pragmatic plans. Though it aimed, through subsidies and other devices, to get more housing built for moderate-income groups in the central city, it also made it possible for the renewal program to include other activities besides housing.

But there were still many difficulties. Land use plans and workable programs were produced hurriedly since they were prerequisites for qualifying for the subsidies. Consequently, they were frequently makeshift and flimsy and more honored in the breach than in the practice. Yet federal officials were loathe to challenge them, for why penalize cities for their lack of experience or staff or adequate data or efficient analytical techniques. Moreover, renewal proceeded slowly, far more so than clearance. Many operations took several years, some even a decade, before they were completed. Small wonder then that to many local officials the hoped for augmentation of local revenues seemed to have been only a mirage.

Rehabilitation, in particular, proved to be of little value. Only about 46,000 rehabilitated dwelling units were "completed" in 1966. This was less than 3 percent of total construction. In addition, FHA rehabilitation loans, which had financed about 10 percent of total residential expenditures before 1955, declined to "about 7½ percent from 1955 through 1963, and . . . to 5½ percent by 1965."[56] Public housing–renewal activities were even more discouraging; they involved less than 1,000 units for the period from July 1965 through December 1966. Total dwelling unit costs (for land, building, rehabilitation, and other expenses) varied for different types of buildings. Though rehabilitated units were less expensive than new construction in most central cities, the process was "time consuming, complex and relatively costly [and it required substantial] subsidies to produce housing for the poor."[57] Moreover, the burden of the renewal programs still fell most heavily on the poorest, most disadvantaged groups in the community.

As the program moved ahead, the net effect seemed to be the jacking up of rents for many low-income families, and not only for those that lived in the rehabilitated housing or areas where the renewal took place.

The Emergence of a Metropolitan Perspective

While efforts to aid the central cities were being broadened, the government was also being pressed to help suburban communities to finance the public facilities and services which they needed. The precedents for such assistance could be traced back to the public works program started in the 1930's. Originally a "make work" effort of the Works Progress Administration, it became a "pump priming" tool under the Public Works Administration, and later an accepted government activity assigned to the Federal Works Agency. The program had concentrated on constructing local sewer and water projects, public buildings, schools, and other public facilities. This experience turned out to be unexpectedly useful during World War II when many small cities and towns found themselves unable to provide with their own resources the essential facilities required for expanding war production activities. To end bickering and bottlenecks, the federal government gave some help in the form of loans and subsidies, but this assistance was reduced to a pittance after the war.

Fear of unemployment in the postwar years prompted efforts to prepare a postwar public works program. A series of acts passed in 1944, 1949, and 1954 authorized interest-free loans for financing technical studies and specifications for specific public works programs. As in the case of the public facility loans, these acts did not have "as a major, or even a significant, goal the comprehensive and orderly development of suburban and metropolitan areas as a whole."[58] The aim was quite limited. At the outset, it was to have a "shelf" of public works; later, the objective was to have more information about public works plans as a guide for the programming of federal public works; and still later, it was to encourage "preliminary planning, as distinct from full planning, because it was found that rapidly changing technology made overly detailed plans and specifications obsolete between the time of planning and the time of construction."[59]

In the fifties the vast building activity in suburban areas once again stoked up the pressures to obtain grants or at least easy federal credit for public works. Eventually this led to the enactment in 1955 of a new public facilities loan program administered by the Community Facilities Administration of HHFA.[60] Moreover, under the same 1954 legislation that provided interest-free advances for preliminary public works planning, the federal government set up matching grants to encourage state, metropolitan, and regional agencies to undertake comprehensive planning studies of metropolitan or regional areas. This was only a start since there were no comparable incentives to ensure comprehensive planned *development*. Nonetheless, the new legislation supported two strongly held views of development specialists: the need to prepare capital budgets scheduling long-range capital improvements[61] and the desirability of encouraging a metropolitan and regional framework for urban planning.

Once the metropolis was accepted, at least at the federal level, as the appropriate unit for land use planning, it was only a matter of time before Congress would enact "a series of laws that . . . aimed directly at assisting orderly metropolitan development."[62] The first such legislation was passed during the Kennedy administration and involved the issues of mass transportation and open space. In 1961 Congress authorized loans to help localities acquire and improve mass transportation facilities, but as a condition for the loans, "area-wide" comprehensive planning was required. There were also grants (two-thirds federal and one-third local) for experiments and demonstrations designed to improve transportation. Congress also approved federal grants up to 20 percent of cost to help states and localities acquire parks and undeveloped land in urban areas. Its aims were to curb "urban sprawl" and to assure "more economic and desirable urban development." But grants could be increased to 30 percent if the local agency was a party to an agreement to establish an open space policy program for "the entire local area"; and, here too, a condition for the grants was area-wide comprehensive planning.[63]

Later refinements provided more generous grants and extended the policies to public works, recreational areas, beautification programs, advance land acquisition, and large-scale land management[64]—but always with a proviso or an incentive for

246

area-wide planning agencies.[65] Finally, in 1966 efforts were made to transform metropolitan planning agencies from purely plan-making organizations to advisory bodies with some power. The new legislation stipulated that a local area-wide planning agency had to "review applications for Federal assistance for development projects in metropolitan areas and comment on them to the Federal Agency involved."[66] There was a complementary requirement that "where projects [were] proposed by local special-purpose bodies, such as sewer commissions or park authorities, the proposal [had to] be submitted for comment to the county, municipality, or other unit of general local government having jurisdiction over the project areas."[67] There were even special supplementary grants to ensure coordinated scheduling of the land use, financial, and operational plans for development throughout the region.[68]

THE TREND TOWARDS AN URBAN GROWTH POLICY

Unfreezing Past Policies

The concerns of the early sixties were quite different from those of the late forties when the first "comprehensive" housing legislation was adopted. Once the production of houses had gotten into full swing and had eased the housing shortages facing middle-income families, housing issues receded from the center of the stage. The low-income housing program became, in effect, an appendage of urban renewal. By the sixties HHFA dealt with the rehabilitation of older neighborhoods as well as with new housing. It was also involved with such varied issues as public works, community facilities, open space, and mass transportation, as well as with state and regional aids for planning and the relationships of the central city and the intermediate grey areas to the growth of the metropolitan region.

Over the years, many of the earlier federal housing programs were reshaped to meet new needs and perspectives. Thus, the special role in urban renewal which FHA acquired in 1954 was further extended in 1961.[69] The amended legislation made it even easier to purchase low-priced sales housing (by lower down payments and even longer amortization periods) and to finance rental housing (by below the market interest rates, waived insurance premiums, and arrangements for FNMA mortgage purchases at par). The liberalized terms were offered to all low and moderate-income families, not just to those who were displaced from renewal areas. True, for many years, the FHA bureaucracy betrayed a formidable lack of zeal for some of these social aims, and many financial institutions declined to make these loans when there were other more attractive alternatives. Nonetheless, the encouragement of moderate and even low-income housing in central cities and in many of the areas between the suburbs and the central cities was becoming almost as important a role for FHA as the servicing of the mass market in the suburbs for large-scale builders. By the mid-sixties, approximately 40 percent of FHA's insured home loans were for properties in central cities.[70] Incessant criticisms since the war also brought about substantial alterations in the terms of FHA insurance. These new provisions made it easier for moderate-income families to obtain mortgage credit and to buy homes, although they likewise increased the risks for these families and to some extent the price levels of the housing provided by the building industry.[71]

On the public housing side, too, new approaches were being cautiously investigated. This was a significant change. For a long time alternatives had not been freely explored. Leading proponents of public housing were not unaware of the inadequacies of the program, but they knew that many of the worst problems had been foisted on the program by an intransigent opposition. It was this opposition which had insisted on low housing standards and on the demeaning supervision of tenants and the eviction of families whose income rose. Moreover, in the long, losing struggle to salvage the program, public "housers" had often overreacted—virulently and negatively—to proposed alternatives. But it was clear, even to the "housers," that the projects that they were forced to build and manage were creating problems as bad or even worse than those they replaced. And so alternatives were being gingerly explored.

In principle, it was conceded that many families required income more than housing, or special social and welfare services as well as better housing, or an environment more attuned to their circumstances and values than the grim, sanitary accommodations thought appropriate by middle-class America. But even in the early 1960's, family allowances, negative income taxes, and policies which put more stress on environmental facilities or services than on housing were not seriously considered or fully appreciated. The measures that were explored were pragmatic, unexciting adaptations in response to the most obvious needs and possibilities.

As a first step, cooperative agreements to coordinate welfare and other social services for low-income families were worked out between HHFA and the Department of Health, Education and Welfare, and still later with the Office of Economic Opportunity and other federal agencies. Limited in scope, they furnished points of departure rather than guidelines for the future. There was also renewed interest in the possibilities of rehabilitating existing housing for low-income families. The hope was that code enforcement and neighborhood rehabilitation would minimize the uprooting of families and conserve and expand the existing stock of housing. Some persons even believed that such a program could stimulate a national or regional market of sufficient volume to attract efficient builders and more effective rehabilitation methods.

There were also attempts to tap the resources of private builders. Under one approach, the "turnkey" method, developers improved existing houses or built new housing and then, usually after reaching agreement in advance on the site, the plans, and the prices, sold the dwellings to the local authorities. Under another formula, local housing agencies did the building and then turned the projects over to cooperatives or even to private firms for management. Sometimes agencies leased a portion of private or cooperative housing projects for low-income families and supplemented the gaps in ability to pay with rent subsidies. In other experiments, there were rent ownership options making it possible for the dwellings to be acquired eventually by the tenants or even purchased directly by low-income families. But though the trends were clearly away from public ownership or management, public housing was still the principal instrument for providing new low-rent housing—especially in smaller communities where the projects were built on a more modest scale and where much energy was expended in trying to "deinstitutionalize" their appearance.

The maze of new and old housing programs, and the changes in the traditional roles of agencies and in the perspectives on development, underscored the need for a general reassessment of both policies and programs. All that was required was the leadership and the opportunity. With the election of President Kennedy and the rediscovery of the poor in the early 1960's both the leadership and the moment seemed opportune; but the victory at the polls was not quite decisive enough to spark searching evaluations or to push through major legislative innovations. These became possible only with the overwhelming victory of President Johnson in 1964 and the creation of a solid Democratic majority in Congress.

There then began an extraordinarily energetic drive to push through the programs of the "Great Society." In regard to urban policy, it was now possible for the new administration to effect a change that had been advocated since the mid-fifties: the creation of a Department of Housing and Urban Development (HUD) with a cabinet-level Secretary. HHFA's new title and the elevation of its status were not achieved without bitter struggle, yet, in retrospect, these actions simply recognized the significance of the urban component of the agency's activities and the growing importance of urban issues in the affairs of the nation.[72]

The establishment of the new Department precipitated an internal reappraisal of the various HHFA programs and the beginnings of an evaluation of their relative effectiveness in relation to the mission of HUD. A reorganization plan was prepared which reflected the revised perspectives and priorities. The functions of HUD were regrouped into five divisions. Mortgage credit, including the coordination of FHA and FNMA, was placed in one division. Urban renewal, low-rent public housing, relocation, neighborhood facilities, and social services constituted another. The problem of planning for public facilities and for other requirements of metropolitan areas was the responsibility of a third division. The fourth dealt with experiments and demonstrations and federal, state, and local intergovernmental relations and the fifth cut across the other divisions, for it focussed on information systems for management, for policy planning, and for program evaluation.[73]

The reorganization of HUD reinforced changes in urban development policy which had occurred over the past decade. It deemphasized housing as such and stressed instead urban and metropolitan perspectives, intergovernmental relationships, and significant development tools. Still unclear, however, were the actual

250

strategies in behalf of which the new administrative machinery was to be deployed.

The Need for a Growth Strategy

Within a short space of time, a complex and growing system of incentives and controls had been devised to encourage area-wide planning for a wide range of purposes. An equally complex and growing system of incentives had transformed some of the development policies for inner cities: rehabilitation was stressed rather than large-scale redevelopment; rent subsidies and private management — and perhaps ultimately home ownership for the poor — rather than public housing. Both systems had developed independently in response to felt needs and both had initially seemed plausible and even appropriate. Yet, as time passed, they turned out to be increasingly inadequate. One reason, of course, was that the programs lacked significant support and were therefore seriously underfunded. In addition, the programs rested on two highly vulnerable assumptions: the failure to see the interregional dimensions of the problem at hand, especially the close connection between the lagging regions, the growing metropolises, and the migration of the black population from the South.[74] This misjudgment further undermined the very shaky second assumption, that the central city could be made attractive enough to induce dwellers from the outskirts, who were weary of the long journey to work, bored, or otherwise dissatisfied with life in the suburbs, to return.

The vast exodus of the nonwhite population changed radically the issues of growth strategy. Large portions of central cities of the North and West were fast becoming black enclaves surrounded by fearful white neighbors. The size of the black areas and their problems had begun to generate on a large scale all of the automatic fears and reactions of the self-fulfilling prophecy. As the black population increased in these areas, more whites left. Between 1950 and 1960 nonwhite population in central cities rose almost 50 percent (from 6.5 to 9.7 million). White population in the same period rose 4.8 percent (from 45.5 to 47.7 million) and it actually declined in the largest central cities.[75] More specifically, between 1950 and 1960, Chicago's central city experienced a net loss of 399,000 whites and a net gain of 320,000 Negroes; Detroit lost 363,000 whites and gained 182,000 Negroes; New York lost 476,000 whites and gained 240,000 Negroes. At the same time . . . the industrial jobs [were] moving to the suburbs. New York lost 204,000 industrial jobs between 1947 and 1964. Between 1960 and 1964 alone, New York lost 8.2 percent of its manufacturing jobs; Philadelphia lost 4 percent; and Pittsburgh lost 5 percent.[76]

The departures accelerated with rising municipal costs and taxes, deteriorating environment and services, and an increasing lack of safety in the streets. In 1968 the nonwhite population in central cities rose to 11.9 million, a gain of more than 20 percent since 1960, whereas the white population of central cities in 1968 was 45.5 million or about 5 percent less than in 1960. Negroes rose from 16 to 20 percent of the central cities' population, remaining at only 5 percent in the suburbs. For "all 224 central cities considered as a whole, all population growth now consists of gains in Negro population. . . . From 1960 to 1966, 89 percent of all nonwhite population growth was in central cities and 11 percent was in suburbs."[77]

Not surprisingly, the urban poverty problem became largely identified with the black population. Actually, two-thirds of all the nation's poor were white but "the proportion of all metropolitan area whites who were poor (9.2 percent) was less than one-third the proportion of such nonwhites who were poor (32.7 percent)."[78] The welfare burden of the central cities grew particularly acute. Baltimore, for example, had 27 percent of Maryland's population, but contributed 72 percent of the expenditures for dependent children; Boston's population was 14 percent of the total population of its state, but it shouldered 40 percent of the burden for these same expenditures. Similar disproportions existed in New York, Philadelphia, Cleveland, Chicago, and elsewhere. The financial strains soon made themselves felt in other areas as well.

In 1957 the per pupil expenditures in the 37 large metropolitan areas . . . favored the central city slightly—$312 to $303 for the suburban jurisdictions. By 1965, the suburban jurisdictions had forged ahead, far ahead—$574 to $449 for the central cities. . . . [T]he central city school districts [had to] carry a disproportionately heavy share of the educational burden—the task of educating an

252

increasing number of "high cost" underprivileged children. Urban children then who need[ed] education the most [were] receiving the least.

To make matters worse, State aid to school districts actually aggravat[ed] this situation by favoring the rural and suburban districts. . . .

On the municipal service and custodial front, the presence of "high cost" citizens, greater population density, and the need to service the needs of commuters force[d] central cities to spend far more than most of their suburban neighbors for police and fire protection and sanitation services. The 37 largest central cities had a non-educational municipal outlay of $232 per capita in 1965 — $100 greater than their suburban counterparts.[79]

The process of black in-migration and white out-migration differed from the experience of the past in two respects. One was the greater ease with which moderate and middle-income white families, taking advantage of low down payments and long-term amortization arrangements, could and did leave the bleak, run-down zones surrounding the inner core as their incomes and standards of demand rose. On the other hand, despite anti-discrimination regulations, most of the black community faced exceptional resistance in penetrating the outer areas. There was not only growing difficulty in obtaining reasonably priced homes or in finding sites for integrated housing, but also an increasing number of local communities blocked subsidized housing by vetoing rent supplement programs or by neglecting legislative requirements.[80]

The deepening sense of withdrawal and entrapment in the inner city that resulted from these trends produced extraordinary tensions. It led to an increasing concentration in the central cities of a bitterly frustrated black population. Mainly young or middle-aged, unemployed or underemployed, lacking the customary family ties, victims of neglect and discrimination, exposed via television to the mores of twentieth-century violence and to the full view of white middle-class standards — material and otherwise — that they could never hope to possess, they proved increasingly receptive to the ideas articulated by their younger leaders who told them not to accept their accustomed lot and the values of integration because the white world would not change its racist practices.[81] The subsequent explosions of violence in these areas — repeated summer

253

after summer—hardened attitudes on both sides, threatened future investment in the inner city zones, and made the movement of middle-income families back into the central cities even more remote a possibility than ever.

These altered prospects were further underscored by anticipated population trends. The evidence pointed to a rapid growth of nonwhite population in central cities and higher growth rates for jobs in the outer areas. Migration and population increase were expected to raise nonwhite population in 1980 to over 50 percent of the population in Chicago, Philadelphia, St. Louis, Detroit, Cleveland, Baltimore, Oakland, and Trenton.[82] Moreover, in comparison with 1964, when they made up more than half of the total metropolitan area population, and more than one-third of metropolitan area employment, the non-central city portions of metropolitan areas were expected, by 1985, to double their population and make up more than half of total metropolitan area employment.[83] Adequate access to these jobs was likely to be very difficult for a population living within the limited horizons of a ghetto. As John Kain's studies have suggested, "as many as 24,000 jobs in Chicago and 9,000 in Detroit may be lost to the black community because of housing segregation."[84]

The prospects profoundly disturbed those who sought integration and the elimination of racism in American society. Almost no one doubted the role of discrimination in fixing these patterns. One study estimated that, on the basis of black employment locations and of low-income white residential choice patterns, as many as 40,000 Detroit black workers and 112,000 Chicago black workers would move out of the central ghettoes in the absence of racial segregation.[85]

But to favor movement to the suburbs now began to arouse the suspicions of many militant black leaders. It smacked too much of a sophisticated version of urban development via Negro clearance. These leaders saw the chance of winning significant political influence in the central city and, therefore, of controlling a little better the conditions of their lives. Along this route lay perhaps the means of improving their education, housing, social and physical facilities, and, perhaps most important of all, their self-esteem and their status. They started to question or discount the evidence that their youngsters performed better in mixed schools.[86] They were

254

willing to turn their backs on the fact that many of the best jobs and facilities were located in the suburbs. Regarding themselves as a colonial population, systematically exploited and deprived of strong cultural and family support and the means of self-improvement for more than two centuries, they no longer trusted the promises of "whitey," liberal or not. They had no inclination to give up the semblance of some political power, even if only in the form of political and administrative decentralization. They were equally ready to reject the integration ideal which they now considered dubious at best, for it appeared to condemn them to a permanently visible, second-class minority status with negligible influence.

Meanwhile, the communities in the outer areas, troubled by their own problems, were hardly inclined to change their policies. In the past, part of the costs of new development at the edge of the city (for schools, water, and utilities) had been shouldered by the central city. Lacking this assistance, many of the newer suburbs sought help from the federal government, and through promotion campaigns, building, zoning, and subdivision controls and other devious devices, they engaged in "internecine warfare" to attract income producers or to preserve or enhance their vaunted advantages. Many of these communities were struggling to keep their costs down. This was especially necessary for communities with a high proportion of young families of modest income, living in new but inexpensive single-family homes, for their tax-paying ability was low and the costs of their school, street, water, and service requirements were high and rising. Despite these difficulties, the majority of these families had won, or saw the prospect of winning, a little "lebensraum" for the kids and themselves and did not want any of their hard-earned gains jeopardized by the central city's political machine or the central city's tax burdens or the central city's crime rates. Most of them had no intention of leaving the suburbs or allowing their communities to change significantly, least of all while their youngsters were still at home.

The attitudes of the local suburban officials simply mirrored these views. They were reluctant to surrender their sovereignty and precious tax havens for the benefits of comprehensive metropolitan planning. This resistance was reinforced by threats, real or imaginary, to their values and style of life. Their rallying cry, therefore, became local autonomy, and, because the automobile and modern technology were steadily erasing the need for close ties to the central city, the odds seemed to be in their favor.

Caught in the middle, disliked or distrusted by both the poor blacks and the suburban whites, and far less powerful in this conflict than they cared to admit, were the elite elements of the metropolitan community: the financial leaders, the downtown interests, the leading families, the clergy, the opinion and taste makers, the leading universities, and the "liberals"—all of whom were wedded by interest and sentiment to the central city. The most influential were persuaded that the bulk of the whites and the nonwhites still shared basically the same American dream of a mixed and upwardly mobile society for all. In their judgment, there would be a very positive response on the part of a large majority of nonwhites if somehow it could be made clear that the white community was prepared to "pay" substantial "reparations" and that "the rules of the game" would be significantly altered to permit nonwhites to participate on reasonably fair terms. And so organizations such as Urban America, and others representing these interests, began searching for ways of breaking the impasse and the self-reinforcing mechanisms that gave rise to it.[87]

In this highly simplified model of the parts played by the different participants in the urban crisis, the role of the federal government was crucial. This was because of the leverage it could exercise with tax and other incentives, with block grants, and with funds for housing, transportation, education, public facilities, and welfare. The critical question confronting the government seemed clear: it was not whether the present development pattern needed to be changed, but how?

The Failure to Devise an Adequate Strategy

Unfortunately, the desire to rise to the challenge was frustrated by the inability to do so. Little could be done at best as long as the government's financial freedom of action was substantially impaired by its growing commitment to the intensely unpopular war in Vietnam. Nonetheless, key advisors of the administration, anxious to do something, shocked and affronted by the mounting fury of the conflict between the black and white communities, turned their attention to the conditions of life in the ghettoes. The main answers they gave, in so far as development strategy was concerned, was to put such resources as were available into comprehensive programs for improving specific ghetto areas and to provide further incentives for building large subdivisions and new cities in the metropolitan region. The *Demonstration Cities and Metropolitan Development Act of 1966* and the program for new communities included in the *Housing and Urban Development Act* of 1968, were the principal new tools expressly designed for these ends.

Under the *Model Cities* program authorized in the 1966 act, a city could experiment with solving the physical, economic, and human problems of the disadvantaged in one of its blighted areas. Here it could apply all of the tools and funds available under past and current legislation for planning, housing, urban renewal, job training, education, recreation, health, and welfare. The city could also obtain a supplemental grant from the federal government equal to 80 percent of the local share of the cost of the federal grant-in-aid programs applied to upgrading the selected area. These additional funds might be used for any purpose desired in backing up the demonstration effort, but the plans had to be approved in Washington. Originally, the first round of grants was intended to serve the poverty neighborhoods of no more than a handful of large metropolitan areas. But to get the legislation passed, the number had to be raised substantially. As a consequence, 75 cities were approved the first year (including a fair number of small urban areas) and a total of 150 cities the next year.

The aim of the Model Cities program was to develop a broad, flexible approach, one which would use, yet not be tied to, existing agencies and one which could be largely shaped by the citizens directly affected, particularly the black population. To encourage further experimentation, HUD financed studies by independent consultants to propose changes on every aspect of urban problems and made special arrangements to monitor what was actually done and learned in the Model Cities program.

As for the legislation on new cities, the emphasis was on insuring loans for the purchase and improvement of land, first for large-scale subdivisions (1965) and then for community development in the metropolitan areas (1966). In 1968, the Congress expressly grappled with the problem of heavy fixed charges during the development period when the project earned no income. To help overcome this difficulty, the 1968 law provided for federally guaranteed cash-flow debentures which would be large enough to cover major costs (site acquisition, site improvement, construction, and fixed charges) until the development could generate income from the sale of lots, homes, and non-residential properties. The law also authorized a small amount of supplementary grants to encourage the use, in connection with the new communities, of existing federal grant programs for water, sewer, and open space projects. Aside from the desire to tap the bond rather than the mortgage market and thus attract more ample private capital,[88] the legislation had two other aims: to assure future outlets to the suburbs for the black population and other minorities and to provide additional ways of accommodating the vast increase of population that the cities would have to accommodate in the future.

In addition to these two major pieces of legislation, immediately following the assassination of Martin Luther King in the spring of 1968, President Johnson pressed for stronger "open occupancy" legislation to combat discrimination in the renting or the sale of multi-family private housing. Along with these efforts, the federal government discouraged almost all new large-scale clearance programs, and it subsidized mass transportation systems to provide better access for the poor to jobs in the suburbs. It also, at the prodding of Robert Kennedy, EDA, and others, began to examine tax incentives to employers and other ways of increasing job opportunities for minorities, and to encourage housing rehabilitation and new economic activities in central cities.[89]

The programs were ambitious, judged in terms of either past efforts or existing staff resources and capabilities—and perhaps even on the basis of what Congress and the country generally wanted at the time. The programs were, nonetheless, overwhelmingly inadequate. This judgment is not an unfair one even if we recognize that the Model Cities program was only a "demonstration," that it took extraordinary White House support and pressures and legislative skill to get this bill and subsequent legislation through Congress, and that in time the scale of the program may be more commensurate with the problems.[90] For the

258

real flaw in these efforts was a paralyzing fear of the explosive racial issue, and thus a reluctance which eventually crystallized into an inability to confront the basic needs and to respond to them. This was why the government—or for that matter, the nation—did not devise an effective development strategy or muster the necessary support for it.

Essential Elements of an Urban Growth Strategy

It has become increasingly clear that a successful urban growth strategy now has to go beyond enrichment programs for the central city, for such efforts attract newcomers and only tend to perpetuate the ghetto. The strategy has to do more than emphasize dispersal or measures designed to spread ghetto residents among many suburban communities to allay the fear of invasion in any one community. Substantial dispersal will certainly be necessary, but even with the most ambitious programs, the ghetto will be with us for at least another generation and probably much longer. Indeed, merely to keep central city ghettoes in 1975 at their estimated 1970 level, there would have to be

an out-movement of 1.9 million Negroes into the suburbs. This amounts to 380,000 per year. From 1950 to 1960, the suburban Negro population of all U. S. metropolitan areas grew a total of only 60,000 per year. . . . From 1960 to 1966, the Negro population growth in all suburban areas declined sharply to a rate of 33,000 per year. In fact, there was actually inmigration of Negroes from suburbs to central cities.[91]

The trends were reversed between 1966–1968. During this period, Negro population in the suburbs rose by 220,000 a year. Even if we take the figures at face value and ignore the fact that much of the movement represented the overflow of black population into inner suburbs, the migration levels were still substantially below the required outward movement.

A combination of dispersal and enrichment would also be inadequate, for these policies might still be hobbled by a sudden rise in the flow of migrants from small towns as well as from rural areas into a few critical metropolitan centers. This, as Professor Kain and others have observed, is what occurred in Detroit when

259

word got around about that city's effective job creation program for the hard-core unemployed.

The key to an effective growth strategy in the United States, as in Britain, France, Venezuela, Turkey and still other countries, is a simultaneous three-sided attack on all of these problems. First, new opportunities must be provided for the relocation of the black population in expanding suburbs and new cities. Second, the social, physical, and economic conditions of the central cities must be enhanced, essentially through a reorganization of metropolitan growth patterns, an increase of the income of the cities and of their residents, a reduction of the excessive concentrations and high densities in the black ghettoes, and a general improvement of ghetto conditions. Third, a few large growth centers must be developed in the lagging regions. These centers must not only spur the reconstruction of the surrounding areas, but also serve as attractive opportunity areas for black as well as white migrants. Of course, it might be possible to solve urban problems even if adequate opportunities could not be created in southern growth centers; but the burdens on the northern cities would be all the more difficult and the moral issues of poverty and discrimination would still continue to haunt the country.

Some of the institutional mechanisms for developing such a strategy exist, at least in principle. EDA programs already encourage urban growth centers in lagging regions. Housing legislation enacted over the past decade makes it possible to improve the poverty areas of our central cities and to encourage more social and economic variety in the composition of the population of our suburban areas. There are also a number of programs which provide management and manpower training and offer grants for mass transportation, health, and educational facilities as well as for planning and a number of other services. These activities need to be strengthened. But, in addition to these tools, three major innovations are still needed.

An end to the fiscal crisis threatening the central cities is long overdue. If the federal government took over the welfare program and substituted family allowances or a negative income tax for the present discredited system, equal assistance (with adjustments for differences in living costs) could be provided for needy families regardless of where they happened to live. As a further step, some form of federal sharing of income taxes with states and cities is essential in order to end the excessive reliance on property and sales taxes and to reduce the pressures for still more federal aid for education, crime prevention, and other services. The idea is certainly not new; and, considering the growing bipartisan support it has been receiving from many prominent leaders, including Walter Heller, Hubert Humphrey, Nelson Rockefeller, and President Nixon, it would appear to be only a matter of time before some version of these ideas becomes the official policy of the government.[92]

More attractive combinations of incentives will also be needed to encourage appropriate development strategies and development organizations in a relatively small number of growth centers in the lagging regions and in the poverty neighborhoods of the major central cities. The tools will have to include rent supplements as well as generous employment and tax incentives. There ought, too, to be more emphasis on spreading the effects of growth outward to the lagging areas in the hinterlands and inward to the lagging poverty areas in the central cities. One way of doing this would be to build expanded or new cities in a lagging region, linked when appropriate to the decentralization plans of a congested metropolis. Another way would be to broaden the idea of Model Cities to include perhaps the creation of New Towns "in-town." Subsidized transportation, educational and vocational training, and improved job counseling and information services are still other ways of realizing some of these effects. In addition, exceptional grants might be provided for housing, education, and open space, and for water and sewage facilities in new and existing communities in the outer areas of the metropolis. These grants might even be proportioned to the success of communities in developing more integrated living patterns.[93]

Finally, an agency needs to be created in the Executive Office of the President to evaluate urban growth issues. Such an activity would require a small number of high level research specialists and policy staff. Although this function might be discharged by a small secretariat serving a Cabinet committee presided over by the President, a preferable arrangement would be to set up a permanent agency, modelled on the Council of Economic Advisors, reporting to the President and the Congress. Whatever organizational framework is decided upon, the minimum role must be to formulate urban growth policy and priorities, to review periodically the general problems and trends of urban development, and to devise appropriate indicators to facilitate this evaluation.

Action along these lines presupposes vast changes in attitudes, for as Anthony Downs has emphasized, it would not be feasible unless accepted by influential segments of private enterprise, the white middle-class, and the nonwhite population. Such a program would require a whole new level of investments and financial assistance to attract the necessary economic activities to the central cities and the regional growth centers and equally vast sums — for rent or ownership payments, for transportation and schools, for employment and training premiums, and for other public facilities — to change significantly the patterns of population settlement in metropolitan areas. It is not possible to say what the final bill would total. A very rough estimate is that minimum to moderate outlays for approximately a decade or longer, not making deductions for the multiplier effects or for the lower human and social costs, would be about 6 to 35 billion dollars annually. In other words, the outlays might range from one to three percent of the projected GNP or somewhere between the 1967–68 expenditures for space research and technology and the expenditures for the Vietnam War.[94]

Some of these costs could be defrayed by increases in GNP and by the savings which would follow the end of war in Vietnam. But only an exceptional crisis and exceptional leadership could persuade the nation of the need for such a strategy, and for the kind of effort, cost, and transfer of income it would entail. At present, however, though the crisis is manifest, the leadership is not.

The magnitude of the urban crisis was revealed in the Kerner Commission's *Report of the National Advisory Commission on Civil Disorders* published in the spring of 1968, which examined at least a few of the leading issues relating to ghetto enrichment and dispersal strategies.[95] Even the more intransigent elements of the black community read the report with respect, and it received an overwhelmingly favorable reception in the press. But the war, the election that loomed ahead, and the fear of a white backlash led the administration to greet with faint praise this ardent plea for leadership. Despite numerous discussions and much private action, there was no decisive government response. Sheer exasperation caused Anthony Downs, one of the principal contributors to the study, to charge that

> future non-white population growth will continue to be concentrated in central cities unless major changes in public policies are made. Not one significant program of any federal, state, or local government is aimed at altering this tendency or is likely to have the unintended effect of doing so. . . .
>
> Almost all current public policies tend to further concentration, segregation and non-enrichment. . . . The few supposedly anti-concentration devices adopted, such as open occupancy laws, have proved almost totally ineffective.[96]

By the end of 1968, however, views had begun to change and new efforts were made to end the war in Vietnam. Both the old and new administrations manifested increased concern about the urban crisis. Just before the Johnson administration left office, members of his cabinet sponsored a major symposium on national growth and its distribution with a special emphasis on the communities of tomorrow.[97] Then — as in Britain and France — a new administration, searching for attractive, ripe ideas to implement, hit upon the formulation of a national urban policy as both a logical next step and as a means of underscoring the failings of the previous incumbents. Even a Republican administration, committed to the rhetoric of minimum federal intervention in American life, found it easy to reconcile its traditional shibboleths with the demands of an urban strategy.

The first act of the Nixon administration was the establishment of an Urban Affairs Council. The Executive Order issued by the President on January 23, 1969 noted that

> the American national government has responded to urban concerns in a haphazard, fragmented, and often woefully short sighted manner (as when the great agricultural migrations from the rural South were allowed to take place with no adjustment or relocation arrangements whatever). What we never had is a policy: coherent, consistent, positive as to what the national government would hope to see happen; what it will encourage, what it will discourage.
>
> Having a policy in urban affairs is no more a guarantor of success than having one in foreign affairs. But it is a precondition of success. With the creation of the Urban Affairs Council we begin to establish that precondition: the formulation and the implementation of a national urban policy.[98]

The new Council, presided over by the President, included the Attorney General, the Secretary of Agriculture, the Secretary of Labor, the Secretary of Health, Education and Welfare, the Secretary of Housing and Urban Development, and the Secretary of Transportation, as well as other heads of departments and agencies whom the President might appoint to the Council when needed. There was, of course, a commitment to coordinate programs and to facilitate decentralization and intergovernmental cooperation. But the functions of the new Council were vague enough to provide ample scope for its efforts. The Executive Order creating it asserted "that policies concerning urban affairs shall extend to the relations of urban, suburban and rural areas, to programs affecting them and the movement of population between them"; and it specified that the main function of the Council was "to assist the President in the development of a national urban policy, having regard both to immediate and to long-range concerns, and to priorities among them." [99]

Also significant was the release a few weeks earlier of a report by the Advisory Commission on Inter-Governmental Relations. Published with the assistance of the Economic Development Administration and other agencies, it recommended the "immediate establishment of a national policy for guiding the location and character of future urbanization. . . ." [100] The study, based on an extensive analysis of migration, industrial location, and urban growth trends, linked for the first time in a major policy document the critical problems of the central cities and the lagging regions and the need for an intra-metropolitan and interregional urban growth policy. It proposed the creation of an executive agency and outlined a possible agenda for such an agency. It also suggested various ways of shaping federal policy to influence the mobility of people, to neutralize factors producing continued excessive population concentrations and to encourage alternative location choices." [101] Some of the specific proposals called for were: resettlement allowances; augmented on-the-job training grants; inter-area job placement; tax, value-added, and employment incentives; an evening out of interstate variations in welfare eligibility and benefit standards; and the utilization of federal procurement controls and construction projects to foster growth in specific areas. Although the proposal naturally skirted some delicate issues, such as where growth should be encouraged, and the effects of discrimination in limiting income and economic opportunity in various states and regions, it did make clear that the need for action was now widely recognized and that there were feasible ways of dealing with these problems.[102]

Finally, during this same period, the mounting concern about the growth of population won new adherents for an urban strategy. There is likely to be about a half-billion more people in the world in the next ten years. This astonishing rate of increase of world population was given more vivid and concrete meaning by the spate of studies exploring possible "alternative futures" for the year 2000. One fact received special notice: that the United States would have to accommodate another 100 million persons—about three-quarters of them in metropolitan areas—in about thirty years. To cope with these prospects, the National Committee on Urban Growth Policy recommended the building of a hundred new cities of about 100,000 persons each and ten major metropolitan areas averaging about one million persons.[103] Even if this proposal were accepted, however, it would only accommodate "a mere one fifth of the expected thirty year increase."[104] Nonetheless, the implications were sufficiently sobering to lead President Nixon to propose the appointment by Congress of a Population Growth Commission to review the trends and their effects.

CONCLUDING OBSERVATIONS

Unlike Britain and France, there has been no effort in the United States to joust against the big city. Nor have there been any attempts to tie urban growth strategy to the needs of both the less and more prosperous regions or even to formulate an industrial location or migration policy. Metropolitan planning has been encouraged but nowhere has it gotten out of the creeping stage. As might be expected, the most successful federal policy has been the encouragement of the growth of the suburbs (which would have taken place anyhow) and the least successful of its policies has been the attempt to arrest the suburban exodus of population and activities out of central areas.

The main programs dealing with these problems have become more internally consistent and versatile, and more socially responsible. EDA, in dealing with lagging regions, has moved away, at least in principle, from a policy of scatter to one of concentrating on urban growth poles. It is now exploring national development policy for regions and the problems of how to handle the lagging regions of the central city. Urban programs, too, have moved ahead. FHA is no longer overwhelmingly biased against "inharmonious groups" and overwhelmingly in favor of the suburbs. Urban renewal is much less a tool for the clearance of disliked minorities and for the dislocation of the poor. Public housing is less doctrinaire and somewhat less public in ownership and management. There are programs today for mass transportation which may some day balance the previous emphasis on roads. There are also a variety of new tools for land acquisition, public works, recreation and open space programs, and for encouraging large-scale subdivisions and community development in the outer areas. On the whole, the legal battle against discrimination has been won; and there is much more concern than in the past for the needs of the poor and the nonwhite population. There is still other evidence of progress: the rise of family income, the smaller proportion of families below established poverty levels, the decline in the number of dilapidated housing units, and the reduction of school dropouts and of several forms of crime.[105]

On all these counts, there exist some grounds for satisfaction. Indeed, despite a growing sense of foreboding in many quarters, there are those who deprecate the language of crisis in discussing urban problems.[106] They cite the evidence of tangible improvements and question whether changing the physical environment by building New Cities or better subdivisions or by rehabilitating neighborhoods and improving housing and community facilities would solve the problems of poverty, crime, pollution, and inadequate public services. At the heart of their criticism lies the aperçu that manipulating the physical environment is a cumbersome and ineffective way to solve many critical urban problems. They espouse simpler policies, such as family allowances (or a negative income tax), transfer payments, block grants to cities, user charges, and the like.

Unquestionably, the measures advocated would not only put a floor on income, ease the fiscal burdens of central cities, and permit families to make more of their own choices, but would be easier to administer. They would also facilitate a more equitable allocation of costs and benefits within metropolitan regions. One of the great merits of these proposals is their useful reminder that there are many problems *in* cities and *of* cities which can be solved or ameliorated simply by giving people or cities more money. We can avoid some unnecessarily painful administrative headaches if we remember this basic fact.

However, the simple solution of giving cities or families more money has always been regarded in the past as alien to American traditions and corrosive of American character. The same view never prevailed in regard to subsidies for "productive" activities— for tariffs, for rail and road building and to encourage homesteads and western development. Although this illogical distinction appears to be rapidly losing support, it is certainly one reason why the United States has not as yet switched to these more "efficient" alternatives.

Moreover, even if environmental changes have turned out to be relatively ineffectual in the past, this is not necessarily a sound basis for discounting their significance in the light of new policies or new problems. There is also reason to believe that black-white polarization, now the most critical domestic issue which the country faces, is, to a very large extent, an outgrowth of failures to transform the growth patterns within and between regions.

We are now on the verge of an effort to effect some of these changes. When this does occur, as all the signs suggest it will, we can expect the nation to resort to the typical tools of urban growth policy, especially incentives to rebuild and improve the central areas of the metropolis and to steer some of the population and economic activities from the more congested portions to urban growth centers in the outer areas of the metropolis and to urban growth poles in the less prosperous regions. In the process, new cities, expanded cities, and improvements of central cities are likely to prove indispensable. The great uncertainty is not the technical feasibility of these ideas, although they would surely bring in their train new problems, such as reconciling the pressures to bring economic activities to the ghettoes and to the lagging regions and avoiding the emergence and spread of "grey" areas. The great question is whether this opportunity may come to naught because of the absence of imaginative leadership over a sustained period of time. If such leadership does manifest itself, however, the period ahead could well become one of the greatest eras of building and rebuilding in the nation's history.

Urban Growth Strategies Reconsidered

In the case studies that we have examined, we have seen how urban growth strategies came into being in different countries. We have also seen how the character of current strategies and ways of thinking about these problems have changed with new ideas, experience, and changes in the environment. But another purpose of examining the case studies was to compare the various experiences, particularly the similarities and differences in environments and germinating conditions. And we have not yet tested and amplified some of our initial observations about urban growth strategies. Nor ought we to conclude without some speculation about the next stage of urban growth strategies.

GERMINATING CONDITIONS

Two conditions generate urban growth strategies: growth problems must be recognized as critical; they must also appear capable of solution. Otherwise it would be hard to persuade the central government to redefine its aims and to reorganize its tools and organizations. Governments, like people, shy away from abstract issues and certainly do not bestir themselves very much unless an issue threatens to be persistent, prominent, and likely to cause trouble if ignored. Once an issue acquires these characteristics, however, it becomes part of the agenda of government and takes the status of what Hirschman has called a "privileged" problem. Urban growth strategies are especially interesting because they are in a transitional stage. They are on the verge of becoming privileged problems.

None of the central governments examined began to think in terms of such strategies until a wide range of specific and obdurate problems—of cities, within cities, and between cities— had become highly visible. At first they dealt with components of the problems, such as housing, industrial location, transportation, recreation, and education. Only later did they grapple with the more basic problems of suburban growth and of the relationships between metropolitan regions and central cities. At approximately the same time, the problems of poverty and of lagging regions came to be treated as specific components of the larger, more complex problem of managing the economy. The efforts to deal with the growth of cities and with the lagging regions proceeded independently at first, but they eventually converged. This convergence was accelerated once the essential interdependence of these programs began to be more fully appreciated. This, in turn, resulted in a quest for the elimination of inconsistencies, for more coherence, and for more effective means of execution.

Extreme phases of the economic cycle, particularly prosperity, also reinforced efforts to help lagging regions. This had not been true in the past—when economic crises as a rule diverted attention from the problem. More recently, however, they have not only spurred (or curtailed) building and development programs, but they have also highlighted regional discrepancies and problems of programming infrastructure investments equitably and efficiently. A modicum of political stability, a moderately effective civil service, and some control or influence over capital allocations as well as tax policy sufficed to make the efforts appear practicable. All that was necessary to spark action was the conviction of key decision-makers that they could do something to correct a serious imbalance and produce more efficient or more socially desirable patterns of development. This sense of need and opportunity impelled Great Britain to ring London with New Towns, spurred France to counter Paris with equilibrium metropolises, prompted the United States to confront the suburbs with urban renewal, led Venezuela to exploit its oil economy to foster the regional development of Guayana, and induced Turkey to try to offset the growth of the Marmara by encouraging urban development in other regions.

Since this blend of circumstances is tantamount to a complex set of preconditions, the strategies evolved very gradually. This is not true for cases where there may be an extraordinary response to a special opportunity or need, such as in the relocation of a capital or in the decision to make massive investments to exploit the resources of a particular region. These efforts, because they are massive, constitute national policies even if they are only implicit. But they do not necessarily lead to systematic, formal policies and programs for the development of other cities and regions. In Turkey, under Mustafa Kemal and Inönü, they did not. The establishment of the new capital and the stress on urban development were important experiences and served as a reminder that new growth centers could be established. But the problem still had to be tackled afresh a generation later. On the other hand, in Britain, France, the United States, and Venezuela (and in Turkey, after the revolution of 1959), the adoption of national policies led to the creation of intellectual beachheads, of administrative mechanisms and staff which could spread the essential ideas to strategic points inside and outside the government. Over time, the increasing awareness of the commitments, the greater visibility of the policies and programs, and the egalitarian pressures on governments led to the extension of these policies and programs. In all five countries, it took at least a generation before goals and policies were even roughly articulated; and it will take many years, perhaps another decade or a generation, before these ideas are translated into effective, systematic strategies.

Nonetheless, we can expect more rapid introduction of programs to guide urban growth in the future, for most of the essential components are now known. Whether one is concerned with policies, organizations, or instruments, there are now a number of operating models. They offer a starting point for thinking about a wide range of urban growth problems and of ways of dealing with them: the choice of goals and development alternatives; the administrative machinery; the incentive, control, and review mechanisms; the inescapable constraints; and the appropriate relationships between development and planning agencies at different levels of government. The existence of such models accelerates similar efforts elsewhere. This is evident by the speed with which underlying ideas are spreading. The notion of New Towns, basically British in origin, is now in vogue almost everywhere; and so are the ideas of urban renewal, an innovation of the United States, and of growth poles, a French doctrine, although none of these ideas were bruited about before the end of World War II.

The popularity of these ideas, however, is not at all a measure of their success. Actually, the difficulties encountered suggest that the problems of managing growth are formidable and are likely to evade easy solution. Britain has wrestled with some of them for more than a generation, and is only now perhaps on the verge of achieving its objectives. The French started earlier but still have a long way to go—probably further than the British—even though their formal administrative machinery appears more highly developed and their strategy of promoting equilibrium metropolises more explicit. Venezuela and Turkey are even further behind France.

One could roughly rate these and other countries on the relative sophistication of their efforts on a number of counts: the adequacy of machinery to define development goals, not only aggregatively but by sectors and regions; the means that exist to coordinate development programs by sectors and by regions; the explicitness of the basic urban and regional development strategies; the quality of staff and training programs; the effectiveness of programs enlisting contributions from the private sector; the linkages that exist among social, economic, and physical elements; the capacity of local and regional organizations to handle their responsibilities; and the provisions for evaluation and improvement of performance as the program continues. What is especially noteworthy is that, although such an examination would point up serious shortcomings in each of these countries, it would also disclose that the concern in each country was with how to refine policies and to improve mechanisms, not with how to get rid of them.

In short, gaps in the understanding of theoretical and pragmatic relationships have not precluded the adoption of such strategies. On the contrary, when the need to act was agreed upon, then the disposition was either to experiment and to learn or, as Hirschman suggests, to follow "The Principle of the Hiding Hand"[1]—that is, to underestimate the difficulties or to overestimate the benefits. In all of the cases studied, recourse to action on a significant scale sooner or later began to spur the necessary theoretical and applied research to sustain and extend these efforts. Moreover, because of the rapid spread of knowledge and experience, future experiments with development policies and programs will acquire more of an adaptive character than an innovative one. This likelihood should further reduce the period between the initiation of such programs and the development of more explicit, systematic policies and provisions for their implementation.

THE ENVIRONMENT FOR URBAN GROWTH STRATEGIES

Britain, France, Turkey, the United States, and Venezuela differ in size, climate, resources, and location. They range from small to large, tropical to temperate, meagerly to well-endowed, and peripheral to central in their location. The five countries also differ in their institutions. Politically, they range from relatively centralized (France and Turkey) to relatively decentralized (United States). Socially, their cultures vary from relatively egalitarian (United States) to relatively hierarchical (Great Britain). All have varying elements of homogeneity and heterogeneity, depending on the criteria used for measurement. None of these differences have precluded the adoption of urban growth strategies, although they have influenced the effectiveness with which they were carried out.

The economies of these countries also differ widely. Some are poor, others rich; some are narrowly diversified, others widely. Turkey and Venezuela are in the take-off stages of industrialization; the others are highly industrialized and service-oriented. France, Britain, and Turkey face serious and immediate economic strains; the others do not. France had slow population and industrial development for more than a century; the others experienced the reverse. Both the more and the less economically developed countries are trying to spur national economic growth through the encouragement of growing regions. However, the advanced countries are also trying to arrest the decline of some regions, a decline stemming from changes in the location of industries, whereas the poorer countries are trying to induce development in primitive hinterlands. The lagging regions are prominent issues, particularly in the poorer countries, because of their magnitude and because a few of these regions may have very significant growth potentials.

These economic differences can affect urban and regional development strategies in fairly obvious ways. The most important involve the opportunities and constraints inherent in having relatively limited or relatively ample resources or in having a vigorous private sector and mature economic institutions[2] or the reverse. Another involves the differing psychological, as well as economic, significance of opening a hinterland rather than arresting its decline. What is intriguing, however, is that even though these differences have affected opportunities for development, they have not otherwise changed the main outlines of the urban and regional strategies adopted or the more general definitions of the problems on which they are based. Each of these countries believes it suffers from overconcentration in congested cities in some areas, underconcentration in others, and from undesirable and unnecessarily large regional differences in levels of social and economic development. All believe that they need to change the way the metropolis grows and to promote urban growth centers in the less prosperous regions.

Institutional differences can be significant factors also. An urban growth strategy involves controls, incentives, and pressures to influence the scale and pattern of development of metropolitan regions. It requires priorities for regional development and measures to implement them. It means favoring a West or a North against an East or a South. Even if the measures do not go counter to dominant trends or powerful interests, they presuppose choices among alternatives which will shift costs and benefits for cities and regions and arouse stormy conflicts. Such policies ought to be easier to work out in countries with centralized governments, hierarchical social systems, and homogeneous cultures. In point of fact, they are—but subject to a number of important reservations. In a country with a weak local system of government, opposition to the central government policy is crippled; but it is also harder to carry out the policy effectively in the field without able local or regional organs of government. The urban and regional aspects of growth strategy in Turkey and Venezuela betrayed serious weaknesses because of failings at this level. On the other hand, a weak national system of government is unable to develop a strong central policy for regional development, except through powerful incentives, relatively effective local, state, or provincial governments, or a vigorous system of private enterprise. The existence of any or all of these conditions is exceptional. But they did prevail in the United States in the nineteenth century and were responsible, in part, for its phenomenal Western development.

A hierarchical social and political system—where the governing class is accustomed to govern, where other classes are accustomed to acquiesce, and where private interests have relatively less power—can more readily evolve urban and regional growth policies at the national level than systems under the sway of the market, local political jurisdictions, or egalitarian political processes. This is one reason why urban growth policies burgeoned earlier in France and Britain than in the United States. But a hierarchical system—whether social or administrative, or both—has serious weaknesses in execution. It generally suffers from "apoplexy at the center and anemia at the edges," problems which both France and Britain as well as Turkey and Venezuela are struggling to solve. On the other hand, if problems become serious enough (or simply appear to be serious enough), national strategies will emerge even in market-oriented environments. For example, the current furor over the problems of the central city in the United States, and, to a lesser extent, over the problem of energizing less prosperous areas, is prompting the government to follow roughly the same course taken in the more hierarchical and centralized environments—albeit with significant adaptations to take account of racial issues and differences in planning institutions.

All told, the adoption of variants of the same strategies in a wide range of different environments underscores the common problems and trends and conventional ways of thinking about these matters. Even more significant, perhaps, is the fact that in all of these countries, the common denominator is the conviction that the guidance of urban growth strategy cannot—or, rather, must not— remain only at the local level.

CONCEPTS AND GOALS

The urban growth strategies of nations are hardly mature, but one can already speak of a "traditional" approach to urban growth issues and of problems characteristic of this approach. It has become increasingly customary for development specialists to consider the role different cities and regions might or ought to play in the development of a country, and hence in the programming of infrastructure and in the shaping of industrial and other development policies. In Britain, France, and Venezuela this definition of roles has led to quite different decisions about development priorities, and such differing results comfort planners who want urban and regional considerations taken more explicitly into account.

Nonetheless, there are difficulties imbedded in these ideas which need to be faced. Most planners, for example, are disposed to believe that development efforts will eventually founder if basic concepts are hazy and if development aims are obscure. Based on these assumptions, the future prospects of urban growth strategies are unattractive. This is because these strategies rest on two "fuzzy" assumptions—the disadvantages of big cities and the feasibility of promoting growth centers—which no one to date has been able to define operationally. We do not really know when a city is too big or too congested, rather than merely poorly organized. And we have, as yet, learned little more than the rudiments of how to convert an urban center into a growth center and how to radiate the effects of such growth centers over surrounding hinterlands. But, this is not the first time (and probably not the last) that decision-makers have to manipulate forces which they do not fully understand.

The situation may appear to be all the more discouraging because development aims are defined obscurely in all the countries studied, and not just in the United States whose aims have scarcely been formulated at all. The British goals, for example, of encouraging growth centers and reducing unemployment in the lagging regions are still so vague that they hardly provide an adequate basis for evaluating progress, or even for gauging how much of the changes in the character of urban development can be attributed to the measures undertaken. The French goals appear to be more explicit. The notion of equilibrium metropolises identifies the metropolitan regions where growth is to be encouraged and defines the strategy to build up large cities to compete with Paris. But conflicting national aims, not to mention pressures from other cities and regions, drain away much of the substance of this policy, so that in France, too, it is difficult to say what level of performance would represent satisfactory progress in carrying out its strategy within a reasonable period. The objectives in Turkey are far vaguer still. There are no explicit commitments, only general intentions of encouraging growth centers and correcting imbalance between growing and lagging regions. Plans are prepared which are supposed to be backed up by the Turkish government and private investments in the designated regions, but, more often than not, this fails to occur.

The sole exception, perhaps, is the experience of Venezuela. Plans for Guayana were incorporated into the national plan, and specific, staged targets for regional investment, production, and exports were linked to plans for national development. But this was true only for the Guayana region. Indeed, the success of Venezuela's policy was possible only by focussing on one region whose development had national significance and by systematically exploiting the unique resource endowment of the region with relatively ample capital resources. Even under these highly favorable circumstances, the projected targets aggregated many important elements and were meaningful and well-implemented only in comparison with the way regional plans were prepared elsewhere.

The experiences of these nations indicate the ambiguity and the range of variation that might be expected in the definition of aims in the early years of such a planning venture, and perhaps for many years thereafter. They suggest that it may be impossible — at least at the outset — for a government to formulate adequate or precise national goals for urban and regional development. What appears to be a far more feasible approach is the preparation of some general guidelines which can later be successively redefined. It may also be possible to work out somewhat more adequate and more detailed development goals and programs in one or two regions. These can then be tried and evaluated and serve as a training ground and as a guide for efforts elsewhere.

Of course, it is more customary, and attractive, to argue that clear goals should be set from the start. But this does not appear to be an option. It is very hard in the early stages to devise solutions to complex problems or to obtain backing for new ways of dealing with them. However odd it may seem, it is easier and often more realistic to fix precise goals in the middle or toward the end of a program. Effective goals presuppose awareness of what is feasible and desirable. They are in effect the fruition of much thought and experience and substantial consensus. This implies a learning process, often stretching over a decade or two. During this period, however, vague formulations and limited efforts, for all of their inadequacies, serve a useful purpose. They indicate general directions and invite the necessary initial critiques and refinements of goals and methods. In the course of these efforts, the bureaucracy and the public are given time to familiarize themselves with the issues and time to devise ways and means of dealing with unsuspected difficulties, or of avoiding further entanglements.

Despite the relatively obscure objectives indicated in the case studies, the kinds of measures deployed in these different environments have been fairly limited. The principal ones involve changing the rate of growth of a major city and encouraging development in growth zones within metropolitan regions and in other areas. The traditional instruments for these purposes range from controls to a variety of incentive schemes for public and private investment programs. Of course, it makes a difference how these measures are applied: whether there are many loopholes in the controls, whether the incentives are significant enough to induce the desired outcomes, whether all or only some of these instruments are deployed, whether the diverse efforts are made by one organization or by several, whether the policies are reinforced by other policies and programs of the national government. The pattern to date—in Britain, France, and the United States and to a lesser extent in Turkey and Venezuela—is for simple, limited measures to be initiated at the outset, out of prudence and ease of innovation and possibly also out of lack of conviction or clarity either about the goals or the efficacy of the means.

This prudence is understandable. With a relatively new policy where it is difficult to foretell the problems that may be encountered or the consequences of policy choices, the best the decision-maker can do in the beginning is to develop simple analytical and administrative machinery that may be made more efficient with time and to avoid major and relatively inflexible commitments until there is more of a consensus, or until the decision-maker is more certain about what is likely to happen. Later, as goals become clearer and if they still seem worth pursuing, he can either improve the tools (tighten or extend the controls, enlarge the premiums, change the definition of areas, perfect the coordinative mechanisms) or devise new tools to make the efforts more successful. He may also decide that the aims are wrong or, more probably, that they could be realized more efficiently by still other means; in that case, he might then relax controls and place more reliance on other tools, such as the price system. But such a reversal of official attitudes seems unlikely in any of the five countries studied.

This orientation today toward more controls and larger subsidies is all the more striking since, as we have observed, the experience with controls and incentives has been until recently somewhat disappointing. They have generally proved to be inadequate as a means of reversing a powerful force such as the expansion of a capital or a dominant metropolis. The opportunities for evasion are legion and the strain of enforcement on the administrative apparatus is severe. In Britain and France, after a generation of effort, the controls and incentives are working better—but still not adequately. The principal justification for controls and incentives today is not that they prevent congestion or successfully induce new growth. It is rather that in a territory which contains several development possibilities, a well-designed system of controls and incentives will prompt many firms and ministries to take advantage of these other possibilities.

A national system of incentives and controls to reinforce an urban growth strategy can be evolved in many ways. One possibility is to start at the top, create an intelligence unit close to the chief executive, and then develop a national strategy for area development. This is doubtless the most appealing approach from one point of view, for it is certainly possible now, in principle, for a small group of specialists to devise a fairly comprehensive strategy: to spell out goals, write legislation, formulate policies, fashion administrative mechanisms, and devise means to carry them into effect. Doubtless this can be done all the more quickly and elegantly if there is a national planning organization. But unless there is a large backlog of experience on these matters, not to mention adequate staff and resources, such efforts are apt to bog down. The ideas won't be fully understood and therefore will not gain necessary backing in different quarters, especially in the local regions. The programs in Britain, the United States, Venezuela, and even France did not evolve in this way; and the brief experience of Turkey with planning from the top down suggests that when such an approach is followed, it will not be effective. However simple and direct the centralized style may appear, the lack of an adequate analytical, administrative, and political base outside the political center often turns out to be a crucial weakness. It would take a rare group of administrators, indeed, to overcome it.

An alternative approach is illustrated by the experience of Venezuela or by the later stages of the regional planning program in Turkey. In these two cases, the emphasis was on promoting one or more metropolitan regions; at the same time, or at some reasonable period thereafter, these programs were linked into national development plans and policies. This approach built up the necessary experience and trained staff and gradually familiarized key elements of the public and the government with the program and the issues. A basic assumption here is that the essential ideas of the program have merit and will win further support, that they will survive despite inconsistencies and conflicts between regions, and that over time they will generate pressures for complementary programs.[3]

Despite the clarity of a nation's goals, political pressures can complicate and dilute the effectiveness of development policies. The issue of dispersal or concentration is an illustration of this. In the past, and even today, the pressure to satisfy political requirements hobbled programs in Britain, France, and the United States (not to mention Italy and other countries in western Europe). Dispersal was more effectively resisted in Venezuela, due to a political leadership which created an extraordinary national consensus about an exceptional region; and it was also successfully resisted in Turkey under the leaderships of Kemal and Inönü, but not thereafter. In general, however, the free market tends to favor concentration, whereas making the issues explicit often tends to consolidate political pressures and to favor dispersal. Thus, the great task of urban statesmanship is to develop the necessary political imagery to steer a middle course for a reasonable period in the future. This, however, is extremely difficult. To date, the issue of dispersal or concentration has proved so inflammatory and the way it is resolved so critical to the success of any policy of development that governments have often found it necessary to talk one way and to act another. And although it is easier politically to advocate dispersal and then allocate resources otherwise (or allow such allocations to occur), the experience of France suggests that on occasion this process may be reversed. There, lip service has been paid to the ideology of concentration, but as yet this has imposed very few constraints on a far more permissive allocation policy.

THE NEXT PHASE OF URBAN GROWTH STRATEGIES

Urban growth strategies now address themselves to the curbing of metropolitan growth in one or more areas and to the promotion of growing points elsewhere. In the future, however, we can expect this emphasis to be modified in four ways.

The first change in emphasis will involve the responses of nations to the emergence of sprawling metropolitan areas along major transportation corridors forming massive linear megapolitan clusters. Such patterns are already being formed along the Caracas-Valencia-Maracay axis in Venezuela and along the Istanbul-Izmit-Ankara sector in Turkey. They are visible in France along the east-west and north-south regional axes extending outwards from Paris; and they are even more in evidence in Great Britain in the linear belt extending from London to Birmingham, Liverpool, Manchester, and Glasgow. Their most publicized expressions, of course, are the spreading metropolitan growth complexes along the eastern and western coastal areas of the United States and along the Great Lakes. Even New Towns, which have been increasingly favored as instruments for linking decentralization and economic growth strategies, are no longer thought of as self-contained communities, but rather as growing points generally connected on some linear pattern to larger urban complexes "along a band of communications, [or like] ... beads on a string."[4]

The markets created by these vast concentrations of population and economic activity and the relative flexibility, compactness, and ease of extension of such patterns of development make it likely that the linear megalopolis form of growth will continue. Only inter-metropolitan and national policies can cope with the common problems facing such areas. The most important of these problems will concern transportation, water and sewage facilities, the handling of open space and recreational policies, and such special questions as air pollution and relationships with depressed areas, in addition to the general guidance of growth and development.

A second area of future concern will involve the building up of the resources and capabilities of local governments. At present, almost everywhere, local revenues are hopelessly inadequate, pay and staff poor, and local services in education, transportation, housing, recreation, social service, and basic information in need of massive improvements. There are several reasons why the problems of local capability have not played a major role so far in national policy in relation to urban growth strategies. In the poorer nations, central governments have been in no position to transform local government services; nor have these problems been as pressing in the short run as the monetary, exchange, general development, or minority problems which have faced the central governments. Moreover, in most of these countries, there exists no tradition of strong local government. Often, there are powerful landed or regional interests—vestiges of feudalism—which the central governments are trying to combat. These conditions, coupled with meager resources and inadequately trained professional staff, have made it unlikely for central governments to have either the capacity or the desire to strengthen local or regional independence. But overloaded central staffs, and the need to stir local initiative, will eventually spur efforts to solve these problems through some form of decentralization.

In the more developed countries, such as the United States, France, and England, the local governments had, or have acquired, greater responsibilities for territorial planning and development. But even these powers have proved inadequate. The mounting obligations accompanying increases in population, in welfare services, and in development responsibilities have compelled persistent efforts on the part of national governments to strengthen local capabilities. During the past generation, these efforts took the form of matched grants from the central government for specific services or of encouraging local public development corporations to build and manage housing, transportation, and other services. The current trend is toward enlarging local government boundaries, as in France and Great Britain, and toward providing unrestricted block grants to local communities, as in the United States.

One effect of these measures will be the weakening of the power of the central government to guide developmental strategy within the region. If communities do not require financial assistance, they will not be especially receptive to unpopular national policies. However, block grants and changes in boundaries will not alter the need for national efforts to induce desired changes in interregional or intra-regional patterns of development. Therefore, national incentives are likely to be increased in order to aid lagging regions, to underwrite urban renewal, to siphon off population growth and industries from congested areas, and to support other programs favored by the central authorities.

Still a third question which will be of growing concern in the future is how to ensure that the groups who should benefit from growth will actually do so. Providing assistance from the well-to-do regions to the poorer regions via the central government often ends up with the giver as the principal beneficiary. It has therefore been urged that regions, and in particular the people of these regions, be given a greater voice in the administrative and political process. Mainly dissident minorities have expressed these views to date, but the ideas reflect the mood of the age and are neatly attuned to prevailing circumstances. It is hardly surprising that they are spreading and bid fair to become the conventional wisdom of the future.

One can see these tendencies in a number of different political and social contexts. For example, in the Guayana region of Venezuela, the dissidents stressed the importance of having the Guayana Development Corporation consult the views and needs of the local population: the merchants and political leaders and even the humbler elements of society. They wanted a greater emphasis placed on achieving high employment than on attaining a high rate of growth. They favored low density, more self-help, and owner-occupied housing in places where migrants could find jobs and learn more easily about new opportunities. They objected to the criteria used for housing selection and welfare, which some of the local populace considered to be inappropriate for many of the families the programs were intended to serve. A growing awareness of the discrepancy between the needs of the population and the policies of the administrators soon led some of the local leaders to explore ways of effecting change by pressures and other processes and even by violence.[5] Finally, on some matters, such as the distribution of public land to the local community, the Guayana Development Corporation was forced to reverse its position in response to the pressures of the local leaders.

Other national programs have also been modified by local demands. In Turkey, despite the disdain for local views and a highly centralized administrative tradition, local and regional pressures have forced more attention to be paid to development in the East, though "participation" is still a long way off. In Britain, on the other hand, the claims for regional autonomy in Scotland and Wales have been asserted with increasing intensity. In France, even more than in Britain, the emphasis has changed from simply helping the lagging regions to providing more opportunity for their participation in the decision-making process. These views, expressed often enough before the revolutionary outbreaks in May and June of 1968, were clearly a reaction to the paternalistic and heavy-handed tutelage of the French administrative process. For a long time they were dismissed as contrived political pressures encouraged by an intractable opposition; but after the events of May and June, and even after the subsequent elections which gutted the opposition, the government radically reversed its position and supported the creation of regional assemblies as well as a gradual movement toward eventual fiscal autonomy. Moreover, the government favored these measures on the grounds that the people in the regions would thereby be more apt to pursue vigorous measures in their own behalf.[6]

As for the United States, although its long established pattern of decentralized state authorities has been dwindling in importance, new pressures for more local control have arisen from certain militant leaders of the poor and the black. Only such power, it has been contended, will allow vigorous efforts at self-improvement, and only the possession of such power will transform the black population's image of itself and of its status. These views have come to the fore at approximately the same time that several experiments have been undertaken to encourage "maximum feasible participation" by low-income families in a variety of economic development, educational, and housing assistance programs designed to help them improve their conditions. The ambiguity of the language and the inadequacies of certain programs have led some persons to dismiss such efforts as impractical and misguided. But it is far from certain that the programs have failed or that their limitations have been due to inherent weaknesses rather than to inexperience and limited resources.[7]

In any case, the evidence seems to suggest that, in the future, urban growth strategies will not be simply efforts of the central governments to aid lagging regions through incentives and controls. These strategies will be characterized by pressures and demands on the part of the populations of these lagging areas and their supporters for a greater share in the planning and administration of policies. Indeed, if these views prevail, the big question will be how to ensure that the programs undertaken will prove responsive to those groups which they were designed to benefit.

The fourth set of issues will stem from the changed role of cities in the future. In the past, the basic functions of cities were economic. They still are. Cities provide a favorable location for all kinds of economic activities. And big cities, up to a scale which we cannot yet identify with precision, tend to be the most favorable locations because of their markets, their wide range of public and private services, and the various opportunities and stimuli which accompany their growth and diversification. These, on balance add up to the advantages and "external" economies which families and firms find in cities.

But cities also affect the way we live and enjoy ourselves and our capacity to change and grow. These functions are latent: they involve roles not usually associated with the city's *raison d'être*. But they are becoming more important. People today are increasingly present- and pleasure-oriented. Preferred styles of living and sheer enjoyment rank far higher than they used to in the locational decisions of families and of firms, largely because they can now afford these preferences.

The educational function of cities is also receiving more recognition. In countries in transition from rural, traditional societies, the city concentrates and transmits a new tempo and values. This effect is all the more significant in the poorer countries, since schools reach only a limited portion of the population for a relatively short period. Even in the more developed countries, the city plays the role of educational center for in-migrants from rural areas.

Not the least important role of the city of the future, however, will be to help direct the evolution of its own economy and culture. To be sure, a city's capacity to assist in its own transformation will be subject to serious constraints. Nonetheless, this role will become more crucial as our wealth increases and as we improve our tools and intelligence mechanisms and as we more avidly explore feasible "alternative futures."

Given these prospects of the changing roles of the city, what are the implications for urban growth strategies? In general, we can expect still more emphasis on programs for renewal and for the control of the size or relative growth rates of the very largest cities—because of the anticipated amenity and educational effects. There will also be renewed interest in optimum-sized cities. But the quest will not prove any more amenable to analysis in the future; and as a by-product of this, attention may well shift to the problems of establishing critical *minimum* sizes for cities, especially in lagging regions, to sustain growth and to help cities become more interesting. In addition, we can count on efforts not only to spread the influence of the city to the hinterland, but also to expand the vistas of the city's own population, to get them to experience the whole city and the surrounding region. For, as John Dyckman has noted,

> the West Side Puerto Rican or the Harlem Negro knows that he does not have access to the full meaning of the city of New York. Both the physical space apprehended by the individual and the Lewinian "life space" would have to be expanded. We make much

of the city as a center of communication, but the information in the messages is received by a few while to the many the communication content is chiefly noise.[8]

Finally, there is sure to be much more exploration of the future for the purpose of guiding present national urban growth strategies. We live in an age, many people believe, in which we can successfully accomplish most of what we seek to accomplish if we can only agree on what it is that we want. This faith, especially in the United States, is in large measure an outgrowth of the successes we have achieved in the realm of science and in the growth of our economy. Daniel Bell has even argued that

> perhaps the most important social change of our time is the emergence of a process of direct and deliberate contrivance of change itself. Men now seek to anticipate change, measure the course of its direction and its impact, control it, and even shape it for predetermined ends.[9]

It is not at all certain that the response to this challenge will fortify the faith. The success of a national urban and regional growth strategy involves achieving consensus on values and resource allocation and resolving social conflicts which do not easily lend themselves to technical solutions. Nonetheless, the effort will surely be made: indeed no other aspect of our culture will receive more searching examination in the next generation.

APPENDIX A

Translations of Titles of French Agencies and Administrative Devices

Caisse des Dépôts et Consignations (CDC)	Deposit and Consignment Bank
Centre d'Études et de Recherche d'Aménagements Urbains (CERAU)	Center of Study and Research for Urban Planning
Centre d'Études et de Recherches Mathématiques sur la Planification (CERMP)	Center of Mathematical Studies and Research on Planning
Centre de Recherche et de Documentation sur la Consommation (CREDOC)	Center for Research and Documentation on Consumption
Centre de la Recherche d'Urbanisme (CRU)	Center for Research on Urbanism
Centre de Recherche Économique et Social (CRES)	Center for Economic and Social Research
Collectivités locales	Local authorities
Comité Consultatif Économique et Social de la Région de Paris (CCESRP)	Economic and Social Advisory Committee of the Paris Region
Comité d'Expansion Économique (CEE)	Committee of Economic Expansion
Comité des Plans Régionaux (CPR)	Committee for Regional Plans
Comité de Régionalisation du Plan (CRP)	Committee on the Regionalization of the Plan
Comité Interministériel pour les Problèmes d'Action Régionale et d'Aménagement du Territoire (CIPARAT)	Interministerial Committee for the Problems of Regional Action and Territorial Development
Comité National d'Orientation Économique (CNOE)	National Council of Economic Orientation
Commissariat Général du Plan d'Équipement et de la Productivité (CGP)	General Planning Commission of Equipment and Productivity
Commission de Développement Économique Régional (CODER)	Commission on Regional Economic Development

287

Commission D'Équipement Urbain (CEU)

Commission of Urban Equipment

Commission Départementale d'Équipement (CDE)

Departmental Equipment Commission

Commission Interministérielle de Décentralisation (CID)

Interministerial Commission for Decentralization

Commission Nationale de l'Aménagement du Territoire (CNAT)

National Commission for Territorial Development

Commission Régionale d'Équipement (CRE)

Regional Equipment Commission

Compagnie Nationale d'Aménagement de la Région du Bas-Rhône et du Languedoc (CNARBRL)

National Company for the Planning of the Lower Rhone and Languedoc Region

Conférence Administrative Régionale (CAR)

Regional Administrative Board

Conseil Supérieur du Ministère de la Construction (CSC)

Superior Council of the Ministry of Construction

Délégation à l'Aménagement du Territoire et à l'Action Régionale (DATAR)

Delegation for Territorial Development and Regional Action

Délégation au District de la Région de Paris (DDRP)

Delegation to District of the Paris Region

Délégué Général au District de la Région de Paris (DGDRP)

Delegate General to the District of the Paris Region

Direction de l'Aménagement Foncier et de l'Urbanisme (DAFU)

Directorate of Land and Urban Development

Fonds de Développement Économique et Social (FDES)

Economic and Social Development Fund

Fonds d'Intervention pour l'Aménagement du Territoire (FIAT)

Fund for Territorial Development

Fonds National d'Aménagement Foncier et d'Urbanisme (FNAFU)

National Fund for Land and Urban Development

Fonds National d'Aménagement du Territoire (FNAT)

National Fund for Territorial Development

Groupe Central de Planification Urbaine (GCPU)

Central Urban Planning Group

Groupe d'Ethnologie Sociale à l'École Pratique des Hautes-Études (GESEPHE)

Social Ethnology Group of the Practical School of Higher Studies

Groupe Interministériel d'Aménagement du Bassin Parisien (GIABP)	Interministerial Group for Development of Paris Basin
Inspecteurs Généraux de l'Administration en Mission Extraordinaire (IGAME)	Inspector Generals of Administration on Extraordinary Mission
Institut d'Aménagement et d'Urbanisme de la Région Parisienne (IAURP)	Institute of Development and City Planning of the Paris Region
Institut de Science Économique Appliquée (Économie Régionale) (ISEA)	Institute of Applied Economic Science (Regional Economic Section)
Institut de Sociologie Urbaine (ISU)	Institute of Urban Sociology
Institut d'Urbanisme (IU)	Institute of City Planning
Institut National de la Statistique et des Études Économiques (INSEF)	National Institute of Statistics and Economic Studies
Ministère de la Construction (MC)	Ministry of Construction (formerly the Ministry of Reconstruction and Urbanism)
Ministère du Plan et de l'Aménagement du Territoire (MPAT)	Ministry of Planning and Territorial Development
Organisme Régional d'Étude de l'Aire Métropolitaine (OREAM)	Metropolitan Area Regional Study Organism
Plan d'Aménagement et d'Organisation Générale de la Région Parisienne (PADOG)	Plan of Development and General Organization of the Paris Region
Service Technique Central d'Aménagement et d'Urbanisme (STCAU)	Central Technical Service of Development and Urban Planning
Services des Études Économiques et Financières (SEEF)	Financial and Economic Studies Services
Société Centrale pour l'Équipement du Territoire (SCET)	Central Territorial Equipment Company
Société de Développement Régional (SDR)	Regional Development Society
Société d'Économie Mixte (SEM)	Joint Venture Society
Zone à Urbaniser par Priorité (ZUP)	Priority Urbanization Zone

APPENDIX B

Sources of Figures

1–4. Venezuela; Ciudad Guayana, 1961; Ciudad Guayana, 1970: Programmed Land Uses; Ciudad Guayana: Pattern of Residential Growth

L. Rodwin, *Planning Urban Growth and Regional Development: The Experience of the Guayana Program of Venezuela* (Cambridge: M.I.T. Press, 1969).

5. Turkey, 1960

R. Keleş, *Türkiyede Şehirleşme Hareketleri, 1927-60* [Urbanization Movements in Turkey] (Ankara: University of Ankara, 1961).

6. Proposed Development Strategy for Eastern Marmara

Department of Regional Planning, *Doğu Marmara Bölgesi Ön Plâni* [Preliminary Plan for the Eastern Marmara Region] (Ankara: Ministry of Reconstruction and Resettlement, 1963).

7. Zonguldak

Department of Regional Planning, *Zonguldak Bölgesi Ön Plâni* [Preliminary Plan for the Zonguldak Region] (Ankara: General Directorate of Planning and Reconstruction, Ministry of Reconstruction and Resettlement, 1963).

8. Adana Region

Adapted from maps prepared for the Department of Regional Planning by the Çukurova Regional Planning Project (Ankara: Department of Regional Planning, General Directorate of Planning and Reconstruction, Ministry of Reconstruction and Resettlement).

9. Great Britain: New Towns and Development Areas, 1969

Adapted from maps and information provided by the Ministry of Housing and Local Government, London; the Distribution of Industry Division of the Board of Trade, London; the Scottish Development Department, Edinburgh; and the Welsh Office, London.

10. New Towns and Expanding Towns in England and Wales, 1969

Adapted from maps and information provided by the Ministry of Housing and Local Government, London, and the Welsh Office, London.

11. Timetable of Principal Measures Used in British Policy for Development Areas

Adapted from G. McCrone, *Regional Policy in Britain* (London: G. Allen and Unwin, Ltd., 1969).

12. French Regional Planning Organization Chart

Prepared by Lloyd Rodwin.

13. Spheres of Influence of Paris and the Equilibrium Metropolises

Adapted from J. Hautreux and M. Rochefort, *La Fonction Régionale dans l'Armature Urbaine Française* [The Regional Function in French Urban Structure] (Paris: Commissariat Général du Plan d'Équipement et de la Productivité and Ministère de la Construction, et al., 1964).

14. United States, 1960: Density of Population and Cities Over 50,000

Adapted from N. Ginsburg, H. Fullard, and H. C. Darby (eds.), *Aldine University Atlas* (Chicago: Aldine Publishing Company, Scott Foresman and Company, 1969).

15. Regions, Districts, and Redevelopment Areas of the Economic Development Administration, 1968

Adapted from "Economic Development Districts, July 1, 1968" and "U.S. Department of Commerce Qualified Areas, Sept. 1, 1968." These maps were prepared by the Office of Development Districts, Economic Development Administration, U.S. Department of Commerce, Washington, D.C.

Maps by John V. Morris

FOOTNOTES

Introduction

1. E. Weissmann, "The Urban Crisis in the World," *Urban Affairs*, vol. 1, no. 1 (1965), pp. 66–67.

2. A. O. Hirschman, *Journeys Toward Progress* (New York: Twentieth Century Fund, 1963), chaps. 4, 5.

3. L. Rodwin, *The British New Towns Policy* (Cambridge: Harvard University Press, 1956).

Chapter I

1. These ideas were first developed in a paper prepared in 1957. See L. Rodwin, "National Urban Policy for Developing Countries," *Papers and Proceedings of the Regional Science Association*, vol. 3 (1957). They were subsequently revised and extended in my article "Metropolitan Policy for Developing Areas," *Daedalus*, Journal of the American Academy of Arts and Sciences, vol. 90, no. 1 (1961), pp. 132–146; and this version was reprinted in W. Isard and J. H. Cumberland, eds., *Regional Economic Planning* (Paris: European Productivity Agency of the Organisation for European Economic Cooperation, 1961). Several important additions and revisions have been made in this new version.

   Since 1957 there has been an increasing number of articles describing experiences and problems of different countries which call for the equivalent of urban growth policies. Some recent examples are: L. Jakobson and V. Prakash, "Urbanization and Regional Planning in India." *Urban Affairs Quarterly*, vol. 11, no. 3 (1967), pp. 36–65; J. Friedmann, "The Strategy of Deliberate Urbanization" (1967) and Friedmann, "The Role of Cities in National Development" (1968) [both mimeographed papers published by the Ford Foundation, Urban and Regional Advisory Program in Chile, Santiago, Chile]; and S. H. Robock, "Strategies for Regional Economic Development," *Papers of the Regional Science Association*, vol. 17 (1966), pp. 129–161. See also International Union of Local Authorities, *Urbanization in Developing Countries: Report of a Symposium Held in December, 1967, at Noordwijk, Netherlands* (The Hague: Martinus Nijhoff, 1968) pp. 11–106.

2. For example, see R. Vining, "A Description of Certain Spatial Aspects of An Economic System," *Economic Development and Cultural Change*, vol. 3, no. 2 (1955), pp. 147–195; E. M. Hoover, "The Concept of a System of Cities: A Comment on Rutledge Vining's Paper," *Economic Development and Cultural Change*, vol. 3, no. 2 (1955), pp. 196–198, and W. F. Stolper, "Spatial Order and the Economic Growth of Cities: A Comment on Eric Lampard's Paper," *Economic Development and Cultural Change*, vol. 3, no. 2 (1955) pp. 137–146.

3. See E. E. Lampard, "The History of Cities in Economically Advanced Areas," *Economic Development and Cultural Change*, vol. 3, no. 2 (1955), pp. 81–136; B. F. Hoselitz, "Generative and Parasitic Cities," *Economic Development and Cultural Change*, vol. 3, no. 3 (1955), pp. 278–294; and B. Harris, "Urbanization Policy in India," *Papers and Proceedings of the Regional Science Association*, vol. 5 (1959), pp. 181–207. For a different source of suggestive ideas, see F. Perroux, "Note sur la Notion de 'Pôle de Croissance,' " *Économie Appliquée*, vol. 8, nos. 1 and 2 (1955),

pp. 307–320; and *L'Économie du XXème Siècle* (Paris: Presses Universitaires de France, 1964), Deuxième Partie, chaps. 2–7.

4. Overhead capital and infrastructure are employed as interchangeable terms. Paul Rosenstein-Rodan supplied the figures cited. The estimates are based on data for several countries, and of course the figures vary for each country. See P. N. Rosenstein-Rodan, "Les Besoins des Capitaux dans les Pays Sous-Développés," *Économie Appliquée*, vol. 7, nos. 1 and 2 (1954), pp. 77–89; and Rosenstein-Rodan, "Reflections on Regional Development," mimeographed memorandum, C/63-25 (Cambridge: Center for International Studies, M.I.T., 1963). Another interesting statistic is provided by Lowdon Wingo who is conducting a major study for Resources for the Future, Inc. on the relationship of infrastructure to national and regional economic development, urbanization, and programming strategy. In an informal memorandum he has observed that "counting in depreciation, or effective life, and obsolescence, it seems likely that in the course of the next generation Latin America will have to put in place a gross stock of fixed social capital in its cities equal to five times the size of that now in existence just to maintain existing service levels. Such an effort will make large demands on the financial resources of the region, so that their efficient employment will have direct consequences for the overall rates of growth" (L. Wingo, "Determinants of Urban Infrastructure Investment in the Less Developed Countries: A Research Memorandum," preliminary draft, 1964, p. 4).

5. C. B. Wurster, "The Nature and Cost of Minimum Acceptable Living Conditions in Different Types of Indian Urban Community," mimeographed (Berkeley: Department of City and Regional Planning, University of California, 1958). The main flaw in this argument is that it is often more important to increase returns than to cut costs.

6. C. Haar, B. Higgins, and L. Rodwin, "Economic and Physical Planning: Coordination in Developing Areas," *Journal of the American Institute of Planners*, vol. 24, no. 3 (1958), p. 169.

7. A. O. Hirschman, *The Strategy of Economic Development* (New Haven: Yale University Press, 1958), pp. 184–185. Hirschman shrewdly goes on to explain that

> the reason for this tendency—perhaps implicit in the phrase 'nothing succeeds like success'—must be sought in the realm of social psychology. The progressive sectors and regions of an underdeveloped economy are easily overimpressed with their own rate of development. At the same time, they set themselves apart from the less progressive operators by creating a picture of the latter as lazy, bungling, intriguing and generally hopeless. There seems to be a cliquishness about progress when it first appears that recalls the same phenomenon among adolescents! The girls who menstruate and the boys who shave have an acute sense of their superiority over those who cannot yet claim such achievements. . . .
>
> Even though the initial success of these groups may often be due to sheer luck or to environmental factors such as resource endowment, matters will not be left there. Those who have been caught by progress will always maintain that they were the ones who did the catching; they will easily convince themselves or attempt to convince others that their accomplishments are primarily owed to their superior moral qualities and conduct. It is precisely this self-righteousness that will tend to produce its own evidence: once these groups have spread the word that their success was due to hard work and virtuous living, they must willy-nilly live up to their own story, or at the least will make their children do so. In other words, there is reason to think that

the 'Protestant ethic,' instead of being the prime mover, is often implanted *ex post* as though to sanctify and consolidate whatever accumulation of economic power and wealth has been achieved. To the extent that this happens, a climate particularly favorable to further growth will actually come into existence in the sectors or regions that have pulled ahead, and this will confirm the economic operators in their preference for these regions and make it somewhat less rational.

(Ibid., pp. 185–186.)

8. See the discussion on growth centers in Chapter II of this book. Cf. also F. Perroux, *op. cit.,* fn. 3. Perroux's ideas have stimulated a sizeable literature. For a brief introduction, see J. R. Boudeville, ed., *L'Espace et les Pôles de Croissance* (Paris: Presses Universitaires de France, 1968); P. Aydalot, "Note sur les Économies Externes et Quelques Notions Connexes," *Revue Économique,* vol. 16, no. 6 (1965), pp. 944–972; and N. M. Hansen, *French Regional Planning* (Bloomington: Indiana University Press, 1968), chaps. 5, 6. See also C. Ponsard, *Économie et Espace,* École Pratique des Hautes Études, Observation Économique, no. 8 (Paris: SEDES, 1954), Book 2, pp. 334–450.

9. Hirschman, *op. cit.,* pp. 190–197.

10. Throughout this book the term "physical planners" is used as a synonym for city and regional planners.

11. Haar, Higgins, and Rodwin, *op. cit.,* p. 168.

12. See P. G. Frank, "Economic Planners in Afghanistan," *Economic Development and Cultural Change,* vol. 1, no. 5 (1953), p. 339; and the International Bank for Reconstruction and Development, *The Economic Development of Mexico* (Baltimore: Johns Hopkins Press, 1953), pp. 150–151.

Chapter II

1. The initial ideas for this chapter were first formulated in a lecture delivered in the spring of 1961 at the Case Institute of Technology under the sponsorship of the Program in Planning and Policy Sciences. The ideas were then revised and published in C. J. Friedrich and S. E. Harris, eds., *Public Policy* (Cambridge: Graduate School of Public Administration, Harvard University, 1963) and then reprinted in J. Friedmann and W. Alonso, eds., *Regional Development and Planning* (Cambridge: M.I.T. Press, 1964). Several additions and revisions have been made in this new version.

2. H. B. Chenery, "Comparative Advantage and Development Policy," *The American Economic Review,* vol. 51, no. 1 (1961), p. 20. It may be, however, that today the potential gains from comparative advantage tend to be neglected. Despite the greater realism of the growth economists' approach, Chenery thinks they underrate the risk in ignoring comparative advantage both for countries with a shortage of capital and foreign exchange and for smaller countries with a limited range of production possibilities. On this point, as well as on the others for which Chenery is cited, this paper leans heavily on Chenery's perceptive article cited above.

3. Chenery, *op. cit.,* pp. 20–22. See also R. E. Caves, *Trade and Economic Structure: Models and Methods* (Cambridge: Harvard University Press, 1960); R. Nurske, *Problems of Capital Formation in Underdeveloped Countries* (Oxford: Oxford University Press, 1953); A. O. Hirschman, *The Strategy of Economic Development* (New Haven: Yale University

Press, 1958); and W. W. Rostow, *The Stages of Economic Growth* (Cambridge: Cambridge University Press, 1960).

4. Hirschman, *op. cit.*, chap. 6.

5. W. Isard, *Location and Space Economy* (Cambridge: The Technology Press of the Massachusetts Institute of Technology, 1956; New York: John Wiley and Sons, 1956), p. 183.

6. *Ibid.*

7. See Chenery, *op. cit.*, pp. 25–46. The programming techniques can accommodate other constraints besides capital, such as labor, foreign exchange, and the supply of particular factors and commodities. They can also handle certain sequential effects including the impact on import prices of investment in supplying sectors and the revision of initial calculations of opportunity costs, labor, capital, and foreign exchange. In addition, the techniques can take into account different processes of production as well as the effects of those indirect benefits and costs which can be specified in quantitative form. *Ibid.*

8. Hirschman, *op. cit.*, chaps. 2, 4; Chenery, *op. cit.*, p. 40.

9. B. Stevens, "Interregional Linear Programming," *Journal of Regional Science*, vol. 1, no. 1 (1958), pp. 61–62.

10. L. Lefeber, *Allocation in Space, Production, Transport and Industrial Location* (Amsterdam: North-Holland Publishing Company, 1958), p. 134; and Stevens, *op. cit.*, pp. 60-98; see also W. Isard, *Methods of Regional Analysis* (Cambridge: The Technology Press of the Massachusetts Institute of Technology, 1960; New York: John Wiley and Sons, 1960), chap. 10; and L. H. Moses, "General Equilibrium Model of Production, Interregional Trade and Location of Industry," *The Review of Economics and Statistics*, vol. 42, no. 4 (1960), pp. 373-396. Roughly the same limitations noted for Lefeber's and Stevens's papers apply to Moses's stimulating paper, too.

11. Lefeber suggests that

> in a detailed analysis of larger areas, a fruitful approach might be to work out a skeleton system based on the main flows of prime materials. Then, as a second step, one may work out the allocation patterns in the different regions, with suitable aggregation, taking the skeleton system as given. By considering several feasible skeleton systems and their corresponding regional adjustments, one may approximate that overall pattern for spatial allocation that yields the highest level of welfare.
>
> The empirical investigation of spatial general equilibrium adjustment presents difficulties which should not be underestimated. The insufficiency of basic data, the problem of aggregating flows, and the limitations of existing forecasting methods may prove to be the most difficult obstacles to overcome. Nevertheless, it is believed that the analytical approach developed in this work is a step in the right direction.
>
> (*Ibid.*, p. 134.)

12. Stevens, *op. cit.*, pp. 89–90.

13. Alas, I have lost track of the source of this quotation.

14. E. M. Hoover, "The Concept of a System of Cities: A Comment on Rutledge Vining's Paper," *Economic Development and Cultural Change*, vol. 3, no. 2 (1955), p. 196. The rank size rule conforms to a Pareto distribution with an exponent greater than one. The function has the form:

$$y \cdot x^a = b$$

where y is the number of cities greater than a specified size a; and x is the size of a specified city. The constants are a and b; or alternatively expressed, y is the rank and x is the size of a given city and b may be the population of the largest city. See also J. Q. Stewart, "Empirical Mathematical Rules Concerning the Distribution and Equilibrium of Population," *The Geographical Review*, vol. 37, no. 3 (1947), pp. 461–485; G. K. Zipf, *Human Behavior and the Principle of Least Effort* (Cambridge: Addison-Wesley Press, 1949); M. Jefferson, "The Law of the Primate City," *The Geographical Review*, vol. 29, no. 2 (1939), pp. 226–232; G. R. Allen, "The 'Courbe Des Populations': A Further Analysis," *Bulletin of the Oxford Institute of Statistics*, vol. 16, nos. 5 and 6 (1954), pp. 179–189; B. J. L. Berry and W. L. Garrison, "Alternate Explanations of Urban Rank Size Relationships," *Annals of the Association of American Geographers*, vol. 48, no. 1 (1958), pp. 83–91; Berry, "City Size Distributions and Economic Development," *Economic Development and Cultural Change*, vol. 9, no. 4 (1961), pp. 573–587; C. H. Madden, "On Some Indication of Stability in the Growth of Cities in the United States," *Economic Development and Cultural Change*, vol. 4, no. 3 (1956), pp. 236–252; Madden, "Some Spatial Aspects of Urban Growth in the United States," *ibid.*, vol. 4, no. 4 (1956), pp. 371–387; Berry, "Cities as Systems Within Systems of Cities," *Papers and Proceedings of the Regional Science Association*, vol. 13 (1964), pp. 147–164; M. Beckman, "Some Reflections on Lösch's Theory of Location," *Papers and Proceedings of the Regional Science Association*, vol. 1 (1955), pp. N1–N8; and Beckman, "City Hierarchies and the Distribution of City Size," *Economic Development and Cultural Change*, vol. 6, no. 3 (1958), pp. 243–248. Beckman multiplies the rank of the city in the midpoint of its class and its population, and concludes that "after a fair number of such multiplications, the product itself will show a distribution pattern. . .[in which] the steps in the rank size diagram are thus smoothed out, the distinctness of the size classes is lost, and [the rank size rule] applies in effect throughout the size classes" (*ibid.*, p. 245). For a critical view of Beckmann's work, see J. B. Parr, "City Hierarchies and the Distribution of City Size: A Reconsideration of Beckmann's Contribution," *Journal of Regional Science*, vol. 9, no. 2 (1969), pp. 239–254.

15. H. Simon, "On a Class of Skew Distribution Functions," *Biometrika*, vol. 42 (1955), Parts 3 and 4, pp. 425–40. This proposition requires other questionable assumptions, such as a net increase of urban population by natural increase, which we can ignore for the purposes of this discussion. See also B. Mandelbrot, "A Class of Long Tailed Probability Distributions and the Empirical Distribution of City Sizes," in F. Massyik and P. Ratoosh, *Mathematical Approaches in Behavioral Science* (Homewood, 111.: R. D. Irwin and the Dorsey Press, 1965), pp. 322–332.

16. Berry, "City Size Distributions and Economic Development," 573–587. See also F. T. Moore, "A Note on City Size Distributions," *Economic Development and Cultural Change*, vol. 7, no. 4 (1959), pp. 465–6; and C. Stewart, "The Size and Spacing of Cities," *The Geographical Review*, vol. 48, no. 2 (1958), pp. 222–245.

17. A. Fleisher, "On Prediction and Urban Traffic," *Papers and Proceedings of the Regional Science Association*, vol. 7 (1961), pp. 43–50. Arguing against changing the exponent for a gravity model, Fleisher emphasizes that "the matter is not merely one of throwing in another adjustable constant. . . . Properly, the problem requires the best fit with the least number of ad hoc constants, for in this way degrees of freedom are conserved. This is precisely the same problem that arises in the elaboration of a prediction rule" (*ibid.*, p. 47). The same objection applies to adjustments of the exponent of the rank size rule. However, Michael J. Woldenberg suggests that the convergent mean—the area between the arithmetic and the geometric mean—

generally provides a better fit. See M. J. Woldenberg, "Energy Flow and Spatial Order—Mixed Hexagonal Hierarchies of Central Places," *The Geographical Review*, vol. 58, no. 4 (1968), pp. 552–574.

18. Hoover, *op. cit.*, p. 198.

19. For another view, see Vining, *op. cit.*, pp. 187–195.

20. N. S. B. Gras, *An Introduction to Economic History* (New York and London: Harper and Bros., 1922), p. 185.

21. B. F. Hoselitz, "Generative and Parasitic Cities," *op. cit.*, pp. 278–294.

22. *Ibid.* See also Stolper, "Spatial Order and the Economic Growth of Cities: A Comment on Eric Lampard's Paper," *Economic Development and Cultural Change*, vol. 3, No. 2 (1955), pp. 141–2.

23. Stolper, "Spatial Order and the Economic Growth of Cities."

24. For some suggestive hypotheses on this subject, see T. W. Schultz, *Economic Organization of Agriculture* (New York: McGraw-Hill, 1953), chaps. 9, 10; Lampard, *op. cit.*, pp. 131–2; W. H. Nicholls, "Research on Agriculture and Economic Development," *American Economic Review, Papers and Proceedings*, vol. 50, no. 2 (1960) pp. 629–635; Nicholls, "Accommodating Economic Change in Underdeveloped Countries," *ibid.*, vol. 49, no. 2 (1959), pp. 156–168; Nicholls, "Industrialization, Factor Markets and Agricultural Development," *Journal of Political Economy*, vol. 69, no. 4 (1961), pp. 319–340; V. W. Ruttan, "The Impact of Urban-Industrial Development on Agriculture in the Tennessee Valley and the Southeast," *Journal of Farm Economics*, vol. 37, no. 1 (1955), pp. 38–56; and A. M. Tang, *Economic Development in the Southern Piedmont, 1860–1950—Its Impact on Agriculture* (Chapel Hill: University of North Carolina Press, 1958). See also P. Pottier, "Axes de Communication et Théorie de Développement," *Revue Économique*, vol. 14, no. 1 (1963), pp. 113–114; J. Pautard, *Les Disparités Régionales dans la Croissance de l'Agriculture Française* (Paris: Gauthier-Villars, 1965), pp. 108–18, 147–175; and B. F. Hoselitz, "The Role of Cities in the Economic Growth of Underdeveloped Countries," *The Journal of Political Economy*, vol. 61, no. 3 (1953), pp. 195–208. See *Economic Development and Cultural Change*, vol. 3, no. 1 (1954), pp. 3–77, and especially R. Redfield and M. B. Singer, "The Cultural Role of Cities," *ibid.*, pp. 53–73 for some qualifications of the points raised above; and D. C. North, "The Spatial and Interregional Framework of the U. S. Economy: An Historical Perspective," *Papers and Proceedings of the Regional Science Association*, vol. 2 (1956), pp. 13–1, 13–9.

25. Schultz, *op. cit.*; and Schultz, "Reflections on Poverty Within Agriculture," *Journal of Political Economy*, vol. 58, no. 1 (1950), pp. 1–15. See also J. Friedmann, *Regional Development Policy: A Case Study of Venezuela* (Cambridge: M.I.T. Press, 1966), chap. 1; G. M. Meier and R. E. Baldwin, *Economic Development: Theory, History, Policy* (New York: John Wiley and Sons, 1957), Part 2; H. Perloff and L. Wingo, "Natural Resource Endowment and Regional Economic Growth" in J. J. Spengler, ed., *Natural Resources and Economic Growth* (Washington, D. C.: Resources for the Future, 1961), pp. 204–205; S. A. Stouffer, "Intervening Opportunities: A Theory Relating Mobility and Distance," *American Sociological Review*, vol. 5, no. 6 (1940), pp. 845–867; Isard, *Location and Space Economy*, pp. 64–65, fn. 13; and C. D. Harris, "The Market Factor in the Localization of Industry in the United States," *Annals of the Association of American Geographers*, vol. 44, no. 4 (1954) pp. 315–348.

26. S. R. Dennison, *The Location of Industry and the Depressed Areas* (London: Oxford University Press, 1939); and J. F. Kain and J. J. Persky, "The North's Stake in Southern Rural Poverty," in *Rural Poverty in the United States: A Report by the President's*

National Advisory Commission on Rural Poverty (Washington, D. C.: *Department of Agriculture*, 1968), chap. 27, pp. 288–308. On the other hand, see H. S. Perloff et al., *Regions, Resources and Economic Growth* (Baltimore: Johns Hopkins Press [published for Resources for the Future], 1960), pp. 600–607; and G. H. Borts, "The Equalization of Returns and Regional Economic Growth," *The American Economic Review,* vol. 50, no. 3 (1960), pp. 318–347.

27. F. Perroux, "Economic Space, Theory and Applications," *Quarterly Journal of Economics,* vol. 6, no. 1 (1950), pp. 90–91; and N. M. Hansen, French Regional Planning (Bloomington: Indiana University Press, 1968), pp. 102–122. Chapter 5 of Hansen's book gives the best short review in English on this literature. See also L. H. Klaassen, "Growth Poles—An Economic View," Paper prepared for the Expert Group on Growth Poles and Growth Centers, United Nations Research Institute for Social Development (Geneva) and the European Coordination Center for Research and Documentation in Social Sciences (Vienna), Toulouse, May, 1969; and P. Bernard, *Les Pôles et Centres de Croissance en tant qu'Instruments du Développement Régional et de la Modernisation,* Rapport Préliminaire (Geneva: Institut de Recherche des Nations Unies pour le Développement Social, 1969), pp. 79–119.

28. For valuable starts in this direction, see Perloff, et al., *op. cit.,* Part 4; Tang, *op. cit.;* Nicholls, "Industrialization, Factor Markets and Agricultural Development;" Perloff and Wingo, *op. cit.;* R. A. Elletson, "City-Hinterland Relationships in India," in R. Turner, *India's Urban Future* (Bombay: Oxford University Press, 1962), chap. 5; and R. D. Lambert, "The Impact of Urban Society Upon Village Life," *ibid.,* chap. 6.

29. The concept of dynamic external economies is used by Scitovsky to indicate the effect of investment in one sector on the probability of investment in another sector via increased demand or reduced costs. These economies are particularly induced by urbanization, through improved infrastructure, demand increases in other sectors, economies of scale, better financial services, education, and formal and in-service training. These economies cannot be gauged by means of sector by sector analysis. See T. Scitovsky, "Two Concepts of External Economies," *Journal of Political Economy,* vol. 62, no. 2 (1954), pp. 143–151; and Chenery, *op. cit.,* pp. 20–21, 24–25.

30. Chenery emphasizes on the basis of the experience of southern Italy "that a change in the productive structure must be put on a par with an increase of total investment as an immediate objective of development policy. The development of overhead facilities is only one aspect of the total change that is needed." See H. B. Chenery, "Development Policies for Southern Italy," *Quarterly Journal of Economics,* vol. 76, no. 4 (1962), pp. 515–548.

31. For some suggestive notions on the effects of regional developments on traditional attitudes, see Stouffer, *op. cit.;* D. Lerner, *The Passing of Traditional Society* (Glencoe: The Free Press, 1958), chap. 1; Lampard, *op. cit.;* and L. R. Peattie, *The View From the Barrio* (Ann Arbor: University of Michigan Press, 1968), chaps. 10, 11.

32. Chenery points out that "leading sectors are likely to be industries in which import substitution becomes profitable as markets expand and capital and skills are required. Even in Japan, the most successful of the low income countries in increasing exports, import substitution accounted for nearly 40% of the rise of industry (from 23% of the GNP to 33% between 1914 and 1954) as compared to less than 10% for exports" (H. B. Chenery, "Patterns of Industrial Growth," *The American Economic Review,* vol. 50, no. 4 [1960], p. 651).

33. The difference between goals and constraints is often moot or meaningless. See R. Dorfman, "Operations Research," *American Economic Review,* vol. 50, no. 4 (1960), p. 609; and J. Margolis, "The Evaluation of Water Resources Development," *ibid.,* vol. 49, no. 1 (1959), pp. 99–100.

34. For an interesting example of an effort to devise a simple pragmatic inter-industry model to analyze regional development proposals, see J. H. Cumberland, "A Regional Inter-Industry Model for Analysis of Development Objectives," *Papers of the Regional Science Association,* vol. 17 (1966), pp. 65–94. Cf. also Chapter III of this book which discusses in more detail how regions might be studied. See, too, A. Mayne, "Designing and Administering a Regional Economic Development Plan with Specific Reference to Puerto Rico," in Isard and Cumberland, *op. cit.,* chap. 7.

35. For a discussion of some of these problems, see T. A. Reiner, "Organizing Regional Investment Criteria," *Papers and Proceedings of the Regional Science Association,* vol. 11 (1963), pp. 63–72.

36. Rosenstein-Rodan, "Reflections on Regional Development," p. 9. For further discussion of the different types of regions and the kinds of policies that might be applied, see Friedmann, *Regional Development Policy, A Case Study of Venezuela,* chaps. 3–5, 9.

37. N. M. Hansen, "The Structure and Determinants of Local Public Investment Expenditures," *Review of Economic Statistics,* vol. 47, no. 2 (1965), pp. 150–162; and Hansen, *French Regional Planning,* chaps. 7, 8.

38. Hirschman, *Journeys Toward Progress,* pp. 276–297.

Chapter III

1. This chapter is based on the writer's experience as Director of the Guayana program of the Joint Center for Urban Studies of MIT and Harvard University. It is an abbreviated, updated, and substantially rewritten version of *Urban Planning in Developing Countries* (Washington, D. C.: Department of Housing and Urban Development, 1965). The writer prepared this monograph for the Department of Housing and Urban Development at the request of the Agency for International Development. The substance of this chapter appeared in a more popular article ("Ciudad Guayana—A New City," *Scientific American* [vol. 213, no. 3, 1965]) which was subsequently republished with minor changes in L. Rodwin & Associates, *Planning City Growth and Regional Development: The Experience of the Guayana Program of Venezuela* (Cambridge: M. I. T. Press, 1968), chap. 1.

2. The reader ought to be warned that a description of planning processes is likely to create an image that is less confusing than the actuality. Studies and plans are made—not by machines but by human beings—thinking, discussing, arguing and testing their ideas. Planners are always learning as they go, particularly when they are working in a foreign country within an unfamiliar institutional framework. Since no strict series of steps can be formulated in advance, what we have chosen to do instead is to report on the more important studies and actions and sequences which shaped the planning of Ciudad Guayana.

3. In drawing up this list, the economists took into account the demand in Venezuela and elsewhere for each industry's products; the linkages between the industries; the effect of economies of scale; transportation costs; and the influence upon each potential industry of the existence in their initial stage of development of a hydro-power facility, and integrated iron and steel complex, and a basic aluminum smelting project. For more detail, see R. Alamo Blanco and A. Ganz, "Economic Diagnosis and Plans," in Rodwin and Associates, *op. cit.,* pp. 60–90.

4. Blanco and Ganz, *op. cit.* The total estimated private investment was expected to approximate 365 million dollars for the 1965–1968 period and 1,483 million dollars for the 1969–1975 period. The data are based on material on the Guayana Region

Development Program prepared for the *Plan de la Nación, 1965–1968* and on other long-range estimates made by the Economic Research and Planning Division of the Corporación Venezolana de Guayana and the MIT-Harvard Joint Center Guayana Project.

5. D. Appleyard, "City Designers and the Pluralistic City," in Rodwin & Associates, *op. cit.*, pp. 422–452.

6. L. R. Peattie, *The View from the Barrio* (Ann Arbor: University of Michigan Press, 1968), p. 5. For further detail on some of these issues, see Rodwin & Associates, *op. cit.*, chaps. 12, 18, 20–25.

7. For further discussion of this question, see Rodwin & Associates, *op. cit.*, chaps. 20–25.

8. R. Soberman, "An Economic Evaluation of the Urban Transportation Plan: August 1964" (Report prepared for the Economic Research and Planning Division of the Corporación Venezolana de Guayana and the MIT-Harvard Joint Center Guayana Project), p. 9.

9. División de Estudios Planificación e Investigación Planeamiento Físico, *Plan de Desarrollo Ciudad Guayana,* Corporación Venezolana de Guayana, pp. 36, 56–60. This document incorporates the results of a number of studies and conclusions of the staff of the Urban Design Section of the Corporación Venezolana de Guayana and the MIT-Harvard Joint Center Guayana Project. The author's discussion of the industrial, business, and civic centers is based to a large extent on these studies and reports.

10. *Ibid.*, p. 62. See also Wilhelm von Moltke, "The Evolution of the Linear Form," in Rodwin & Associates, *op. cit.*, pp. 126–146.

11. División de Estudios Planificacióne Investigación Planeamiento Físico, *op. cit.*, pp. 67–69.

12. K. Lynch, "Some Notes on the Design of Ciudad Guayana" (Report prepared for the Urban Design Section of the Corporación Venezolana de Guayana and the MIT-Harvard Joint Center Guayana Project), pp. 1–11.

13. Appleyard, *op. cit.*, pp. 422–452.

14. K. Lynch, *The Image of the City* (Cambridge: The Technology Press and Harvard University Press, 1960), p. 2.

15. Division de Estudios Planificación e Investigación Planeamiento Físico, *op. cit.*, p. 67. See also R. B. Mitchell, "Memorandum to Lloyd Rodwin on Caracas Visit of May 11–16, 1964 (Cambridge: Joint Center for Urban Studies of MIT and Harvard University), p. 4.

16. Some of the land for Alta Vista was owned by the Orinoco Mining Company, and acquisition involved delicate negotiations, especially since the company was involved in a dispute with the government on taxes and related matters. The administrative style of the Venezuelan officials also influenced the pace of the operation.

17. A. Fawcett, "Implementation of the Physical Plan" (Preliminary draft report prepared for the División de Estudios Planificación e Investigación, MIT-Harvard Joint Center Guayana Project) [1964], pp. 21–28.

18. *Ibid.*, pp. 31–32.

19. R. Corrada and L. Ayesta, "Investment Opportunities in Housing, Construction and Financing and in Housing Materials Manufacture" (Report prepared for the División de Estudios Planificación e Investigación and the MIT-Harvard Joint Center

Guayana Project) [1963]. See also R. Corrada, "The Housing Program," in Rodwin & Associates, *op. cit.*, pp. 236–251.

20. It turned out that the migrants rarely settled in these areas when they first arrived. Instead, they stayed initially with friends and relatives or in already built housing. Only later, after finding a job and a mate and after becoming oriented in the community, did they decide to search for land and a more permanent home. Since the planners did not know enough about this initial stage to do much about it, they concentrated on meeting the needs of the more established families. See L. R. Peattie, "Memorandum to L. Rodwin, W. Doebele and R. Corrada," August 26, 1963 (Cambridge: Joint Center for Urban Studies of MIT and Harvard University), pp. 1–2.

21. One aim was to discover how responsive migrant families would be to various forms of assistance. To the great surprise of the directors of the program, the most important factor in spurring housing improvement in El Roble turned out to be the construction of streets. Provision of streets, more than schools or electricity, seemed to imply a stage of urbanization that distinguished city life from the countryside and apparently justified investments by these families in significant improvements. This discovery may have interesting implications if future migrants react in the same way. See R. Corrada, "Housing Program for 1964," Memorandum to Colonel Rafael Alfonzo Ravard, November 18, 1963 (Cambridge: Joint Center for Urban Studies of MIT and Harvard University), pp. 1–5.

22. R. G. Davis, "Strategy for Human Resource Development in the Distrito Caroní: A Summary" (Report prepared for the Human Resource Section of the Corporación Venezolana de Guayana and the MIT-Harvard Joint Center Guayana Project) [1964]. See also R. G. Davis and N. F. McGinn, "Education and Regional Development," in Rodwin & Associates, *op. cit.*, pp. 270–285.

23. Davis, *op. cit.*, p. 10

24. *Ibid.*

25. R. G. Davis and N. F. McGinn, *Build a Mill, Build a House, Build a School: Industrialization, Urbanization and Education in Ciudad Guayana*, Part 3 (Cambridge: Harvard University Press, 1969).

26. J. Zucotti, "Municipal Ordinance Project—Preparatory Memo" (Report prepared for Desarrollo Humano and the MIT-Harvard Joint Center Guayana Project) [1964], pp. 1–5, 8–14.

27. Summer Study Group in Public Administration, "Governing Guayana, Roles and Responsibilities in the Public Management of Santo Tomé" (Staff working paper prepared for the Corporación Venezolana de Guayana and the MIT-Harvard Joint Center Guayana Project) [1963].

28. Real Estate Research Corporation, "Summary of Conclusions—Land Development Strategy Analysis, Ciudad Guayana, Venezuela" (Report prepared for Corporación Venezolana de Guayana) [1964].

29. *Ibid.*, pp. 30–37. CVG balked at the last recommendation on the grounds that it was too difficult to implement. See also A. Downs, "Creating A Land Development Strategy for Ciudad Guayana," in Rodwin & Associates, *op. cit.*, pp. 202–218.

30. For further details on the application of these policies to specific firms, see Alamo and Ganz, *op. cit.*, pp. 25–26. See also R. Alamo Blanco and A. Ganz, "The Promotion of Economic Activity," in Rodwin & Associates, *op. cit.*, pp. 163–177.

31. The economists decided that, given the existing and prospective level of building, a construction materials wholesaling business offered attractive prospects. They also

explored methods of easy financing for the self-help housebuilder. Contacts were established with leading builders and industrialists interested in this market. While these potential investors conducted their own feasibility studies, the staff examined the terms on which long-term and short-term construction financing could be obtained, the possibilities of expanding the assets of existing savings and loan associations in Ciudad Guayana, and the kinds of guarantees and other assurances builders would require before initiating operations in this environment.

Meanwhile, the work on the heavy machinery complex was in a pre-promotional stage. CVG did make a contract with the Batelle Memorial Institute to evaluate the specific production processes, costs, and organizational framework for the management of this group of activities. In the interim, the staff made preliminary efforts to identify the attitudes of various firms which might wish to be associated with this complex. See N. Fitts, "Recommendations for Action: Organization and Activities of the Promotion Staff," Memorandum to Lloyd Rodwin, Rafael Corrada, and Alexander Ganz, July 1, 1964 (Cambridge: Joint Center for Urban Studies of MIT and Harvard University). See also Blanco and Ganz, "The Promotion of Economic Activity."

32. For further detail, see P. E. Beach, Jr., "The Business Center," in Rodwin & Associates, *op. cit.*, pp. 219–235.

33. Establishment of promotional offices abroad was not considered high priority by CVG since other agencies of the Venezuelan government (such as the Venezuelan Corporation for Development [CVF] and the foreign consulates) were already engaged in such efforts. The staff wanted a specialized firm engaged in this activity. CVG also dragged its heels on making bids for labor-intensive activities because labor costs in Guayana were so high and the efforts required to establish such activities were so time-consuming. It was also hoped that much of this employment would be supplied by the service industries, and the construction of housing and the dam. For some of the critical views on this subject, see E. Moscovitch, "Employment Effects of the Urban-Rural Investment Choice," and L. Peattie, "Social Mobility and Economic Development," in Rodwin & Associates, *op. cit.*, pp. 400–410.

34. L. Peattie, "Urban Design in the Underdeveloped Countries," mimeographed (Cambridge: Joint Center for Urban Studies of MIT and Harvard University, 1964), p. 4.

35. The Joint Center of Urban Studies of MIT and Harvard University has financed a series of studies on different aspects of this program. Those published to date are: J. Friedmann, *Regional Development Policy* (Cambridge: M.I.T. Press, 1966); R. Soberman, *Transportation and Technology for Developing Regions: A Study of Road Transportation in Venezuela* (Cambridge: M.I.T. Press, 1966); Rodwin & Associates, *op. cit.;* Davis and McGinn, *op. cit.;* and L. Peattie, *The View from the Barrio.*

36. A. O. Hirschman, *The Strategy of Economic Development* (New Haven: Yale University Press, 1958), p. 210.

37. As a result of the apparent success of CVG, urban and regional programs are becoming more popular in Venezuela. The idea has spread that such growth strategies are more effective than political "pull" or pressure in producing regional improvements. Partly as a consequence of the Guayana program, a Zulia Planning Council was set up in 1963 to help counteract the decline of the city of Maracaibo and its surrounding region. In addition, in 1964 a semi-autonomous authority was established for the depressed region of the Andes and a private foundation set up to promote the development of the communities and surrounding areas of the west central part of Venezuela. These programs may be the prelude to sustained efforts

to develop other cities and regions in Venezuela. For furthur discussion of this subject, see Friedmann, *Regional Development Policy: A Case Study of Venezuela*, chap. 7.

38. See L. Rodwin, "Reflections on Collaborative Planning," in Rodwin & Associates, *op. cit.*, pp. 482–489.

Chapter IV

1. For general background studies in English of contemporary Turkey, especially its politics and development policies, see F. W. Frey, *The Turkish Political Elite* (Cambridge: M.I.T. Press, 1965); K. H. Karpat, *Turkey's Politics—The Transition to a Multi-Party System* (Princeton: Princeton University Press, 1959); Z. Y. Herschlag, *Turkey, An Economy in Transition* (The Hague: Van Kenlen, 1961); B. Lewis, *The Emergence of Modern Turkey* (London: Oxford University Press, 1961); R. D. Robinson, *The First Turkish Republic: A Case Study in National Development* (Cambridge: Harvard University Press, 1963); State Planning Organization, *First Five Year Development Plan, 1963–1967* (Ankara: State Planning Organization, 1963); M. V. Thornburg, G. Spry, and G. Soule, *Turkey, An Economic Appraisal* (New York: The Twentieth Century Fund, 1949); J. M. Barker and Associates, *The Economy of Turkey, An Analysis and Recommendations for a Development Program*, Report of a mission sponsored by the International Bank of Reconstruction and Development in collaboration with the Government of Turkey (Washington, D.C.: Johns Hopkins Press, 1951); and F. Baade, *Exports and Invisible Receipts in Turkey* (Paris: Organization for Economic Cooperation and Development, 1961).

For a tabulation of the data summarizing urban trends since the establishment of the Republic, see Mark Fortune, "Toward a National Policy of Urbanization for Turkey," unpublished report (Ankara: Department of Regional Planning, Ministry of Reconstruction and Resettlement, 1964); R. Keleş, *Türkiyede Şehirleşme Hareketleri, 1927–60* [Urbanization Movements in Turkey, 1927–60] (Ankara: University of Ankara, 1963). This doctoral dissertation was done under the general direction of Prof. F. Yavuz of the University of Ankara and partly under my direction when Mr. Keleş was at M.I.T. during 1959 and 1960. See also B. Kastarlak, "Programming Organization for Turkey: An Institutional Concept for Effective Implementation of Annual Development Programs" (M.C.P. diss., Massachusetts Institute of Technology, 1965); M. Rivkin, "Regional Development in Turkey," (Ph.D. diss., Massachusetts Institute of Technology, 1964); S. Rosen, "Labor in Turkey's Economic Development," (Ph.D. diss., Massachusetts Institute of Technology, 1959).

2. To promote industrialization, a Law for the Encouragement of Industry was passed in 1927. Under its terms, appropriate industries could obtain free land up to ten hectares, substantial reductions in rail and sea transport rates, subsidies of production costs, guaranteed markets, monopoly privileges, and bonuses or price reductions from goverment factories. By 1932 almost 1500 firms operated under the provisions of this legislation, but the number of firms dropped by more than one-fifth by 1939. This law was repealed in 1942. See Robinson, *op. cit.*, p. 106; Herschlag, *op. cit.*, p. 163; A. Bonne, *State and Economics in the Middle East, A Society in Transition* (London: Routledge and Kegan Paul, 1960), p. 276; and A. P. Alexander, "Industrial Entrepreneurship in Turkey, Origins and Growth," *Economic Development and Cultural Change*, vol. 8, no. 4 (1960), pp. 349–365.

3. A five-year industrial plan was prepared in 1934, a four-year mineral plan in 1936, and another five-year plan in 1938. Development corporations were created to

establish public enterprises largely in coal, tobacco, iron and steel, chemicals, cellulose, paper, salt, sugar, tea, and matches (all activities where the government held a monopoly) and in textiles, cement, brick and tile, lignite, mining, and leather (where there were also some private activities). Government monopoly often resulted from the lack of private enterprise, not the outlawing of private activity. See Herschlag, *op. cit.,* chap. 10; Robinson, *op. cit.,* pp. 129–130; and A. H. Hanson, *Public Enterprise and Economic Development* (London: Routledge and Kegan Paul, 1959).

4. Nonetheless, about 61 percent of the population of school age and older in Turkey were illiterate in 1957 and 48 percent in 1965. For other dramatic indicators of Turkey's backwardness in relation to other countries, see State Planning Organization, *First Five-Year Development Plan,* pp. 7–53; State Planning Organization, *A Summary of the Second Five-Year Development Plan of Turkey (1968–1972),* Part 2, Social Planning Draft (Ankara: State Planning Organization, 1967), p. 2; and Robinson, *op. cit.,* p. 122.

5. For descriptions of the growth of Ankara, see Fehmi Yavuz, "The Development of Ankara," *Journal of the Town Planning Institute,* vol. 38, no. 10 (1952), pp. 251–252; Tuğrul Akçura, "Ankara et ses Fonctions Urbaines," *La Vie Urbaine,* vol. 27, no. 2 (1960), pp. 89–128; and Fortune, *op. cit.,* Table 1.

The data on the locational trends of urban growth in Turkey were examined in terms of seven regions: the Marmara, the Aegean, Central Anatolia, the Mediterranean, the Black Sea, Eastern Anatolia, and Southeast Anatolia. The regions are described in more detail in Keleş, *Türkiyede Şehirleşme Hareketleri, 1927–60.* See also R. Keleş, "Regional Disparities in Turkey," *Ekistics,* vol. 15, no. 91 (1963), pp. 331–334.

Note that the Census Bureau uses a definition of urban population different from that of cities of 10,000 or more. However, this difference in definition does not lead to substantially different urban ratios. If the Census definition is used, the urban population of Turkey would be 21.7 percent and 28.7 percent in 1950 and 1960, respectively compared with 18.9 percent and 25.7 percent otherwise. For further discussion of the differences, see Fortune, *op. cit.,* pp. 1–8.

6. The greatest increases occurred in the largest cities. Those of 100,000 and over increased by 105 percent; those of 50,000 to 100,000 by 90 percent; and those of 10,000 to 50,000 by 57 percent. For further information on these points, see Fortune, *op. cit.,* Tables 1 and 2; and Rivkin, *op. cit.,* pp. 167–168.

7. Alexander, *op. cit.,* p. 354.

8. The growth of Ankara was assured by the concentration of resources in developing the capital, the creation of new cultural institutions, transportation, and linkages, and the promotion of ancillary activities and industries. The industrial support of Adana (the fourth largest city in the south) came from the prosperous cotton economy, which financed textile processing and export activities. Later, when cotton prices sagged in the postwar period, truck garden crops, citrus fruits, cereals, and other crops supported its economy.

9. Farm to market roads increased 50 percent, the number of kilometers of national highways which were hard-surfaced rose more than 100 percent, and the total kilometers of all roads tripled. See Rivkin, *op. cit.,* p. 212.

10. See Robinson, *op. cit.,* pp. 221, 240 ff.; Hanson, *op. cit.,* p. 123; R. S. Lehman, "Building Roads and Highway Administration in Turkey," in H. M. Teaf and P. G. Franck, eds., *Hands Across Frontiers, Case Studies in International Cooperation* (Ithaca: Cornell University Press, 1955), pp. 363–405; and State Planning Organization, *First Five Year Development Plan,* pp. 14–21; Rivkin, *op. cit.,* chap. 4.

11. State Planning Organization, *First Five Year Development Plan*, p. 7; see also Fortune, *op. cit.*, Table 3.

12. State Planning Organization, *First Five Year Development Plan*, pp. 14, 24–5.

13. See F. W. Frey, *The Mass Media and Rural Development in Turkey*, Rural Development Research Project, Report No. 3 (Cambridge: Center for International Studies, M.I.T., 1966); D. Lerner, *The Passing of Traditional Society* (Glencoe: The Free Press, 1958), chap. 1; and Rosen, *op. cit.*, p. 69. See also Evner Ergun, "The Scope of Social Planning in the Second Five Year Plan," in *International Colloquium on the Technical Aspects of Turkey's Second Five Year Plan* (Ankara: State Planning Organization, 1966), pp. 6–9.

14. Many of the migrants were absorbed in the burgeoning medium-sized urban centers of 50,000 to 100,000 people. The number of small-scale enterprises in consumer activities in these cities more than doubled during this period—an increase that roughly matched the growth in population.

15. Net regional emigration occurred only from the regions of the Black Sea and East Anatolia. Cf. fn. 5. Tables summarizing these trends may be found in Keleş, *Türkiyede Şehirleşme Hareketleri*, Appendix.

16. The designation "largest cities" refers to those of 500,000 people or over. See Fortune, *op. cit.*, pp. 1–11 and Tables 1–3; and Rivkin, *op. cit.*, pp. 241–245.

17. For a sensitive description of this process, see Lerner, *op. cit.*, chap. 1.

18. Fortune, *op. cit.*, pp. 11–13.

19. The Ministry of Reconstruction and Resettlement was created by Law No. 7116, enacted September 5, 1958. Before 1957 there was a small Regional Planning Bureau within the City Planning Office of the Ministry of Public Works. The key officials who helped prepare the legislation were Mithat Erçetin, Director of the Construction Department of the Central Bank; Mithat Yenen, the Assistant General Director of the Central Bank; and Medeni Berk, a successful bank administrator who became the first administrator. Also consulted were Orhan Alsaç, head of the Building and Planning Department of the Ministry of Public Works; Esat Turak, Director of the Regional Planning Directorate within the Department; and Aydïn Germen, a member of this Directorate. For further detail, see E. Turak, "Regional Planning in Turkey—Brief Historical Note," mimeographed, November 1968; and İlhan Tekeli, "Regional Planning in Turkey and Regional Planning in the First Five Year Development Plan," in S. İlkin and E. İnanç, *Planning in Turkey*, Middle East Technical University, Faculty of Administrative Sciences, Publication No. 9. (Ankara, 1967), pp. 254–273.

20. The regions were roughly but not precisely equivalent to those discussed earlier. See fn. 5.

21. L. Rodwin, *Report No. 1 on EPA Mission to İmar Ve İskân Vekâleti*, General Directorate of Planning and Reconstruction. (Ankara: Ministry of Reconstruction and Resettlement, 1959). See also Rodwin, *Report No. 3 on OEEC/EPA Mission to General Directorate of Planning and Reconstruction* (Paris: Organization for European Economic Cooperation, 1960), p. 14.

22. See Rodwin, *Report No. 2 on OEEC/EPA Mission to General Directorate of Planning and Reconstruction* (Ankara: Ministry of Reconstruction and Resettlement, 1960); Rodwin, "Analysis of Functions, Proposed Organization and Staff Requirements of Bölge Plânlama," mimeographed (Ankara Ministry of Reconstruction and Resettlement, 1960); and Rodwin, *Report No. 3*.

23. The local officials, however, were influenced by their Italian consultant, Mr. Luigi Piccinato. Although the Ministry's staff would have liked to encourage growth centers elsewhere, they were persuaded that the Marmara region was the most influential directly and indirectly. See Rodwin, *Report No. 4 on OEEC/EPA Mission to General Directorate of Planning and Reconstruction*, Ministry of Reconstruction and Resettlement (Paris: Organization for European Economic Cooperation, 1960), p. 2.

24. The State Planning Organization has subsequently noted some administrative advantages in regional planning. In a report it declared:

> Regional analysis makes it possible to obtain fuller information on resources and problems and to consider the complementary aspects of investments so that the National Plan may be based on sounder foundations. Regional studies are also useful in the preparation of projects and programmes which constitute the basis of the Plan.
>
> It must be pointed out that besides contributing to the preparation of the National Plan, regional planning is important at the implementation stage. In the implementation of plans and programmes, cooperation at the regional level between the various executive organs will help to achieve success. It is certain that the consideration of problems at this level will bring important new elements into the implementation of the plan. . . . Furthermore, one must bear in mind that regional implementation may also help to mobilize resources which cannot be taken into account at the national level.
>
> *(Turkish Experience in Regional Planning*
> [Ankara: State Planning Organization, 1963], pp. 31–32.)

25. Law No. 91 was enacted September 30, 1960. Actually, the law which established the State Planning Organization made regional planning the responsibility of the Economic Planning Department. However, the Social Planning Department was given the authority to deal with this subject because of the special interest in the subject of the first—and later the second—director of the Social Planning Department. Those aspects of planning under the direct responsibility of the Social Planning Department are: population, manpower, employment, education, labor, social security, social services, cultural affairs, sports, scientific research, health, family planning, village affairs, youth affairs, community development, urbanization and settlement, housing, technical assistance administration, and research on social structure.

26. Rodwin, *Report No. 4*, pp. 12–15; and Rodwin, *Report No. 5 on OEEC/EPA Mission to General Directorate of Planning and Reconstruction* (Paris: Organization for European Economic Cooperation, 1961), p. 11.

27. The resident consultants were Gian Carlo Guarda, Loretta Guarda, and Malcolm Rivkin. Mr. Guarda served as advisor on the Marmara planning studies. Mrs. Guarda was the population and land use planning specialist. Mr. Rivkin was the assistant to the chief consultant. Later, he served also as advisor on the Zonguldak planning studies. The U.N. resident consultants assigned to the program included Samuel Joroff, who served as a specialist on zoning and infrastructure studies in the Marmara region, and Ernest Jurkat, who served first as advisor on economic base studies for the Marmara region and then on general studies of interregional economic relationships. The first three resident consultants renewed their one-year term of service. When they left—roughly at the end of their second year—a new group of Organization for Economic Cooperation and Development (OECD) resident advisors, more senior in status and experience, were brought to Turkey. The new group of advisors were: Mark Fortune, who served in Ankara as an assistant to the chief consultant and resident advisor to the Department of Regional

Planning on a variety of assignments, including the Zonguldak and Çukurova planning studies; Ralph Kaminsky, who served as advisor on economic studies for Zonguldak and Çukurova and on urban migration trends; and Blaise Gillie, who served as a resident advisor on land use planning in the Çukurova region. Later OECD resident consultants included Frank Earwaker, who studied the industrial development potential of the Keban Region among other subjects, and several junior consultants. Arrangements were also made at a later date for some short-term consultant assistance on specialized problems. Thus, Desmond Heap of Great Britain was brought to Turkey to advise on procedures related to the adoption of plans and land use controls, and Philippe Bernard came from France to deal with administrative problems in light of the experience of French regional planning. The resident advisors reported in writing twice a month to the chief consultant. They also prepared formal reports three times a year. These reports accompanied the chief consultant's reports to the OECD.

28. Rodwin, *Report No. 5.* See especially the reports of Gian Carlo Guarda and Loretta Guarda in Appendices B1 and B2.

29. *Ibid.,* especially Appendices A1 and A2, containing the reports of Malcolm Rivkin to the chief consultant.

30. *Ibid.*

31. The purpose of this brief summary is to give some sense of the problems examined and the approach taken. The study is the work of the Istanbul Directorate under the leadership of Tuğrul Akçura and his associates, and under the direction of the two previous directors of the Regional Planning Department, Aydïn Germen and Evner Ergun. The work owes much, of course, to the efforts of the resident consultants, especially Mr. and Mrs. Guarda. For further details, see Department of Regional Planning, *Doğu Marmara Bölgesi Ön Plâni* (Ankara: Ministry of Reconstruction and Resettlement, 1963). See also State Planning Organization, *Five Year Development Plan,* p. 445.

32. They expected to do this mainly through control of capital allocations and tax benefits in order to achieve a better distribution of population and income between regions. See State Planning Organization, *First Five Year Development Plan,* section 2. In a note to the author, dated January 13, 1969. Evner Ergun, former Director of the Department of Social Planning of the State Planning Organization, emphasized that "although no priority was established among the objectives of the First Five Year Development Plan, in practice to achieve the 7% growth rate of GNP became the major concern and influenced the overall development strategy a great deal. Most of the 'economic' investments went to the developed regions. Undeveloped regions, however, had a better share of the 'social' investments."

33. The results were summarized in charts, diagrams, and other graphic materials. One of the most ambitious was the territorial land use map of the eastern Marmara (at 1:100,000), which provided the best available picture of the distribution of urbanized areas, major transportation networks, forests, and agricultural land uses. Another was an urban land use survey (at 1:5,000) which provided an authoritative inventory of the location and nature of the major land uses in the city of Istanbul and its surrounding area.

34. The purpose of this brief summary, as in the case of the Marmara proposals cited above, is only to provide some idea of the problems examined and the approach taken. Credit for the study belongs to the Ankara office of the Department of Regional Planning under the leadership of Evner Ergun, the director of the Department, and Yiğit Gölöksüz, leader of the Zonguldak project team and their associates. The work owed much, of course, to the efforts of the consultants who

participated, especially Malcolm Rivkin. Further details may be found in Department of Regional Planning, *Zonguldak Bölgesi Ön Plāni* (Ankara: Ministry of Reconstruction and Resettlement, 1964). This report is a substantially revised version prepared by İlhan Tekeli with the help of the Ankara staff of the Department of Regional Planning. For a resumé in English, see İlhan Tekeli, *op. cit.*, pp. 265–270; and Yilmaz Gürer, "Interrelations of Planning and Regional Planning—Zonguldak Regional Plan," in Turkish Society for Housing and Planning, *Regional Planning, Local Government and Community Development in Turkey*, Papers of the Eighth Seminar on Housing and Planning, December 14–18, 1964 (Ankara: Turkish Society for Housing and Planning, 1966), pp. 51–64.

35. The initial phases of the Istanbul and Zonguldak studies were discussed in June 1961; the second phases were considered at meetings held for Zonguldak in January 1962 and for Istanbul in June 1962. See Rodwin, *Report No. 6 on OEEC/EPA Mission to General Directorate of Planning and Reconstruction* (Paris: Organization for European Economic Cooperation, 1961); Rodwin, *Report No. 7 on OECD Mission to General Directorate of Planning and Reconstruction* (Paris: Organization for Economic Cooperation and Development, 1962); and Rodwin, *Report No. 8 on OECD Mission to General Directorate of Planning and Reconstruction* (Paris: Organization for Economic Cooperation and Development, 1962).

36. F. Yavuz, *A Survey of the Financial Administration of Turkish Municipalities* (Ankara: University of Ankara, Faculty of Political Sciences, 1962).

37. See fn. 27.

38. See fns. 32 and 34.

39. The Antalya program was a Special Fund Project of the United Nations. The executive agency was the Food and Agriculture Organization (FAO) and counterparts were provided by the State Planning Organization. The study was called the Antalya Preinvestment Survey. This region, containing the provinces of Burdur, Isparta, and Antalya, was first recommended by the FAO for an agricultural development program. The project proved controversial. It was reluctantly accepted by the Turkish authorities, and it was subsequently reorganized as a special regional development study under the sponsorship and with the collaboration of the State Planning Organization.

40. Rodwin, *Report No. 8*, p. 15. For a more detailed description of the technical plans of the project by the resident coordinator, see H. Teoman Baykal, "The Çukurova Regional Plan," in Turkish Society for Housing and Planning, *op. cit.*, pp. 65–79.

41. Friction persisted, however, and the embittered relationships finally led to the ousting of the Head of the Department of Regional Planning and the eventual resignation of the Chief Consultant. See Rodwin, *Report No. 9 on OECD Mission to General Directorate of Planning and Reconstruction* (Paris: Organization for Economic Cooperation and Development, 1963), pp. 5–9; and Rodwin, *Report No. 10 on OECD Mission on Turkish Regional Planning Problems* (Paris: Organization for Economic Cooperation and Development, 1963), pp. 6–7.

42. A summary of this policy has appeared in several reports of the State Planning Organization. For example, the following view appeared in *Turkish Experience in Regional Planning:*

> ... One of the most important problems in achieving balanced regional growth is that of reconciling social and economic objectives by assigning appropriate weights to the measures necessary to their implementation. The conflicting aspects of the two basic objectives can thus be minimized and the complementary aspects maximized. Therefore, the Plan tried to strike a

balance between economic and social goals and the principle was accepted that backward regions will be given a definite priority only with respect to social service investments. At the same time, in the selection of investment projects at the different stages of sector studies and project analysis, the regional factor will be taken into consideration, since certain appropriate projects may be a means of reducing excessive income disparities between regions. Priorities will be given to economically and socially backward regions in such a way as to reduce as far as possible the sacrifice of productivity. The regional development policy should not try to create artificial development conditions in areas having minimal development potential, otherwise the implementation of such policy would entail the transfer of income gained in productive regions to unproductive parts of the country.

However, it must be stressed that what the Turkish Development Plan provides is not a pure equalization policy but a principle of balancing the development of various parts of the country. What it does want to do is to minimize the backwash effects of the already developed metropolitan regions and to maximize their spread effects so that the largest numbers of small cities, towns and villages lacking even minimal social services may receive them. This principle has grown out of an observation on the overgrowth of certain urban areas, particularly Istanbul. With a population of more than 2 million, Istanbul is absorbing today whatever the other parts of the country produce and possess. Capital and human resources, entrepreneurship are sucked into the city and its environs. As stated in a preliminary Regional Development Plan prepared for the Eastern Marmara (İmar Ve İskân Bakanlīgī, *Doğu Marmara Bölgesi Ön Plânī*, 1963, p. 8) this region attracts capital to such consumption sectors as housing and real estate. Housing, urban traffic, primary and secondary educational institutions suggest that certain external diseconomies have already been started from the point of view of the quality of these social services.

As may be noticed, the problem Turkey faces is not only to encourage underdeveloped regions to reduce their backwardness, but to provide minimum social services to inhabitants of every part of the country and to try to take measures necessary in preventing the large disparities which may arise in the long run. To assure the essential harmony between social and economic goals, the State should take into consideration the levels of economic activity and income and the social services in the geographical distribution of expenditures and investments. These measures will, in the long run, influence economic activity and assure development which will not conflict with the principles of balance and social justice.

(State Planning Organization,
Turkish Experience in Regional Planning, pp. 11–12.)

A still more advanced view appeared in a draft document on Social Planning which appeared in 1967. That document stated:

a) In order to realize balanced inter-regional development, investments will be directed to the less-developed regions. The productive investments will be concentrated in strategic urban centers which have high growth potentials in the regions mentioned above.

b) Urbanization will be encouraged as a potential pushing forward of the economy and as a means of development.

(State Planning Organization,
A Summary of the Second Five Year Development Plan of Turkey
[1968–1972], Part 2, Social Planning, Draft, pp. 85–87.)

However, most of these views were blurred or omitted in a later summary document published by the State Planning Organization entitled *Planning in Turkey,* Consortium Report on The Second Five Year Development Plan (Ankara: State Planning Organization, 1968).

43. The government offered tax and other concessions for investments made in the poorer regions. It also exercised simple controls. Thus, more than one location had to be considered for large investment projects. In addition, projects located in less developed regions received higher priority if they had equal ratings in terms of other investment criteria. But even in those regions there was considerable emphasis on the urban growth prospects.

44. For example, some of the studies subsequently conducted by SPO and the Ministry dealt with such matters as trends of public investment and industrial location, criteria for evaluation of different locations for investment (especially urban growth centers), patterns of internal migration, changes in village structure and mass communications, comparative productivity of various industries, their prospective responses to incentives geared to location, and feasible long-term policies for the development of East and Southeast Anatolia (i.c., the eighteen provinces in the east and southeast, which are the poorest and most volatile of the provinces in Turkey).

45. State Planning Organization, *Annual Program of the Five Year Development Plan* (Ankara: 1965), pp. 383–384; and İlhan Tekeli, *op. cit.,* p. 263. For the figures on the proportion of public investment in the region in the next paragraph, see N. Ölçen, "The Geographical Distribution of Public Investments," in İlkin and İnanç *op. cit.,* pp. 274–278.

46. For example, more work was done on the industrial plan for the metropolitan area. Also, a French team made some studies of eastern Thrace. See Association Bretonne de Géographie Appliquée, *Rapport Sur un Programme de Développement Économique et Social de la Thrace Orientale* (1966).

47. This 7.5 million figure was in addition to the 1 million known disguised unemployed in agriculture even in peak periods. See State Planning Organization, *A Summary of the Second Five Year Development Plan in Turkey (1968–1972),* Part 2, Social Planning, Draft, pp. 12–16.

48. See Ergun, *op. cit.,* pp. 1–26. See also State Planning Organization, *A Summary of the Second Five Year Development Plan of Turkey (1968–1972),* Part 2, p. 87.

49. Census data for the period from 1960 to 1965 tend to support these projections. They also indicate both a continuation and a reversal of some of the dominant trends in the earlier periods. Total population of Turkey continued its rapid growth, rising to an estimated 31.4 million in 1965. Approximately 30 percent of the population was urban. There are now 30 cities of 50,000 or over; the three new ones are now located in the Marmara region. The number of cities of 50,000 to 100,000 increased from 6 to 16 between 1950 and 1960, but these cities lost 8 percent of their population between 1960 and 1965. The highest percentage of increases occurred in cities of 100,000 and over (a jump from 4 to 14 in number and a population increase of 66 percent). Most of them were in the orbit of the larger metropolitan centers. Istanbul's population increase of 19 percent was higher than the average urban population increase of 13 percent (and the figure vastly understates the growth occurring in the outskirts of the city and in the Marmara region). More movement is now occurring between the regions experiencing the greatest population losses and the regions experiencing the greatest population increases. See *Census of Population* (Ankara: Institute of Statistics, 1965), Table No. 4,

p. 6; State Planning Organization, *A Summary of the Second Five Year Development Plan of Turkey (1968–1972)*, Part 2, pp. 1–8, 85–87; and Fortune, *op. cit.*, pp. 13–16 and Tables 3, 4, 5.

50. I am indebted for this point to Mr. Evner Ergun. For more details, see State Planning Organization, *Planning in Turkey*, pp. 104–106.

51. The situation improved somewhat in the mid-1960's. Arrangements were then made for OECD, UN, and other technical assistance agencies to aid the regional planning education program at the Middle East Technical University.

52. This point was called to my attention in a number of memoranda prepared by Mark Fortune. An interesting example of reoriented attitudes can be found in the critical appraisal of regional planning experience in Turkey by İlhan Tekeli, *op. cit.*, pp. 254–273. This article is one of the more severe evaluations in English by one of the younger Turkish regional planners subsequently trained in the United States. It shows an understandable impatience with some of the limitations of past regional planning but not an equally sensitive understanding of the constraints that produced these limitations. This is not to say that he is unaware of these constraints. Indeed, Professor Tekeli finds that, as of September 1968, he can still function more effectively in the university than in the Turkish civil service where his skills are in very short supply.

53. C. Haussmann, "When Foreign Student Scholarships are Misused," *Saturday Review*, August 12, 1965, pp. 48–50, 62–63.

Chapter V

(HMSO: Her Majesty's Stationery Office)

1. For the rest of this chapter, references to the North and South will be based on these definitions, unless otherwise indicated.

2. The Home Counties include Bedfordshire, Buckinghamshire, Essex, Hertfordshire, Kent, Middlesex, and Surrey. This area extends about forty miles from Central London. For data from 1801 to 1901, see *Report of the Royal Commission on the Distribution of the Industrial Population*, Cmd. 6153 (henceforth referred to as the *Barlow Report* [London: HMSO, 1940]), Table 1, p. 22. The ratios for 1961 are based on data in Tables 3–6 in Ministry of Housing and Local Government, *The South East Study* (London: HMSO, 1964), pp. 120–123. For data on England, Wales, and London from 1801 to 1891, see A. F. Weber, *The Growth of Cities* (New York: Macmillan, 1899), p. 46. Note that data for the population in England and Wales [in *The South East Study*, p. 125] varied irregularly from 35 to 39 percent during the period from 1801 to 1961. See also Peter Hall, *London, 2000* (London: Faber and Faber, 1963), pp. 78–82; and "England in 1801," unpublished draft of manuscript which will appear in H. C. Darby, *Historical Geography of England in 1900* (forthcoming).

3. S. R. Dennison, *The Location of Industry and the Depressed Areas* (London: Oxford University Press, 1939), p. 125. This section of the chapter dealing with the early policy for the less prosperous regions leans heavily on the able dissertation of Professor Dennison.

4. Dennison, *op. cit.*, p. 129. See also "Definition of Backward Areas," in *Regional Disequilibria in Europe* (Brussels: L'Institut de Sociologie, Université Libre de Bruxelles for the European Coordination Center for Research and Documentation in the

Social Sciences, 1968). [Henceforth this memorandum will be cited as "The Backward Areas of the United Kingdom."]

5. From 1921 to 1931 the South East "gained 615,000 people by migration, this being equivalent to 50% of its 1921 population. Most other regions lost population by migration, the most notable case being that of Wales which lost about 242,000 people or 12.3% of its original population" (Dennison, *op. cit.,* p. 150).

6. The minimum financial support covered subsistence costs for the workers and their dependents until they could get jobs in these areas. This was essential if only to compensate the worker for loss of unemployment insurance benefits during the transfer period. British workers still draw the same scale of unemployment benefits in all parts of the country, regardless of occupation or living costs. Wilson believes that this impedes mobility in the poorest regions, especially if unemployment benefits are coupled with allowances for larger families and housing. See T. Wilson, *Policies for Regional Development,* University of Glasgow Social and Economic Studies, Occasional Papers, no. 3 (Edinburgh and London: Oliver and Boyd, 1964), p. 23.

7. Dennison, *op.cit.,* p. 176. For more recent discussions, favoring taking workers to the jobs, see A. T. Peacock and D. M. Dosser, "The New Attack on Localized Employment," *Lloyd's Bank Review,* no. 55 (1960), p. 21; and H. W. Richardson and E. G. West, "Must We Always Take Work to the Workers," *Lloyd's Bank Review,* no. 71 (1964) pp. 35–48.

8. Actually, a large proportion of workers, to avoid the requirements and for other reasons, tended to migrate without taking advantage of these services. Testimony before the Barlow Commission indicated, for example, that, from January 1936 to June 1937, 30,000 men were transferred while 61,600 moved on their own. See testimony of the Ministry of Labour in *Minutes of Evidence,* taken by the Royal Commission on the Distribution of the Industrial Population, cited by Dennison, *op. cit.,* p. 172.

9. Dennison, *op. cit.,* pp. 126–127.

10. The main trading estates initiated by 1939 were: Team Valley in Tyneside, Treforest in South Wales, and small estates in Sunderland and Southwest Durham. By September 1958 the English commissioner's

> total financial commitments amounted to almost seventeen million pounds, about one-half of which had already been spent. The total commitments were distributed as follows:
>
> 1) Grants to assist industry. £5,152,000
> 2) Grants for land settlement 3,260,000
> 3) Grants toward public health schemes 6,112,000
> 4) Other grants. 2,246,000
> (See Dennison, *op. cit.,* p. 162.)

11. The findings were published in the *Barlow Report.* There is also a wealth of detail in the twenty-six volumes of testimony gathered in the *Minutes of Evidence* taken by this commission in 1938. See, for example, the testimony of Sir Malcolm Stewart, *Minutes of Evidence,* E 646 ff.

12. L. Needleman and B. Scott, "Regional Problems and Location of Industry Policy in Britain," *Urban Studies,* vol. 1, no. 2 (1964), p. 161.

13. This legislation applied to new activities developed by local firms in the Development Areas as well as new firms coming to these areas.

    Although the policy on loans can in specific cases be quite flexible, in general the Board of Trade has tended to regard £1500 per new worker employed as a maximum unless there is a special justification. See *Seventh Report* from the Estimates Committee, Administration of the Local Employment Act, 1960 (London: HMSO, 1963), pp. viii–xi. Cited in Wilson, *op. cit.*, p. 37. Note also that the power over building licenses ended on November 11, 1955.

14. See W. Ashworth, *The Genesis of Modern British Town Planning* (London: Routledge and Kegan Paul, 1954).

15. E. Howard, *Garden Cities of Tomorrow* (London: Faber and Faber, 1945); and L. Rodwin, *The British New Towns Policy* (Cambridge: Harvard University Press, 1956), chap. 2.

16. Ministry of Local Government and Planning, *Town and Country Planning, 1943–1951,* Cmd. 8204 (London: HMSO, 1951), p. 4.

17. See the *Report of the Committee on Land Utilization in Rural Areas,* Cmd. 6378 (London: HMSO, 1942); and *Report of the Expert Committee on Compensation and Betterment,* Cmd. 6386 (London: HMSO, 1942).

18. P. Abercrombie, *Greater London Plan 1944: A Report Prepared on Behalf of the Standing Conference on London Regional Planning* (London: HMSO, 1945).

19. Cited in *Town and Country Planning 1943–1951,* p. 1.

20. Although the Town and Country Planning Act of 1947 consolidated basic planning powers in the hands of 145 counties and county boroughs, it also provided for delegation of these powers to lesser authorities and for joint action where necessary to deal with still larger areas. This aspect of the legislation has produced some discontent. There was strong feeling (in 1965) among some key planners in Great Britain that because of the widespread delegation of authority, the results were the opposite of what was intended and that the net effect was to increase the number of planning authorities and to impair the quality of local plans and private participation.

21. In 1953 an act was passed that ended this program. This act did not abolish the provision that all development rights were vested in the community and that all development was subject to local planning authority permission. The act abolished the £300 million fund used to defray compensation costs and also the charge levied on developers to represent the amount of betterment resulting from development. For some background discussions on some of these points, see C. M. Haar, *Land Planning Law in a Free Society* (Cambridge: Harvard University Press, 1951); W. Wood, *Planning and the Law* (London: P. Marshall, 1949); D. Heap, *An Outline of Planning Law* (London: Sweet and Maxwell, 1963), chaps. 2–5, 14, pp. 1–75, 175–183; W. O. Hart, "Control of the Use of Land in English Law," in *Law and Land,* ed. C. M. Haar (Cambridge: Harvard University Press and MIT Press, 1964); and D. Heap, "English Development Plans for the Control of Land Use," in C. M. Haar, *Law and Land;* see also P. Brenikov, "The Conurbations;" H. R. Parker, "Finance;" C. M. Haar, "Planning Law;" and J. P. Reynolds, "The Changing Objectives of the Drawn Plan;" in *Land Use in an Urban Environment,* ed. Department of Civic Design, University of Liverpool (Liverpool: At the University Press, 1961).

22. Two evaluations of the New Towns have been prepared by Ray Thomas. The first is "London's New Towns, A Study of Self-Contained and Balanced Communities," Broadsheet 510, *Political and Economic Planning,* vol. 35, April 1969. The second deals with the seven New Towns in the rest of Great Britain and will be published shortly. See also Rodwin, *op. cit.;* H. Orlans, *Utopia Ltd.* (New Haven: Yale University Press, 1953) [published in the United Kingdom under the title *Stevanage: A*

Sociological Study of a New Town (London: Routledge and Kegan Paul, 1952)]; and F. J. Osborn and A. Whittick, *The New Towns—The Answer to Megalopolis* (London: Leonard Hill, 1963). For more details on the development programs of the individual towns in England, Wales, and Scotland, see the annual *Reports of the Development Corporations* (London: HMSO) and the annual *Reports of the Development Corporations* (Edinburgh: HMSO).

23. Apparently this problem is still serious for the New Towns of the North. According to Ray Thomas, "there has not been the same integration of regional and national policies as in the case of London's New Towns." Moreover, Glasgow and most of the other local authorities' actively oppose the "export" of their employment. See Thomas, "Seven New Towns," Draft Broadsheet, *Political and Economic Planning*, mimeographed (1969), pp. 86–92. See also P. Self, *The Planning of Industrial Location* (London: University of London Press, 1953), p. 29, and *Cities in Flux* (London: Faber & Faber, 1961), chap. 6; and *First, Second, Third,* and *Fourth Reports from the Committee of Public Accounts* (London: HMSO, 1950–1951), Appendix 16, "Distribution of New Industries Between Development Areas and New Towns," pp. 630–631.

24. W. Thomas, "The Growth of the London Region," *Town and Country Planning*, vol. 29, no. 5 (1961), pp. 185–193; F. J. Osborn, "Success of the New Towns," *Town and Country Planning*, vol. 22, no. 117 (1954), pp. 10–12; and A. G. Powell, "The Recent Development of Greater London," *The Advancement of Science*, vol. 17, no. 65 (1960), pp. 76–86.

25. Central Office of Information, *The New Towns of Britain* (London: British Information Services, 1964), Appendix 1. See also Rodwin, *op. cit.,* Table 1.

26. Rodwin, *op. cit.,* chaps. 8, 9. The Town Development Act of 1952 provided for the extension of financial and technical assistance to smaller communities for those land improvement costs (sewers, water, land drainage, and site preparation) which resulted from the community's rapid expansion in the course of absorbing the overspill population from congested areas. These crowded metropolitan areas, unable to expand because of limited space and the maximum densities set by their physical development plans, were asked to negotiate agreements with small communities in neighboring areas to serve as receiving centers for the "excess" population. The agreements vary, but in general they fix the amounts and kind of development, the specific reception areas, whether the exporting or reception authority will do the building and subject to what conditions, and the financial assistance that will be given by the exporting authority or authorities, by the county council, etc. Unfortunately, negotiations are often excruciatingly time-consuming and in almost half the cases come to naught. Time elapsed between the start of negotiations and the commencement of housebuilding for Greater London schemes range from one to seven years, with four to five years representing the typical length of time required compared with a year or more for the schemes of other metropolitan areas.

27. By the end of 1962, a little more than 13,000 local authority houses were completed in expanded towns of Greater London, almost 6,400 in Staffordshire (Birmingham, Walsall, and Wolverhampton), and 5,600 in the other towns, or a total of about 25,000 units in the first ten years since the legislation was enacted. At the start of 1968, about 30,800 houses had been built in the London region, 5,300 in Birmingham, 4,300 in Wolverhampton, 1,500 in the Liverpool region, 2,100 in Manchester, 1,100 in Newcastle, 2,300 in Bristol, and 4,500 in Salford. In short, close to 60 percent was in the towns of the London region and a little less than 20 percent in

FOOTNOTES

Birmingham and Wolverhampton. (The data in this footnote and in fn. 26 are based on two unpublished typewritten memoranda supplied to me by officials of the Ministry of Housing and Local Government.)

28. Rodwin, *op. cit.*, p. 26.

29. Board of Trade, *The Movement of Manufacturing Industry in the United Kingdom 1945–1965* (London: HMSO, 1968), pp. 13, 35–36. See also G. McCrone, *Regional Policy in Britain* (London: George Allen and Unwin, 1969), chap. 11.

30. Wilson, *op. cit.*, p. 26. Hatfield and Hemel Hempstead were the two principal towns with employment deficits.

31. A. E. Holmans, "Industrial Development Certificates and Control of the Growth of Employment in South East England," *Urban Studies*, vol. 1. no. 2 (1964), pp. 144, 147.

32. *Ibid.*, p. 140.

33. *Ibid.*, p. 149.

34. A. E. Holmans, "Restriction of Industrial Expansion in South East England: A Reappraisal," *Oxford Economic Papers*, n.s., vol. 16, no. 2 (1964), p. 252.

35. Holmans, "Industrial Development Certificates and Control of the Growth of Employment in South East England," p. 149.

36. Needleman and Scott, *op. cit.*, pp. 165–166. See also Scottish Development Department, *Central Scotland, A Programme for Development and Growth*, Cmd. 2188 (Edinburgh: HMSO, 1963), p. 12; G. McRobie, "A Development Plan for Scotland," *Political and Economic Planning*, vol. 29, no. 476 (1963), p. 411; and *The North-East—A Programme for Regional Development and Growth*, Cmd. 2206 (London: HMSO, 1963), pp. 12–13.

37. Needleman and Scott, *op. cit.*, p. 164 and Table 2.

38. "The Backward Areas of the United Kingdom," p. 8; and Department of Employment and Productivity, *Statistics on Incomes, Prices, Employment and Production*, no. 25 (London: HMSO, 1968), p. 95 and Table E7.

39. Needleman and Scott, *op. cit.*, pp. 153, 166–170; and "The Backward Areas of the United Kingdom," p. 8. See also Wilson, *op. cit.*, chap. 5; The National Economic Development Council, *Conditions Favourable to Faster Growth* (London: HMSO, 1963), paras. 59–61; J. Sykes, "Remedies for Localized Unemployment," *The Manchester School*, vol. 19, no. 1 (1951), pp. 71–88; and M. W. F. Hemming, "The Regional Problem, "*The National Institute Economic Review*, no. 25 (1963), pp. 40–57.

40. The Board of Trade considers a gross public outlay of £1500 for each job a reasonable average figure, and only in exceptional circumstances are expenditures of more than £2,500 per job considered reasonable. According to Needleman and Scott, the actual average gross outlay was just under £900, but the total additional jobs provided were only about two-thirds of the number directly sponsored by the government, so that the gross outlay per job was more in the neighborhood of £1,350. Citing the National Economic Development Council's estimate that non-returnable costs only come to about £340, Needleman and Scott contrast this figure with the costs of unemployment, which comes to £1200. The latter is calculated to be £115 for taxes forgone, direct and indirect, on an average income of £621, and £290 for assistance payments. The total, if capitalized at 6 percent for a five-year period, amounts to £1200. The output of such a person, if employed, averages about £621 a year, which capitalized for five years amounts to £2,500. (For somewhat similar calculations and analysis see Wilson, *op. cit.*, chap. 5.) Needleman and Scott

also argue that the discrepancy between costs and outlays would be even greater if one added the higher labor and land costs in the South which increase infrastructure outlays, and if one deducted a certain amount of infrastructure investment, which would be inescapable in the North for social and political reasons, regardless of the scale of development. See Needleman and Scott, *op. cit.,* pp. 166–170.

41. Holmans, "Restriction of Industrial Expansion in South East England: A Reappraisal," pp. 240–245.

42. Holmans believes that even the argument of a potential labor shortage—presumably evinced by lower unemployment rates in the region and underlined as a major problem in Britain's first Five-Year Plan—could be questioned as a serious consideration. He suggests that this claim is much less persuasive when tested on the basis of estimated growth trends of the working-age population in the South, the availability of a redundant labor force from the declining activities of the region, and the higher activity rates of the southern force generally and of their women in particular. He also objects to the arguments of labor shortage and waste of social capital: first, because there is no evidence of an increasing shortage of labor in the South; and, secondly, because the social capital in the North is in many respects obsolete and ready for replacement. *Ibid.,* pp. 240–245. On the other hand, Professor Robertson and his colleagues feel that "the British economy is short of labour. The target for economic growth over the next five years is four times greater than the expected increase in manpower." He adds that although there are "in most of the less developed regions, no sizeable reserves of skilled male labour, the prospect of getting labour is, however, better than in the Southeast of England. Manpower is underutilized also in the sense that participation rates are lower particularly among married women. ... And the activity rate reflecting the proportion of people reaching retirement age who are prepared to stay in employment, tends to be lower in the less prosperous regions" ("The Backward Areas of the United Kingdom," pp. 11–12). See also Needleman and Scott, *op. cit.,* pp. 155–7; and South East Economic Planning Council, *A Strategy for the South East* (London: HMSO, 1967), chap. 2.

43. M. Posner has suggested that "the amount worth spending on providing jobs for workers in their home regions can ... be defined as any sum less than the cost of moving the labour, together with their families, to alternative locations, account being taken of all the relevant social (economic) costs." He adds in a footnote (on the same page) that "this rule is subject to the constraint that the [marginal addition to] total expenditure must not exceed the value of the [marginal addition to] output it generates" (M. V. Posner, "Regional Economic Policy in the United Kingdom," *The New Atlantis,* vol. 1, no. 1. [1969], p. 63).

44. McCrone, *op. cit.,* chap. 5.

45. Central Office of Information, *Regional Development in Britain* (London: HMSO, 1968), p. 10.

46. After the first twenty-one years, economic rents are charged. Wilson, *op. cit.,* p. 62.

47. Cited in Wilson, *op. cit.,* p. 60. See *Seventh Report of the Estimates Committee* (London: HMSO, 1963), pp. xii–xiii, 194 ff.

48. Needleman and Scott, *op. cit.,* p. 162; Wilson, *op. cit.,* chaps. 3, 4; and "The Backward Areas of the United Kingdom," p. 31.

49. Wilson, *op. cit.,* pp. 67–70. See also McCrone, *op. cit.,* p. 200.

50. Department of Economic Affairs, "Industrial and Regional Progress Report," no. 1 (1965). Note that the Minister of Economic Affairs serves as Chairman of the

National Economic Development Council. The new Department cut across the jurisdiction of several other Ministries, especially the Treasury and Housing and Local Government. As of September 1968, it appeared to be highly unpopular in some quarters. There were even predictions that it would not survive a new administration. Others claimed that these were problems of an earlier "teething" period that were no longer a cause for serious concern.

51. For previous efforts made by the Labor Government in the early postwar period, see R. Vance Presthus, "A Note on British Town Planning Coordination," *Journal of Politics*, vol. 14, no. 3 (1952), pp. 471–87; P. Self, *Regionalism: A Report on Local Government* (London: Fabian Publications and George Allen and Unwin, 1949); and R. B. Black, "Town and Country Planning in England's Northeast Section," *Journal of the American Institute of Planners*, vol. 15, no. 3 (1951).

52. There are now eight regions in England: Northern, Yorkshire and Humberside, North West, East Midlands, West Midlands, South West, South East, and East Anglia. Northern Ireland has set up an Economic Council and the Orkney and Shetland Islands are Development Areas. The Chairman of the Scottish Planning Board is appointed by the Secretary of State for Scotland, and the Chairman of the Welsh Planning Board is appointed by the Secretary of State for Wales.

53. See, for example, South East Economic Planning Council, *A Strategy for the South East* (London: HMSO, 1967); South West Economic Planning Council, *A Region with a Future, A Draft Strategy for the South West* (HMSO, 1967); Northern Economic Planning Council, *Challenge of the Changing North* (HMSO, 1966); Yorkshire and Humberside Economic Planning Council, *A Review of Yorkshire and Humberside* (HMSO, 1966); East Midlands Economic Planning Council, *The East Midlands Study* (HMSO, 1966); West Midlands Economic Planning Council, *The West Midlands: Patterns of Growth* (HMSO, 1967).

54. The Location of Offices Bureau is a Commission whose members are appointed by the Minister of Housing and Local Government. In 1968 the Commission was shifted to the Board of Trade. The program may be extended to the rest of the South East and elsewhere but it started in London. The government pointed out in its White Paper that South East England has one-third of Great Britain's population but accounted for half the increase in employees during the past decade. About three-fourths of this increase occurred in the London Metropolitan Region. London has been increasing its employment at the rate of 40,000 a year, and office employment is estimated to be increasing at the rate of 15,000 a year. The new jobs are requiring additional expansion of rail and road capacity and other infrastructure requirements, and it was for this reason that a curb on growth was imposed. (Note, however, Holmans's evidence that expansion would still continue in the South East, since it constituted only one-fourth of the increase in service employment.) See Holmans, "Industrial Development Certificates and Control of Growth of Employment in South East England," p. 155.

55. *Offices, A Statement By Her Majesty's Government*, November 4, 1964 (London: HMSO); and Control of Office and Industrial Development Act, 1965, chap. 33. The controls, as of 1968, apply to office space of 3000 square feet (gross) or more for the South East, West Midlands, East Anglia, and East Midlands Economic Planning Regions. In July 1967, the exemption was raised to 10,000 square feet for all of the areas designated above except the London Metropolitan Region. To qualify for an office development permit, applicants must satisfy the Board of Trade that the activity cannot be carried on elsewhere; that no satisfactory alternative accommodations can be found; that the project is essential to the public interest; and that in case of modernization or rebuilding, no extra jobs will result. Board of Trade, *Annual*

Chapter V

Report for the Year Ended March 31, 1968 (London: HMSO, 1968), p. 2. See also Wilson, op. cit., pp. 50–57.

56. For the most recent summaries concerning these towns, see Town and Country Planning, vol. 37, nos. 1 and 2 (1969), pp. 43–50. Note that the Minister of Housing and Local Government approved the Northumberland County Council proposals for the New Town of 17,000 population at Killingworth. The proposal is unique, since the sponsoring authority is not a development corporation, an exporting authority, or a housing authority, but the county council. Another New Town is also proposed in the North at Cramlington, to be developed by private enterprise. The Minister has agreed to assist this development.

57. In March 1965, the Minister of Housing and Local Government, R. H. S. Crossman, set up a Committee on Housing Research to advise on an immediate program of urban planning research and on how and where it could best be carried out. Its focus was on problems associated with the rebuilding of old towns and the building of new ones, and it has tried to stimulate and assist specific research projects conducted at universities. The wide range of interests of members of the Committee illustrate the broader approach to the problem. Lord Llewelyn-Davies, Professor of Architecture at University College, London, is Chairman. The other members of the group are: Mr. Leslie Lane, president of the Town Planning Institute; Mr. William Bor, City Planning Officer, Liverpool; Professor D. V. Donnison, Professor of Social Administration, London School of Economics; Professor R. Grieve, Professor of Town and Regional Planning, Glasgow University, now Chairman, Highland Development Board, Scotland; Mr. Peter Cowan, Director of Joint Unit for Planning Research, University College, London; Mr. Christopher Foster, Senior Research Fellow in the Economics and Organisation of Transport, Jesus College, Oxford; and Dr. Peter Hall, Lecturer in Geography, Birkbeck College, London University. The Secretary of State for Scotland and the Minister of Transport are associated with the setting up of the Research Advisory Group and senior officials of the Scottish Development Department and the Ministry of Transport are represented on it as well as the Ministry of Housing. See also Centre for Environmental Studies, First Annual Report (London, 1968).

58. J. R. James, "Regional Planning in Britain," in S. B. Warner, Planning for a Nation of Cities (Cambridge: MIT Press, 1966), chap. 11. The new plans were disclosed at a talk that Mr. James gave to the Land Use Society on July 23, 1965 in London.

59. The Ministry has had to cope in recent years with a volume of planning appeals which rose to 14,000 in 1964 and stood at 12,000 in 1967. More than half were settled by formal inquiry, which takes an average of nine months. See Ministry of Housing and Local Government, Scottish Development Department and Welsh Office, Town and Country Planning, Cmd. 3333 (London: HMSO, 1967), p. 7. The problems and the changes necessary to function more effectively in the future were examined in detail by a planning group advisory to the Ministry. Their report became the basis for the White Paper cited above. It urged that local authorities should submit for ministerial approval only broad policy proposals and that the detailed plans of local authorities should conform with these proposals and with changes the Minister might make in them after hearing objections. The group's sharpest criticism was of delay:

> The attempt to process all these detailed plans through a centralized procedure, including provision for objections (of which there may be hundreds or even thousands on a single plan) and public local inquiry, has inevitably led to very serious delays which tend to undermine public confidence in the system. The average time taken by the Ministry of Housing to deal with a

319

development plan submission is two to three years, but some cases may take considerably longer—some 60 town map submissions have been with the ministry for more than three years. The result of these delays may mean both that necessary development or redevelopment is held up pending approval of the plan, and that the plan once approved is already, in some respects, out of date. The detailed character of the plans may also be a contributory factor in delays at the local authority planning level. Many quinquennial reviews are overdue, some by five years or more. Many town maps have been submitted for small towns, some little more than villages, where no substantial growth or changes is expected. And yet these submissions have to go through the same procedure as the complex and important cases, thus causing delay and themselves incurring delay. . . .

We would stress the function of plans not primarily as a control mechanism but as providing a positive brief for developers and setting the standards. . . .

Thus, for the county boroughs and other urban areas over 50,000 population we propose a new type of urban plan which concentrates on the broad pattern of future development and redevelopment and deals with the land use transport relationships in an integrated way, but which excludes the detailed land use allocations of the present town maps.

Similarly, for the counties we propose a new form of county plan which deals with the distribution of population and employment, the major communications network, the main policies for recreation and conservation, green belts, and the general development policy for towns and villages. The county plan will include urban plans for towns over 50,000 population and other areas of special importance, notably those planned for major expansion.

Both the urban plans and the county plans will be required to identify the *action areas*, which are the areas that require comprehensive planning (for development, redevelopment or improvement) and on which action is to be concentrated over the next 10 years or so. . . .

The Minister's approval of the action areas will be related to the policy proposed and not to detailed design proposals.

The report adds that the types of plans which the group recommends cannot be produced by planning authorities acting in isolation. They must form part of a regional pattern and also a sub-regional pattern. The regional context would be set out in plans prepared by the economic planning boards and councils. See Ministry of Housing and Local Government, *The Future of Development Plans, A Report by the Planning Advisory Group* (London: HMSO, 1965), pp. 7–10, reproduced by permission from the Controller of Her Britannic Majesty's Stationery Office.

60. *The Times,* July 28, 1965, p. 10.

61. Under the Selective Employment Payments Act of 1966, an employer who has paid the Selective Employment Tax on employees in a manufacturing establishment can receive a premium consisting of the amount of tax paid plus a sum of 7s. 6d. a man *per week,* with smaller sums for women, girls, and boys. (In April 1968 this premium was made available only to firms in Development Areas.) The regional employment premiums, described a little later, simply add extra premiums, roughly up to 30s. a man *per week,* with smaller sums for women, girls, and boys, employed in industrial establishments in Development Areas. Department of Economic Affairs, *The Development Areas: A Proposal for a Regional Employment Premium* (London: HMSO, 1967), p. 10. See also Posner, "Regional Economic Policy in the United Kingdom," pp. 60–69.

62. Ships, hovercraft, computers, and mining works also qualify for grants.

63. The Development Districts were areas with high actual or prospective unemployment, defined by the Board of Trade as areas with unemployment of 4.5 percent or more. The new Development Areas were "chosen with reference to the Government's wider regional policies and [to] take account of all relevant economic circumstances including population change, migration, economic growth and unemployment." The boundaries of the Development Areas are:

   1) The whole of Scotland, except Edinburgh, Leith, and Portobello employment exchange areas.

   2) The Northern Development Area consisting of the Ministry of Labour Northern Region, plus the Furness Peninsula (i.e., the Barrow Group, and Ulverston employment exchange area, and Grange-over-Sands sub-office area).

   3) The Merseyside Development Area consisting of the existing development districts with the addition of St. Helens, Runcorn, Ellesmere Port, Neston, and Hoylake employment exchange areas. Skelmersdale New Town, which draws its population mainly from Merseyside, will also qualify for the benefits available within the Development Area.

   4) The Welsh Development Area consisting of the whole of Wales and Monmouthshire, with the exception of the following employment exchange areas:
      a) South East Wales—the Cardiff and Newport Groups, Chepstow, Abergavenny, Cwmbran, and the Monmouth sub-office area; and
      b) North Wales—the Shotton Group and Rhyl, and Colwyn Bay and Llandudno.

   5) The South Western Development Area consisting of the employment exchange areas in Cornwall (excluding Devonport, Saltash, and Gunnislake but including Launceston and Bude), and the North Devonshire employment exchange areas of Bideford, Barnstaple, and Ilfracombe.
   (Investment Incentives, Cmd. 2874 [London: HMSO, 1966], pp. 812–813.)

64. Cairncross, *op. cit.,* p. 21.

65. *Investment Incentives,* p. 15. See also Employment Acts, 1960 to 1966, *Eighth Annual Report by the Board of Trade for the year ended 31st March 1968* (London: HMSO, 1968). [From 1959 to 1968, 181 advance factories were built in Britain (72 in England, 69 in Scotland, and 40 in Wales).]

66. H. F. R. Catherwood, Chief Industrial Advisor, Department of Economic Affairs at the Scottish Branch of the Confederation of British Industry, estimated that the investment grants would cost £300 million less than the depreciation allowances; and Regional Employment Premiums had a ceiling of £100 million. See *The Times,* February 1, 1966, p. 15.

67. For more detail on the regional employment premiums, see fn. 61. See also McCrone, *op. cit.,* pp. 200–202.

68. Department of Economic Affairs, *The Development Areas: A Proposal for a Regional Development Premium,* p. 12.

69. These changes were reported by the London *Times* just as this manuscript was sent to the printer. See D. Wood, "Prime Minister Forms Two New Whitehall Empires," *The Times,* October 6, 1969, p. 1; also the leading article, "A Better Shape," published on the same date on p. 11; and M. Shanks, "Two Cheers for the New Set-Up," *The Times,* October 8, 1969, p. 27.

70. Needleman and Scott, *op. cit.,* p. 151; see also A. J. Odber, "Local Employment and

the 1958 Act," *Scottish Journal of Political Economy*, vol. 6, no. 3 (1959), pp. 211–228; and Needleman and Scott, *op. cit.*, pp. 153, 166–170.

71. Needleman and Scott, *op. cit.*, p. 151.

72. Under the last year of the Conservative Government, however, much of the responsibility for economic planning was shifted from the Treasury to the Secretary of State for Industry, Trade, and Regional Development.

73. "The Backward Areas of the United Kingdom," p. 30.

74. *Report of a Committee of Inquiry into the Scottish Economy, 1960–1961* (Edinburgh: The Scottish Council, 1961). The stress on development growth centers reflected in part the views expressed in the earlier Cairncross Report *(Report of the Committee on Local Development in Scotland 1952)*. Another influential figure was A. J. Odber, Director, Business Research Unit, University of Durham. For a summary of his views, see his article "Regional Policy in Great Britain," in *Area Development Policies in Britain and the Countries of the Common Market* (Washington, D. C.: U.S. Department of Commerce and Area Development Association, 1965).

75. The two White Papers were Scottish Development Department, *Central Scotland: A Program for Development and Growth*, Cmd. 2188 (Edinburgh: HMSO, 1963); and the Secretary of State for Industry, Trade, and Regional Development, *The North East, A Program for Development and Growth*, Cmd. 2206 (London: HMSO, 1963). The other studies are Ministry of Housing and Local Government, *The South East Study: 1961–1981* (London: HMSO, 1964); Department of Economic Affairs, *The North West* (London: HMSO, 1965); Department of Economic Affairs, *The West Midlands* (London: HMSO, 1965); Ministry of Health and Local Government (Government of Northern Ireland), *Belfast Regional Survey and Plan: Recommendations and Conclusions*, Cmd. 451 (Belfast: HMSO, 1963); Great Britain, Ministry of Housing and Local Government, Committee on Depopulation of Mid-Wales, *Depopulation in Mid-Wales* (London: HMSO, 1964).

76. Some of these growing points were Irvine, the Grangemouth-Falkirk area, and other industrial areas (such as the Vale of Leven, the Lothians, central Fife, and North Lanarkshire.

77. Ministry of Housing and Local Government, *The South East Study: 1961–1981*, pp. 51–79.

78. The New Town in Essex which would have been at Stansted has been abandoned because the proposal to situate the airport there has been dropped. The final site for the airport is still under review by a commission.

79. The number of long distance commuters working in Central London had increased by an average of approximately 30,000 a year in the decade before 1963. The cost of accommodating these additional half million commuters was estimated to have been more than £100 million for British Railways and at least the equivalent for internal London transportation. See Standing Conference on London Regional Planning, *Report of the Technical Panel on Population, Employment and Transportation*, October 1963, cited in P. Self, "Regional Planning and the Machinery of Government," *Public Administration*, vol. 42, Autumn (1964), p. 229.

80. *The Times*, February 1, 1966, p. 11.

81. W. F. Luttrell, *Factory Location and Industrial Movement* (London: National Institute of Economic and Social Research, 1962), vol. 1, p. 300. Wilson also emphasizes that "even if the industrial inducements so reduce the capital costs of a firm in the development districts of Great Britain as to give it a margin of 20 percent as compared with a firm elsewhere, and if, moreover, annual costs amount to as much

as 20 percent of total costs, the margin in favor of the grant aided firm will come to only 4 percent of its annual outlays" (Wilson, *op. cit.*, p. 69).

82. Wilson, *op. cit.*, p. 38.

83. The figures apply to all industrial projects including some not classified to industrial activity. Board of Trade Statistics Division, *Industrial Building (By Regions and Subdivision)* [London: Board of Trade, 1968].

84. Wilson, *op. cit.*, pp. 53–57.

85. Cited in McCrone, *op. cit.*, pp. 201–202.

86. H.F.R. Catherwood, *op. cit.*, p. 15. For an evaluation of the pro's and con's of these subsidies, see McCrone, *op. cit.*, pp. 191–202; K. Keith, "A Misuse of Economic Resources," *The Times*, May 23, 1967, p. 23; "Seven Year Regional Premiums," *The Times*, June 6, 1967, p. 7; Sir R. Hall, "The Labour Bonus: A Powerful New Weapon," *The Times*, May 11, 1967, p. 25; Posner, *op. cit.*; A. Crosland, "A Progress Report on the Development Areas," *Board of Trade Journal*, March 29, 1968, pp. 1–4; and P. Shore, "A Policy to Keep Pace with Industrial Change," *The Times*, July 3, 1969, p. 25.

87. F. Cairncross, "Grape-shot Regionalism," *The Times*, July 28, 1967, p. 21.

88. See fn. 66.

89. McCrone, *op. cit.*, pp. 193–194.

90. Secretary of State for Economic Affairs, *The Intermediate Areas, Report of a Committee under the Chairmanship of Sir Joseph Hunt*, Cmd. 3998 (London: HMSO, 1969), p. 92.

91. This disproportion may appear exaggerated, since gross total capital expenditure in the Development Areas is in the neighborhood of £260 million a year, of which £100 million are for REP and another £25 million for SET. However, because of tax effects, "the present capital grants lower the effective price of fixed capital in the development areas by about 25 percent compared with elsewhere whereas REP and SET reduce labour costs by 9 percent" (Secretary of State for Economic Affairs [London: HMSO, 1969], p. 43). See also "Note of Dissent of H. J. Brown," in *The Intermediate Areas*, p. 163 and Appendices H, I and J.

92. *The Intermediate Areas*, p. 44.

93. Board of Trade Statistics Division, *Industrial Building (By Regions and Subdivisions)*, (London: Board of Trade, 1968). See also R. Lambert, "Bonus in a Move," *The Times*, March 4, 1968; and fn. 42. Note that the figures on jobs are the annual average for the periods 1960–64 and 1966–67, whereas the data on gross financial outlays are for the periods 1964–65 and 1967–68. In interpreting these data the reader should bear in mind that it is generally risky to estimate anticipated employment. Moreover, knowledge of the number of jobs lost through closures is essential to get a view of net change. Since the Board of Trade's data have been criticized for being overly optimistic, such data must be used with caution. Subject to these qualifications, the data presented give some insight on orders of magnitude and relative change. Thus, a study by the Board of Trade, "made at the end of March 1968, showed that the projects included in the sample, which accounted for about 63 percent of the potential employment in projects offered assistance in the five years [to the end of March 1965] had, so far, provided 91,250 jobs. This was 75 percent of the jobs which the firms estimated, at the time they applied for assistance, would eventually be provided when recruitment was completed. If the progress of recruitment had been similar in the projects not covered by the enquiry, the total number of jobs created by March 1968 in all projects offered assistance to the

end of March 1965 would be over 144,000. The total amount of assistance in all forms offered for these projects was £141 million, and the firms concerned estimated originally that they would provide 192,000 jobs." Cost per job at the 144,000 estimate would be £979, and £734 for the 192,000 estimate. See *Local Employment Acts—1960 to 1966, Eighth Annual Report By the Board of Trade for the year ended 31st March 1968* (London: HMSO, 1968), p. 10.

94. McCrone, *op. cit.*, p. 198.

95. James, *op. cit.*, pp. 206–207.

96. "The analysis covers the opening of new manufacturing establishments in new locations (whether in new or existing premises) where a firm had not manufactured previously. The terms 'movement' and 'moves' cover both the opening of additional branches by a firm and the complete transfer of a firm's activities from one area to another (lock, stock and barrel moves). By far the majority of moves are the opening of additional branches." *(The Intermediate Areas, p. 36.)*

97. McCrone, *op. cit.*, p. 165. See also chap. 6.

98. *Ibid.*, pp. 150–151.

99. R. W. Shakespeare, "North Preparing Its Case for Special Treatment," *The Times,* August 1, 1967, p. 17. See also "Regions Quarrel over Development Area Policies," *The Times,* February 5, 1968, p. 19; "Reports Criticize the Government's 'Grey' Area Policies," *The Times,* March 15, 1968, p. 23; and J. Chartres, "Grey Areas in Uphill Battle," *The Times,* March 25, 1968, p. 30.
The Lancashire and Merseyside Industrial Development Association cited ten factors which it felt should influence the need for investment grants. They include "persistently high unemployment[;]. . . substantial population loss and distortion of the population structure; contraction of traditional industries; narrow employment structure resulting in undue vulnerability; bad environment with a large amount of outworn property, spoil heaps, disused factory premises and other forms of industrial dereliction; inadequate communications; excessive travel to work; low earnings and productivity; and a low rate of new industrial building" (Shakespeare, *The Times,* March 15, 1968, p. 23).

100. *The Intermediate Areas*, pp. 1–88.

101. The present South East Economic Planning Region excludes East Anglia, where many new development schemes are to take place. This partly accounts for the slowdown in the migration figures.

102. South East Economic Planning Council, *A Strategy for the South East*, pp. 1, 4–5. For an interesting study showing that the New Towns had reduced the journeys to London and had in fact become more self-contained than other suburban towns, especially in terms of the journey to work, see R. Thomas, "London's New Towns," *op. cit.*, fn. 22.

103. These views were expressed in a letter to the author dated March 26, 1969. Prof. Self added that the policy entailed

either pushing more industry out of London or uprooting industries in the metropolitan ring which (as I know) naturally feel resentful having space there to expand. The problems of running both these horses, at any rate until the mid-70's, have become increasingly important. They have accounted for the dropping of the proposed new city at Ashford, Kent; and for considerable anxieties among the new cities as to where they are to get employment from.

There is also a conflict over office employment. The preferred locations for dispersing firms are within a 40 or 50 mile radius from London. But to the extent that they can be pushed further (and perhaps they can to a greater extent) there is obvious conflict between the needs of these South East cities and places like Liverpool, Leeds or Newcastle. This also is increasingly apparent since the planners in 'Housing and Local Government' put a lot of weight on getting offices to these new cities. In point of fact, earlier ideas of switching office development to suitable cities in the "regions at risk" have now largely been dropped by the DEA, largely because of pressure from interests in the South East including the South East Council which has demanded recently (and secured) a relaxation of office development controls outside London itself. There is also pressure now to relax these controls within London.

There is an interesting conflict of strategy between expansion of the outer Metropolitan region which would fit in best with development area policy and stretching out the poles of growth to these proposed new cities. . . . These issues are still very much alive, and worth comment, because the fate of the countermagnet policy is very uncertain. Milton Keynes and Northampton are going ahead but are anxious about employment in the short run, and the new airport may be sited in that sector. Ashford has been dropped, Ipswich still uncertain. Peterborough is anxious, and the Solent City idea has been scaled down to a joint study by the local planning authorities which will probably exclude the original idea of London overspill. In the long run, the poles of growth in the South East are still certainly to be stretched considerably, but how quickly is dubious. Airport location and port development are critical factors here.

104. The work of the South East Council has been criticized on the grounds that it did not take adequate account of social trends and likely changes, some of which have been explored by The Standing Conference on London and South East Regional Planning.

The Standing Conference is an organization of constituent authorities of the South East Region set up to collect information on basic trends, evaluate major development issues, develop recommendations on joint policy, and coordinate subsequent action. Its reports constitute imaginative efforts to break with past traditions of land use planning, and some of the technical studies are extremely provocative. See Standing Conference on London and South East Regional Planning, "The Conference Area In The Long Term," Agenda Item 11, LRP 780 (London: Standing Conference on London and South East Regional Planning, 1967); and "The South East—A Framework for Regional Planning," Agenda Item 18, LRP 1180 (London: Standing Conference on London and South East Regional Planning, 1968).

105. "A high proportion of the jobs remaining in the region (205,000) and of those moving to East Anglia (13,000) were to new and expanding towns" *(The Intermediate Areas,* p. 94). See also Board of Trade, *The Movement of Manufacturing Industry in the United Kingdom 1945–65* (London: HMSO, 1968), pp. 35–36. The South East received 45 percent in the 1953–1959 period and only 29 percent in the 1960–1966 period; but the volume of employment is expected to be the same. *Ibid.,* p. 22.

106. *The Intermediate Areas,* p. 97.

107. *The Times,* April 17, 1968, pp. 11, 24, reproduced from *The Times* by permission. See also *The Times,* March 2, 1968, p. 13; and *The Intermediate Areas,* pp. 98–9.

108. McCrone, *op. cit.*, p. 127. The government felt that this assistance was "a relatively small price to pay for the acquiescence—albeit the reluctant acquiescence –of the mining industry and the mining unions in the loss of up to 46,000 jobs a year" (C. W. Roberts, "Regional Policy in Britain" mimeographed [London: Board of Trade, 1969], p. 16).

109. Brown, *op. cit.*, pp. 155–165; T. Lambert, "Regions Quarrel over Development Policies," *The Times,* February 5, 1968, p. 19; and *The Times,* March 2, 1968, p. 13. There were already differences in the application of the incentives before 1967. Thus, in Northern Ireland, the 45 percent rates apply to building as well as to plant and machinery, and the exact rates are subject to negotiation depending on the number of jobs, the type of product, and the place. K. Withers, "Industrial Incentive Policy Pays Off," *The Times,* November 20, 1967, p. 1.

110. *The Intermediate Areas,* chaps. 6–11.

111. The seven intermediate areas are: the Yorkshire coal field, northeast Lancashire, parts of Humberside, the Nottingham-Derbyshire coal field, limited parts of southeast Wales, the Plymouth area, and Leith. It is not at all certain the government's program will be enacted by Parliament in the form now proposed. For a description of the government's position and some of the critical reactions, see P. Shore, "A Policy to Keep Pace with Industrial Change," *The Times,* July 3, 1969, p. 25; R. W. Shakespeare, "Merseyside Calls for Action on Hunt Report," *The Times,* May 21, 1969, p. 22; "7 s. 6 d. Refund on SET Will Stop for 'Grey' Areas Redevelopment," *The Times,* June 26, 1969, p. 19; and "Depressing Drift in Regional Policy," *The Times,* June 26, 1969, p. 25.

112. As one might expect, it is the large firms which are able to make the long distance moves. They represent only 22 percent of the firms but 76 percent of the jobs. See *Annual Report, 1964–1965* (London: Location of Offices Bureau, 1965), p. 18; and *Annual Report, 1966–1967* (London: Location of Offices Bureau, 1967), pp. 6, 9.

113. *Annual Report, 1966–1967,* p. 19.

114. *Ibid.,* p. 19.

115. The Treasury, until recently, has been responsible for government dispersal policy. (These responsibilities have now been taken over by the new Civil Service Department.) In testifying before the Sub-Committee of the Select Committee on Estimates the Treasury pointed out that

> The policy of dispersing Government offices from London was first seriously considered in the late 1930's. This was soon superseded by the large-scale evacuations of the war. In the late 1940's the question which of the evacuated offices should return to London became merged with a further examination of fresh dispersal. Some substantial projects were decided upon including the establishment in Newcastle of much of the headquarters of what is now the Ministry of Social Security.
>
> The policy did not receive a further significant boost until 1962 when the Government was particularly concerned about congestion in London, though an appreciable amount of dispersal continued. Sir Gilbert Flemming was appointed to review the possibilities. He reported to Treasury Ministers; and in July, 1963 the Chief Secretary to the Treasury announced in Parliament that, in the light of the Flemming Report, the Government planned to move about 13,500 jobs away from London and another 4,500 from Central London to the London periphery.
>
> Decisions in detail have been taken on all the recommendations of the Flemming Report, in most cases some time ago. But not all the decisions

have been fully implemented because this has to be done over a period, particularly when new building is involved. . . . Figures of actual performance have to be read against the background of the existing disposition of the Civil Service, a much larger proportion of which than is generally realised is already outside London. Of the whole non-industrial Civil Service (including the G.P.O.), numbering (on 1st July, 1967) some 866,000 some 584,000 or 67 per cent, are already outside London.

(This reference was supplied to me by C. W. Roberts, Board of Trade, Distribution of Industry Division, in a letter dated August 29, 1969.)

116. H. G. Wells, *Anticipations* (London: Harper and Bros., 1901), p. 52. See also Hall, *London, 2000*, chaps. 5–7 and pp. 207–209.

117. Subsequent to the preparation of this chapter, I encountered three suggestive discussions bearing on the ideas sketched in the text. The first, by Kenzo Tange, dealt with the need for a linear development strategy to handle Japan's urbanization prospects. The second, by J. R. James, dealt with linear patterns as the essential underlying idea of the plans for the growth of different urban regions in Britain. The third, by R. H. Best, noted that "the main area of urban growth was in a belt of country, shaped rather like a dumb-bell and extending from Lancashire and the West Riding, diagonally down through the Midlands, to the London Region, which has been termed Megalopolis England." See K. Tange, "The Japanese Archipelago In the Future—The Creation of the Tokaido Megalopolis" (pp. 79–93), and J. R. James, "The Future of Urban Forms" (pp. 205–212). in *The Papers and Proceedings of the International Symposium on Regional Development* (Hakone: Japan Center for Area Development Research, 1967); and R. H. Best, "Extent of Urban Growth and Agricultural Displacement in Post-War Britain," *Urban Studies*, vol. 5, no. 1, p. 77.

118. *The Scottish Economy 1965–1970, A Plan for Expansion*, Cmd. 2864 (Edinburgh: HMSO, 1963), p. 56 (my italics).

119. Standing Conference on London and South East Regional Planning, "The Conference Area in the Long Term." Similar exercises are likely on a national scale. The new perspectives on development have already led the Ministry of Housing and Local Government and the Department of Economic Affairs—independently—to propose a drastic reorganization of local government. On the grounds that current boundaries are thoroughly obsolete for basic planning and development programs, the Ministry and the Board urged the establishment of thirty to forty city regions having principal responsibility for land use and transport planning, collection of local taxes, supervision of the priority and timing of capital projects within the region (subject to the determination of policy and the overall financial aggregates by the central government), and a number of other basic services such as education, police, and fire services. For further details, see Royal Commission on Local Government in England, *Written Evidence of the Ministry of Housing and Local Government* (London: HMSO, 1967), especially Part 2; and *Written Evidence of the Department of Economic Affairs* (London: HMSO, 1967), pp. 1–4; and Department of Economic Affairs, *Minutes of Evidence*, January 19, 1967 (London: HMSO, 1967), pp. 3–20.

On June 11, 1969, the Royal Commission on Local Government, headed by Lord Redcliffe-Maud, presented its recommendations to Parliament. The main proposals, as summarized by *The Times*, were that

England (outside London) should be reconstructed into 61 new local government areas grouped in eight provinces. In 58 of these local government areas single authorities (called unitary authorities by the commission) would be responsible for all services. Each would cover town and surrounding country.

In the three conurbations of Birmingham, Liverpool and Manchester, as in Greater London, responsibility for services would be divided between a metropolitan authority and a number of metropolitan district authorities. The metropolitan authority would have the overriding functions of planning, transport and major development; the second tier of district authorities would be responsible for education, personal social services, health and housing.

Superimposed on this local government structure would be the eight proposed provincial councils. These would be elected by the authorities in the unitary and metropolitan areas (including Greater London for the Southeast), although there would also be coopted members.

The function of the provincial councils would be to determine provincial strategy and planning, and the unitary authorities would have to conform to the strategic framework they prescribed.

(D. Wood, "Plan for 61 Main Local Authorities,"
The Times, June 12, 1969, p. 1.)

The recommendations were not unanimous, however. A minority proposal was submitted by Derek Senior. He proposed 37 regional authorities and 150 district authorities with services and functions divided between the two. The aim of his recommendations was to accommodate the desire for self-government of those communities which had an established tradition and capacity for self-government. Not surprisingly, there were differences of opinion between the Prime Minister and the leader of the Opposition on whether the substance of the proposals would be implemented before 1974 and the changes that were likely to be made considering the controversy the recommendations had stirred. For more detail, see the *Report of the Royal Commission on Local Government in England* (London: HMSO, 1969), vol. 1, *Report of the Commission*, Cmd. 4040; vol. 2, Memorandum of Dissent by Mr. D. Senior, Cmd. 4040–1; and vol. 3, Research Appendices, Cmd. 4040–11; and Royal Commission on Local Government in England, *Local Government Reform* (Short version of the Report of the Royal Commission on Local Government in England), Cmd. 4039 (London: HMSO, 1969).

By September 1969 there was also a report of the royal commission on local government in Scotland and a White Paper dealing with local government in Wales. The latter suggested some amalgamations within the framework of the present system whereas the proposals for Scotland by implication reinforced Mr. Senior's arguments. All of which led *The Times* to exclaim that "the publication of such different sets of proposals, all carefully and persuasively argued, to fit what are basically similar circumstances makes it all the more difficult to pin faith on any one of them" *(The Times,* September 26, 1969, p. 11).

120. This is especially evident in the most recent studies prepared by the regional economic councils.

121. A major study of urbanization in Great Britain, financed by the Ford Foundation and conducted by Political and Economic Planning (PEP), was initiated at the end of 1965.

Chapter VI

1. For regional data on France, see Institut National de la Statistique et des Études Économiques (INSEE), *L'Espace Économique Français,* fascicule 1, Démographie Générale (Paris: Presses Universitaires de France, 1965), pp. 25–26. (Henceforth

referred to as *L'Espace Économique Français.*) See also the yearly regionalized budgets of the state: Délégation à l'Aménagement du Territoire et à l'Action Régionale, Institut National de la Statistique et des Études Économiques, *Statistiques et Indicateurs des Régions Françaises, Projet de Loi de Finances pour 1969, L'Analyse des Situations et des Évolutions des Régions Françaises Statistiques et Indicateurs,* tome 3 (Paris: Imprimerie Nationale, 1969). (Henceforth referred to as *Statistiques et Indicateurs des Régions Françaises.*) For data on England, see A. F. Weber, *The Growth of Cities in the Nineteenth Century* (New York: Macmillan, 1899), pp. 46, 58; and Department of Economic Affairs, *The North West, A Regional Study* (London: HMSO, 1965), p. 125.

2. The percentages in this paragraph are derived from a) Weber, *op. cit.* Table XXXVI, p. 73 (his data by decades up to 1891 are based on *Résultats Statistiques du Dénombrement de 1891,* p. 33); b) *L'Espace Économique Français,* pp. 25–35; and Tables 1–3 and R1–4, pp. 62–63. France reached a population of 50 million about the end of 1968. For details, see *Le Monde,* September 26, 1968, p. 32. The reasons for the low birth rate during the nineteenth century are still somewhat obscure. The explanations have ranged from emphasis on the desire of the French peasant to avoid parcellization of his land to conjectures about the effects of war and revolution and the expression of deep rooted preferences and values. See A. Sauvy, *Richesse et Population* (Paris: Payot, 1943); *La Montée des Jeunes* (Paris: Calmann-Lévy, 1960); C. P. Kindleberger, "The Postwar Resurgence of the French Economy," In *France: Change and Tradition* (London: Victor Gollancz, 1963), pp. 132–133, 414–415, and fns. 5, 7; and C. P. Kindleberger, *Economic Growth in France and England, 1851–1950* (Cambridge: Harvard University Press, 1964), pp. 72–80.

3. Many explanations have been offered for France's slow industrialization and economic growth. The most important are: lack of natural resources (especially coking coal and plentiful labor); diversion of savings from domestic capital formation to foreign political loans; domination of enterprises by family firms; social conflicts; overcentralized and misguided governmental intervention; and deep-seated values favoring high-quality consumption and limited family size. As Kindleberger has observed, these hypotheses "overlap and are not mutually exclusive. The importance which one attaches to each factor will differ among observers, depending on one's view of the processes of economic growth, the relative weight of economic and non-economic factors and the tolerable limits of government economic activity" (Kindleberger, "The Postwar Resurgence of the French Economy," p. 120). Kindleberger analyzes the evidence for these hypotheses and attaches most importance to the role of population growth and basic French attitudes towards levels of living.

4. Economic Commission for Europe, *Economic Survey of Europe in 1954* (Geneva: United Nations, 1954), p. 181.

5. J. H. Clapham, *The Economic Development of France and Germany, 1815–1914* (London: Cambridge University Press, 1921), p. 258; and W. C. Baum, *The French Economy and the State* (Princeton: Princeton University Press, 1958), pp. 229–236.

6. Kindleberger, *Economic Growth in France and Britain,* Table 9, p. 166 and Table 13, p. 169.

7. Clapham, *op. cit.,* p. 53.

8. Celia von der Muhl, "The Urban Structure of France" (unpublished seminar paper), pp. 3–10 and Table II: "Growth Rates of Major French Cities."

9. *Ibid.,* pp. 6–7. See also for further general discussion of the functions of the cities and regions, P. George, *La Ville* (Paris: Presses Universitaires de France, 1952); and R. E. Dickinson, *The West European City* (London: Routledge and Kegan Paul, 1947). More than a dozen regional histories have been published by the Presses Univer-

FOOTNOTES

sitaires de France in its series "Que Sais-je." For a discussion of the regions from the point of view of territorial planning, see J. F. Gravier, *L'Aménagement du Territoire et l'Avenir des Régions Françaises* (Paris: Flammarion, 1964).

10. H. Ormsby, *France, A Regional and Economic Geography* (London: Methuen, 1931), p. 7.

11. For data on cities see Institut National de la Statistique et des Études Économiques, *Villes et Agglomérations Urbaines Recensement de 1962* (Paris: Direction des Journaux Officiels, 1964).

12. *L'Espace Économique Français*, Table R–1–1, pp. 58–59.

13. *Ibid.*, pp. 58–59.

14. The economic activities which were especially concentrated in Paris were banking, insurance and exchange, automobile manufacturing, aeronautical and radio-electrical construction, armaments, and science and market-oriented activities. Industry generally has expanded more rapidly in Paris than in the rest of France. See Kindleberger, *Economic Growth in France and Britain*, chap. 11.

15. *L'Espace Économique Français*, Table 5, p. 36; and p. 44. Since the cumulative effects of the migration was to increase the age and to reduce the fecundity of the population in the regions and départements exporting their populations, the persistence of the trends indicates how deeply they were imbedded in the social and economic features of the region.

16. The three major growth regions were Provence-Côte d'Azur, Rhône-Alpes, and Paris—particularly the latter. *Ibid.*, Tables R 1–3 and R 1–4, p. 62. Following the war, however, seventy-two départements experienced a population increase. This major reversal was due to the fact that the growth of population during this period (1946–62) was almost double that of the preceding eighty years. *Ibid.*, p. 34.

17. *Ibid.*, p. 42. More specifically, about 25 percent came from neighboring regions, about 25 percent came from abroad, and about 50 percent from more distant regions within France. Of the migrants who came from distant regions between 1954 and 1962, more than 40 percent made the move in one jump. For data supporting the statements in this paragraph, see Tables R 6–1–1, p. 121; and R 6–2–4, p. 131; and pp. 41–2, 44.

18. *Ibid.*, p. 30.

19. *Projet de Loi de Finances pour 1966, Annexe, Régionalisation du Budget d'Équipement pour l'Année 1966 et Coordination des Investissements Publics au Regard des Objectifs de l'Aménagement du Territoire*, vol. 2, tome 1, Rapport, pp. 13–14, 19. (Henceforth referred to as *Projet de Loi [1966]*, Annexe, vol. 2, tome 1.)

20. J. R. Boudeville, *Problems of Regional Economic Planning* (Edinburgh: University of Edinburgh, 1966), pp. 52–74.

21. *Ibid.*, p. 71.

22. The figures reflect, in part, the different rates of urbanization. See *IVᵉ Plan de Développement Économique et Social 1962–1965* (Paris: Imprimerie des Journaux Officiels, 1962). (Henceforth referred to as *IVᵉ Plan*.) This observation is based on a survey conducted by INSEE; see also *Projet de Loi (1966)*, Annexe, vol. 2, tome 2, pp. 263, 265, 267; M. Béaud, "Une Analyse des Disparités Régionales de Croissance," *Revue Économique*, vol. 17, no 1 (1966) pp. 55–91; *idem*, "Analyse Régionale-structurale et Planification Régionale," *Revue Économique*, vol. 17, no. 2 (1966), pp. 264–287; and N. M. Hansen, *French Regional Planning* (Bloomington: University of Indiana Press, 1968), chap. 6.

330

23. *L'Espace Économique Français*, Table V, p. 36. M. Béaud, "Une Analyse des Disparités Régionales de Croissance," pp. 75–83.

24. Some scholars even argued that normal growth of the tertiary employment of other cities of France, especially in the basin of Paris, was arrested by the preference for location in Paris. For further details, see Béaud, *op. cit.*, pp. 79–80. See also J. F. Gravier, *Paris et le Désert Français* (Paris: Flammarion, 1947); and Gravier, *L'Aménagement du Territoire*, pp. 146–157.

25. Data are not available for the Paris agglomeration for 1801 and 1891. Therefore, the comparison for the two earlier periods is based on the population within the corporate limits of the city.

26. Kindleberger, *Economic Growth in France and Britain*, p. 255. See also Jean Labasse, *Organisation de l'Espace* (Paris: Hermann, 1966), pp. 566–592.

27. United Nations, *Economic Survey of Europe in 1954*, p. 183.

28. *L'Espace Économique Français*, p. 31.

29. F. Bloch-Lainé, "Justification des Choix," in *Urbanisme (Métropoles d'Équilibre)*, vol. 34, no. 89 (1965), p. 6.

30. Kindleberger, "The Postwar Resurgence of the French Economy," pp. 123–126.

31. Moreover, most of the public expenditures in Paris for investment and maintenance were high relative to those in the rest of France. See N. M. Hansen, *French Regional Planning*, p. 31.

32. *IVe Plan*, p. 130.

33. Gravier, *Paris et le Désert Français*. For the work done by the team of geographers during the war, see Délégation Générale à l'Équipement National, *Rapports et Travaux sur la Décongestion des Centres Industriels, 1944–45* (Paris: Ministère de l'Économie Nationale), vols. 1–9. For a more recent study which corrects but also confirms some of the conclusions, see *La Décentralisation Industrielle et le Bassin Parisien* (Paris, Cahiers de l'Institut d'Aménagement et d'Urbanisme de la Région Parisienne, 1966), vol 6. This study notes that at the beginning of the nineteenth century the periphery of Paris (the ring within 200 kilometers of Paris but excluding Paris) had twice the population of the center; and in 1963 the center had twice the population of the periphery. See p. 103.

34. Joseph Lajugie, "Aménagement du Territoire et Développement Économique Régional en France (1945–1964)," *Revue d'Économie Politique.* (Développement Économique Régional et Aménagement du Territoire), vol. 74 (1964), p. 273.

35. E. Claudius-Petit, *Pour un Plan National d'Aménagement du Territoire* (Paris: Ministère de la Reconstruction et de l'Urbanisme, 1950).

36. For a more detailed citation and review of some of the decrees and regulations noted in this and the following paragraph, see *Industrialisation et Aménagement du Territoire*, Notes et Études Documentaires, La Documentation Française, no. 3508 (Paris: Secrétariat Général du Gouvernement, 1968) pp. 5–16; A. Trintignac *Aménager l'Hexagone* (Paris: Éditions du Centurion 1965), chap. 10; J. Fourastié and J. P. Courthéoux, *La Planification Économique en France* (Paris: Presses Universitaires de France, 1968), chap. 8, pp. 218–231; Jacques de Lanversin, *L'Aménagement du Territoire* (Paris: Librairies Techniques, 1965), Deuxième Partie, chap. 2; Lajugie, "Aménagement du Territoire et Développement," p. 268; and J. Faucheux, *La Décentralisation Industrielle* (Paris: Éditions Berger-Levrault, 1959), chaps. 1–4. Note that a 1966 decree gave the Minister of Equipment, on the advice of a commission

located in Lyon, the right to control new industrial construction or extensions of 1000 square meters or more, in the Lyon region.

37. Ministère de la Construction. *Plan d'Aménagement et d'Organisation Générale de la Région Parisienne* (PADOG) [Paris, 1960]. The Plan intended to keep population in the neighborhood of 9 million but population of the region was already 8.4 million. See pp. 7, 115. See also F. Choay, "Pour Sauver Paris: l'Opération Banlieue," *Observateur* May 5, 1960, pp. 14–15. On the other hand, the population increase in the period from 1962 to 1968 was a third lower than projected, so that the population in 1968 was 9.24 million. See *Le Monde*, September 1 and 2, 1968, p. 15.

38. Decrees establishing and gradually extending these powers were passed in 1948, 1953, 1954, 1955, and 1957. Trintignac, *op. cit.*, pp. 238–39. Half the funds come from the local public bodies, another 10 to 20 percent from private sources, such as chambers of commerce or of agriculture, and the rest from specialized financial institutions. "The examination of existing statistics shows the preponderant place of equipment [joint ventures] in the execution of land planning operations. In the month of April, 1965, of 122 urban priority zones being studied or in course of execution, 94 were handled by the societies. Of 123 programmed industrial zones assisted by FNAFU in 1964 and 1965, 93 were handled by these societies. Finally, 40 industrial zones out of 58 which had benefited in 1964 by a loan from the Caisse des Dépôts were executed by joint societies" (*Projet de Loi [1966]*, Annexe, vol. 2, tome 1, p. 37). See also J. E. Godchot, *Les Sociétés d'Économie Mixte et l'Aménagement du Territoire* (Paris: Berger-Levrault, 1966), chaps. 1–7.

39. SCET was the joint creation of the Caisse des Dépôts et Consignations (CDC), a credit bank with resources from pension and social security funds and deposits of savings banks, which supplies most of the long-term funds borrowed by local authorities and which often engages in joint ventures with private capital and other leading financial institutions, including the Crédit Foncier, the Caisse Nationale de Crédit Agricole, the Caisse Nationale des Marchés de l'État, and the Banque de France. The Administrative Council includes the government administrators concerned with development, notably the assistant Director of the General Planning Commission, the head of the Delegation for territorial development, and representatives of the Ministries of Construction and Finance. Among other things, CDC manages the postal savings, social security and pension funds, and the surplus funds of savings banks.

40. John and Ann-Marie Hackett, *Economic Planning in France* (London: George Allen and Unwin, 1963), pp. 65–68; Dixième Rapport du Conseil de Direction du Fonds de Développement Économique et Social, *Statistiques et Études Financières*, no. 198 (Paris: Imprimerie Nationale, 1965), pp. 968–971.

41. The societies received exemptions from the taxes on corporations and on distributed profits; and they obtained a guarantee from the Ministry of Finance, on the recommendation of FDES, to provide minimum dividends to shareholders for twelve years. The minimum subscribed capital was originally 2 1/2 million francs. For further details on the operations of FNAFU, FDES, SCET, and SRR, see J. Milhau, "Le Financement de l'Expansion Régionale," in *Revue d'Économie Politique* (Développement Économique Régional et Aménagement du Territoire), vol. 74 (1964), pp. 111–135; Lajugie, "Aménagement du Territoire et Développement," pp. 278–335; and P. Bauchet, "Regional Development Policies in France," in Area Development Administration, *Area Development Policies in Britain and the Countries of the Common Market* (Washington, D.C.: Department of Commerce, 1965), pp. 83–170.

42. See *Rapport Général sur le Premier Plan de Modernisation et d'Équipement.* (Paris: Commissariat Général du Plan de Modernisation et d'Équipement, 1946); and *Deuxième*

Plan de Modernisation et d'Équipement (1954–1957) (Paris: Imprimerie des Journaux Officiels, 1956).

43. They involved not only fiscal and exchange issues but also failures in carrying out proposed decentralization policies. An example of such failures is the fact that between 1945 and 1954 some 270 new firms were established in the region of Paris whereas only about 50 important firms were relocated in the provinces during the same period. See Lajugie, "Aménagement du Territoire et Développement," p. 289.

44. *Troisième Plan de Modernisation et d'Équipement (1958–1961), Journal Officiel,* no. 1129 (1959), pp. 88–97.

45. Hackett, *op. cit.,* pp. 25–33: and Kindleberger, "The Postwar Resurgence of the French Economy," pp. 147–158. For another view, see S. Wellisz, "Economic Planning in the Netherlands, France and Italy," *Journal of Political Economy,* vol. 68, no. 3 (1960), pp. 279–280.

46. The prestige associated with the new committees also made it possible to encourage broader representation (i.e., to draw upon professional, craft, and agricultural organizations as well as local chambers of industry and commerce). Hackett, *op. cit.,* pp. 91–92; de Lanversin, *op. cit.,* pp 80–85; and Trintignac, *op. cit.,* pp. 221–223.

47. Lajugie, "Aménagement du Territoire et Développement," p. 293.

48. Teams were formed to study the key problems and to frame development proposals with the aid of staff from different ministries. These programs were drafted by rapporteurs of the Commissariat and reviewed by the prefects, the local officials, the Comités d'Expansion, and other organizations. The programs and the evaluation were then referred back to Paris for review and reformulation by a group responsible for the synthesis. Next came a scrutiny by the Comité National d'Orientation Économique (consisting of representatives of professional organizations and syndicates) and final review by an Interministerial Committee.
    For a more detailed description of these programs, see the following articles by J. Lajugie: "Décentralisation Industrielle, Reconversion, Aménagement du Territoire," *Revue Juridique et Économique de Sud-Ouest,* Série Économique, no. 2 (1956), pp. 355–413; and "La Politique Française de Développement Régional de 1958 à 1963," *Revue Juridique et Économique de Sud-Ouest,* no. 2 (1963), pp. 255–297.

49. Plans have been published for Lorraine, Corse, Languedoc, Midi-Pyrénées, Rhône-Alpes, Franche-Comté, Auvergne, Provence-Côte-d'Azur, Bourgogne, Limousin, Picardie, Champagne, Centre, Bretagne, Basse Normandie, Aquitaine, and Pays de la Loire.

50. For examples of the regional plans of the Ministry of Construction, see P. Dufournet, *Aménagement de la Bretagne* (Paris: Ministère de la Construction, 1961); R. Puget, *Région Auvergne,* Rapport Préliminaire (Paris: Ministère de la Construction, 1959); and I. Wiener, *Normandie, Étude Analytique* (Paris: Ministère de la Construction [no date indicated]).

51. Lajugie, "Aménagement du Territoire et Développement," pp. 304–309; Trintignac, *op. cit.,* pp. 215–216.

52. The zones were Nord (Avesnes-Fourmies); Calais (Calais and Béthune); Vosges and Bas Rhin (Vallée des Vosges); Loire Atlantique (Saint Nazaire-Nantes); Hérault (Montpellier, Sète, Béziers); and Haute Vienne (Limoges). In 1961 Nord, Calais, Vosges, and Bas Rhin were dropped from the list. Lajugie, "Aménagement du Territoire et Développement," pp. 324–330.

53. *Ibid.,* p. 328 (my translation).

54. The activity had to involve a minimum number of twenty jobs. However, the offer of a 20 percent lump sum grant was substantially qualified by a ceiling of 5,000 to 7,500 francs (1,000–1,500 dollars) per job depending on whether it involved an extension of an existing operation or a new establishment. The Préfet of the département where the investment was to occur had to comment on the proposal, but the critical decision was the one made by the appropriate committee of FDES. These benefits were available in approximately the same areas formerly designated as critical zones, with somewhat privileged treatment for the Massif Central, the Midi, and regions likely to experience critical employment problems. Within the critical zones, there were still conversion areas where the grants of 15 to 20 percent remained in force as well as the simplified accelerated procedures. The areas so designated were Nantes-Saint Nazaire, Limoges, and Montpellier, but later Brest and Lorient were added to the list. See Pierre Viot, "Regional Aspects of French Planning," unpublished paper for Regional Planning Conference, sponsored by The National Institute for Physical Planning and Construction Research, Dublin, 1965, pp. 19–22. Note that rates were changed to 8500 to 11,000 francs (1700 to 2200 dollars) in 1962. Also, a somewhat similar program was devised for agricultural regions suffering from serious overpopulation and rural emigration. Lajugie, "Aménagement du Territoire et Développement," p. 329.

55. During the revolutionary outbreaks of May–June 1968, key civil servants concerned with regional planning in France put out a perceptive publication indicating their views on the need for more regional autonomy and decentralization. Their first sentence declared: "Few countries have been able to make such perfect pyramids of their institutions as those fashioned in France in the course of three centuries of centralization" (author's translation). See "2000," Partage des Pouvoirs, Partage des Décisions: Essai sur la Participation, Autonomie et Solidarités, Numéro 9, "Special" (1968).

56. Trintignac, op. cit., pp. 209-211; and M. Crozier, Le Phénomène Bureaucratique (Paris: Éditions du Seuil, 1963), pp. 322-342, 382-386.

57. The government also pressed the Comités d'Expansion to tailor their jurisdictions to the new regional boundaries, and it began to explore ways and means of reducing or eliminating discrepancies between the new regional boundaries and those of the other administrative services of the state and of adapting its statistical services accordingly. See the two perceptive articles by Serge Antoine: "L'Aménagement du Territoire et l'Expansion Régionale: Les Institutions: Analyse-Critique" (February-March 1958); and "L'Aménagement du Territoire et l'Expansion Régionale: Propositions pour une Réforme des Institutions Administratives" (August-September 1958), published in Études et Documents du Centre de Recherches Économiques et Sociales. See also Lajugie, "Aménagement du Territoire et Développement," pp. 314-316.

58. Ministère de la Construction, Bulletin Statistique Mensuel, nos. 7–8 (1965), Table: "Permis de Construire Industriels Plus de 500 M^2 Délivrés de 1949 à 1962," pp. 98–101. The figures record intentions, not actual moves. No study has been made to determine the discrepancy between actual and intended moves.

59. Lajugie, "Aménagement du Territoire et Développement," p. 334.

60. Hackett, op. cit., p. 258.

61. Another 377,000 square meters was simply abandoned and could again serve the same purpose. Trintignac, op. cit., p. 186.

62. Although seventy-eight départements benefitted from one or more decentralization moves, twenty-seven of these départements received twenty or more of these establishments, and most of them were located in the periphery of the Paris region. The regions which benefitted most were Picardie, Haute-Normandie, Centre, and Bour-

gogne; those which barely benefitted were Midi-Pyrénées, Languedoc, Limousin, and Provence. Ministère de la Construction, *Bulletin Statistique*, nos. 7–8 (1965), p. 77 and Table 2, p. 78.

63. Lajugie, "Aménagement du Territoire et Développement," p. 321.

64. Hackett, *op. cit.*, p. 251.

65. *Projet de Loi (1966)* Annexe, vol. 2, tome 1, pp. 37–40.

66. Hansen, *French Regional Planning*, chaps. 3, 9 and p. 71. See also *La Politique d'Incitation* (Paris: Bureau de Recherches et d'Action Économique, 1960); M. MacLennan, "French Planning: Some Lessons for Britain," vol. 24, no. 475 (1963), pp. 365–366; Viot, "Regional Aspects of French Planning," pp. 22–23; and R. Millot, "Rapport pour Avis Présenté au Nom de la Section des Économies Régionales," Avis et Rapports du Conseil Économique et Social, *Journal Officiel*, November 13, 1964, p. 907.

67. In the postwar period, local authorities had prepared urban plans with the financial assistance and guidance of the Ministry of Construction (previously known as the Ministry of Reconstruction and Urbanism). The typical plans had two parts. The first examined the main physical, social, and economic characteristics and trends of the community; the other sketched out recommended land uses and densities, the principal networks for transportation and services, and the areas to be reserved for public open spaces. Although the plans influenced urban development of the city somewhat and provided some assistance to the Ministry of Construction and other government agencies in the location of their investments, their general impact was uncertain and often negligible. They were simply optional guides which could be ignored when it proved convenient. From the point of view of the Commissariat du Plan, however, the plans' principal weaknesses were the absence of any cost estimates, time dimensions, or financial proposals for implementing the programs. Since CGP was particularly anxious about the costs and coordination of the community facilities and the financial arrangements for building new urban zones and for the improvement of older areas, it set up in 1959 a new procedure for estimating the investment requirements. The amounts involved turned out to be huge. With urbanization proceeding at the rate of 2 percent a year, loans for urban equipment approached one billion dollars in 1961, and urban equipment subsidies from the central government amounted to about 30 percent of total capital investments. The prospects were that these costs would increase, given the emphasis of the Fourth Plan on "collective consumption." The anticipated strain on local finance stirred passionate discussion but little action, other than admonitions from central government officials to raise more money locally, and steady increases in the scale of government credits and subsidies. Almost inescapably, local action programs were forced to rely on special ad hoc administrative districts and joint societies to handle development projects requiring autonomous action, special financing, and more qualified management. See *Projet de Loi (1966)*, Annexe, vol. 2, tome 1, p. 40; J. Dreyfus, "Publications Françaises sur l'Urbanisme: Revue Bibliographique," mimeographed, 1968, p. 2; *V* Plan de Développement Économique et Social, 1966-1970, Annexes, tome 2, pp. 383–410. (Henceforth referred to as *V* Plan.) Local communities derived most of their direct income from sales taxes. This was inadequate especially with obligations and costs increasing. Since property taxes were anathema, the local governments found themselves in a financial straitjacket and in a general condition of penury, as well as dependent on the central government for grants, particularly for education, housing, police, water supply, and drainage. The entire system of local government required overhauling. See P. B. M. James, "Regional Economic Planning in France," mimeographed, 1965, pp. 110–14; and

Ecole Nationale d'Administration, *L'Adaptation de l'Organisation Administrative Française aux Problèmes d'Aménagement des Grandes Agglomerations Urbaines* (Seminar directed by P. Viot, Chief of the Urban and Regional Division at the Commisariat Général du Plan), mimeographed (Paris, March 1966), pp. 19–46; and Centre de Recherches et de Documentation sur la Consommation (CREDOC), *Étude Méthodologique sur les Programmes d'Équipements Urbains Réalisés à ce Jour* (Paris, 1961); and V. Bourrel, *Rapport de la Commission d'Étude des Finances Locales à M. le Premier Ministre* (Paris: Imprimerie Nationale, 1965).

68. Hackett, *op. cit.*, pp. 99–102.

69. *Ibid.* See also Lanversin, *op. cit.*, pp. 77–9.

70. "If the number of words spent on discussing regional problems was counted," the Hacketts observed, "it would probably exceed those devoted to all other subjects put together. The enthusiasm of parliamentarians of whatever political leaning for more regional elements in the Plan seemed to have no limits" (Hackett, *op. cit.*, p. 198).

71. M. Astorg, "Sur les Principes et les Structures de la Planification Régionale," (*Exposé Présenté par la Délégation Française* les 5 et 6 Octobre 1965 et Résumé des Discussions auxquelles Ils Ont Donné Lieu au Groupe de Travail de Comité de l'Industrie) [Paris: Organization of Economic Cooperation and Development, 1965], pp. 39–59. (Henceforth cited as *Exposé Présenté par la Délégation Française.*) See also *Organisation des Services de l'État dans les Départements et les Circonscriptions d'Action Régionale et Déconcentration Administrative*, Textes d'Intérêt Général, no. 64–40 (Paris: *Journaux Officiels*, 1964, pp. 6–19; and *Organisation des Services de l'État dans les Circonscriptions d'Action Régionale*, Textes d'Intérêt Général, no. 64–40 (Paris: *Journaux Officiels*, 1964), p. 6.

72. Viot, "Regional Aspects of French Planning," p. 12. See also Alphonse Thelier, "Les Comités d'Expansion Régionaux Sont-ils Condamnés à Disparaître?" *Le Monde*, June 19-20, 1966, pp. 11, 14.

73. The new organizations were furnished with a small operating subsidy and enlarged. They now have fifty members.

74. Astorg, *op. cit.*, pp. 60–61. Unfortunately, the same criticisms leveled at the Comités d'Expansion still seem to be leveled against the new commissions. Many of the older committees are still in existence, and it is uncertain whether they will have a significant role to play in the future.

75. Viot, "Regional Aspects of French Planning." The functions of the Committee on Regional Plans were spelled out more precisely in a decree of July 17, 1965. Members consisted of the Commissaire Général (CGP), the Délégué of DATAR, and key representatives of other ministries. *Journal Officiel*, July 25, 1965, p. 649. See also Hansen, *French Regional Planning*, chap. 4.

76. See fn. 137. See also L. Fauré, "Ou en Est la Mue Administrative et Économique Régionale," *Le Monde*, May 7-8, 1967, pp. 11, 14; Viot, "Regional Aspects of French Planning," pp. 5-9; James, *op. cit.*, pp. 16–26; and "Les Missions Régionales Cherchent un Second Souffle," *Le Monde*, June 25, 1969, p. 17.

77. Conseil Superieur du Ministère de la Construction, *Plan d'Aménagement du Territoire*, (CSC/621) [Paris: Ministère de la Construction, 1962]. This report was prepared by Philippe Lamour, Vice-President of the Council, at the request of Pierre Sudreau, the Minister of Construction from 1958 to 1962. Lamour subsequently became President of CNAT when that organization was created in 1963.

78. Lajugie, "Aménagement du Territoire et Développement," pp. 307–314; and Trintignac, *op. cit.*, pp. 246–268.

79. These were the reasons specifically spelled out in the "Rapport du Premier Ministre au President de la République," requesting Décret No. 63-112 du 15 Février, 1963 creating a Délégation à l'Aménagement du Territoire et a l'Action Régionale, and fixing the responsibilities of the Délégué. *Journal Officiel*, February 15, 1963, p. 544. (Henceforth referred to as "Rapport du Premier Ministre.") See also Décret No. 63-113 du 14 Février, 1963 modifying the powers of the CGP, *Journal Officiel*, February 15, 1963, p. 553. For the decrees dealing with these matters and the changes made in the role of the Conseil Supérieur of the Ministry of Construction, see *Aménagement du Territoire et Action Régionale, Décrets et Arrêtés du 14 Février, 1963* Textes d'Intérêt Général (Paris: *Journal Officiel*, 1963), no. 63–27, pp. 541–589. (Henceforth referred to as *Décrets et Arrêtés du 14 Février, 1963.*)

80. *Décrets et Arrêtés du 14 Février, 1963*. The basic studies for CNAT are prepared by the staff of CGP.

81. It was without doubt effective politically to be able to help out on the building of a bridge here, a road there, or an educational institution somewhere else. The rest of the funds were presumably to be supplied by more specialized or more customary financial channels such as FNAFU. The focus of these investments was especially on the equilibrium metropolises and the lagging regions. Among the activities which received assistance were economic and planning studies, establishment of technical colleges, transport and airline improvements, de-pollution, irrigation, and mosquito control schemes. See *Projet de Loi (1966)*, Annexe, vol. 2, tome 1, pp. 34–35.

82. For further background on some of these changes, see Olivier Guichard, *Aménager la France* (Paris: Laffont-Gonthier, 1965), pp. 177–231; and *Décrets et Arrêtés du 14 Février, 1963*, especially pp. 543–553. For criticisms of the political role of DATAR, see Fourastié and Courthéoux, *op. cit.*, pp. 203–205.

83. The District was a compulsory association of 1,305 communes of the Paris region. The District included the city of Paris which had one-third of the total population (about 2.7 million inhabitants) and one-hundredth of the area. Extending over an area of approximately 5,000 square miles, only one-tenth of which was built up, it was governed by a board (originally 28, now 54, members). Half of the members of the board were councillors elected by the councils of the départements and the mayors of the communes, and half of them were selected by the central government from the members of the local councils. There was also an Economic and Social Advisory Council appointed by the board for a three-year period. Funds were raised by a special tax levied by Parlement on the inhabitants, a tax which could be raised but not lowered. It amounted to roughly 573 million francs (115 million dollars) in 1968. Most of the necessary studies were undertaken by the Institut d'Aménagement et d'Urbanisme de la Région Parisienne (IAURP), which was created in 1960 and is now one of the largest research organizations of its kind in the world today.

84. The Préfet de la Région Parisienne will have three assistants—also prefects. One will deal with law; a second with problems of urban equipment; the third is the chef de cabinet (head of his office). The other prefects for the départements of Paris will also work with him in the same way that département prefects now work elsewhere with the Préfet de la Région. *Le Monde*, July 28, 1966, p. 16.
    For a review of the problems of planning the region by the Délégué Général, see Paul Delouvrier, *L'aménagement de la Région de Paris*, Paris, Conférences des Ambassadeurs, 1966, nouvelle série no. 21, Collection Dirigée par André David, Guy David, et Jean Epstein; and for a brief description of the mechanics of the operation by the Assistant to the Délégué Général, see M. Piquard, "Organization and Planning of the Paris Region," *Public Administration*, vol 43, Winter (1965),

pp. 383–393. For some sharp criticisms of the lack of control of the Préfet de la Région by the Council of the District and of the problems associated with the Délégué being the same person as the Préfet de la Région, see *Le Monde*, January 3, 1968, p. 9, and January 23, 1968, p. 6.

85. *IVe Plan*, pp. 129–139.

86. *Ibid.*, pp. 139–151.

87. *Ibid.*, p. 132.

88. For a brief summary, see Trintignac, *op. cit.*, pp. 139–145. See also *Urbanisme*, vol. 34, no. 86 (1965) [Loisirs-Languedoc-Roussillon], pp. 11–72; and M. Larrue, "La Mise en Valeur Touristique de Littoral Languedoc-Roussillon," in *Exposé Présenté par la Délégation Française*, pp. 73–105.

89. These would involve: a) in the South, connecting the valley of the Garonne and the Lower-Languedoc from Bordeaux to Marseille; b) in the Center, connecting the valley of the Loire and the Berry going around the Morvan by the South or the mountains of Forey by the North; c) in the North, working out the most convenient connection between the Nord to Lorraine and Alsace. In addition, the lower valley of the Seine would be connected either with the transversal axis of the North through the valley of the Loire and beyond or with the transversal axis of the Center by the valley of the Loire or beyond, or possibly both. See also Trintignac, *op. cit.*, pp. 264–269; and Conseil Supérieur du Ministère de la Construction, *Plan d'Aménagement du Territoire*, February (1962), chap. 4.

90. *Ve Plan*, pp. 126–129. See also *L'Axe de Transport par Voie d'Eau entre le Nord-Est de la France et la Méditérranée*, Rapport du groupe de travail au Premier Ministre, Notes et Études Documentaires, La Documentation Française, no. 2874, April 2, 1962, and Trintignac, *op. cit.* The Ministries of Public Works, Industries, Finance, and the CGP opposed the proposals. In favor were the Ministries of Interior, Foreign Affairs, Construction, and Agriculture.

91. The départemental investments—in housing, roads, and elementary schools—were examined only in terms of the lump sum totals for the period of the Plan. Proposed national investments within the region were also noted or commented on, but these matters were beyond their control and were decided at the national level. See *La Régionalisation du Budget de l'État et l'Aménagement du Territoire 1966*, Notes et Études Documentaires, La Documentation Française, no. 3,243, December 7, 1965, p. 6. See also Guichard, *op. cit.*, pp. 222–225. For a critical evaluation of the methodology of these economic background studies, noting especially the weaknesses of the projections and the need to distinguish more clearly between probable and intended outcomes, see M. Béaud, "Technical Problems of Regional Planning in France," *The New Atlantis*, vol. 1, no. 1 (1969), pp. 23–38.

92. In approving the Fourth Plan in 1962, Parlement prescribed that the law dealing with finance should spell out the investments planned for the different regions. This requirement reflected the uneasiness that had been produced by the previous allocations. At the 1962 session, representatives from the poorer regions expressed the fear that projected budget cutbacks would hurt their regions. To ensure an adequate volume of investment they sought a "Programme Law." (This was a device to allow investment planning for several years. Program laws stipulated the total authorized expenditure for a program; and program credits authorized funds for each year varying with the requirements which were sanctioned by the Program Law.) The aim in this case was to authorize for a number of years a certain level of expenditures for the different programs in their regions. After much political pressure, the proposals were provisionally accepted by the Minister of Finance, though opposed

by his technical staff. At the last moment, however, the President of the Republic rejected the arrangement as an unwise precedent which favored some lagging regions at the expense of others and which imposed inflexible and perhaps undesirable burdens on future budgets.

93. Some items, such as primary schools, represent needs roughly proportionate to population. Others, such as universities, roads, or scientific research, are "selective" and favor some regions directly, others indirectly. So do certain policies, such as placing more emphasis on complementary than on propulsive measures, or vice versa. Despite the great interest in the subject, it is not yet feasible to draw valid inferences on past or current allocations because the data are difficult to compile.

94. For a general summary of the trends revealed by these reports, see Ve *Plan*, Annexes, tome 2, pp. 433–471. For an analysis of the social and administrative problems associated with the introduction of the regional portions of the budget, see the articles by C. Roig, "L'Administration Locale et les Changements Sociaux," pp. 11–34; J. L. Quermonne, "Planification Régionale et Réforme Administrative," pp. 87–125; C. Palazzoli, "Partis Politiques et Régions Autonomes," pp. 130–141; and B. Pouyet and P. De Montbrison-Fouchère, "La Régionalisation dans le IVe Plan: l'Experience des Tranches Opératoires," pp. 147–228. These articles were published by the Institut d'Études Politiques de l'Université de Grenoble in *Administration Traditionelle et Planification Régionale* (Paris: Librairie Armand Colin, 1964). See also Hackett, *op. cit.*, pp. 94–96; Astorg, *op. cit.* pp. 39–57; and Boudeville, *op. cit.*, chaps. 3, 6, 7. For an example of such a report, see *Rapport sur les Principales Orientations du Ve Plan en Haute Normandie* présenté par P. Chaussade, Préfet de Région, April 1965. Michel Béaud argues that projections and goals are not distinguished as sharply as they might be, nor are they related to the probable effects and needs. See Béaud, "Technical Problems of Regional Planning in France," *The New Atlantis*, vol. 1, no. 1 (1969), pp. 23–38.

95. *Projet de Loi (1966)*, Annexe, vol. 2, tome 1, p. 53. In 1966 CGP and DATAR published the regional budgets together with the reports on the execution of the Fifth Plan for the years 1964 and 1965. The budget for the year 1966 provides the transition between the Fourth and Fifth Plans, and the regional budget shows the disposition of the investments by region.

96. The report by INSEE, *L'Espace Économique Français,* is an example of a general study commissioned for this purpose. Examples of more specialized studies by CREDOC are Aménagement du Centre des Villes (Paris: June 1965); Note Technique sur des Études d'Armature Urbaine Régionale (Paris: January 1965); and Synthèse des Études d'Armature Urbaine Régionale (Paris: March 1966).

97. See Ve *Plan*, tome 1, p. 124; and Pierre Viot, "L'Aménagement du Territoire," in *Exposé Présenté par la Délégation Française*, pp. 7–15. For an example of the analyses of alternatives, see Commissariat Général du Plan d'Équipement et de la Productivité et Commission Nationale de l'Aménagement du Territoire, *Essai de Régionalisation de l'Économie Française, en 1985 en Trois Grandes Zones Géographiques* (Paris, 1964). The perspective studies went beyond the usual projections of population, national product and income, consumption, etc. They tried also to estimate the effect of leisure, urban trends, change of taste, health, etc. See, for example, *Réflexions pour 1985* (Paris: La Documentation Française, 1964).

98. The older PADOG plan was deemed obsolete because it was intended to serve a projected population of 9.4 million by 1970. However, it should be noted that the Schéma Directeur's population projection of 11.6 million in 1985 is not consistent with that of 14 million in the year 2000. It was put forward, I have been told, to

reduce the fears of many people. Actually 12 million people are projected for 1985. For further details, see Viot, "L'Aménagement du Territoire," pp. 13–14. The Comité Consultatif Économique et Social de la Région de Paris observed that "In effect, only to the extent that the 35 cities of over 20,000 inhabitants of the Paris Basin, which comprised two million three hundred thousand inhabitants in 1962, will surpass five million inhabitants around the year 2000, will they contribute to the limiting of the population of the Paris region to fourteen million inhabitants, i.e., to a population larger by only two-thirds of what it is today, while the urban population of France as a whole will have doubled. The schéma directeur must in no way incite an accelerated development of the Paris region. It is only a development framework adapted to an eventuality whose realisation does not depend on the will of Parisians but on choices which will be made for the provinces" *(Le Monde,* July 21, 1966, p. 8 [author's translation]).

99. Délégation Générale au District de la Région de Paris, *Schéma Directeur d'Aménagement d'Urbanisme de la Région de Paris* (Paris: Premier Ministre, 1965). The Schéma Directeur is vague on the actual number and location of new towns. This was partly to avoid problems of land speculation and objections from other cities and regions. Eight are often referred to, but at present preliminary efforts have started in Évry (in Essonne) with a projected population of 300,000; and in Pontoise-Cergy (in Val d'Oise) with a projected population of 340,000. Both were initiated in July 1966. Trappes (in Yvelines) is the third. It was initiated in December 1967 and has a projected population of 470,000 inhabitants. The preliminary studies for a fourth town, Vallée de la Marne-Noisy-le-Grand (in Seine-St. Denis and Seine-et-Marne), and for a fifth in Tigery-Lieusaint (in Seine-et-Marne), are well advanced and the setting up of a study mission is expected in 1969. However, there is a difference of opinion as to whether it is wise or feasible to proceed with the development of all of the towns. (See fn. 140.) In any case, provisions have been made in 1969 to reduce land taxes and ease industrial relocation procedures for fourteen industrial sites in Pontoise-Cergy, Évry, Tigery, and Noisy-le-Grand. See "Le Gouvernement Prend les Mesures pour Harmoniser la Croissance Industrielle de la Région Parisienne" *(Le Monde,* January 23, 1969, p. 8).

100. *Le Monde,* July 5, 1967, p. 6; and Piquard, *op. cit.,* p. 392. See also P. Merlin, *Les Transports Parisiens* (Paris: Masson, 1966).

101. *Projet de Loi (1966),* Annexe, vol. 2, tome 1, p. 53.

102. These general aims were to modernize agriculture, industrialize public services and urban centers, improve the national network of communications and transportation, cope with the problems of water pollution and water shortage, and generally promote regional and resource development. The sectoral priorities were expressed equally vaguely—mainly as government commitments to spend increased funds in a number of sectors. However, the government, in response to a Parliamentary request, did agree to develop indicators for the general criteria of income and standard of living which could help to measure future variations in disparities between regions. Viot, "Regional Aspects of French Planning," p. 19. For an example of these efforts, see *Statistiques et Indicateurs des Régions Françaises.*

103. See fn. 77.

104. J. Hautreux and M. Rochefort, *La Fonction Régionale dans l'Armature Urbaine Française,* Commission Nationale de l'Aménagement du Territoire (Groupe V), Commissariat Général du Plan et Direction de l'Aménagement Foncier et de l'Urbanisme (Paris: Ministère de la Construction, 1964). See also J. Hautreux, J. Lecourt, and M. Rochefort, *Le Niveau Supérieur de l'Armature Urbaine Française,* mimeo-

graphed (Paris: Commissariat Général du Plan d'Équipement et de la Productivité et Ministère de la Construction, 1963). For an earlier expression of some aspects of this idea, see P. Bauchet, "La Compatibilité Économique Régionale et Son Usage," *Économie Appliquée,* vol. 14, no. 1 (1961), pp. 71–74.

105. The answers to this question will vary for different people because of the critical values and imponderables involved. For a brief review of some of these difficulties, see L. Rodwin, *The British New Towns Policy* (Cambridge: Harvard University Press, 1956), pp. 32–35.

106. For the articulation of P. George's views, see Hautreux and Rochefort, *op. cit.,* p. 2, and for more details on the indices, see Annexes 1–8.

107. In the North and the East, the larger number of cities limited the zone of influence or dominance of any single metropolis, though one or two cities at the frontier appeared destined to play a far more significant role with the emergence of the Common Market. Beyond the zone of influence of the regional metropolises, there was also a vast area where the facilities, the services, and the zone of influence of the communities within this area were stunted due, it was believed, to the dominance exerted by Paris. These included cities like Caen in Normandy, Rennes in Bretagne, Limoges and Clermont-Ferrand in Auvergne, and Dijon in Bourgogne. Finally, within the Paris region, there were also a ring of satellite cities (Amiens, Tours, Bourges, and Orléans) which appeared destined to serve as limited sub-regional centers for the decentralization of activities from the capital city. For a description of a subsequent plan for follow-up research on Hautreux and Rochefort's ideas, see Commissariat Général du Plan d'Équipement et de la Productivité, *Note Technique sur les Études d'Armature Urbaine Régionale* (Paris: CREDOC, 1965).

108. The Groupe Intérministeriel d'Aménagement du Bassin Parisien (GIABP) was set up in July 1966 to deal with the problems in the basin within 200 kilometers of Paris. Its responsibility was to help build new towns, orient relationships with neighboring regions and cities, organize university development in Orléans, Rouen, and Reims, encourage decentralization policy for tertiary activities in the area, and develop land reserves for urban development. In June 1966 the government decided to prepare a development plan for the basin. In a preliminary report, *Réflexions pour un Livre Blanc,* GIABP recommended that growth and diversification be encouraged in eight cities: Caen, Rouen, Le Havre, Amiens, Reims, Troyes, Orléans, Tours, and Le Mans. See *L'Aménagement du Territoire en France,* Notes et Études Documentaires, La Documentation Française, no. 3461, February 9, 1968, p. 30; and "Le Bassin Parisien en 1985," *Le Monde,* February 12, 1969, p. 15. The Paris Basin includes, in addition to the District of Paris, the following départements: Oise, Somme, Aisne, Marne, Aube, Yonne, Loiret, Loir et Cher, Indre et Loire, Eure et Loir, Sarthe, Eure, Orne, Calvados, and Seine-Maritime.

109. For a presentation of the main elements of the official policy, see *Ve Plan,* tome 1, pp. 131–4; and Commission Nationale de l'Aménagement du Territoire, *Premier Rapport,* Commissaire Général du Plan d'Équipement et de la Productivité, September 1964, pp. 81–91. For a stimulating group of articles analyzing different aspects of these ideas, see *Urbanisme (Métropoles d'Équilibre),* vol. 34, no. 89 (1965), pp. 6–34.

110. *L'Aménagement du Territoire en France,* Notes et Études Documentaires, La Documentation Française, no. 3461, February 9, 1968, pp. 28–34.

111. These metropolitan areas were selected on the grounds that they suffered the most severely from this problem and that, if the policy proved satisfactory in these cities,

the example could be followed elsewhere. See "Adoptation de Projets Instituant Quatre Communautés Urbaines à Lille, Lyon, Bordeaux et Strasbourg." *Le Monde,* June 10, 1966, p. 24. For a description of some of the current problems of metropolitan areas, see École Nationale d'Administration, *op. cit.,* pp. 19–46; and *Projet de Loi (1966),* vol. 2, tome 1, pp. 31–37.

112. Decisions of the new communities require a two-thirds vote of the new councils. The latter are elected by the communes, the number of seats being roughly proportional to population with some adjustments to assure representation for the smallest communes. The new communities have responsibility for a wide range of functions including urban planning, land reserves, development of industrial zones, housing, transport, teaching at the secondary level, water, gas, electricity, sanitation, and cemeteries. Other functions (roads, cultural facilities, sports) can be taken over at the request of the communities or at the initiative of the tutelage power of the state. *Le Monde,* June 12–13, 1967, p. 6; June 15, 1967, p. 8; and December 5, 1967, p. 9.

Le Conseil Général de la Seine declared that "the project in question is proof of a deliberate desire of the administration to suppress progressively local freedom and autonomy, a desire against which the départemental assemblies strongly raise their voice." (*Le Monde,* July 8, 1966, p. 10 [author's translation]); and the mayors of the département of Lyon protested "this anti-constitutional enterprise aimed at the suppression of the prerogatives of the mayors and the disappearance of the communes" (*Le Monde,* June 30, 1966, p. 7 [author's translation]); see also *Le Monde,* December 13, 1966, p. 19.

113. On June 8, 1969, this requirement was extended to cities of 10,000 or more. *Le Monde,* June 10, 1969, p. 25. For summaries of the debates in the Assembly and Senate see daily issues of *Le Monde,* October 6, 1966; April 20, 1967; June 21 until July 2–3, 1967; November 8, 12 and 13, 1967; December 2, 1967; and January 4, 1968. See also, A. Levy-Soussan and B. Pelpel, "La Loi D'Orientation Foncière— L'Histoire de Son Élaboration et Ses Thèmes," (STCAU), Direction de l'Aménagement Foncier et Urbain, Ministère de l'Équipement, January 1969.

114. To increase local revenues, the system of taxation was modified to provide extra local revenues by giving local communities a portion of the tax on salaries in lieu of other local (consumption) taxes. It was anticipated that "when the new system [went] into effect, local governments [would] receive 400 million francs ($80 million) more in revenues than would have been obtained under the present system" (Hansen, *French Regional Planning,* chap. 11). See also *Le Monde,* November 8, 1967, p. 6. However, the new tax which was supposed to come into effect in 1968 was suppressed in November of that same year. See A. Verholes, "La Fiscalité Locale n'Evolue Pas dans le Sens d'une Plus Grande Autonomie des Communes et des Départements," *Le Monde,* April 15, 1969, pp. I and III.

115. In a 1963 survey, two-thirds of the respondents from other areas of France favored curbing the growth of Paris. A still higher proportion of the respondents who lived in Paris also favored restriction. *Sondages,* no. 4 (1963), p. 26. See also Alain Girard and Henri Bastide, "Les Problèmes Démographiques devant l'Opinion," *Population,* vol. 15, no. 2 (1960), pp. 246–288. For criticisms of the restrictions on the growth of Paris, see M. Drancourt, "Plaidoyer pour Paris," *Réalités,* no. 222 (1964), p. 76; District de la Région de Paris, *Paris en Question* (Paris: Presses Universitaires de France, 1965), p. 29; and R. Nungesser, "L'Aménagement du Territoire Ne Peut Se Faire contre Paris," extract du *Journal Officiel,* no. 132, November 28, 1963, p. 16.

116. One survey of opinion showed that the idea of having seven or eight cities of a million or more in about forty years was considered unreasonable by 40 percent of the respondents and folly by another 17 percent. Some 61 percent felt it should be avoided at any price. The same proportion disagreed also with the proposition that there were not enough cities containing over 500,000 inhabitants. See "L'Aménagement du Territoire et l'Action Régionale," *Sondage* (Revue Française de l'Opinion Publique), vol. 27, no. 1 (1965), pp. 64–66.

However, three out of four persons expressed the view, in a subsequent survey, that most of the big cities would be filled with skyscrapers by the year 2000. Cf. *"2000,"* Revue de l'Aménagement du Territoire et du Développement Régional, vol. 1, no. 6 (1967), p. 17.

117. This was later transformed into a chair of urban studies; and in 1967 a chair in urban sociology was set up at the new Faculty of Letters and Human Sciences of the University of Paris at Nanterre. However, the Institute of Urbanism was replaced by a new institute in March 1969 following a long strike of students protesting against the obsolete program. New urban programs were also started at this time in other universities. See "L'Urbanisme Entre à l'Université Mais Cherche Encore Sa Voie," *Le Monde,* November 11, 1969, p. 14.

118. École Nationale d'Administration, *op. cit.*, p. 10.

119. *Ibid.*, p. 7. See also Commission Nationale de l'Aménagement du Territoire, "Les Obstacles à la Politique d'Aménagement du Territoire," pp. 4–9. For more information about the Schéma Directeur of the region of Paris see Piquard, *op. cit.*, p. 387; and "Rapport d'Avis de la Société Française des Urbanistes sur le Schéma Directeur d'Aménagement et d'Urbanisme de la Région de Paris," *Revue de la Société Française des Urbanistes*, 2 trimestre, 1966, pp. 4–16. The Schéma Directeur of the region of Paris was eventually approved by the government and by the President of the Republic. On the other hand, the Schéma Directeur of the city of Paris prepared in 1965 by l'Atelier Parisien d'Urbanisme (created in 1967 under the authority of the Préfet de Paris) was even more savagely criticized and has not yet received the approval of the government. See *Le Monde,* September 15, 1965, p. 16; September 19–20, 1965, p. 8; January 14, 1966, p. 18; July 5, 1967, pp. 1, 6; July 26, 1968, p. 10; and April 9, 1969, p. 8.

120. Since the development of the planning system in France, a number of new organizations collect essential data and carry out certain basic studies. Some were created explicitly to help the national economic planning efforts. Two already mentioned are INSEE (established shortly after the liberation of France) and CREDOC. Others are organizations, or parts of organizations, created since 1958 because of either the general extension of the Plan's activities or their extension to urban and regional problems. These include the regional or urban divisions of CREDOC, INSEE, and SEDES (Société d'Étude et de Développement Économique et Social), and also SEMA (Société d'Économie et de Mathématiques Appliquées) and CERAU (Centre d'Études et de Recherches d'Aménagement Urbains) which combined the urban parts of CREDOC and SEDES. Still other agencies handle local studies. The most important are IAURP, which handles the studies for the Paris region, and OREAM (Organismes Régionaux d'Études d'Aires Métropolitaines), created in 1965 by DATAR and the Ministry of Equipment to make the planning studies of major metropolitan areas, including Marseille, Nord, Metz-Nancy, Nantes-Saint Nazaire, Basse Seine, and Lyon–St. Étienne-Grenoble. In addition there are ODEAM (Organisme Départemental d'Étude des Alpes Maritimes), OREAV (Organisme d'Étude et d'Aménagement

des Vallées), and STCAU (Service Technique Central d'Aménagement et d'Urbanisme). STCAU was created in 1966 within the framework of the Ministry of Equipment to make studies for the city of Paris. There are also scholarly organizations, such as CRU (Centre de la Recherche d'Urbanisme), ISU (Institut de Sociologie Urbaine), ISEA (Institut de Science Économique Appliqué) [Économie Régionale], and GES (Groupe d'Ethnologie Sociale), which promote more independent research efforts.

Although these organizations produced a considerable amount of basic data and many illuminating studies, the intelligence services for decision making are still generally acknowledged to be inadequate. Much of the research conducted has been superficial in quality and in scope. Many cities and regions have not been covered at all. True, some twenty or more university-based regional research institutes which have mushroomed since the war have conducted studies of their regions, mainly of regional structure and trends. But most of these institutions, including two of the most highly regarded (Bordeaux and Montpellier), are run on the proverbial shoestring. For further details, see *Documents Relatifs à l'Organisation des Études d'Aménagement des Aires Métropolitaines*, Paris, Premier Ministre, Délégation à l'Aménagement du Territoire et l'Action Régionale, October 1966. See also "Études Réalisées par la Direction des Études et Recherches à l'IAURP," mimeographed (Paris, 1968). Many of these studies are published in the Cahiers de l'IAURP (Paris: L'Institut d'Aménagement et d'Urbanisme de la Région Parisienne), vols. 1–15. For some criticisms of the intelligence services for decision making, see École d'Administration, *op. cit.*, pp. 11–12. See also J. Dreyfus, "Recherche et Aménagement Urbains," *Consommation*, no. 1 (1966), pp. 6–114; R. Millot, "Rapport pour Avis Présenté au Nom de la Section des Économies Régionales," in *Avis et Rapports du Conseil Économique et Social*, pp. 690–697. For more information on university based regional studies, see Institut d'Économie Régionale du Sud-Ouest, "L'Organisation et les Tendances des Études d'Économie Régionale en France," typewritten manuscript (Bordeaux, 1966), pp. 1–26. For a review of the problems of obtaining good data for regional economic accounting, see J. Ousset, "Les Travaux Français de Comptabilité Économique Régionale," in *Aménagement du Territoire et Développement Régional*, pp. 61–104. For a discussion of the plans to improve the system of regional information, see J. P. Trystram, "Système d'Accumulation des Données et Information Régionale," in *Aménagement du Territoire et Développement Régional*, pp. 161–178.

121. A study of 1,277 establishments was recently made by M. Vieugue of l'Inspection Générale de l'Économie Nationale. It dealt with the fulfillment of obligations contracted under FDES loans and grants made available to firms for the period 1956–1963. The study showed that: 1) only 7 percent of the firms receiving assistance failed and about 60 percent of the firms receiving assistance had increased their total activity; 2) 56 percent of the grants went to firms that fulfilled their obligations whereas the failure to do so led to the partial annulment of 30 percent of the grants and the total annulment of 14 percent of the grants; 3) the larger firms were the ones most capable of responding to the forms of assistance rendered. *Le Monde*, August 9, 1969, p. 9.

122. The choice of other equilibrium metropolises was also questioned. For example, Nice considered itself at "war" with Marseille, and Rennes with Nantes–St. Nazaire. See *Le Monde*, April 2, 1969, pp. 24–27; and Gravier, *L'Aménagement du Territoire*, pp. 321–322.

123. "Les Grands Travaux pour les Métropoles Lorraine et Marseillaise Commenceront en 1971," *Le Monde*, January 5–6, 1969, pp. 1, 13. For a description of some of the physical problems of development, see "Contribution à l'Établissement d'un

Programme pour la Métropole Lorraine," *Urbanisme,* vol. 34, no. 89, pp. 50–59. See also Serge Antoine and Gérard Weill, "Les Métropoles et Leur Région," *ibid.,* pp. 11–19.

124. As late as September 1966, three years following the establishment of DATAR, only four *métropoles d'équilibre* (Marseille, Lyon, Nantes–St. Nazaire, and Metz-Nancy) had technical staffs to make plans and studies for their regions, and these staffs were minimal in number and had only recently been recruited. Partly for this reason, there were constant criticisms of the Schéma Directeur for the Paris region by spokesmen for other regions. See, for example, the critical comments of the advisory council to the national plan complaining about the effects of the publicity received by these plans on development elsewhere. *Avis et Rapports du Conseil Économique et Social,* Projet de Rapport Général sur le Ve Plan, Session de 1965, *Journal Officiel,* October 14, 1965, pp. 651, 665–666; 690–696; also Gravier, *L'Aménagement du Territoire,* p. 57; and Hansen, *French Regional Planning,* chap. 10.

125. The suspicion is hardly surprising: trickling down is hardly ever attractive, especially to those who are at the bottom of the queue. See 'Gravier, *L'Aménagement du Territoire,* p. 51; and Hansen, *French Regional Planning,* chap. 10.

126. Moreover, the needs seemed to be expanding at a rate higher than that of the supply. *Ve Plan,* tome 2, pp. 347–84.

127. Since the decentralization of government agencies was proceeding far too slowly, the government decided at the end of 1959 to clear all proposals for the expansion of facilities with the committee for the study of decentralization facilities. The measure to shift the schools was intended to dramatize and provide firm evidence of the government's new policies. The schools involved included schools of engineering (Lyon, Grenoble, St. Étienne); aeronautics, aeronautical construction, and civil aviation (Toulouse); public health (Rennes); maritime studies (Brest); telecommunications and electronics (Nantes); higher judicial studies (Bordeaux); taxation (Clermont); treasury (Dijon); Institute of Applied Scientific Studies (Lyon, Lille, Toulouse); new faculties of science (Nantes, Nice, Reims); new schools of arts and crafts (Bordeaux, Clermont-Ferrand, Le Havre). See Lajugie, "Aménagement du Territoire et Développement," pp. 324–5. (One of the readers of this manuscript, J. Dreyfus, has remarked that INSA "constitutes an original kind of creation; their localization does not result from a decentralization" [author's translation].)

128. The issue was especially important in the West where investment in social overhead capital and, in particular, in the strengthening of educational facilities, ranked among the most important ways of building up the human capital of the region. Hansen, *French Regional Planning,* chap. 7. See also Hansen's articles: "The Structure and Determinants of Local Public Investment Expenditures," *The Review of Economics and Statistics,* vol. 57, no. 2 (1965), pp. 150–162; and "Regional Planning in a Mixed Economy," *The Southern Economic Journal,* vol. 32, no. 2 (1965), p. 187.

129. For Zone 1, there are fixed and automatic rates, currently 25 percent for investment in "privileged agglomerations" in the West of France; 15 percent in the extreme West (Bretagne and neighboring départements), and 12 percent in other regions of the West and Southwest. These grants are available for investments of at least 300,000 francs (60,000 dollars) and the creation of at least thirty jobs. This was changed to twenty jobs in 1965. There are smaller grants for extensions. These must enlarge the activity by 30 percent or by an increase of one hundred persons. There are also special adaptation grants to favor industrial diversification. These

are for areas of declining industries and high unemployment (principally mining, textile, and rural renovation areas [Zone 2]). They apply only to investments of 300,000 francs (60,000 dollars) involving at least twenty jobs, although in special cases these conditions can be waived. The grants vary from 0 to 25 percent depending on the circumstances, but there are ceilings of 11,000 francs (2,200 dollars) and 6,000 francs (1,100 dollars) per job created. The higher rates apply to new activities; the lower rates to extensions and partial conversions. Special fiscal exemptions (rapid amortization, reduction of property transfer taxes) which are automatically provided for the two zones above are also available for certain areas (Nord and Lorraine) suffering from economic dislocations which warrant some public assistance but no subsidies (Zone 3). There are also standard subsidies designed to cover the costs of transfer for firms decentralizing from the Paris region. To facilitate administration, grants for investment of less than 1 million francs (200,000 dollars) can be approved directly by the prefect of the region. Also, investments of more than 40 million francs (8 million dollars) creating at least 800 jobs can receive the maximum subsidies if they are located near the zones of adaptation and help to provide jobs for persons employed in these zones. See *Projet de Loi de Finances pour 1969, Annexe, Régionalisation du Budget d'Équipement pour 1969 et Aménagement du Territoire* (Paris: Imprimerie Nationale, 1968), tome 1, pp. 22–23. (Henceforth referred to as *Projet de Loi pour 1969*, tome 1.) See also *Industrialisation et Aménagement du Territoire*, La Documentation Française, pp. 20–24.

130. Viot estimated that less than a third of the decentralization operations from Paris in 1960 and 1961 took advantage of these grants. See Viot, "Regional Aspects of French Planning," p. 20. See also IAURP, *La Décentralisation Industrielle et le Bassin Parisien*, pp. 62–65. Most of the firms were of average size and the moves were mainly to the South and West. It was primarily the very large firms which moved to the provinces and they tended to move to the large metropolitan areas. See *Industrialisation et Aménagement du Territoire*, La Documentation Française, Tables I and II, pp. 24–25; and Table VII, p. 27. See also Ministère de la Construction, *Bulletin Statistique* (1963), pp. 80–101. The difficulties were further compounded by the pressures for industrial consolidation and by the prospects for relocation in the new cities publicized by the Schéma Directeur for the Paris region. Moreover, the data, as indicated earlier, do not take account of the expansion of smaller and average-sized firms in Paris and the fact that most of the decentralization operations are taking place in the peripheral ring of small cities between 80 and 200 km. from Paris; nor do the data make clear that most of this decentralization or expansion would be likely without economic assistance because of the pressures of high rents, congestion, and the controls on new construction. Cf. also *Projet de Loi (1966)*, Annexe, vol. 2, tome 1, p. 29; James, *op. cit.*, pp. 5–6; and Délégation à l'Aménagement du Territoire et à l'Action Régionale, *Aides au Développement Régional* (Paris, 1965).

131. *Projet de Loi (1969)*, tome 1, pp. 23–24; Table 1, p. 77; *Le Monde,* June 12–13, 1966, p. 10; and *Industrialisation et Aménagement du Territoire*, La Documentation Française, p. 32. See also Fourastié et Courthéoux, *op. cit.*, pp. 226–231; J. Monod and Gerard Weill, "Paris et la France," *La Table Ronde*, no. 245 (1968), p. 37; and *Le Monde,* June 15, 1966, p. 19. The most recent data on the number of decentralized operations was reported by J. Monod in a report to an interministerial committee concerned with the industrial growth of the Paris region. See "Le Gouvernement Prend des Mesures pour Harmoniser la Croissance Industrielle de la Région Parisienne," *Le Monde,* January 23, 1969, p. 8.

132. DATAR argued that it was important to see that the assistance provided by France was reasonably in line with the assistance provided by other European

countries because of the need to harmonize policies of the Common Market countries and because of the competition to attract U. S. firms to the lagging regions. See F. Grosrichard, "Le Montant des Aides Régionales à l'Industrie est Plus Faible en France qu' à l'Étranger," *Le Monde*, August 8, 1969, p. 3; and "Aménagement du Territoire," *Le Monde*, August 28, 1969, p. 16.

133. See *Projet de Loi (1969)*, tome 1, pp. 27–28. A study of permits to build office space in the period from February 1962 to July 1966 showed that permits for new office space in the Paris region exceeded office space abandoned (but generally re-utilized by others) by a factor of more than 6 to 1. That factor was a composite of about 10 to 1 for public office space and more than 4 to 1 for private office space. There was likewise an increase by factors ranging from 2-6 to 1 for different categories of service activities in Paris (with the exception of private commercial and administrative office space where there was a slight increase of abandoned office space); and there was an even higher proportion of permits to build in the suburbs compared with space abandoned in the suburbs. The reason for this discrepancy was the difference in attitude of the private and public committees responsible for decisions on requests for space. About twice as much floor space was refused by the public committee as by the private committee. (The reverse was true, however, for industrial space.) It was partly for this reason that the two committees were dissolved in 1967 and a single committee set up to deal with both the public and private sectors. See *Documents Relatifs à la Décentralisation des Activités Tertiaires*, Premier Ministre, Délégation à l'Aménagement du Territoire et à l'Action Régionale, La Documentation Française, 1968, Tables on pp. 27–37 and text of decrees, especially pp. 57–58; and *Le Monde*, January 23, 1969, p. 8.

134. Monod and Weill, *op. cit.*, p. 38. See also "35% des Emplois Tertiaires Sont Créés dans la Région Parisienne," *Le Monde*, August 2, 1968, p. 13; and November 26–27, 1968, p. 8. Note, however, that Paris had 26 percent of the *urban* population in 1968 compared with 29 percent in 1962. *Le Monde*, January 26–27, 1969, p. 19.

135. The grants cannot exceed 13,000 francs (2,600 dollars) per job unless the investment exceeds 10 million francs (2 million dollars) or the subsidy is less than 10 percent; and the amount of the real estate investment including land purchase cannot exceed 40,000 francs per job created. See "Seize Villes Bénéficieront des Primes de Décentralisation des Activités Tertiaires," *Le Monde*, July 31, 1968, p. 14. See also *Documents Relatifs à la Décentralisation des Activités Tertiaires*, pp. 57–60. In January 1969 the controls were applied to all new or expanded building of more than 1,000 square meters. *Le Monde*, January 23, 1969, p. 8.

136. *Le Monde*, September 1–2, 1968, p. 15. In October 1968, P. Delouvrier, Préfet de Région, claimed that the first studies indicated that migration had declined due to the recession and other problems and would probably resume again. *Le Monde*, October 20–21, 1968, p. 7. See also *Projet De Loi (1969)*, tome 1, p. 13.

137. Three pioneering studies of these regional organisms have recently been completed by some able sociologists under the direction of Michel Crozier. They are part of a larger research effort concerned with the behavior of organizations. The focus of these three studies is on the transformation of the political and administrative system for territorial planning. See P. Gremion, *La Mise en Place des Institutions Régionales* (Paris: Centre de Recherche de Sociologie des Organisations, 1965), pp. 7–151; P. Gremion and J. P. Worms, *Les Institutions et la Société Locale*, Groupe de Sociologie des Organisations (Paris: Centre National de la Recherche Scientifique, 1968), pp. 21–198; and 245–255; J.-Claude Thoenig and F. Danserau, *La Société Locale Face à une Institution Nouvelle d'Aménagement du Territoire; Le Cas de la*

Métropole d'Équilibre Lorraine, Groupe de Sociologie des Organisations (Paris: Centre National de la Recherche Scientifique, 1968), pp. 1–8; and 57–79. See also P. Gremions et J.-P. Worms, "La Concertation Régionale-Innovation ou Tradition" in *Aménagement du Territoire et Développement Régional* (Grenoble: Institut d'Études Politiques, 1968), pp. 35–60; and B. Gournay, "Les Dirigeants des Municipalités Urbaines," in *Aménagement du Territoire et Développement Régional,* pp. 155–160. The government is aware of the criticisms of CODER and has promised to consult the organizations more effectively before and after adoption of the Plan. Note also that at the 15th Congress of Le Conseil National des Économies Régionales, M. Georges Pompidou announced that the progress of the regional policy "will be completed progressively by the separation of the regional prefect from the prefect of the département's capital city" *(Le Monde,* June 21, 1966. p. 22 [author's translation]). M. Pompidou was then Premier Ministre of France.

138. In the past, the government was reluctant to set up elected assemblies on the ground that many able people would not participate in these regional efforts on this basis. *Le Monde,* April 28–29, 1968, p. 7; February 3, 1967, pp. 1, 6; and February 4, 1967, p. 8. For an interesting document reflecting the views expressed during the "revolutionary" period, see "2000," *Partage des Pouvoirs, Partage des Decisions: Essai sur la Participation, Autonomie et Solidarités.* See also "De Nombreuses Mesures Illustrent la Volonté de Déconcentration du Gouvernement," *Le Monde,* December 1–2, 1968, p. 8; E. Pisani, "La Région . . . pour quoi Faire?" (Bonnes Feuilles), *Le Monde,* March 26, 1969, p. 10; and E. Pisani, "Réforme Régionale et Réforme Communale," *Le Monde,* April 25, 1969, pp. 1, 16; M. Duverger, "La Réforme Régionale et l'Article 72," *Le Monde,* March 2–3, 1969, pp. 1, 7; "L'Avant-projet de la Loi qui Sera Soumise au Referendum du 27 Avril, 1969," *Le Monde,* February 26, 1969, pp. 2–5; also *Le Monde,* December 13, 1968, pp. 2–3; March 25, 1969, p. 8; March 26, 1969, pp. 1–7; April 9, 1969, pp. 6–7; April 11, 1969, p. 6; April 12, 1969, pp. 1–6; April 13–14, 1969, p. 7; and April 23, 1969, p. 13.

139. More than ten of the present regions have less than 1.5 million inhabitants. See Gravier, *L'Aménagement du Territoire et l'Avenir des Régions Françaises,* pp. 162–3. See also *Le Monde,* November 17, 1965; Hansen, *French Regional Planning,* chap. 4; J. L. Quermonne, "La Régionalisation et l'Aménagement du Territoire en France," *Aménagement du Territoire et Développement Régional,* pp. 1–34;. and M. Béaud, "Une Analyse des Disparités Régionales de Croissance," *Revue Économique,* vol. 17, no. 1 (1966), pp. 55–91.

140. See "Le Gouvernement Prend des Mesures pour Harmoniser la Croissance Industrielle de la Région Parisienne," *Le Monde,* January 23, 1969, p. 8. The provincial authorities are aware of the stakes and there are increasingly tart reminders of the earlier pronouncements and presumed commitments. It is partly for this reason that—although the central authorities are personally convinced that Paris must grow and the new towns must proceed, and have taken steps to ensure the preparation of plans and the acquisition of sites for centers for several of the new towns—no adequate financing arrangements have yet been worked out, and no adequate administrative machinery has yet been established to promote these enterprises. Also, the CCESRP and the GIABP have publicly disagreed with the Préfet de Region of Paris on the number of new towns that could reasonably be built and equipped with rail and road transportation as well as other services during the period of the Sixth Plan (1971–1975). The Council feels that only three new towns (Évry, Pontoise-Cergy, and Trappes) could be reasonably developed. They have also noted that only 40 percent of the equipment deemed essential for the 1966–1970 period has actually been provided. See *IVᵉ Plan (1962-5),* p. 132;

Ve *Plan*, pp. 124–134; and *Schéma Directeur d'Aménagement et d'Urbanisme de la Région de Paris*, pp. 67–68. The Comité Interministériel (according to *Le Monde*, July 24–25, 1966, pp. 1, 12) decided that the nine cities of the Paris Basin would be favored to decentralize industry from Paris and to temper the migration to Paris. The implications for the proposed new towns are ominous if this should prove to be a firm decision. As Alain Vernholes observes, "But would the Schéma Directeur have been what it is if a view of the comprehensive development of the Paris Basin had existed at the time of its elaboration?"(*Le Monde*, July 24–25, 1966, p. 1 [author's translation]). See also "La Préparation du VIe Plan, Une Seconde Chance pour le Schéma Directeur," *Le Monde*, July 2, 1969, p. 17; E. Mallet, "Alors que les Premiers Chantiers S'ouvrent les Villes Nouvelles Attendent Encore un Statut," *Le Monde*, February 5, 1969, p. 15; and *Le Monde*, March 27, 1969, p. 12. See also P. Bernard, *Les Pôles et Centres de Croissance en tant Qu' Instruments du Développement Régional et de la Modernisation;* Rapport Préliminaire (Genève: Institut de Recherche des Nations Unies pour le Développement Social, 1969), pp. 120–121.

141. P. Delouvrier, "Sept Ans de Vie de la Région Parisienne et de Son District," *Le Monde*, January 26–27, 1969, p. 19.

142. J. Lajugie, "Les Conditions d'une Politique de Développement Régional pour les Pays du Marché Commun," in *Revue d'Économie Politique*, vol. 69, no. 3 (1959), pp. 264–334.

143. Alain Prate, "Marché Commun et Politique Régionale," in *Revue d'Économie Politique*, vol. 74, no. 1 (1964), pp. 169–191. See also Political and Economic Planning, *Regional Development in the European Economic Community* (London: Political and Economic Planning, 1962), pp. 55–56; and Hansen, *French Regional Planning*, chap. 2.

144. See *Projet de Loi de Finances pour 1969, Annexe, Exécution du Ve Plan 1966–1967 et 1968*, vol. 1, *Première Partie, la Politique Économique et l'Exécution du Ve Plan* (Paris: Imprimerie Nationale, 1968), pp. 43–46; and *Projet De Loi (1969)*, tome 1, pp. 14–29. Note, however, that the global data require cautious interpretation. There are wide differences "between Aquitaine and Limousin or Bretagne and Midi-Pyrénées [which] are sometimes more important than between East and West," *Projet de Loi (1966)*, Annexe, vol. 2, tome 1, p. 15. For the most recent comparative statistics, see *Statistiques et Indicateurs des Régions Françaises*, pp. 21–37, 164–190.

145. See, for example, S. Antoine, "Les Français et l'Aménagement du Territoire" in *Aménagement du Territoire et Développement Régional*, pp. 105–133; and P. Massé, *Le Plan ou l'Anti-hasard* (Paris: Gallimard, 1965), chaps. 1, 3–5.

146. See M. Béaud, "Technical Problems of Regional Planning in France," pp. 23–38.

147. See, for example, Délégation à l'Aménagement du Territoire et l'Action Régionale, *Études de Moyens de Formation dans le Domaine de la Planification Régionale aux États Unis*, (Paris, 1966) troisième partie. See also fn. 117.

148. The aim is not to prepare a physical plan, but to consider the interrelationships of the principal programs in different regions and to consider the implications for these programs of innovations in information systems, decision-making, and other areas of technology. See "Le Schéma Général d'Aménagement de la France," *Le Monde*, October 29, 1968 (supplement to number 7,400), p. 1. See also Commission Nationale de l'Aménagement du Territoire, *Les Obstacles à la Politique d'Aménagement du Territoire*, and École Nationale d'Administration, *op. cit.*; and *Projet de Loi (1969)*, tome 1, pp. 10–11.

Chapter VII

1. The regions referred to are the Atlantic seaboard, the Lower Great Lakes, the Texas-Louisiana-Central Gulf Coast, and the Pacific seaboard. For other definitions, see J. P. Pickard, "Trends and Projections of Future Population Growth in the United States, with Special Data on Large Urban Regions and Major Metropolitan Areas, for the Period 1970–2000," presented to the Ad Hoc Subcommittee on Urban Growth, Committee on Banking and Currency, U.S. House of Representatives, Washington, D.C., July 22, 1969. The Urban Land Institute has published earlier projections indicating that 55 percent of the U.S. population will be living in the four major urban regions by 1980 and about 60 percent by the year 2000. See J. P. Pickard, *Dimensions of Metropolitanism*, Urban Land Institute, Research Monograph 14 (Washington, D.C., 1967), p. 23. For other descriptions of trends in these large regions, see H. S. Perloff *et al.*, *Regions, Resources, and Economic Growth* (Baltimore: Johns Hopkins Press [published for Resources for the Future], 1960); and E. Ullman, "Regional Development and the Geography of Concentration," *Papers and Proceedings of the Regional Science Association*, vol. 4 (1958), pp. 179–198.

2. Bureau of the Census, *Trends in Social and Economic Conditions in Metropolitan Areas*, Series P-23, no. 27, February 7, 1969, Washington, D.C., p. 3. See also Urban Ghetto Study Program, *Ways of Providing New and Improved Job Opportunities for the Urban Ghetto Poor* (Cambridge: Laboratory for Environmental Studies, M.I.T., 1968), p. 6 and Table 17, p. 28.

3. The block grant is allocated for general expenditures and not for a particular purpose such as housing or roads. It rests on the assumption that the central government can raise revenues more equitably and efficiently than other levels of government. Britain and other European countries have employed this form of revenue raising for at least a generation.

4. This section is based largely on the excellent evaluation of the early ARA legislation by S. R. Levitan, *Federal Aid to Depressed Areas* (Baltimore: Johns Hopkins Press, 1964). For another view of some of these problems, see M. R. Levin, "The Economic Development Districts—New Planning Regions," *Urban Affairs Quarterly*, vol. 3, no. 3 (1968), pp. 80–102.

5. Senator Paul Douglas, one of the key Democratic leaders, had been profoundly stirred by some of the conditions in the poorer areas which he had visited in southern Illinois during his statewide election campaign. Following his election, he found himself in an exceptional position to exercise leadership on these matters by virtue of his appointment to the chairmanship of the Joint Economic Committee, the prestigious committee which reviews the work and policies of the Council of Economic Advisors.

   His bill provided for rapid tax amortization of new plants, including equipment and machinery, for firms in these areas, but the idea was later abandoned. It also set up two revolving funds: one to provide industrial and commercial loans for urban and rural areas (200 million dollars), the other to finance the construction of public facilities (100 million dollars). There were additional authorizations of grants to reduce the costs of public facilities and to finance programs for vocational training, subsistence payments, and federal assistance.

6. Levitan, *op. cit.*, p. 21; see also pp. 12–13; and Levin, *op. cit.*, pp. 85–86.

7. Levitan, *op. cit.*, p. 123. During the first two years of operation, ARA's investment per job amounted to 3,000 dollars. Loans in excess of 1 million dollars, however, involved an average investment of 6,300 dollars per job. *Ibid.*, pp. 111, 121.

The loans could cover 65 percent of the investment in land, buildings, and equipment; and interest was based on Treasury borrowing rates plus a small service fee and insurance charge. The maximum term was 25 years.

Applicants had to show that funds could not be secured from conventional sources. They also had to supply 10 percent of the needed capital. This "local participation" requirement was burdensome for it made repayment of the local investment subordinate to the repayment of the ARA loan, and in effect obliged the local community to support the program via a long-term deferred loan, if not a subsidy. Maximum investment per job could vary substantially depending on whether the loans were made for labor or capital—intensive activities. In cases where the investment was high, ARA took account of the wages paid and indirect employment effects. There were also other criteria, such as new uses of indigenous natural resources, the possibility of attracting other industries, and alternative opportunities for development in the area.

Public loans could be made for a period of 25 years for any purpose which might help to attract industrial and commercial firms. But for the public loans, too, there had to be evidence that the funds were not otherwise available at reasonable terms. Interest was very moderate—indeed even lower than on the loans to business— being based on the average Treasury rates on all obligations of the government (then 3.25 percent) plus one-fourth of 1 percent as a service charge.

8. *Ibid.*, pp. 124–130.

9. A dispute arose concerning the criteria for determining a community's ability to pay. The Community Facilities Administration of the Housing and Home Finance Agency, which processed most of the applications, favored the use of relative tax rates and debt burdens as general guidelines. ARA favored a formula based on differences in charges for a facility, based on fair user rates and actual costs. Levitan, *op. cit.*, pp. 141–146.

10. In the former, ARA paid for the services of a private consulting firm to provide technical assistance in preparing plans for the Upper Peninsula region. The other involved a grant to the University of Pittsburgh to assist the President's Appalachian Regional Committee in developing a program for Appalachia and in evaluating the feasibility of setting up an Appalachian Institute.

11. Congress coupled this authorization with standby authority for tax reduction—to help provide immediate jobs in communities faced with substantial unemployment. One-third of the funds was for rural and small urban areas. Larger areas were eligible if the unemployment rate exceeded 6 percent in nine of the twelve preceding months. Projects had to serve essential public needs and not conflict with local land-use plans. Levitan, *op. cit.*, pp. 152–154.

12. *Ibid.*, pp. 60, 79, 109.

13. *Ibid.*, p. 109. Eligibility depended on several criteria spelled out in the legislation. However, the administrator was also authorized to designate areas based on other criteria that might appear appropriate. For urban areas, eligibility was based on a sliding scale of excess unemployment above the national average as follows: 1) Unemployment in the area had to average at least 6 percent during the qualifying period; and 2) either a) 50 percent above the national average for three of the preceding four calendar years, or b) 75 percent above the national average for two of the three preceding years, or c) 100 percent above the national average for one of the preceding two calendar years. This included not only major labor market areas but even small ones with a labor force of less than 15,000. Rural areas were designated on the basis of income levels, manpower, availability for "supplemental

employment," migration, and the previous location of rural development projects by the Department of Agriculture. More than 300 rural counties were selected on the basis of low income or low level of farm production, and another 230 counties were chosen by the Dept. of Agriculture under its rural redevelopment program. Another twenty four counties were added to the unemployed and underemployed category in areas contiguous to designated areas; furthermore, two counties qualified by disaggregating a larger area which did not qualify unless broken into two smaller labor market areas. *Ibid.,* pp. 55–56.

14. *Ibid.,* p. 109.

15. *Ibid.*

16. *Ibid.* The business loans were mainly for food processing, lumber, and wood products, though approximately 25 percent served recreational and tourist developments. The public facilities were generally industrial parks, sewerage systems, water mains, and research, recreation, and port facilities.

17. *Ibid.,* p. 151. In areas where unemployment exceeded 12 percent of the work force, grants accounted for five-sixths of ARA contributions to public facilities. These areas received a third of the total funds allocated in grants for 5(a) [larger industrial areas] but only 4 percent of the total loans. The average ARA investment in public facilities per job was 1800 dollars. This average varied significantly by size of project: for projects of less than 250,000 dollars, it amounted to 600 dollars, compared with 7,000 dollars on projects of 1 million dollars or more.

18. U.S. Department of Commerce, Area Redevelopment Administration, "The Overall Economic Development Program—Policies and Procedures," December 20, 1962, mimeographed (Washington, D.C.). Levin points out that "more often than not, OEDP's were hodge-podges of hastily prepared statistical material dwelling at length on the area's chronic economic problems but sparse in realistic interpretations and analyses" (Levin, *op. cit.,* pp. 91–92.)

19. The most significant modifications of the machinery concerned loans and grants for public facilities, i.e.: 1) provision of 50 percent direct grants, plus as much as 30 percent more in supplementary grants for projects involving immediate economic benefits, such as water and sewer projects, and access roads for specific sites in industrial areas; 2) to enable EDA to assist projects not otherwise financially feasible, loans for the public works programs were more specifically designed to help the local community raise their matching share of the cost, "not an uncommon situation in areas requiring assistance the most—such as Alaska, the Cumberland Plateau, the Appalachian Highlands and the Mississippi Delta region". Statement of Eugene P. Foley, House of Representatives, *Hearings Before the Special Subcommittee on Economic Development Programs of the Committee on Public Works,* 89th Congress, 2nd Session, 1966 (Washington, D.C.: Government Printing Office, 1967), p. 10. (Hereinafter cited as Foley, *Testimony at Hearings.*)

20. *Ibid.,* p. 10.

21. The area could be either a county, a labor area as defined by the Department of Labor, a city of over 250,000 population, or an Indian reservation of at least 1,000 persons.

22. Substantial unemployment was defined to be a 6 percent or higher annual average rate during the most recent calendar year and 50 percent above the national average for three of the last four years or 75 percent above for two of the last three years, or 100 percent above for one of the preceding two years. Foley, *Testimony at Hearings,* p. 16. Lack of employment opportunity was interpreted administratively to

be a 25 percent or more net population loss and 50 percent or less of the national median family income. *Ibid.,* p. 16.

23. Approximately two-thirds (or 600) of the designated areas qualified on July 1, 1966 on the basis of unemployment. Only 10 percent (or 98) qualified because of low family income; and another 6 percent (or 55) qualified because of sudden rise in unemployment. Practically all of the remainder were Indian reservations. *Ibid.,* Table 1, p. 26.

24. *Ibid.,* p. 19. The Governors of the states propose the districts, and EDA and the Governors have to approve the boundaries.

25. *Ibid.,* p. 22. The Commissions are set up following the designation of the region by the Secretary of Commerce with the concurrence of the states concerned.

26. The Department of Commerce assists these Commissions by covering their administrative expenses during the first two years and 50 percent of their expenses thereafter. The Department also finances the remainder of the fiscal year in which the Commissions are established.

27. For example, the central office of EDA has contracted for a series of studies summarizing the state of the art of regional economic development. It has also contracted for the development of an information data system which will record and predict public investment expenditures on a county by county basis and it is compiling information on the many different types of federal programs which have a significant impact on regional economic development. Foley, *Testimony at Hearings,* p. 23.

28. *Ibid.,* p. 25.

29. *Ibid.,* p. 26. There was, in addition, an Employment Review Board including representatives from EDA, labor and management, plus a majority representing the community committees in the hard-core target areas of Oakland which set up a monthly review of the adequacy of these plans.

   The programs ran into many difficulties, particularly on the training side. But imaginative administration and cooperation with the local militant leadership did much to "cool" Oakland while other cities were "burning." See A. Bradford, *Oakland's Not For Burning* (New York: David McKay, 1968), pp. 149–214.

30. Foley, *Testimony at Hearings,* pp. 25–26.

31. *Ibid,* p. 24.

32. S. Miller, D. Gaskins, and C. Liner, "Evaluation of the ARA-EDA Loan Program," Economic Development Administration, verifax memorandum, November 10, 1968 (Washington, D.C.), p. 18. The estimate assumed no growth in payrolls of loan-assisted firms, a discount rate of 10 percent, and an income multiplier of 1.2. The subsequent data in the paragraph in the text come from the same memorandum.

33. Urban Ghetto Study Program, *op. cit.,* p. 18.

34. G. L. French, "An Analysis of EDA's Training Division," Economic Development Administration, verifax memorandum, September 1968 (Washington, D.C.), p. 18. The data in the next paragraph also come from this memorandum, including the Appendix on Limited Benefit Cost Analysis.

35. As stated by E. P. Foley, the former head of the program, EDA's aim was "to provide opportunities at the major growth centers within a region [in order] to minimize the social cost of migration. From the standpoint of the individual, it is far better to move as far as 200 to 300 miles to a viable city within his region of birth

than it is to migrate to a metropolis a thousand miles away." (Foley, *Testimony at Hearings*, p. 26).

36. Planning Research Corporation, *Evaluation of Alternatives to the Business Loan Program* (prepared for the Economic Development Administration) PR C R-1108 (Los Angeles and Washington, D. C.: Planning Research Corporation, 1968), p. 5.

37. The data on designated and funded development areas were supplied to me by Gerald Duskin in a letter dated February 26, 1969. Cf. Foley, *Testimony at Hearings*, Table 1, pp. 25–26. See also Levin, *op. cit.*, pp. 98–100. Although 389 areas were no longer eligible for assistance on June 30, 1966, this was because they failed to satisfy the criteria for unemployment, income, or migration. They were dropped because of improvements in economic circumstances rather than a change in principle.

38. Bradford, *op. cit.*, p. 25; E. P. Foley, *The Achieving Ghetto* (Washington, D. C.: The National Press, 1968), pp. 112–115.

39. J. F. Kain and J. J. Persky, "Alternatives to the Gilded Ghetto," *The Public Interest*, vol. 4, no. 14 (1969), p. 76.

40. Urban Ghetto Study Program, *op. cit.*, Part 2, pp. 26, 27. See also Advisory Commission on Inter Governmental Relations, *Urban and Rural America: Policies for Future Growth* (Washington, D. C., 1968), chap. 2, pp. 1–28. For the basic population data, see the following reports of the U. S. Department of Commerce, Bureau of the Census: *Social and Economic Conditions of Negroes*, Current Population Reports, Report no. 332, Series P-23, no. 24 (Washington, D. C.: Government Printing Office, 1967); also *Negro Population: March 1966*, Population Characteristics, Series P-20 (Washington, D.C.: Government Printing Office, 1967); *Recent Trends in Social and Economic Conditions of Negroes in the United States*, Current Population Reports, Report no. 347, Series P-23, no. 26 (Washington, D. C.: Government Printing Office, 1968); and *Trends in Social and Economic Conditions in Metropolitan Areas*, Current Population Reports, Series P-23, no. 27 (Washington, D.C.: Government Printing Office, 1969); and H. T. Eldridge, *Net Intercensal Migration for States and Geographic Divisions of the United States, 1950-1960*, University of Pennsylvania, Population Studies Center (Philadelphia, 1965), Table A-1. Actually, in the period from 1960 to 1965, 80 percent of the net immigration was to nine areas: Los Angeles; Orange County, New York–Northeastern New Jersey; San Francisco-Oakland-San Jose; Washington, D.C.; Philadelphia; Houston; Miami-Fort Lauderdale; San Bernardino-Riverside; and Dallas. In each of the peak years of the fifties and sixties, migration from the South made up roughly half to two-thirds of the country's total. Typically, Negro farmers of the Southeast headed for cities in the Northeast; those of the Mississippi Delta headed primarily for Chicago; those from Louisiana and Texas headed mainly West, to Los Angeles, for example; and those from the middle South and Tennessee headed for diverse destinations in a more diffuse pattern, especially Chicago, Detroit and Cleveland. There was also much white migration from the South. For example, white farmers from the Appalachians made their way to Chicago, Detroit, and especially Ohio; and Mexican Americans made their way mostly to the cities of Texas and Southern California. See *The New York Times*, March 23, 1969, p. 66.

41. Urban Ghetto Study Program, *op. cit.*, p. 2.

42. National Resources Committee, *Regional Factors in National Planning*, 1935; *Our Cities*, 1937; *Urban Planning and Land Policies*, 1939 (all printed in Washington, D.C. by the Government Printing Office).

43. G. Greer and A. H. Hansen, *Urban Redevelopment and Housing* (Washington, D.C.: National Planning Association, 1941). See also A. H. Hansen, "Three Plans for

Financing Urban Redevelopment," in *Hearings Before the Subcommittee on Housing and Urban Redevelopment of the Senate Special Committee on Postwar Economic Policy and Planning*, 79th Congress, 1st Session, Part 9, 1945 (Washington, D.C.: Government Printing Office, 1946), p. 1622. (Hereinafter cited as *Taft Committee Hearings*.) Note that earlier experimental urban redevelopment efforts at the state level bogged down for lack of power to acquire the land or funds to write down the costs to levels which would promote new development.

44. See *Taft Committee Hearings*, Parts 4–15. The Home Loan Bank system represented the building and loan associations and FHA represented their competitors. The building and loan associations saw no justification for commercial banks and insurance companies in this field or for government insurance of the loans of their competitors.

45. A. A. Foard and H. Fefferman, "Federal Urban Renewal Legislation," in J. Q. Wilson, ed., *Urban Renewal—The Record and the Controversy* (Cambridge: M.I.T. Press, 1966), pp. 104–113.

46. R. Vernon, *The Changing Economic Functions of the Central City* (New York: Committee for Economic Development, 1959). For two more recent studies, see A. Granz, "The Urban Growth Context for Transportation Requirements," paper presented to M.I.T. Project Transport Summer Study Group, April 20, 1967; National Planning Association, *Economic and Demographic Projections for 224 Metropolitan Areas*, Regional Economic Projections Series, Report no. 67-R-1, Washington, D.C., May 1967, and the summary paper by J. W. Lee, "The Dimensions of U. S. Metropolitan Change," in *Looking Ahead*, monthly report of the National Planning Association, vol. 15, no. 5 (1967).

47. M. Millspaugh, "Problems and Opportunities of Relocation," *Law and Contemporary Problems*, School of Law, Duke University, vol. 26, no. 1 (1961), p. 20.

48. From 1950 to 1960, dilapidated housing declined from 14.8 to 8.8 million units, a decrease from 35 percent to 17 percent of the occupied inventory. Nonwhite families living in substandard housing numbered 2.3 million, or one-fourth of the national total. Also, the percent of nonwhites living in substandard housing was roughly double the percent of whites. See W. G. Grigsby, "Housing Markets and Housing Policy," in J. Q. Wilson, ed., *Urban Renewal: The Record and the Controversy*, Table 1, and p. 30.

49. See J. Margolis, "Metropolitan Finance Problems: Territories, Functions and Growth," in National Bureau of Economic Research, *Public Finances: Needs, Sources and Utilization* (Princeton: Princeton University Press, 1961), pp. 229–293; Dick Netzer, *Economics of the Property Tax* (Washington, D.C.: Brookings Institution, 1966), chaps. 1–3; and L. F. Schnorr, *The Urban Scene* (New York: The Free Press, 1965), Parts 3–5.

50. The local burden was eased further by allowing local public improvements, such as schools, playgrounds, or other facilities near the redevelopment area, to be counted in whole or in part as the local share of the capital grant.

51. For the best collection of articles discussing these problems, see Wilson, *Urban Renewal: The Record and Controversy*.

52. Foard and Fefferman, *op. cit.*, p. 97. See also *The President's Advisory Committee on Governmnent Housing Policies and Programs, A Report to the President of the United States* (Washington, D.C.: Government Printing Office, 1953).

53. Indirect government loans backed up both programs. Private banks serviced the loans for a fee and the Federal National Mortgage Association, a secondary mort-

gaging facility of the government, could buy the mortgages if the banks did not want to hold on to them and could find no other private purchasers. See H. Fefferman, "Federal Role in Urban Affairs," in *Hearings Before the Subcommittee on Executive Reorganization of the Senate Committee on Government Operations,* 89th Congress, 2nd Session, Appendix to Part 1 (Washington, D.C.: Government Printing Office, 1966), pp. 40–48; and 55–69. This excellent report will be cited hereinafter as Fefferman, "Federal Role in Urban Affairs."

54. The 1954 act also restricted additional public housing to those low-income families who had to be relocated from redevelopment or renewal areas. In addition, it provided matching grants to finance state, regional, and metropolitan planning studies to guide the urban renewal efforts (Section 701) and grants (up to two-thirds of the cost) for developing and evaluating new ways of preventing or arresting blight. In 1959 Congress approved long-range programming and scheduling for all of the urban renewal needs of a city; and for this purpose, localities could obtain grants up to two-thirds of cost.

55. The change occurred in 1956. It is no longer even necessary for a substantial number of the dwellings to be substandard if the locality officially asserts that redevelopment for predominantly non-residential uses is necessary for the proper development of the community. Still other

> exceptions to the predominantly residential requirement have been made with respect to economically depressed areas, disaster areas, and college, university or hospital expansion activity in or near the project areas. In effect, the Congress has broadened urban renewal goals to the point where it is fruitless to attempt to distinguish whether non-residential renewal is now a primary, or still a secondary goal of the program.
>
> These changes in the enabling legislation were made as a congressional response to the actual needs of cities as expressed by the cities themselves. (Fefferman, "Federal Role in Urban Affairs," p. 59.)

56. U.S. Senate Committee on Banking and Currency, *Rehabilitation Problems:* A Report submitted to the Committee by the Department of Housing and Urban Development, 80th Congress, 1st Session, August (1967), pp. 4, 26, 38. For some statistics on the high costs of such programs, see *The Report of the President's Committee on Urban Housing, A Decent Home* (Washington, D.C.: Government Printing Office, 1968), pp. 100–101. (Hereinafter cited as *A Decent Home.*) One exceptional case is the rehabilitation program which took place in Roxbury, Boston. The experience is described in detail in a study for the Joint Center for Urban Studies of M.I.T. and Harvard University. See. L. Keyes, "The Boston Rehabilitation Program," mimeographed draft (Cambridge: Joint Center for Urban Studies of M.I.T. and Harvard University, 1969). Details on another experiment which fared less well may be found in R. Bolan, "Rehabilitating New York's Multiple-Dwelling Tenements" (Cambridge: Joint Center for Urban Studies of M.I.T. and Harvard University, 1968).

57. See *A Decent Home,* p. 100. See also Wilson, *Urban Renewal: The Record and the Controversy,* chaps. 10–14.

58. Fefferman, "Federal Role in Urban Affairs," p. 71.

59. *Ibid.,* p. 71; and pp. 70–77.

60. *Ibid.,* p. 71.

61. See fn. 54.

62. See fn. 54.

63. See fn. 54.

64. For example, the Urban Mass Transportation Act of 1964 proportioned the subsidy to the relative progress in meeting the requirements. Thus, the federal government offered to foot half the costs if there was reasonable evidence of transportation and area-wide planning and two-thirds of the cost if the requirements were fully satisfied ("either at the time of the original grant or within three years"). The open space program was similarly reinforced with the scale of the federal grants raised to 50 percent. Still other grants were provided for the beautification of urban areas and to help make open spaces more usable for parks, recreation, and other purposes. But the planning requirements were tightened to ensure that the acquired open space was part of a comprehensively planned development of the urban area.

    In 1965 the federal government set the same conditions for public works. It offered to pay half the costs for water and sewerage facilities and to waive five years interest on financing land needed for future public works—provided these activities were part of area-wide land use, financial, and operational plans for development. See Fefferman, "Federal Role in Urban Affairs," pp. 70–77.

65. The legislation increased the grants (set up in the 1954 Housing Act) to state, regional, and metropolitan planning agencies, and to state planning agencies which furnished planning assistance to municipalities with populations of 25,000 or less. It raised the federal share from one-half to two-thirds, and in some cases to three-fourths, of costs. Assistance was also broadened to include

    > municipalities of up to 50,000; areas of either rapid urbanization or substantial reduction in employment because of Federal actions; economic redevelopment areas; disaster areas; Indian reservations; and in 1966, new communities.
    >
    > A 1965 amendment authorized grants to organizations for local public officials representative of the political jurisdictions within a metropolitan area to develop regional plans and programs, and to consider regional problems, even though they were not in a position to carry out a full comprehensive planning program.
    >
    > *(Ibid., p. 74.)*

66. *Ibid.,* p. 75.

67. *Ibid.,* p. 75.

68. They were "only for projects in those metropolitan areas that maintain and follow current area-wide comprehensive planning and programming adequate for evaluating and guiding all actions, both public and private, of metropolitan-wide or inter-jurisdictional significance. The grants would be available only to those public bodies in the eligible metropolitan areas that are carrying out, in accord with area-wide planning and programming—the location and scheduling of their public facilities; their zoning and other sub-division control actions; and their other policies and actions of metropolitan-wide or inter-jurisdictional significance" *(Ibid., p. 75)*.

    These grants could amount to 20 percent of the cost of federally aided projects for transportation, water and sewer facilities, recreational areas, open space, libraries, and hospitals.

69. FHA's mission was broadened both earlier and later. Thus, FHA was empowered to insure loans on more favorable terms for veterans in 1946, prefabricated housing in 1947, cooperative housing in 1948, military housing in 1949, persons displaced in urban renewal areas in 1954, the elderly in 1956, self-contained new communities in 1966, and still others.

    The Home Loan Bank System, which was remarkably successful in attracting savings and providing long-term amortizable mortgage loans for middle-income families, managed to wrest itself loose from HHFA and acquire anew its independence in 1955. It therefore escaped the obligation to adapt its program to serve the special needs of moderate-income families, which was the original aim and historic contribution of the early building and loan associations.

70. FHA has halted its practice of arbitrarily excluding some neighborhoods from its mortgage insurance programs because the neighborhoods were blighted and, therefore, "economically unsound." See Fefferman, "Federal Role in Urban Affairs," p. 45. However, one indication of the difficulties encountered in changing attitudes of the FHA staff is provided by the declaration by P. J. Maloney, Deputy Assistant Secretary of FHA, that the agency's underwriters and district directors "have been measured and found wanting." He objected especially to the failure to enforce the provision of the 1962 Executive Order forbidding discrimination in federally insured housing. "Their record," he added, "was unimpressive." He cited many metropolitan areas where Negroes made up far more than 11 percent of the population (which is the national proportion of Negroes to total population) and yet offices in these areas had supplied virtually no housing for Negroes through FHA. R. F. Semple, "FHA Asks Aides to Get Housing for Minorities," *The New York Times*, November 21, 1967, p. 30.

71. Of all homes in the mid-sixties which sold for less than $15,000 about four out of every ten were FHA-aided. However, the FHA and Veterans Administration share of the total private nonfarm housing market dropped from 41 percent in 1955 to 17 percent in 1965. This was partly because of the shift in FHA's functions and partly because of the adoption of some of FHA's more customary terms—excluding the insurance premiums—by conventional lenders and by building and loan associations.

72. U.S. Senate, *Hearings Before the Subcommittee on Executive Reorganization of the Committee of Government Operations*, 89th Congress, 1st Session, 1965 (Washington, D.C.: Government Printing Office, 1965); and U.S. Senate, *Establishment of a Department of Housing and Urban Development*, Report of the Committee on Government Operations, S 1599, 89th Congress, 1st Session, 1965, Report no. 536 (Washington, D.C.: Government Printing Office, 1965).

73. President Johnson also sponsored an Urban Institute to expand urban research. In November 1969 the Nixon Administration regrouped several functions. It put all housing production and rehabilitation functions under Housing Production and Mortgage Credit; housing management, rehabilitation, and urban renewal functions under Renewal and Housing Management; comprehensive planning, community facilities, intergovernmental relations, and land use programs (including new communities, open space, urban parks, and beautification) under Metropolitan Planning and Development.

74. We have already noted that about 3.7 million black people had left the South between 1940 and 1966, most of them settling in the central cities of the larger metropolitan areas of the North and West. Though the migration has dropped substantially in very recent years, it is likely to rise again. More than half the nonwhite population still lives in the South, close to three-fifths of them in poverty conditions; and despite the terribly inadequate conditions in the northern metropolitan areas, the Negro there has a higher income than Negroes living elsewhere. That fact alone may continue to act as a magnet. Even if the scale of movement out of the South continues at its present low level, however, the size of the northern ghettoes will increase, because their populations have expanded sufficiently to make natural increase rather than migration their main source of growth. Cf. fns. 36 and 83; and Urban Ghetto Study Program, *op. cit.*, Part 1, p. 16;

and Part 2, p. 26. See also R. Langendorf, "The Negro and the Metropolis" (Ph.D. diss., M.I.T., 1967), chap. 3, p. 124; and J. F. Kain and J. J. Persky, "The North's Stake in Southern Rural Poverty," in *Rural Poverty in the United States*, a Report by the President's National Advisory Commission on Rural Poverty (Washington, D.C.: U.S. Department of Agriculture, 1968), chap. 17, pp. 288–308.

75. Bureau of the Census, "Social and Economic Conditions of Negroes in the United States," p. 8; and A. Downs, "Alternative Futures for the American Ghetto," reprinted by permission from *Daedalus*, Journal of the American Academy of Arts and Sciences, vol. 97, no. 4 (1968), p. 1332.

76. Foley, *The Achieving Ghetto*, p. 56. Despite the high rates of Negro migration from the South, "less than half of the non-white residents living in the North and West were born in the South. Furthermore, many who came from the South came from urban areas in the South" (Langendorf, *op. cit.*, p. 42).

77. See Bureau of the Census, *Trends in Social and Economic Conditions in Metropolitan Areas*, pp. 2–5; and Downs, *op. cit.*, p. 1332. See also Ganz, *op. cit.*, p. 46 and Table 29; and Kain and Persky, "Alternatives to the Gilded Ghetto," p. 26. In 1966 there were 12.5 million nonwhites living in all central cities of the United States; of these, 12.1 million were Negroes.

78. Systemetrics, *A Framework for Federal Policies and Programs Concerning Urban Problems* (Washington, D.C., 1969), p. 12. (Systemetrics is a divison of the Real Estate Research Corporation.) See also Langendorf, *op. cit.*, pp. 53–55.

79. Advisory Commission on Intergovernmental Relations, *op. cit.*, p. 26; and Foley, *The Achieving Ghetto*, pp. 26–27.

80. Langendorf, *op. cit.*, pp. 124–125; D. P. Moynihan, "Toward Equality as a Fact and as a Result," A Program of Foundation activity in Negro American Affairs (typewritten and undated report prepared for the Carnegie Foundation); and U.S. Department of Labor, *The Negro Family* (Washington, D.C.: Government Printing Office, 1965), chap. 4. For a review of the evidence that the conditions of most Negroes have improved, see N. Glazer, "America's Race Paradox," *Encounter*, October (1968), pp. 9–18.

81. For two significant early expressions of these views, see S. Carmichael and C. V. Hamilton, *Black Power* (New York: Vintage Books, 1967); and Malcolm X, *The Autobiography of Malcolm X* (New York: Grove Press, 1965).

82. The outbreak of riots in 1966, however, affected the movements in and out of the central city. Before 1966, whites moved at an average rate of 140,000 a year. Between 1966 and 1968, the rate climbed to nearly a half-million a year. However, the rate at which Negroes moved into central cities *decreased* even more dramatically. From 1960 to 1966, Negro populations in central cities grew at an average of 370,000 per year. Between 1966 and 1968, however, growth dropped to only about 100,000 per year and this could be attributed largely to natural increase. See Bureau of the Census, *Trends in Social and Economic Conditions in Metropolitan Areas*, p. 3. See also Langendorf, *op. cit.*, chap. 5, pp. 233–234; and Downs, *op. cit.*, p. 1333.

83. Urban Ghetto Study Program, *op. cit.*, p. 42; and J. F. Kain, "The Distribution and Movement of Jobs and Industry," in J. Q. Wilson, ed., *The Metropolitan Enigma* (Washington, D.C.: U.S. Chamber of Commerce, 1967), pp. 1–39.

84. J. F. Kain, "Housing Segregation, Negro Employment and Metropolitan Decentralization," *Quarterly Journal of Economics*, vol. 82, no. 2 (1968), pp. 175–197.

85. Kain and Persky, "Alternatives to the Gilded Ghetto," p. 76; and J. R. Meyer,

J. F. Kain, and M. Wohl, *The Urban Transportation Problem* (Cambridge: Harvard University Press, 1965), pp. 164–165.

86. J. Coleman *et al.*, *Equality of Educational Opportunity* (Washington, D.C.: U.S. Office of Education, 1966); and U.S. Civil Rights Commission, *Racial Isolation in the Public Schools* (Washington, D.C.: Government Printing Office, 1967); see also J. S. Coleman, "Equal Schools or Equal Students," *The Public Interest*, vol. 1, no. 4 (1966), pp. 70–75; and Langendorf, *op. cit.*, chap. 4.

87. Andrew Heisskell, Board Chairman of Urban America, Inc., has characterized Urban America as a

nonprofit organization dedicated to improving the quality of life in the Nation's cities. It was founded in 1965 as a continuation and expansion of the American Planning and Civic Association, one of the Nation's pioneer urban improvement organizations, and later that year merged with ACTION - the American Council to Improve Our Neighborhoods. Urban America has a broadly representative board and membership. It represents no particular interest group. Its involvement with the problems of cities is a totally independent one—independent, but by no means detached. Urban America and its late president and founder, Stephen Currier, were instrumental in conceiving and forming the Urban Coalition, which is composed of leaders in business, labor, religion, civil rights, and local government.
(Testimony of Mr. Heisskell in *Hearings Before the Subcommittee on Housing and Urban Affairs of the Committee on Banking and Currency on Proposed Housing Legislation for 1968*, U.S. Senate, 90th Congress, 2nd Session, Part 1, pp. 441–442 [Washington, D.C.: Government Printing Office, 1968.])

See also R. Vernon, *The Myths and Reality of Our Urban Problems* Cambridge: Harvard University Press, 1966.

88. Testimony of Mortimer Zuckerman, *Hearings Before the Subcommittee on Housing and Urban Affairs of the Committee on Banking and Currency, Proposed Housing Legislation for 1968*, pp. 794–805. The guidelines for the building of the new communities which were issued by HUD towards the end of 1968 made it clear that "a new community must include a range of housing for families of varying incomes, size and composition," and, more specifically, that "a substantial amount of housing must be included for families of low and moderate income" *(New York Times,* December 22, 1968, p. 52).

89. See Sen. R. Kennedy's "Statement and Testimony," *Hearings before the Subcommittee on Executive Reorganization of the Committee on Government Operations* (Federal Role in Urban Affairs), U.S. Senate, 89th Congress, 2nd Session, Part 1, August 15 and 16 (Washington, D.C.: Government Printing Office, 1966), pp. 25–59. See also Foley, *The Achieving Ghetto,* chap. 3, pp. 103–148. It is also argued that "there has been relatively strong growth of low-skilled job opportunities in the central city (relative, that is, to central city growth), and much evidence that not all unemployment traces to unsuitability of the work force and, therefore, that efforts to eliminate bias and ignorance must have a very prominent role, since this particular strategy probably has a uniquely high ratio of benefits to costs." See W. Lewis, Jr., "Urban Growth and Suburbanization of Employment—Some New Data," draft (Washington, D.C.: Brookings Institution, 1969), p. 38.

90. For an interesting account of the efforts and pressures required to pass this legislation, see R. B. Semple, Jr., "Signing of Model Cities Bill Ends a Long Struggle to Keep It Alive," *The New York Times,* November 4, 1966, pp. 1, 44. The program was subsequently embraced by the Nixon administration, after certain changes were

made. One change was to permit mayors, after the first year of the program, to expand the model neighborhoods to embrace all poverty areas. The programs also emphasized participation, not citizen control.

91. Downs, *op. cit.*, p. 1350. Source of statistics quoted in the following paragraph is: U.S. Bureau of the Census, *Current Population Reports, Population Characteristics, Population of the United States by Metropolitan–Nonmetropolitan Residence; 1968 and 1960*, Series P-20, No. 181, April 21, 1969, Tables A and D.

92. The main need is to relieve the burden on the cities and states and to provide more adequate welfare allowances regardless of jurisdiction. Although there is evidence that some of the poor have moved to areas with more generous payments, no one knows to what extent these inducements affect migration, especially of Negroes, who have several reasons for preferring to live in the North.
    For a discussion of the revenue-sharing issue, see H. S. Perloff and R. P. Nathan, eds., *Revenue Sharing and the City* (Baltimore: Johns Hopkins Press, 1968); and Report of the National Commission on Urban Problems to the Congress and the President of the United States, *Building the American City*, House Document no. 91-34, 91st Congress, 1st Session, 1969 (Washington, D.C.: Government Printing Office, 1969), chap. 5, pp. 376-383. Bills dealing with different aspects of these matters were submitted to Congress by President Nixon. One measure submitted in May 1969 requests the power to merge local aid grants into a small number of block grants; the other measure, introduced in August 1969, proposes work and training incentives for welfare recipients and for federal sharing of welfare costs. Both measures are likely to be substantially modified before enactment.

93. It is clear that generous incentives will be required because the experience to date is that most investments to create jobs or housing in inner city blighted areas involve high risk and low yield. See J. Herbers, "Development of Blighted Inner City Areas is Running Into Snags," *The New York Times*, May 4, 1969, p. 72. See also, for a discussion of the application of the New Towns idea to inner cities, H. S. Perloff, "New Towns Intown," *Journal of the American Institute of Planners*, vol. 32, no. 3 May (1966), pp. 155-162.

94. Systemetrics, *op. cit.*, pp. 180-182. These estimates do not include the costs for growth centers in lagging regions.

95. *Report of the National Commission on Civil Disorders* (New York: Bantam Books, 1968).

96. Downs, *op. cit.*, pp. 1333, 1357-1358.

97. U. S. Department of Agriculture (in cooperation with the Department of Commerce; Department of Health, Education and Welfare; Department of Housing and Urban Development; Department of Labor; Department of Transportation), *National Growth and Its Distribution* (Washington, D.C.: Government Printing Office, 1967).

98. Executive Order 11452 Establishing the Council for Urban Affairs, Office of the White House, January 23, 1969.

99. *Ibid.*

100. Advisory Commission on Inter Governmental Relations, *op. cit.*, chap. 45, pp. 129–130. The Commission is a twenty-six man body of federal, state, and local officials which advises the President and Congress on ways to avoid stresses in the federal system. Some of the members of the Commission were: Farris Bryant (Chairman), Price Daniel (Vice-Chairman and Director, U.S. Office of Emergency Planning), Henry Fowler (Secretary of the Treasury), Senators Karl E. Mundt and Edmund S. Muskie, Governor Nelson A. Rockefeller, and

Jesse M. Unruh (Speaker, California Assembly). In still another set of proposals submitted in February 1969, the Commission favored a tax-sharing plan with no-strings-attached access by states and cities to the federal treasury and streamlining the 400 categories of federal aid into several "block grants."

101. *Ibid.*, p. 131; also pp. 137–8.

102. *Ibid.*, pp. 137–138. It also advocated strengthening the existing voluntary federal-state programs of family planning information for low-income persons and under certain conditions federal involvement and assistance (such as to assure an adequate range of housing) for large-scale urban and new community development; and it suggested a number of specific ways in which state credit, controls, and development policies could reinforce and extend the federal urban growth policies. *Ibid.*, pp. 138-173.

103. National Committee on Urban Growth, "Key National Leaders Recommend Large Program of New Cities for the U.S.," Washington, D.C., Urban America, Inc., news release dated May 25, 1969. (The release was based on the book *The New City* [New York: Praeger, 1969], edited by D. Canty, the editor of *City* [the bimonthly publication of Urban America, Inc.].)

104. Message from the President of the United States Relative to Population Growth, House of Representatives, 91st Congress, 1st Session, 1969, Document no. 91-139, p. 4. See also E. Weissmann, *op. cit.*; and C. P. Snow, "Excerpts from Lecture on World Problems," *The New York Times,* November 13, 1968, p. 29. Subsequently J. P. Pickard, Director of Program Analysis and Evaluation Staff of HUD, presented estimates to the Ad Hoc Subcommittee on Urban Growth of the House Banking and Currency Committee (July 22, 1969) indicated a potential of 272 large new communities ranging from 50,000 to 500,000 in size—assuming that 30 percent of the projected 100 million population increase would go into such cities. See J. P. Pickard, "Trends and Projections of Future Population Growth in the United States."

105. Glazer, *op. cit.*

106. J. Q. Wilson, "The War on Cities," *The Public Interest,* no. 3, Spring (1966), pp. 27–44.

Chapter VIII

1. A. O. Hirschman, *Development Projects Observed* (Washington, D.C.: Brookings Institution, 1967), chap. 1.

2. Examples are varied credit mechanisms and business and consumer services.

3. "Good" ideas do not always win further support: witness the limited success of TVA in the United States. Also, there is no guarantee, of course, that the eruption of conflicts and pressures will, in fact, prove benign.

4. J. James, "The Future of Urban Forms," *The Papers and Proceedings of the International Symposium on Regional Development,* Hakone, Japan, April 1967, p. 211. See also in the same collection K. Tange, "The Japanese Archipelago of the Future," pp. 79–92.

5. L. R. Peattie, *The View From the Barrio* (Ann Arbor: University of Michigan Press, 1968), chaps. 6, 7.

6. L'Équipe de la Revue "2000," *Essai sur la Participation, Autonomie, et Solidarités,*

numero 9, "Special," Paris, June 1968. See also remarks of Premier Ministre Couve de Murville and General de Gaulle, cited respectively in *Le Monde*, December 15–16, 1968, p. 6; and February 4, 1969, p. 2.

7. D. P. Moynihan, *Maximum Feasible Misunderstanding* (New York: The Free Press, 1969); P. Marris and M. Rein, *Dilemmas of Social Reform, Poverty and Community Action in the United States* (New York: Atherton Press, 1967); and J. A. Califano, Jr., "Moynihan: The Lasting Value is Dubious," *The Washington Post*, February 6, 1969, p. B 7.

8. J. W. Dyckman, "The Changing Uses of the City," in L. Rodwin, ed., *The Future Metropolis* (New York: Braziller, 1961), pp. 161–2.

9. D. Bell, "Notes on the Post-Industrial System," *The Public Interest*, vol. 2, no 6 (1967), p. 25.

ACKNOWLEDGMENTS

I have received generous assistance from many quarters during the past decade when I was studying or working professionally on different aspects of urban growth strategies of nations.

I owe special thanks to the Olivetti Foundation, the Joint Center for Urban Studies of M.I.T. and Harvard University, and the Guggenheim Foundation. The Olivetti Foundation made a generous grant to the Joint Center to help finance three studies dealing with the urban problems of developing countries. I received a portion of these funds from the Joint Center to help defray the major part of the expenses of spending a year abroad studying urban growth strategies, mainly those of Great Britain and France. In addition, the Guggenheim Foundation awarded me an unrestricted fellowship to cover a portion of the expenses for travel and research.

I am indebted, too, to the Centre International Universitaire for making available a private office to work in Paris from September 1966 to June 1967.

I have also received assistance from many knowledgeable persons while working on each of the case studies in this volume. The persons who helped me most on the assessment of the Venezuelan experience include General R. Alfonzo Ravard, J. A. Vegas, R. A. Blanco, H. Font, and L. Petrie; also R. Corrada, A. Ganz, W. von Moltke, A. Penfold, P. E. Beach, Jr., A. H. Fawcett, Jr., G. A. Marker, L. Peattie, and A. Penfold; and also D. Appleyard, O. T. Boyd, R. G. Davis, J. R. Dodge, W. A. Doebele, A. Downs, A. Fleisher, J. Howes, K. Lynch, M. Meyerson, J. Moore, H. Robinson, R. C. Wood, R. M. Soberman, and B. Wagner. L. Peattie and Messrs. Vegas, Corrada, Ganz, von Moltke, Penfold, and Fleisher read and made helpful comments on earlier versions of the chapter.

In dealing with the Turkish experience, I have received special assistance from T. Akçura and T. Cansever, F. W. Frey, A. German, G. C. and L. Guarda, B. Kastarlak, R. Keleş, M. Fortune, R. Kaminsky, E. Turak, Ü. Üstandağ, and F. Yavuz. Messrs.

Akçura, Keleş, Fortune, and Turak read and made helpful comments on this chapter.

In assessing the British experience, I received valuable help from W. Burns, D. V. Donnison, C. D. Foster, P. Hall, D. Heap, A. E. Holmans, J. James, E. Jones, P. Johnson-Marshall, A. G. Powell, C. W. Roberts, P. Self, A. G. Wilson, D. Robertson, and O. Koenigsberger. Messrs. Hall, James, and Self read and made helpful comments on this chapter.

I was also assisted in exploring the intricacies of French area development policy by S. Antoine, B. Augustin, P. Bernard, J. Boudeville, F. Choay, M. Conan, P. Coulaud, J. Dreyfus, S. Goldberg, N. Hansen, M. Marie, P. Merlin, M. Stern, F. Viot, and the late G. Weil. Messrs. Antoine, Dreyfus, Conan, Merlin, Viot, and Weil read and made helpful comments on this chapter.

In regard to the U. S. experience, I have been especially aided by C. Abrams, A. Altshuler, A. Fleisher, A. Ganz, and H. Fefferman. Messrs. Fefferman and Fleisher read and made helpful comments on the chapter and the manuscript as a whole.

Chapters I, II, and III are revised versions of papers that have been published elsewhere. More detailed information is provided in the initial footnotes of each of these chapters.

I acknowledge with thanks the authorization of the following organizations and publishers to cite passages from their publications:

1.) Controller of Her Britannic Majesty's Stationery Office for permission to quote from *The Future of Development Plans, A Report of the Planning Advisory Group.*

2.) *Daedalus* for permission to quote from A. Downs, "Alternate Futures for the American Ghetto."

3.) National Press, Inc., for permission to quote from E. P. Foley, *The Achieving Ghetto.*

4.) State Planning Organization of Turkey for permission to quote from *Turkish Experience in Regional Planning.*

5.) *The Times* for permission to quote from the leading article of April 17.

6.) *Urban Studies* for permission to quote from L. Needleman and B. Scott, "Regional Problems and Location of Industry Policy in Britain."

7.) Yale University Press for permission to quote from A. O. Hirschman, *The Strategy of Economic Development.*

Several persons—K. W. O'Brien, M. Hipshman, L. Wickens, N. Rodwin, V. Rodwin, and especially Susan Granoff—helped me to edit the manuscript, and Penny Peters, Romin Koebel, and William Porter provided skilled assistance on the maps and charts. R. Bofah prepared the index. H. Sahagian, A. Clement, and J. McBeth typed the successive versions of the manuscript.

Almost needless to say, the book could never have been written without the collaboration and extraordinary patience of Nadine Rodwin.

LLOYD RODWIN

Cambridge, Massachusetts

INDEX

(Continued)

(Continued)

(Continued)

(Continued)

(Continued)

(Continued)

(Continued)

(Continued)

(Continued)

(Continued)

(Continued)

(Continued)